ONE HUNDRED BIBLE LESSONS

ALBAN DOUGLAS

Revised Edition

OMF LITERATURE INC.

One Hundred Bible Lessons
First published (1960)
Three Hills, Alberta
First Philippine edition (1966)
Published by OMF Literature Inc.
Copyright 1966 by Alban Douglas

Reprinted - 1968, 1973, 1975 (twice), 1978, 1979, 1981,
    1983, 1984, 1987

This new edition
One Hundred Bible Lessons - Revised
Copyright © 1988
OMF Literature Inc.

Published (1988) by
OMF Literature Inc.
776 Boni Avenue
Mandaluyong, Metro Manila

Reprinted – 1989, 1990

ISBN 971-511-084-3

Printed in the Philippines

Contents

Preface to the first Philippine edition

These lessons were originally given at the Thursday night Bible class at the Youth Gospel Center, Manila, Philippines — in 1958 and 1959. They were published by the Evangelical Missionary Fellowship, Three Hills, Alberta, Canada, in 1960 — under the title, "Seventy Bible Lessons." The series has since been revised and the selection enlarged to the present one hundred lessons.

Preface to the 1988 Edition

The author is absolutely thrilled at the acceptance and response to this book of Bible Lessons. The translations into several Asiatic languages have been very encouraging. The Chinese, Korean and Indonesian translations have been widely used. The translations into the main languages of India have proved to be of great spiritual blessings.

The English translations printed in the Philippines and North America have been widely sold in the Philippines, in America and Australasia. The author prays that the Lord will abundantly bless this new edition.

Alban Douglas
Prairie Bible College

1

The Existence of God

Introduction

To begin our study in Bible doctrine, we ought to begin with God.

We are constantly challenged by atheists, skeptics and hecklers to prove that there is a God.

It is difficult for natural man to believe in something that he cannot see, touch or feel, 1 Corinthians 2:14.

The problem for the Christian is solved in the first verse of the Bible, "In the beginning God created the heaven and the earth," Genesis 1:1.

The Bible is not a textbook that attempts to prove the existence of God — the Bible opens with a positive fact that God does exist. It did not occur to any other writer of the Bible to prove this fact.

The Bible plainly states that it is the fool who denies the existence of God.

Psalm 14:1 "The fool hath said in his heart, There is no God."

Anyone with any intelligence would acknowledge the evident fact of a living God.

The greatest proof apart from Scripture of the existence of God is our daily fellowship with Him in prayer.

I know that there is a God because I talked to Him today and He heard and answered the prayer of my heart though it was only whispered silently.

I Proof from Scripture

Psalm 19:1 "The heavens declare the glory of God; and the firmament shows His handiwork." The beauty and glory of the heavens speak loudly saying, "God exists."

Romans 1:20 goes farther and suggests that creation even teaches about the eternal power of the Godhead, "For the invisible things of Him from the creation of the world are clearly seen, being understood by the things that are made, even His eternal power and Godhead; so that they are without excuse."

The man who accepts Scripture will readily acknowledge the existence of God.

In addition to the argument from Scripture, we may consider seven other powerful "proofs."

II Proof from Conscience

Man is born with a universal belief in a supreme Being; no tribe has yet been discovered that lacks this. They know that some Being creates and controls.

Romans 2:15 "Who show the work of the law written in their hearts, their conscience also bearing witness, and between themselves their thoughts accusing or else excusing them." The existence of God is written in the human conscience.

Acts 17:23 "For as I passed by, and beheld your devotions, I found an altar with this inscription, To the Unknown God." Conscience told them that there was a God even though they did not know Him personally.

Some atheists may claim that their conscience does not tell them about God.

It is doubtful if genuine atheists can be found, for at best they are men who have silenced their conscience by blatant unbelief.

Some men are so blind that they may deny the existence of the sun in the sky, but that does not alter the fact that the sun exists, rises and sets each day.

None are so blind as those who refuse to see. The honest man will find that the inner still small voice says that God exists and is alive today.

Men deny the existence of God not because they cannot find Him, but because they are afraid to face the responsibility of being accountable to Him after death.

Atheism is one of the devil's tools to put men to sleep without accepting salvation.

If there is no God then I am not responsible to anyone and I can live and die as I please.

But in the quieter moments of reflection the conscience of every man whispers, "There is a God," and only fools deny it. To look up into the heavens and say that there is no God, simply because we cannot see Him, is as ridiculous as seeing a plane and saying that the plane is pilotless because we cannot see the pilot.

Few of us have ever seen our brains, yet we believe that we possess them because of a centralized control system in the body. Because we see creation, we believe in God.

III The Argument from Cause (Cosmological)

The world is here. It must have come from somewhere. Somebody or something must have caused it to come into being at one time or another.

Here is a book. Someone must have written it. No printing press can of itself produce a book, be it ever so modern a press with the latest electrical gadgets.

Someone built this building. Someone created the trees. Someone operates the universe.

If all the pieces of a watch were placed in a can and the can shaken gently for a million years the watch would not be "accidentally" put together and running.

The only sensible answer to the problem of the existence of the world is the existence of an intelligent Being whom we call God.

IV The Argument from Design (Teleological)

A watch not only exists but it has a designer. It was planned for a specific purpose.

A watch was not designed for mosquitoes to live in. It was designed by a keen mind for the purpose of accurately telling the time.

An examination of the world and the things large and small shows that each is designed by an intelligent mind for a specific purpose in life.

The colors of a bird and means of defence of the animals are not accidents. They are the result of a plan of a superior planning mind of the originator.

V The Moral Argument (Anthropological)

Man has an intellectual and oral nature showing that the Creator must not be merely an inanimate force but a living, intelligent moral Being.

Genesis 1:26 " Let us make man in our image, after our likeness."

Genesis 1:27 God created man in the image and likeness of God, that is, patterned after Him.

Psalm 94:9 "He that planted the ear, shall He not hear? He that formed the eye, shall He not see?" God has given to man ears, eyes, knowledge, intelligence, and willpower, for these are the things that He possesses.

Conscience teaches man right and wrong, good and bad; for the Creator is a moral Being-that is holy, and loves righteousness but abhors evil.

VI The Life Argument

Life comes from life and the original life must have come from a Being possessing eternal life, that is, life that existed before physical life was created.

Where can such life be found? It can only be found in God, who possesses eternal life: Psalm 36:9 "For with Thee is the fountain (source) of life."

The apple tree gets its life from the parent tree, the lamb from the mother sheep. But where did *they* get life from? We go back to the original creation.

Jesus said in John 11:25, "I am ... life," — also in John 14:6, "I am ... life," and in John 10:28, "And I give unto them eternal life."

All life proceeds from God. The theory of spontaneous generation has been proved false and completely unacceptable to authoritative science.

Life must have a beginning. The only logical answer is that the beginning was with God.

VII The Argument from Congruity

The theory of atheism solves no problems but only multiplies unsolved mysteries.

The acceptance of the existence of God as Creator of the world is like a magic key that fits all the facts of Scripture, revelation, knowledge and science.

This irrefutable doctrine is held tenaciously by multitudes of souls who are willing both to live and die in the consolation of this assurance.

Conclusion

Atheism, which is only giant doubt and unbelief, can only lead to darkness and despair for the one accepting it.

Acceptance of Genesis 1:1, "In the beginning God," leads a sincere seeker into the path of a fuller revelation of God Himself.

Hebrews 11:6 "He that cometh to God must believe that He is [exists]."

Let us come as children in simple faith, based on the revelation of God in Scripture and nature, believing and trusting Him completely.

Review Questions

1 Did God write the Bible as a textbook to prove His existence? Explain.
2 What is an atheist in the eyes of the Lord?
3 Give two Scriptures to prove the existence of God.
4 Why in Acts 17:23 had the people of Athens built an altar to the unknown God?
5 What is the atheist's real purpose in denying the existence of God?
6 What is the argument from cause to prove the existence of God?
7 What is the argument from design to prove God's existence?
8 How do we know that God is not an inanimate force?
9 What is the life argument that proves God's existence?
10 What is a prerequisite for faith in God?

2

The Person of God

Introduction

The study of God has been the ambition of philosophers for millennia.

Some sit and meditate and try to think into the realm of the eternal Being, but the only true knowledge about God can be gained from the Bible.

John 1:18 "No man hath seen God at any time; the only begotten Son which is in the bosom of the Father, He hath declared Him."

1 John 4:12 "No man hath seen God at any time."

Exodus 33:20 (God speaking to Moses) "And He said, Thou canst not see My face: for there shall no man see Me, and live."

Exodus 33:23 "And I will take away Mine hand, and thou shalt see My back parts: but My face shall not be seen.'

Moses talked to God and saw a part of Him but did not see the Lord's face.

Jesus who is God's Son came from heaven to reveal the Father God to us.

Jesus speaking to Philip, John 14:7-11, says that Jesus is the revelation of God.

Pagan wisdom says, "Man, know thyself," but Jesus says, "Man, learn of the Father."

John 17:3 tells us that to know God and Christ His Son is to have eternal life, "And this is life eternal, that they might know Thee the only true God, and Jesus Christ, whom Thou hast sent."

I God's Personality

Personality is characterized by possessing knowledge, feeling and will power.

An idol is devoid of personality for it neither knows, feels nor responds.

Our God is an individual who is living and has definite characteristics.

God is a Person. He is not an influence or unseen force or power like electricity.

Jeremiah 10:10 "But the Lord is the true God, He is the living God."

Acts 14:15 "Turn from these vanities unto the living God."

1 Thessalonians 1:9 "How ye turned to God from idols to serve the living and true God."

2 Chronicles 16:9 "For the eyes of the Lord run to and fro throughout the whole earth, to show Himself strong in the behalf of them whose heart is perfect."

The moving eyes denote life and personality unknown to idols or false gods.

Psalm 94:11 "The Lord knoweth the thoughts of man," that is, He has knowledge.

II God's Nature

God is a Spirit. A spirit has neither flesh, bones nor blood.

Luke 24:39 "Behold My hands and My feet, that it is I Myself: handle Me, and see; for a spirit hath not flesh and bones, as ye see Me have."

John 4:24 "God is a Spirit: and they that worship Him must worship Him in spirit and in truth."

1 Timothy 1:17 "Now unto the King eternal, immortal, invisible, the only wise God."

1 Timothy 6:16, speaking of God, "...who alone has immortality, dwelling in unapproachable light, whom no man has seen, or can see."

III God's Unity

The Lord our God is one God in contrast to the plurality of pagan gods.

Deuteronomy 6:4 "Hear, O Israel: the Lord our God is one Lord."

Isaiah 44:6 "Thus saith the Lord the king of Israel, and His Redeemer the Lord of hosts; I am the first, and I am the last; and beside Me there is no God."

Isaiah 45:21 "And there is no God else beside Me; a just God and a Savior; there is none beside Me."

IV God's Natural Attributes

An attribute is a quality, property or unique characteristic of something.

We reason that to be God, He must possess certain basic qualities. These include the following:

1   He is eternal. To be the true God He must have neither beginning nor ending.

An idol is disqualified for it was made by someone, thus it had a beginning.

Psalm 90:2 "Before the mountains were brought forth, or ever Thou hadst formed the earth and the world, even from everlasting to everlasting, Thou art God."

1 Timothy 1:17 "Now unto the King eternal, immortal." cf. Psalm 102:24, 27; Isaiah 57:15.

Genesis 1:1 "In the beginning God ... " God has always existed.

2   He is unchangeable. God is so constituted that He cannot change.

1 Samuel 15:29 "And also the Strength of Israel will not lie nor repent: for He is not a man, that He should repent."

Malachi 3:6 "For I am the Lord, I change not."

James 1:17 "Every good gift and every perfect gift is from above, and cometh down from the Father of lights, with whom is no variableness, neither shadow of turning."

3   He possesses all power (omnipotent). To lack this He could not be God.

Genesis 1:1 "In the beginning God created the heaven and the earth." Creative power.

Genesis 1:3 "And God said, Let there be light: and there was light." Power by speaking.

Man makes things out of existing materials. God creates out of non-existent materials, objects that are good and perfect. Genesis 1:4 "It was good."

Job 42:2 "I know that Thou canst do every thing." Job speaking to God.

Psalm 33:9 "For He spake and it was done; He commanded, and it stood fast."

Jeremiah 32:27 "Behold I am the Lord, the God of all flesh: is there any thing too hard for Me?" Certainly not, for He can do anything or everything.

4   He is present everywhere at one and the same time (omnipresent) 1 Kings 8:27.

Psalm 139:7-9 "Whither shall I go from Thy Spirit? or whither shall I flee from Thy presence? If I ascend up into heaven, Thou art there: If I make my bed in hell, behold Thou art there. If I take the wings of the morning, and dwell in the uttermost parts of the sea; even there shall Thy hand lead me.:

Jeremiah 23:23 "Am I a God at hand, saith the Lord, and not a God afar off?"

Ephesians 1:23 "Which is His body, the fullness of Him that filleth all in all."

5 **He has all knowledge (omniscient).** Nothing is hidden from the Lord.

1 Chronicles 28:9 "... know thou the God of thy father ... for the Lord searcheth all hearts, and understandeth all the imaginations of the thoughts."

2 Chronicles 16:9 "For the eyes of the Lord run to and fro throughout the whole earth, to show Himself strong in the behalf of them whose heart is perfect."

Psalm 94:11 "The Lord knoweth the thoughts of man."

Daniel 2:20 "Blessed be the name of God for ever and ever: for wisdom and might are His."

Job 42:2 "No thought can be withholden from Thee."

Isaiah 40:28 "There is no searching of His understanding."

V God's Moral Attributes

1 **God is holy** — Exodus 15:11; 1 Samuel 2:2; Isaiah 6:3; 1 Peter 1:16
2 **God is righteous** — Psalm 116:5; Ezra 9:15; Psalm 145:17; Jeremiah 12:1
3 **God is merciful** — Psalm 103:8; Deuteronomy 4:31; Psalm 86:15; Romans 9:18
4 **God is love** — 1 John 4:8-16; John 3:16; 1 John 3:16; John 16:27
5 **God is faithful** — 1 Corinthians 1:9; 2 Timothy 2:13; Deuteronomy 7:9; 32:4

Also, God is Glorious — Exodus 15:11; Psalm 145:5

Gracious — Exodus 34:6; Psalm 116:5

Jealous — Joshua 24:19; Nahum 1:2

Great — 2 Chronicles 2:5; Psalm 86:10

Invisible — Job 23:8, 9; 1 Timothy 1:17

Upright — Psalm 25:8, Psalm 92:15

Light — Isaiah 60:19; 1 John 1:5

Perfect — Matthew 5:48

Immortal — 1 Timothy 1:17; 6:16

None like Him — Exodus 9:14; Deuteronomy 33:26

Longsuffering — Numbers 14:18; Micah 7:18

Compassionate — 1 Kings 8:23
Unsearchable — Job 11:7; Psalm 145:3
Good — Psalm 25:8; Psalm 119:68
Immutable — Psalm 102:26, 27; James 1:17
True — Jeremiah 10:10
Incorruptible — Romans 1:23
Consuming fire — Hebrews 12:29

Conclusion

Love Him. Worship Him. Serve Him. Obey Him. Fear him.

Review Questions

1   Where can reliable information be obtained about God?
2   What do we mean when we say that God has a personality?
3   What is the nature of God?
4   Is God a plurality or a single unit? Give one Scripture reference.
5   What is meant by the word 'attribute'?
6   List five natural attributes of God.
7   Give one Scripture to prove that God is eternal.
8   Why do we believe that God is all-powerful?
9   How can God be present at all places at the same time?
10   Prove that God knows everything.

God is a Balanced Being

Introduction

God is holy, loving, merciful, faithful, yet just and righteous.

Many people today have a lopsided view of God. Some over-emphasize His love and forget that He is just and holy at the same time.

God's love allows Him to forgive sin and show mercy to a repentant sinner.

The holiness and justice of God demand that sin must be punished to the full extent of the law: Romans 6:23 "For the wages of sin is death" — see also Exodus 18:20.

If God were a mere human being He would be completely frustrated with incompatible emotions and desires, with the two sides in constant conflict.

However God is not a man and these two opposing emotions work together in perfect harmony for the one becomes a balance for the other.

To argue that hell is impossible, for a loving merciful God could not send a helpless human being there forever and ever, is an unbalanced view of God.

To understand the horrors of hell and the blackout at Calvary, meditate much on the holiness and severity of God's wrath against sin, 2 Corinthians 5:11

The holiness of God demands that we be holy. The law of God pronounces eternal damnation on the guilty sinner in accordance with the justice of God.

One of the greatest marvels of our age is that God found a way of salvation that satisfied both the holiness of God and the love of God.

This solution also satisfied the law, yet left man a creature with a free will who could choose salvation or damnation, heaven or hell.

I God is Holy

We cannot imagine a God who could be anything but perfect holiness.

To be holy means to be free from all defilement, to be pure. God is absolutely pure.

Habakkuk 1:13 "Thou art of purer eyes than to behold evil, and canst not look on iniquity." God turned from His own Son dying on Calvary.

Exodus 15:11 "Who is like unto Thee, O Lord ... glorious in holiness."

1 Samuel 2:2 "There is none holy as the Lord: for there is none beside Thee."

Isaiah 6:3 "Holy, holy, holy, is the Lord of hosts."

1 Peter 1:15, 16 "But as He which hath called you is holy, so be ye holy in all manner of conversation; Because it is written, be ye holy; for I am holy."

The holiness of God separated Him from fallen man: Ephesians 2:13 "But now in Christ Jesus ye who sometimes were far off are made nigh by the blood of Christ."

The only way that man can approach this holy God is through the blood of Christ.

God is holy. God hates sin. His holy wrath must punish sin. This is the explanation of Isaiah 53:6, when the Father forsook and punished His Son on Calvary.

God's love to sinners will never be appreciated until seen in the light of His blazing wrath against sin.

The holiness of God demanded punishment for sin. This demand was voluntarily assumed by the Savior on the cross and completely satisfied the Father.

II God is Love

1 John 4:8 "He that loveth not knoweth not God; for God is love."

This is not only a verb saying that God loves but a noun for God *is* love.

If God lives in my heart by conversion then I must love, for I'm indwelt by *love*.

1 John 4:7 "Beloved, let us love one another: for love is of God; and every one that loveth is born of God, and knoweth God."

What is love? Love is a desire for and delight in the welfare of the one on whom the love is bestowed. True love even loves sinners and enemies; Matthew 5:44, 45.

The love of God is manifested toward the Son and all believers in particular.

John 16:27 "For the Father Himself loveth you, because ye have loved Me, and have believed that I came out from God."

God loves the world (John 3:16), which caused Him to think of a plan of salvation to give men the opportunity to escape wrath and damnation.

God as a loving Father manifests His love to the Christian by chastening: Hebrews 12:6

III God is Faithful

1 Corinthians 1:9 "God is faithful, by whom ye were called unto the fellowship."

Deuteronomy 7:9 "Know therefore that the Lord thy God, He is God, the faithful God."

What does the word faithful mean? It means someone who can be safely trusted, who is reliable and dependable. God is faithful for He is honest and never changes.

How great is God's faithfulness? It reaches to the skies: Psalm 36:5 "Thy mercy, O Lord, is in the heavens; and Thy faithfulness reacheth unto the clouds."

All of God's work is done in faithfulness: Psalm 33;4 "For the Word of the Lord is right; and all His works are done in truth."

God's faithfulness is manifested in keeping His promises and fulfilling every Word that He has spoken; God is unchangeable for He neither lies nor repents.

God will keep every promise to protect, assist and guide His child in need.

2 Timothy 2:13 "If we believe not, yet He abideth faithful: He cannot deny Himself."

1 Corinthians 10:13 "God is faithful, who will not suffer you to be tempted above that ye are able; but will with the temptation also make a way to escape that ye may be able to bear it."

IV God is Merciful

Psalm 103:8 "The Lord is merciful and gracious, slow to anger, and plenteous in mercy."

Deuteronomy 4:31 "For the Lord thy God is a merciful God; He will not forsake thee."

Instead of inflicting pain and death as punishment for sin the Lord is merciful and gives many blessings — health, comforts and earthly joys — to the saved and lost.

Matthew 5:45 "He maketh His sun to rise on the evil and on the good, and sendeth rain on the just and on the unjust."

God is sovereign and can choose to whom He desires to show this mercy: Romans 9:15,18. The mercy of God can be shown to the multitudes: Exodus 20:6 "And showing mercy unto thousands of them that love Me and keep My commandments."

How great is the mercy of God? Psalm 103:11, 17 "For as the heaven is high above the earth, so great is His mercy toward them that fear Him. But the mercy of the Lord is from everlasting to everlasting upon them that fear Him."

The Lord extends mercy to those who trust in Him: Psalm 32:10 "He that trusteth in the Lord, mercy shall compass him about."

When the repentant sinner comes to Jesus for forgiveness he claims not merit but throws himself upon the mercy of the Lord.

Psalm 51:1 "Have mercy upon me, O God, according to Thy loving kindness."

V God is Just

Deuteronomy 32:4 ". . . a God of truth and without iniquity, just and right is He."

Psalm 19:9 "The judgments of the Lord are true and righteous altogether."

Our God is just and righteous and will mete out just judgment to each individual.

Isaiah 45:21 "There is no God else beside Me; a just God and a Savior."

God being just, righteous and holy must act in a manner that is just, fair and upright.

1 Samuel 2:3 "The Lord is a God of knowledge, and by Him actions are weighed."

Genesis 18:25 "Shall not the Judge of all the earth do right?" He certainly will.

God's nature or character leads Him to do that which is right at all times.

God as the just One will be the final Judge of all things, 1 Kings 8:32.

Conclusion

How can God be loving and demand holiness at the same time? How can He at the same time be both merciful and just to a guilty sinner?

The answer can only be found in Calvary. Calvary was the expression both of the wrath of God against sin and the mercy of God toward the guilty sinner.

God is love but not that kind of sentimental love that gushes over sin. The love of God is holy and just.

To understand God, His Being, character and nature, study Calvary — and one will begin to understand how God can hate sin and yet love the sinner.

Calvary satisfies the holiness and justice of God by fulfilling all the requirements of the law and permits a sinner to enter heaven legally.

Let us bow in true worship before this great God who is a perfect Being.

Review Questions

1 Name five of the moral attributes of God.
2 Why is God not frustrated by these seemingly contradicting attributes?
3 Does the fact that God is love extinguish the doctrine of hell? Why?
4 What does the word 'holy' mean?
5 What is the practical application of this doctrine, according to 1 Peter 1:15,16?
6 Name three different ones upon whom God bestows His love.
7 How great is God's faithfulness?
8 Why will the mercy of God not finally take everyone to heaven?
9 What do we mean when we say that God is just?
10 Where can we find a balance between the mercy and justice of God? Explain.

4

The Trinity

Introduction

So far we have learned that there is one God — the Creator of the world.

Deuteronomy 6:4 "Hear, O Israel: the Lord our God is one Lord." There is only one God.

But a careful study of the Scriptures will show that God exists in three Persons, that is, a Godhead manifested in three Persons:

Colossians 2:9 "For in Him dwelleth all the fulness of the Godhead bodily."

Objection: How can God be three Persons and one God at the same time? Would that not make three Gods, resembling pagan philosophy and contradicting Deuteronomy 6:4?

Is the doctrine of the Trinity not incomprehensible and contrary to reason?

Isaiah 55:8,9 teaches us that human reason has no bearing in the study of God, "For My thoughts are not your thoughts, neither are your ways My ways, saith the Lord. For as the heavens are higher than the earth, so are My ways higher than your ways, and My thoughts than your thoughts."

Neither the words "Trinity" nor "Triune God" can be found in the Scriptures.

I Basis of the Doctrine of the Trinity

1 In the Baptism of Jesus in Matthew 3:13-17 we see the Trinity at work: God the Father spoke from heaven, "This is My beloved Son, in whom I am well pleased." God the Son, our Lord, Jesus Christ, was being baptized. God the Holy Spirit descended like a dove and alighted on the Savior.

2 The baptismal formula in Matthew 28:19: "Go ye therefore, and teach all nations, baptizing them in the Name of the Father, and of the Son and of the Holy Ghost."

3 The benediction in 2 Corinthians 13:14: "The grace of the Lord Jesus Christ, and the love of God, and the communion of the Holy Ghost, be with you all. Amen."

4 The creation of man uses plural terms: Genesis 1:26 "And God said, Let *Us* make man in *Our* image, after *Our* likeness: and let them have dominion."

In subsequent lessons we will show that the Son Jesus Christ was true God and that the Holy Spirit is God.

II Illustrations of the Doctrine of the Trinity

1 Shamrock — a three-leaved plant said to have been used by Saint Patrick to illustrate this doctrine. It is but one leaf but it has three distinct sections.

2 Water — revealed in three forms — liquid, ice and steam, yet all three have the same chemical formula, H_2O.

3 Light — red heat rays that are invisible picturing the Father, yellow light rays that are seen picturing the Son, blue chemical rays that are seen by their effects, picturing the Spirit.

4 Business firm: (Smith & Co., three brothers, John, Henry and Peter) It is one firm with one name but each brother is head of a department.
   The three work together without friction as a single unit as does the Lord.

5 Alban Douglas. I am only one person but I can be revealed as three persons: My mother sees me as a son. She sees me differently from anyone else and I respond to her in a way that is different from my response to others. My children see me as a father with all that involves. The class sees me as a teacher which is a different relationship. I remain one person but I am revealed as a son, father and teacher at the same time. God is one indivisible God revealed in three separate Persons.

It must be emphasized that the Trinity remains a mystery and that no single illustration can possibly explain everything. However, I believe that we can use these various illustrations to throw some light on this difficult and complex problem.

Because God is a Spirit and we are physical it is hard for us to comprehend God.

God is infinite while we are finite. To attempt a philosophical explanation of the tri-unity of God is an attempt to put the facts of the infinite in finite terms.

We firmly believe that there is one God, eternally existing and manifesting Himself to us in three Persons — Father, Son and Holy Spirit.

III The Trinity Acting in Unity

1 in Creation

God the Father spoke, Genesis 1:3 "And God said, Let there be light."

God the Son was the Word spoken, John 1:1 "In the beginning was the Word."

God the Holy Spirit moved upon the face of the waters, Genesis 1:2; Job 26:12, 13.

2 in the Incarnation

God the Father gave His only Son, John 3:16.

God the Son was born into the world, Luke 2:11.

God the Spirit came upon Mary to cause conception, Luke 1:35.

3 in Redemption

God the Father accepted the sacrifice of Calvary, Hebrews 9:14.

God the Son offered Himself as our substitute, Hebrews 9:14.

God the Spirit — Jesus offered Himself "through the eternal Spirit," Hebrews 9:14.

4 in Salvation

God the Father received the prodigal from the far country, Luke 15:22. The Father welcomes the sinner, forgives him, supplies robes, rings and a feast.

God the Son is the Shepherd that goes to seek the lost sheep, Luke 15:4.

God the Spirit seals the new convert, Ephesians 1:13.

5 in Communion

God the Father invites us to come to Him for fellowship, Ephesians 2:18.

God the Son is the reconciliation, 2 Corinthians 5:19.

God the Spirit effects this union and communion, Ephesians 2:18.

6 in Prayer

God the Father is the One who receives the requests, John 16:23.

God the Son is the One in whose Name we pray, John 16:23.

God the Spirit directs us in our requests, Romans 8:26.

7 in Glory

God the Father is eventually to receive the millennial kingdom, 1 Corinthians 15:24.

God the Son is the One who will change our vile body to one like His,

Philippians 3:21.

God the Spirit gives the invitation, Revelation 22:17.

8 in Regeneration

God the Father records the new name in glory, Luke 10:20.

God the Son cleanses the sin in His precious blood, Ephesians 1:7.

God the Spirit performs the transforming miracle of the new birth, John 3:3-6.

IV The Trinity and the Attributes of God

Attribute	God the Father	God the Son	God the Holy Spirit
1 Eternal	Psalm 90:2	Revelation 1:8, 17	Hebrews 9:14
2 Omnipotent	1 Peter 1:5	2 Corinthians 12:9	Romans 15:19
3 Omniscient	Jeremiah 17:10	Revelation 2:23	1 Corinthians 2:11
4 Omnipresent	Jeremiah 23:24	Matthew 18:20	Psalm 139:7
5 Holiness	Revelation 15:4	Acts 3:14	Luke 1:15
6 Truth	John 7:28	Revelation 3:7	1 John 5:6
7 Benevolent	Romans 2:4	Ephesians 5:25	Nehemiah 9:20
8 Communion	1 John 1:3	1 John 1:3	2 Corinthians 13:14

Conclusion

Do not be troubled if you cannot understand this perplexing doctrine.

"He who would try to understand the Trinity fully will lose his mind. But he who would deny the Trinity will lose his soul." — Lindsell and Woodbridge.

It is a mystery and will remain a mystery until we meet the Lord in glory.

However this does not mean that we cannot *believe* it. We must believe it.

God is so different from us; He is a Spirit and we are human beings.

I believe that God is honored and made happy by our believing this doctrine.

Man, too, is a tripartite being — body, soul and spirit — for we were made in the image and likeness of the Lord.

Let us worship this great God — this One who is so superior to us.

Let us thank each member of the Trinity, the Father, the Son and the Holy Spirit, for that which they have personally done for us.

Review Questions

1   How does Matthew 3:13-17 prove that God is a Trinity?

2   Give two other Scripture references to prove the Trinity.

3   Where is the first hint in the Bible about the Trinity?
4   Give three illustrations of the Trinity.
5   How did the Trinity operate in creation?
6   How did the Trinity operate in redemption?
7   How does the Trinity operate in salvation?
8   How does the Trinity work in regard to prayer?
9   How does the Trinity operate together in the regeneration of a
     sinner?
10   Why is it not possible to completely understand the doctrine of
     the Trinity?

5

Names, Fatherhood and Silence of God

Introduction

We have learned about the existence of God and about His nature and unity.

In Bible lands names had and have a deep significance, and meanings of names in "the Middle East" have a deeper impact than in many Western cultures.

In a study of His Names we learn many things about God.

I The Names of God

The Names of God are found in three forms:

1 Primary, 2 Compound with El, 3 Compound with Jehovah.

1 Primary — One word only: El, Elah, Elohim, Jehovah, Adon, Adonai, God, Lord.

2 Compound with El — Almighty God; Most High God; Everlasting God.

3 Compound with Jehovah — Lord God; Jehovah, the Everlasting God, etc.

Elohim	Genesis 2:4	The One Who is Mighty	The Lord Who Creates
El Elyon	Genesis 14:22	The One Who is Supreme	The Lord Who Owns
Adonai	Genesis 15:2	The One Who is Ruling	The Lord Our Master
El Olam	Genesis 21:33	The One Who is Mysterious	The Lord Who Reveals
Jireh	Genesis 22:14	The One Who Redeems	The Lord Who Provides
Rophi	Exodus 15:26	The One Who Heals	The Lord Who Heals
Nissi	Exodus 17:15	The One Who Fights for us	The Lord Our Banner
Yekaddia	Exodus 31:13	The One Who is Sanctification	The Lord Who Sanctified
Shalom	Judges 6:24	The One Who Gives Peace	The Lord Our Banner
Sabaoth	1 Samuel 1:3	The One Who is Possessing	The Lord of Hosts
Zidkenu	Jeremiah 23:6	The One Who is Justifying	The Lord Our Righteousness
Shammah	Ezekiel 48:35	The One Who is Present	The Lord at Hand
Elyon	Psalm 7:17	The One Who is Blessing	The Lord Who Blesses
Roi	Psalm 23:1	The One Who is Caring	The Lord Our Shepherd

II The Fatherhood of God

"Our Father which art in heaven," Matthew 6:9; This is our happiest conception of God.

Pagan religions know nothing of a God who is a "loving heavenly Father."

Pagan religions portray God as immense, terrible, cruel, and One to be dreaded.

The Bible pictures God as loving, friendly, companionable, approachable and desirable.

It was the Savior who taught us to pray "Our Father" — a new revelation of God.

God is revealed as Father in two ways:

1) As the Father of our Lord Jesus Christ, John 5:17; John 1:14.
2) As the Father of those who believe on the Lord Jesus. John 1:12, "But as many as received Him, to them gave He power to become the sons of God."

The Jews thought of God as their Father in a national or poetical sense:

1) Poetical — Psalm 68:5 "A Father of the fatherless, and a Judge of the widows, is God in His holy habitation."
2) National — Exodus 4:22 "And thou shalt say unto Pharaoh, Thus saith the Lord, Israel is My son, even My firstborn."

Israel did not have a personal consciousness of sonship, as "God is *my* Father."

"Modernism" reasons, "God is my Father and my Father will not harm me, so I will take my ease, eat, drink, and be merry and He will be merciful to me to the end."

John 8:44, Jesus speaking to the Jews said, "Ye are of your father the devil, and the lusts of your father ye will do."

God is the Creator of all, but only the Father of those that are in the family.

2 Corinthians 6:17, 18 "Wherefore come out from among them, and be ye separate, saith the Lord, and touch not the unclean thing; and I will receive you, and will be a Father unto you and ye shall be My sons and daughters, saith the Lord Almighty."

As a Father God gives life to His children; there is no sonship without a new birth.

As a Father God bestows love on His children — to those in the family of God.

This relationship, Father and son, gives a true ideal for work (it is not master and slave).

It is as a Father that He hears and answers our prayers, sifting the requests as a true Father.

III The Silence of God

In times of difficulty men reason, "If there is a loving Father God, why is He silent?" "Why did He allow this to happen?" "Why didn't He prevent this?"

Why does He not prevent disastrous explosions, accidents, typhoons, floods and wars?

An infidel having no faith in the existence of God argues from the silence of God — the greatest problem of our times.

Job 23:3,4 "Oh that I knew where I might find Him! that I might come even to His seat! I would order my cause before Him and fill my mouth with arguments."

Psalm 28:1 "Unto Thee will I cry, O Lord my Rock; be not silent to me: lest, if Thou be silent to me, I become like them that go down into the pit."

Men have devised several answers to this age-old problem:

1 Deism — saying that God is a good God but He has no time to look after the details of life. God is only a spectator of the affairs of this life.

2 Atheism — saying that silence proves that God is a myth. A living God would speak.

3 Materialism — saying that the world is governed by law, without a personal God, and that we are at the mercy of blind chance.

To reject God and the Bible only plunges mankind into greater darkness.

Why, then, is God silent? Is it that God is —

1 Indifferent? No! Christ suffering on the cross cries, "My God, My God." God cared so much for our souls that He continued His wrath upon the Son.

2 Unobservant? No! This is contrary to the omniscient understanding of God.

3 Unloving - No! The parent that truly loves a child will punish him, Hebrews 12:7,8.

4 Unwilling? No! He sees the end from the beginning and plans our whole lives.

If these negative answers are wrong, what, then, is the correct answer?

1   Common sense view — Many difficulties are a result of deliberate sin due entirely to man's carelessness, neglect and folly, such as accidents. Galatians 6:7 "For whatsoever a man soweth, that shall he also reap."

2   Reverent view — Is it right that my puny mind should question the workings of the Almighty God? (Isaiah 55:8,9). Doubtless God's master plan for my life will include sorrow, suffering and pain.

3   The philosophical view — Human free will involves the consequences of those actions. Human freedom means moral responsibility — adultery leads to syphilis or AIDS.

4   Lover's view — God is a jealous lover. Exodus 20:5 "I, the Lord thy God, am a jealous God." He seeks to divorce us from everything and cause us to cling closely to Him.

5   Dispensational view — This is the day of man, the day of sin, the day of grace, when God beckons, "Come Home," but a day of judgment is coming and the silence of God will be broken with audible condemnation. God will yet reckon accounts with men and their relationships with God and society.

6   Faith view — John 13:7 "Jesus answered and said unto him, What I do thou knowest not now; but thou shalt know hereafter." Lord teach me to wait patiently.

7   The testing of my faith — 1 Peter 1:7 "That the genuineness of your faith, being much more precious than gold that perishes, though it is tested by fire, may be found to praise, honor, and glory at the revelation of Jesus Christ."

8   The mysterious works of God — John 9:3 "Jesus answered, Neither hath this man sinned, nor his parents: but that the works of God should be made manifest in him." This is the story of the man that was born blind. Prehaps I may suffer, not for my sin but to be made a blessing to someone else. Those who have passed through suffering and sorrow are uniquely able to comfort others.

Conclusion

Live in a conscious sense of His presence even though He seems to be silent.

Learn to think positively. I know God — I spoke to Him today. He spoke to me through His own precious Word. He spoke through answered prayers.

Live according to the knowledge that we have. Caution: Romans 1:21, "Because that, when they knew God, they glorified Him not as God ..." then read verses 24-32.

Matthew 11:27 teaches that it is the work of the Son to reveal the Father.

The Quiet Hour is our opportunity to deepen our acquaintance with the Lord God.

Psalm 46:10 "Be still and know that I am God."

Review Questions

1   Give three names of God and their meanings.
2   What is our happiest conception of God?
3   What is the price of having a happy relationship with God as our Father?
4   Does the silence of God prove His non-existence or indifference? Why?
5   What is the doctrine of Deism?
6   List three wrong answers given by man to explain God's silence.
7   What is the teaching of materialism in regard to the silence of God?
8   Give five possible reasons for the silence of God.
9   How can I become more God-conscious?
10   When is the best time to deepen our acquaintance with God?

6

The Fear of the Lord

Introduction

This has been a subject that has intrigued me for many years but I've never been able to complete a Bible study on this vital subject.

It seems that there is a wrong kind and a right kind of fear.

One of the precious messages of the Bible is "fear not," — used about fifty times: Genesis 15:1; 26:24; Exodus 14:13; Isaiah 43:1; Luke 2:10; 12:32; Acts 27:24; Revelation 1:17.

Also there are variations, like Jesus' words, "It is I; be not afraid" (John 6:20).

But this lesson is about another kind of fear — the fear of God which we *ought* to have.

Job 28:28 "And unto man He said, Behold, the fear of the Lord, that is wisdom."

Psalm 19:9 "The fear of the Lord is clean, enduring for ever."

2 Samuel 23:3 "He that ruleth over men must be just, ruling in the fear of God."

Lack of absence of this fear can only bring sin and disillusionment, and end in tragedy.

Genesis 20:11, Abraham sinned because, "I thought, Surely the fear of God is not in this place." He mistakenly thought that he was beyond God's fear and was really free.

Romans 3:18 "There is no fear of God before their eyes" — a picture of degenerate man.

I Meaning of "Fear of the Lord" or "Fear of God" Proverbs 14:26-27

Does it mean physical fear where you stand and tremble in the presence of the Almighty?

Dr. C. I. Scofield defines it as meaning "reverential trust with a hatred of evil."

Fear of the Lord means piety. It is used to express our religious duty toward God.

Deuteronomy 4:10 "Gather Me the people together, and I will make them hear My words, that they may learn to fear Me all the days that they shall live upon the earth."

From this we see that it is essential but not inherited. It is something that must be taught to the people including children, that each generation may learn to fear the Lord.

Fear of God is required from each one of us. It is one of the purposes of creation.

Deuteronomy 6:13 "Thou shalt fear the Lord thy God, and serve Him."

Ecclesiastes 12:13 "Let us hear the conclusion of the whole matter: Fear God, and keep ..."

II Things that We are not to Fear

We are not to fear idols or other gods. 2 Kings 17:38 "And the covenant that I have made with you ye shall not forget; neither shall ye fear other gods."

We are not to fear man. 1 Samuel 15:24, Saul's mistake, "I feared the people."

Proverbs 29:25 "The fear of man bringeth a snare." We are to fear the Lord only.

We are not to fear earthly calamities for they signify the near return of our Savior. Luke 21:25-28 "... men's hearts failing them for fear ... then look up ..."

The true believer does not fear future punishments. Hebrews 10:27 "But a certain fearful expectation of judgment, and fiery indignation which will devour the adversaries."

We are not to fear "fear," Job 15:24, "Trouble and anguish shall make him (the unsaved) afraid," but the believer casts all his earthly fears on the Lord.

1 Peter 5:7 "Casting all your care (worries and fears) upon Him ..."

Only one fear remains and that is a holy fear of the Lord God Himself.

III The Fear of God is Commanded

Deuteronomy 13:4 "Ye shall walk after the Lord your God, and fear Him, and keep His commandments, and obey His voice, and ye shall serve Him, and cleave unto Him."

1 Peter 2:17 "Honour all men. Love the brotherhood. Fear God.

Honour the king."

Psalm 22:23 "Ye that fear the Lord, praise Him ... glorify Him; and fear Him."

The earthly disciples set up a noble example in this matter. Acts 9:31 "And walking in the fear of the Lord ... were multiplied."

Cornelius was a man who feared God. Acts 10:2, "A devout man, and one that feared God with all his house," Is it any wonder that God sent Cornelius the Gospel?

2 Corinthians 7:1, the fear of God teaches us to live circumspect lives, "Let us cleanse ourselves from all filthiness of the flesh and spirit, perfecting holiness in the fear of God." This godly fear becomes a powerful motivating force in our lives.

IV Description of the Fear of the Lord

1 It is a hatred of evil. Proverbs 8:13 "The fear of the Lord is to hate evil."

2 It is wisdom. Psalm 111:10 "The fear of the Lord is the beginning of wisdom."

3 It is a treasure. Proverbs 15:16 "Better is little with the fear of the Lord than great treasure and trouble therewith." Isaiah 33:6 "The fear of the Lord is his [believer's] treasure."

4 It is a fountain of life. Proverbs 14:27 "The fear of the Lord is a fountain of life."

5 It is clean. Psalm 19:9 "The fear of the Lord is clean." It is sanctifying.

6 It endures forever. Psalm 19:9 "The fear of the Lord is clean, enduring for ever."

7 It is godly. Hebrews 12:28 "Let us have grace, whereby we may serve God acceptably with reverence and godly fear." There is a difference between reverence and fear.

V What Motives Cause us to Fear God?

1 The holiness of God causes us to fear Him. Revelation 15:4 "Who shall not fear Thee, O Lord, and glorify Thy Name? For Thou only art holy "

2 The greatness of God causes us to fear Him. Deuteronomy 10:12-17 "And now Israel, what doth the Lord thy God require of thee, but to fear the Lord thy God ... for the Lord your God is God of gods, and Lord of lords, a great God, a mighty and a terrible."

3 The goodness of God causes us to fear Him. 1 Samuel 12:24 "Only

fear the Lord, and serve Him in truth with all your heart: for consider how great things He hath done."

4 The forgiveness of God causes us to fear Him. Psalm 130:4 "But there is forgiveness with Thee, that Thou mayest be feared." Praise the Lord for this, too.

5 The wondrous works of God cause us to fear Him. Joshua 4:23,24 Joshua reviews these works.

6 Coming judgments cause us to fear the Lord. Revelation 14:7 "Saying with a loud voice, Fear God, and give glory to Him; for the hour of His judgment is come."

VI The Fear of the Lord is Necessary

1 It is necessary to worship. Psalm 5:7 "In Thy fear will I worship." See Psalm 89:7.

2 It is necessary in service. Psalm 2:11 "Serve the Lord with fear, and rejoice with trembling."

3 It is necessary to keep us from sin. Exodus 20:20 "Fear not: for God is come to prove you, and that His fear may be before your faces, that ye sin not."

4 It is necessary to good government. 2 Samuel 23:3 "He that ruleth over men must be just, ruling in the fear of God." This is lacking in governments today.

5 It is necessary for administration of justice, 2 Chronicles 19:6-9.

6 It is necessary for the perfecting of holiness in our Christian lives, 2 Corinthians 7:1.

VII Results of Fearing the Lord

1 It brings pleasure to the Lord. Psalm 147:11 "The Lord taketh pleasure in them that fear Him, in those that hope in His mercy." Let's bring much pleasure to the Lord.

2 It causes the Lord's pity to increase upon the child of God. Psalm 103:13 "Like as a father pitieth his children, so the Lord pitieth them that fear Him."

3 It brings acceptance with God. Acts 10:35 "But in every nation he that feareth Him, and worketh righteousness, is accepted with Him." Peter to Cornelius and friends.

4 It brings the mercy of God. Psalm 103:17 "But the mercy of the Lord is from everlasting to everlasting upon them that fear Him." O Lord, teach me to fear Thee (Luke 1:50)!

5   It brings blessings. Psalm 112:1 "Blessed is the man that feareth the Lord."

6   It brings confidence. Proverbs 14:26 "In the fear of the Lord is strong confidence."

7   It brings separation from evil. Proverbs 16:6 "By the fear of the Lord men depart from evil." Today there is little fear of God and an abundance of evil.

8   It brings Christian fellowship. Malachi 3:16 "Then they that feared the Lord spake often one to another: and the Lord hearkened, and heard it."

9   It supersedes the fear of man. Isaiah 8:12,13 "... neither fear ye their fear, nor be afraid. Sanctify the Lord of Hosts Himself; and let Him be your fear."

10   It brings answered prayer. Psalm 145:19 "He will fulfill the desire of them that fear Him: He also will hear their cry and will save them."

11   It brings long life. Proverbs 10:27 "The fear of the Lord pro-longeth days."

Conclusion

Let us pray that God will teach us to fear Him. Psalm 86:11 "Teach me Thy way, O Lord; I will walk in Thy truth: unite my heart to fear Thy Name." See Proverbs 15:16; 19:23.

Review Questions

1   Define "fear of the Lord."

2   What do we learn about fearing God from Deuteronomy 4:10?

3   What are the two purposes of man according to Ecclesiastes 12:13?

4   Name four things that we are not to fear.

5   Give two Scriptures to prove that we are to fear God (one from each Testament).

6   Give seven descriptions of the fear of the Lord.

7   Give five motives that cause us to fear God.

8   Why is the fear of the Lord necessary?

9   Give ten results of fearing the Lord.

10   What lesson do we learn from Psalm 86:11?

7

Prophecies and Life of Christ

Introduction

Long before Jesus was born it was prophesied that He would come, Genesis 3:15.

Jesus did not come to earth unannounced. He came in the "fulness of time," Galatians 4:4.

A study of the fulfillment of minute details encourages our faith in a God that not only draws up master plans but the intricate details of the blueprints.

Also, to see that these details are fulfilled exactly as prophesied strengthens our faith in the inspiration of the Scriptures, and shows that the Bible is not an assortment of books by various authors but one Book with one author — God.

To assume that all these things just accidentally happened is an accident too great even for the imagination of an evolutionist!

The child of God prompted by the Holy Spirit gladly accepts their testimony with joy and cries out with Thomas, "My Lord and my God."

Our faith undergirded by the witness of fulfilled prophecy stands firm and unmovable.

I Prophecies Concerning Christ's Origin

1 **Christ would come out of Israel.** Numbers 24:17-19 "There shall come a Star out of Jacob, and a Scepter shall rise out of Israel."

Christ was born a Jew, a descendant of Abraham, Isaac, Jacob and David, Matthew 1:1-17.

2 **Christ would be born of the family of David and of the tribe of Judah.** Genesis 49:10 "The Scepter shall not depart from Judah... until Shiloh come."

Isaiah 11:1 "And there shall come forth a rod out of the stem of Jesse, and a Branch shall grow out of his roots."

These prophecies were fulfilled in our Savior Jesus Christ,

Luke 1:31-33.

3 Christ would be born in Bethlehem. Micah 5:2 "But thou, Bethlehem Ephratah, though thou be little among the thousands of Judah, yet out of thee shall He come forth unto Me that is to be ruler in Israel; whose goings forth have been from of old, from everlasting."

Christ was born in Bethlehem, Luke 2:4-7.

4 Christ would be born of a virgin. Isaiah 7:14 "Behold, a virgin shall conceive, and bear a Son, and shall call His Name Immanuel."

Christ was born of a virgin, Matthew 1:18,22,23.

5 The time of Christ's coming was specified. Daniel 9:24-26 "Seventy weeks are determined upon thy people, and upon thy holy city, to finish the transgression, and to make an end of sins ... and after threescore and two weeks shall Messiah be cut off."

Messiah, Christ, was cut off (crucified) 490 years after the rebuilding of Jerusalem.

Christ was crucified at the precise time. No one earlier or later could be Christ.

6 Christ's coming was announced by a forerunner. Isaiah 40:3 "The voice of him that crieth in the wilderness, Prepare ye the way of the Lord, make straight in the desert a highway for our God."

This prophecy was fulfilled in John the Baptist, Matthew 3:3.

7 The Messiah would be God — the wonderful verse of Isaiah 9:6. "... the mighty God ..."

We have learned from the lesson on the Deity of Christ that Jesus was God, John 1:14.

II Prophecies Concerning Christ's Life

1 He would spend part of His childhood in Egypt. Hosea 11:1 "When Israel was a child, then I loved him, and called My son out of Egypt."

2 He would suffer and make atonement for sin. Isaiah 53:4-6 had to be fulfilled by Christ.

2 Corinthians 5:21 records the fulfillment, "For He hath made Him to be sin for us, who knew no sin; that we might be made the righteousness of God in Him."

3 He would ride into Jerusalem on a colt. Zechariah 9:9 "Behold, Thy King cometh unto thee: He is just, and having salvation ... lowly, and riding upon an ass."

The fulfillment of this on Palm Sunday is told in detail in

Matthew 21:2-5.

4 **He would be given gall and vinegar in His agony on the cross.**
Psalm 69:21 "They gave Me also gall for My meat; and in My thirst
they gave Me vinegar to drink."

This was fulfilled at the cross in Matthew 27:34 by the Roman soldiers.

5 **Not a bone would be broken, contrary to Roman practices.**
Psalm 34:20 "He keepeth all His bones; not one of them is broken."
Not a bone was broken of the Passover lamb, either, Exodus 12:46.
Ordinarily the legs of the crucified prisoners were broken to
prevent them from escaping but they broke custom and didn't
break Jesus' legs or bones, John 19:33-36.

6 **Men would cast lots for His garments.** Psalm 22:18 "They part My
garments among them, and cast lots upon My vesture."

This prophecy was fulfilled precisely as spoken by the soldiers in
Matthew 27:35.

7 **Christ would utter certain words in His dying agony.** Psalm 22:1
"My God, My God, why hast Thou forsaken Me."

This prophecy was fulfilled as the fourth of the "Seven sayings from
the Cross," Mark 15:34.

8 **He would rise again from the dead.** Psalm 16:10 "Thou wilt not
leave My soul in hell; neither wilt Thou suffer Thine Holy One to
see corruption."

Peter affirms that this was literally and actually fulfilled in
Acts 1: 2-3.

III The Life of Christ

1 His pre-incarnate state, as God, Jesus has always existed. He was
before all things.

2 The birth of Jesus of the Virgin Mary is recorded in Matthew and
Luke.

3 Jesus was circumcised at the age of eight days, Luke 2:21.

4 Jesus was taken to the Temple at Jerusalem when He was 12 years
of age, Luke 2:41-48.

5 Jesus spent the early years of His life as a carpenter in Nazareth,
Mark 6:3.

6 Jesus began His ministry in Judea, Samaria and Galilee. This
period lasted six months.

7 Jesus' first miracle was performed at Cana of Galilee, John 2:1; and
His second miracle, the healing of the Nobleman's son, in Capernaum, John 4:46,54.

8 The second stage of Jesus' ministry covered a period of 6 to 8 months in Capernaum and Galilee. He performed miracles, healed the sick and preached the Gospel.

9 The third stage was the later Galilean ministry lasting about a year in and about Galilee. Crowds followed Him. He preached the Sermon on the Mount, etc., Matthew 5, 6 and 7.

10 In the next stage the Pharisees sought to kill Him. Jesus travels to Capernaum, Phoenicia, Bethsaida, Caesarea, Philippi and finally re-enters Galilee.

11 The last six months were spent teaching, preaching and travelling.

12 The last week, Palm Sunday, the Last Supper, Gethsemane, the trials and death by the cross.

13 Three days later, according to prophecy, Jesus rose again from the dead.

14 Forty days after the resurrection He ascended visibly and bodily into heaven, Acts 1:10, 11.

IV The Miracles of Jesus

A miracle is the setting aside of a lower law by a higher law. Lower law is the natural physical law of earth and nature. Only God can do things contrary to this law.

If Jesus truly performed miracles, then He is God, for man cannot perform true miracles.

The Lord Jesus performed miracles not to "show off" or entertain, but to prove His Deity and cause men to believe in Him, His message and His Person, John 2:11; 20:31.

Jesus performed credible miracles over nature. He stilled the tempest, calmed the wind and water. He even walked on the water, Matthew 8:26, 27; 14:25.

Jesus performed miracles over devils, Mark 5:12,13; Matthew 8:28-32; etc.

Jesus performed miracles over disease - cleansed the leper; healed the lame; opened the eyes of the blind; caused the dumb to hear; fevers to depart, Matthew 8:3; 12:10-13; etc.

Jesus performed miracles over death. He raised the dead contrary to all human law that says a dead person must stay dead, John 11:44; Matthew 9:23-25; Luke 7:12-15.

Our Lord's miracles were restrained and are completely believable.

His miracles were performed openly in the presence of many witnesses and recorded by divine inspiration for us to read and believe.

Conclusion

The life of Jesus Christ on earth can be summarized in the words of Acts 10:38, "Who went about doing good, and healing all that were oppressed of the devil."

The Lord Jesus left us an example that we should follow. 1 Peter 2:21 "For even hereunto were ye called: because Christ also suffered for us, leaving us an example, that we should follow His steps."

We are to walk as He walked. 1 John 2:6, Christ came to do God's will and we should too, John 8:29; Hebrews 10:7.

Review Questions

1 Why was Jesus' coming to earth not a surprise?
2 Of what nation was the Savior to come? Of what tribe?
3 When was Messiah to come?
4 Was it accidental that Jesus was given gall and vinegar on the cross? Why?
5 What is the significance of John 19:34?
6 What is the Old Testament prophecy of the resurrection of Christ?
7 What were Jesus' first two miracles?
8 Where does John 13-16 fit into the life of Christ?
9 What is a miracle? Why did Jesus perform miracles?
10 Give three verses to show the kind of life Jesus lived on earth.

The Virgin Birth of Christ

Introduction

In the last lesson we learned that Jesus Christ was Deity — He is the Son of God.

In the Christmas story we learn that Jesus became a man — took upon Himself the form and likeness of man, Philippians 2:5-8.

We believe that since Adam sinned, all born thereafter inherit a sin nature from their parents.

Psalm 51:5 "Behold, I was shapen in iniquity; and in sin did my mother conceive me."

Psalm 58:3 "The wicked are estranged from the womb: they go astray as soon as they be born, speaking lies."

If Christ inherited a sin nature, then He was a sinner and died for His own sin. Even though Christ lived a sinless life, He would be unable to save one soul.

But Jesus Christ was born without a sin nature

If Christ were born without a sin nature, how was this accomplished?

The Father God solved this difficult problem by what is called the "Virgin Birth."

The mystery of the virgin birth is to be believed, adored and accepted by Christians.

Jesus did not have a human father for the Holy Spirit was His Father. Mary was the mother but did not pass on a sin nature to the baby Jesus.

O how wonderful of our God to solve this difficult problem so that we might have a Savior who could truly redeem us from sin on the cross of Calvary.

I The Virgin Birth Foretold in the Old Testament

Genesis 3:15 was the first promise of the Redeemer, given to man after his fall into sin.

Genesis 12:1-3, God calls **Abraham to** be the father of the chosen nation of Israel.

Genesis 49:10, the blessing was to be given through the tribe of Judah.

2 Samuel 7:8-16, the Savior to be born of the family of David; to be a "son of David."

Isaiah 7:14, the actual prophecy, "Behold, a virgin shall conceive and bear a Son, and shall call His Name Immanuel." This is repeated in Matthew 1:23.

Isaiah 9:6, the prophecy that Jesus the human One was to be "born" but Jesus the Divine God was to be "given," for Jesus as God was eternal and could not be born.

II The Historic Fulfillment of this Prophecy

Matthew 1:18-25 records the story as does Luke 2:4-7.

Mary was engaged to Joseph but they were not married yet. Christ was born of a virgin but a betrothed virgin so that she could be married to protect her good name.

Mary's conception was definitely from the Holy Spirit and not from her fiance Joseph or any other man whatsoever. God guarantees this to give us a perfect Savior.

The Lord encouraged Joseph to marry Mary to be a companion and guide to her in order to protect her from the extremity of the law, Leviticus 20:10.

Matthew 1:25 tells us that though Joseph and Mary were married they never lived together as husband and wife until after the birth of the Savior.

God takes special care to insert this verse with this intimate detail to show us that the unborn child could not possibly be contaminated by a human father.

III The Virgin Birth is Taught in Scripture

Some try to maintain that Paul did not teach the virgin birth of Christ. It is true that Paul does not use that exact expression but Paul knew the risen Christ in 2 Corinthians 15:8, and recognized Him as the One fulfilling Isaiah 7:14.

Paul, writing in Colossians 1:15-17, gives a picture of the greatness of the Lord Jesus Christ.

Isaiah prophesied of the Savior's birth 740 years before it actually happened.

Matthew explicitly states that Jesus was conceived by the Holy Spirit and born of a virgin, Matthew 1:18, 20, 23.

Luke, a medical doctor, would be most interested in this medical phenomenon. Every child must have a father. Who was the Father of the baby Jesus? If the father were human, then he had a sin nature and we are yet in our sins.

Luke carefully explains the unusual conception in Luke 1:27,31,34,35.

Luke 1:34 Mary asks the sensible question of the angel, How can I have a child when I am not married and inferred that she was a pure virgin abhorring immorality.

Luke 1:35 the angel carefully explained that the Holy Spirit would be the father.

IV The Purpose of the Virgin Birth

1 To reveal God: John 1:18, Jesus came to declare and reveal the Father to humanity.

2 To bridge the chasm between God and man: 1 Timothy 2:5 "For there is one God, and one Mediator between God and men, the Man Christ Jesus."

3 To save men: Hebrews 2:14, 16, this was the basic purpose that brought Christ to earth.

4 To rescue the whole creation: Romans 8:19-23 "We know that the whole creation groaneth and travaileth in pain together until now ... waiting for ... redemption ..."

V The Importance of the Doctrine of the Virgin Birth

Modernists and liberals attack this doctrine today as they attack the doctrines of the total depravity of man, the deity of Christ and the inspiration of the Scriptures.

If man is totally depraved then he needs a Savior to redeem him. This Savior must be pure and capable. Jesus Christ is the only possible Savior of the world.

The only way that Jesus could become man without a sin nature is by the virgin birth.

A virgin is a lady who has not known a man in marriage. Mary remained a virgin until after the birth of Jesus, until she and Joseph lived together as husband and wife.

Salvation is closely linked with this doctrine. If Jesus was not born of a virgin, then I am a lost sinner still and so are you.

1   It is undeniable truth. It is definitely taught in the Bible. We accept the inspiration of the Scriptures and believe this teaching is absolutely true.

2   It is unchangeable truth. This doctrine stands with the Scriptures and does not change with the changing times, thoughts and theories of mankind, Hebrews 13:8.

3   It is urgent truth. This doctrine is essential to the plan of salvation. Without a virgin--born Savior, the salvation of one soul is utterly impossible.

4   It is undiscernible truth. It is a mystery hidden in God. There is a sense in which all life and birth is a mystery. How can a tree put life into its seed?

   1 Corinthians 4:1, we Christians are to be good stewards of "the mysteries of God."

5   It is unconditional truth. I believe that this truth must be accepted as supreme.

   Romans 10:9, we are to confess Jesus as Lord and if He were not virgin-born, then He cannot be the Savior for He has broken the prophecies of Holy Scripture.

6   It is useful truth for the Almighty God has now entered the world as a man — but a sinless man, a man without a sin nature, a man who can save others. "Emmanuel" means "God with us." This is now true, for God has come to live on earth.

7   It is unavoidable truth for we face it yearly as we hear the Christmas story.

   Let us ceaselessly in our teaching present the virgin-born Savior to the world.

VI   The Significance of the Virgin Birth

Jesus Christ was not a phantom. He was a real human being, truly man, bone of our bone and flesh of our flesh. Philippians 2:7, He has become our "elder brother."

Jesus Christ was also God and remained God because of the Holy Spirit conception.

Jesus Christ was sinless because He was virgin-born without inheriting a fallen sinful, corrupt human nature. He was without original sin.

VII Objections to this Doctrine

1 It is only found in a few places in Scripture. One Scripture is sufficient but it is confirmed by Isaiah, Matthew and Luke, three inspired writers.

2 Jesus did not personally claim to be virgin-born. He infers it in John 6:51.

3 Scientists do not accept it for it is not biologically true. Jesus did not come by natural conception but by a miracle conception.

4 Others reject it because it is miraculous. All life is a miracle, wonderful, mysterious.

5 Liberal theologians do not accept the doctrine. That does not alter the fact that it is true, for it is taught in the Holy Scriptures in prophecy and history.

Conclusion

Make much of Christmas to teach this wonderful truth to our children and students.

Let us thank God that He found a way to bring the Savior into the world without the taint of original sin.

Review Questions

1 Why did Jesus not inherit a sin nature? Psalm 51:5
2 What is the first promise of a Redeemer in the Bible?
3 Give the Old Testament prophecy of the virgin birth.
4 How was this prophecy fulfilled?
5 Give four purposes of the virgin birth.
6 What is the result of denying the deity of Christ and the virgin birth?
7 Why is the mystery of the virgin birth not fully understood?
8 What is the vital link between the deity of Christ and the virgin birth?
9 What is the practical aspect of this doctrine for us today?
10 Why do liberals try to discredit this doctrine?

The Deity of Christ

Introduction

This fundamental doctrine is consistently attacked by Manalistas, Russelites, etc.

Belief in the deity of Christ is essential to salvation. Romans 10:9 RV, "That if thou shalt confess with thy mouth Jesus as Lord . . ." — not merely a good man.

A study of Bible conversions will reveal that many occurred when they recognized Jesus as Lord — Paul in Acts 9:5, the man in John 9:38, etc.

To deny the deity of Christ is to rob mankind of a Savior and condemn us eternally.

In this lesson we present fifteen proofs of the deity of Christ.

I Jesus Christ is Referred to as Lord

Psalm 110:1 "The Lord said unto my Lord, Sit Thou at My right hand until I make Thine enemies Thy footstool." ("The Lord, The Father God, said to my Lord, the Savior . . .")

Jesus referred to this passage in Matthew 22:41-46; Mark 12:35-36; Luke 20:39-44.

Peter referred to it in his sermon at Pentecost, Acts 2:34. It is very important.

The prophecy was the Messiah-Savior would be the Divine Lord Himself.

II The Virgin Birth would be God coming to Live with Men

Isaiah 7:14 ". . .and shall call His Name Immanuel." This is the Savior that was coming.

Matthew 1:23 tells us that Immanuel means "God with us." This came true at Bethlehem.

God in the Person of Jesus Christ came to dwell with man at the Incarnation.

III The Messiah, the Lord Jesus Christ was Given Divine Names in Prophecy

Isaiah 9:6,7 "For unto us a child is born, unto us a Son is given ... and His name shall be called Wonderful, Counselor, The Mighty God, The Everlasting Father, The Prince of Peace." Only the Lord God Himself could be the fulfillment of these names.

Wonderful—Only God is truly wonderful. See Luke 18:19, none good save the Lord God.

Counselor — Only the omniscient God could be the perfect Counselor, Psalm 16:7.

The Mighty God — The One prophesied to be the Messiah was to be God Himself.

The Everlasting Father—John 10:30, Jesus said, "I and My Father are one."

In this text Jesus as man was born but Jesus as God was "given." (God always existed.)

IV The Christ who was Prophesied to Come was to be from "Everlasting"

Micah 5:2 "But thou Bethlehem ... out of thee shall He come forth unto Me that is to be ruler in Israel; whose goings forth have been from of old, from everlasting"

The eternal omnipresent God Himself was to be the Messiah-Savior.

V God and Christ both Gave their Personal Names as "I AM"

Exodus 3:14 "And God said unto Moses, I AM THAT I AM: and He said, Thus shalt thou say unto the children of Israel, I AM hath sent me unto you."

John 8:58 "Jesus said unto them, Verily, verily, I say unto you, Before Abraham was, I AM."

The Jews understood Jesus perfectly and thought that He had committed blasphemy for ascribing the Name of God to Himself. They promptly attempted to stone Jesus.

Death by stoning was the proper death penalty for this particular sin Leviticus 24:12-16.

But Jesus had not sinned for He was truly God. He was the great I AM in person.

VI Jesus Christ Forgave Sins

Mark 2:5 "Son, thy sins be forgiven thee." Only God can forgive sins.

Mark 2:7 "Why doth this man thus speak blasphemies? who can forgive sins but God only."

The Jews were correct for only God can forgive sin, for sin is transgression against the law and only the aggrieved person can forgive the guilty one.

In forgiving sin Jesus either blasphemed or was God. Jesus was God and could forgive.

VII Jesus Claimed Equality with the Father and the Holy Spirit

This is evident in the baptismal formula of Matthew 28:19, and in the benediction of 2 Corinthians 13:14 — the names of God the Father, Son and Holy Spirit are linked together.

VIII Jesus Claimed Omnipresence

To be omnipresent is a characteristic of God Almighty only, not true of angels or men.

Matthew 18:20 Jesus promises to be anywhere, everywhere at one and the same time.

IX Jesus Claimed Omniscience

Omniscience is to know all things and is a characteristic exclusive of God Himself.

This fact is evident in Mark 11:2-6, the description of the colt for the triumphant entry. Jesus exercised the gift of prophecy, too, in Matthew 12:40 and 24:3-31.

X Jesus Claimed Omnipotence

Omnipotence, all power, is another exclusive attribute of the Lord God Almighty.

Matthew 28:18 "All power is given unto Me in heaven and in earth." This claim supersedes the power of man, spirit, angels, demons or supermen.

XI Jesus Christ had Creative Power

To bring something into being from nothing, creation, is possible only to God. Jesus Christ was active in creation and continues to maintain the world, John 1:1-3; Hebrews 1:3.

Jesus used creative power to perform some miracles — water to wine and food for the 5,000.

XII Jesus Christ the true God had Power over the Elements

Luke 8:24 Jesus rebuked the wind and it obeyed Him and there was a great calm at once.

Mark 4:39 Jesus calmed the waves of the raging sea — a power not of man but of God only.

Matthew 14:25, 26 Jesus walked on the water. This ability is denied to ordinary men.

XIII Jesus Christ Received Worship due only to God

John 9:38 the man who had been healed of blindness recognizing the Savior, said, "Lord, I believe. And he worshipped Him." Jesus as God rightfully accepted this worship.

Luke 4:8 Jesus said to Satan at the time of the temptation, "Get thee behind Me, Satan: for it is written, Thou shalt worship the Lord thy God and him only shalt thou serve." To worship anyone but the Lord God is a terrible sin.

When Jesus accepted worship He was saying to the world, "I am the Lord."

XIV Jesus Accepted the Testimony of Thomas

John 20:28 "And Thomas answered and said unto Him, my Lord and my God."

If Thomas had made a mistake, misstatement or overstatement Jesus would have corrected it.

Thomas had told the truth for Jesus was the Lord God, the eternal pre-existent One.

XV The Fact of Jesus' Resurrection

This is the strongest and supreme argument that Jesus is God.

Romans 1:4 "And declared to be the Son of God with power, according to the spirit of holiness, by the resurrection from the dead."

This verse specifically states that the resurrection declares Jesus as the Son of God.

If Jesus were a fake, liar, impostor or a mere man or superman, God would have left Him in the grave until the day of the final judgment and condemned Him to hell.

According to Romans 6:4, it was the Father God, Himself, that raised Jesus from the dead.

The Father God thus proclaims conclusively to the world the deity of Jesus Christ.

Conclusion

We conclude that Jesus is God for He possesses the ten exclusive attributes of God.

1 *Eternal* Micah 5:2 "... from everlasting." Also John 8:58; Colossians 1:17; Revelation 1:8.

2 *Unchangeable* Hebrews 13:8 "Jesus Christ the same yesterday, and today, and for ever."

3 *Omnipotent* Luke 8:24, Jesus stilled the tempest and the sea, also Matthew 28:18.

4 *Omnipresent* Matthew 18:20, 28:20; John 1:48; 3:13.

5 *Omniscient* Mark 11:2-6; John 2:24, 25; Luke 5:22; Matthew 24:3-31.

6 *Holy* Mark 1:24 "Jesus ... the Holy One of God." *Sinless* 1 Peter 2:22; John 19:4.

7 *Just* John 2:14-17, the cleansing of the Temple; Acts 17:31, a righteous Judge.

8 *Loving* John 15:13 "Greater love hath no man than this." Also John 11:36.

9 *Merciful* Titus 3:5 "According to His mercy He saved us." He died for us.

10 *Faithful* 2 Timothy 2:13 "If we believe not, yet He abideth faithful."

The five works of God are ascribed to Jesus — creation, preservation, forgiveness, raising the dead, and judgment — John 1:3; Hebrews 1:3; Luke 7:48; John 5:22; 6:39,

Review Questions

1   Why is the doctrine of the deity of Christ so important?
2   How would you explain Psalm 110:1?
3   Explain how God can be with man from Isaiah 7:14; and Matthew 1:23.
4   List the five names given to the Savior in Isaiah 9:6, 7.
5   Give one prophecy to show that the Savior was to be the eternal one.
6   What is the significance of John 8:58, 59?
7   How does Mark 2:5 prove that Jesus is God?
8   Prove that Jesus possesses the five natural attributes of God.
9   How does Luke 8:24 prove that Jesus is Divine?
10   What is the supreme argument of Jesus' Divinity?

Arguments against the
Deity of Christ

Introduction

This lesson is in addition to lesson nine on the Deity of our Lord Jesus
Christ.

This precious doctrine is attacked mercilessly in this country so it is
good to know the arguments and Scriptures used by these opponents.

The material in this lesson is from the excellent study, *Christ's Deity*,
Efren Alvier.

We list the 21 arguments with brief replies.

The Arguments

Christ is not God, because ...

  I **because He had flesh and bones, and God — being a *spirit***
      — has neither flesh nor bones — John 4:24; Luke 24:39.

Answer: Jesus Christ as man had both flesh and bones but as God He
      was *spirit*. This objection arises from the problem of the
      dual nature of the Savior.

      In order for the invisible God to become visible He must
      become flesh and bones.

      1 Timothy 2:5 Jesus is a dual personality, "The man Christ
      Jesus," (man and God).

      1 Timothy 3:16 "God was manifest in the flesh," in the person
      of Jesus Christ.

  II **Because Christ had a beginning, and God had no beginning**
      — John 8:42; Psalm 90:20

Answer: Jesus as a man had a beginning when He was conceived of
      the Holy Spirit but Jesus as God is without beginning and
      without end. John 8:56-59; Colossians 1:17; John 1:18;
      Isaiah 9:6.

III   Because He has been created, and God has no beginning Colossians 1:15; Revelation 3:14

Answer: A true translation of Revelation 3:14 is something like this, "He was the witness of the beginning of the creation of God," not a creation but a witness of the creation. Proverbs 8:22, 23 speaking of wisdom personified in the person of Christ, "Christ was from everlasting, from the beginning or ever the earth was."

IV   Because Hosea 11:9 says that God is not a man, while Ezekiel 28:2 says that man is not God

Answer: Hosea does not say that God could not assume human form of body and flesh. Nothing is too hard for God, Jeremiah 32:17,18, and He can be manifest in the flesh.

V   Because He called God His Father — Matthew 27:46 and John 20:17

Answer: Jesus as the human Person called God His Father. God in Hebrews 1:8 calls Jesus "God," but that does not lessen the Father's position of deity.

VI   Because the Father sent Him to earth — John 8:42

Answer: The Father sending the Son to earth (Jesus volunteered to come) does not lessen His position as being the Almighty God. Luke 19:10; 1 Timothy 1:15; Galatians 4:4,5.

VII   Because He appeared with flesh — 1 John 4:23; 2 John 7. Since Jesus is flesh, bones and blood, He is merely a man and no more

Answer: Jesus assumed flesh, bones and blood merely for the incarnation. As God He is eternal but to be our Redeemer it was necessary that He become partaker of humanity.

VIII   Because God is His head — 1 Corinthians 11:3

Answer: In a triumvirate it is necessary that one be the chairman but that does not mean that he is greater than the other two. The Father, Son and Holy Spirit are equal but for administrative purposes the Father acts as the executive administrator.

IX   Because He is called man — John 8:40; 1 Timothy 2:5

Answer: Jesus was both true God and true man in one person without an intermingling of the two natures. Emmanuel means "God with us."

X   Christ is not God, but He is a Son of God, just as we may become sons of God

Answer: By conversion we become a "son of God" (John 1:12), but Jesus Christ is the "only begotten Son of God" (John 3:16), a unique and special position.

God's Son is equal to the Father, Philippians 2:6, and the saint becomes an heir with Christ.

XI   Because the Father gave Him power — Matthew 28:18

Answer: In Philippians 2:5-8 the Son surrenders this power and God restores or returns it to Him after the resurrection. It was always His but He voluntarily yielded it.

XII   Because He was made Lord by God — Acts 2:36

Answer: It is not made in the sense of a promotion for though He always was God, the Father takes this opportunity to proclaim this fact to all humanity.

XIII   Because He is subject to God — 1 Corinthians 15:28

Answer: This does not refer to Christ's nature but rather to His position.

Christ voluntarily chose subjection. It was not imposed on Him against His will.

XIV   Because Christ died and God is immortal and cannot die — 1 Timothy 1:17; Luke 23:46 and Acts 2:32

Answer: Jesus as man died but Jesus as God could not and did not die, Hebrews 2:9, 14. It is the physical body that dies. The spirit does not die for it returns to God.

XV   Because He was conceived by the Holy Spirit — Matthew 1:18-20. As a creature of the Holy Spirit He is therefore neither God nor Creator

Answer: The humanity of Jesus Christ was conceived of the Holy Spirit. The deity of Christ has always existed, John 1:1,2. Jesus existed long before the Virgin Mary.

XVI Because He said "I ascend unto my Father and your Father: and to my God and your God"-- therefore the two must be quite distinct — John 20:17

Answer: The Father and Son are two persons but one God, "I and My Father are one," John 10:30. See also John 17:11, 21, 22.

XVII Because He prayed to the Father and addressed Him as the only true God — John 17:3 and 1 Corinthians 8:6

Answer: This objection ignores the fact that the Son co-exists with the Father. They are one. They are one in nature (eternal Spirit), but distinct as to office and responsibilities. The Father and Son are indivisibly linked together, Matthew 11:27; Luke 10:22; John 12:45.

XVIII Because if He were God, then there would be more than one God

Answer: This objection is dealt with in lesson 4, under the Trinity.

XIX Because He was only an "idea," "will" or "purpose" of God, having no material existence or material form in the beginning

Answer: This is perhaps a play on the words in John 1:1,2, but verse 1 answers it definitely and authoritatively, The Word (Jesus) was God."

XX   Because He says, "My Father is greater than I" — John 14:28

Answer: This refers to His position and certainly not to His being or nature.

Positionally Jesus has chosen a position in subjection to His Father God.

XXI Christ is not God, because though He is One with God, that refers merely to Pastoring (shepherding), Teaching and Judgment, but not Godhead

Answer: The Father and Son are one God (but two persons), co-existing as one Jehovah God.

The Father was the Jehovah of the Old Testament, Psalm 23:1, Jesus in the New Testament, John 10:11; Hebrews 13:20; 1 Peter 2:25; Revelation 7:17.

Conclusion

Jesus Christ is God. He is Jehovah. The Lord Jesus Christ is God Almighty. Though we cannot satisfactorily answer all queries we believe that Jesus is God.

Review Questions

1 How can Jesus be God and possess flesh and bones? John 4:24; Luke 24:39

2 How can Jesus be God when He had a definite day that He was begotten or conceived? Psalm 2:7; 90:2

3 How can Jesus be God and the first being that was created? Revelation 3:14

4 Hosea 11:9 says that God is not a man. How then can Jesus be God?

5 In 1 Corinthians 11:3 God is distinctly called the head of Christ. How then can Christ be subservient and God at the same time?

6 We are all sons of God by the new birth but that does not make us gods. How then does Jesus as "Son of God" become God too?

7 If there was a specific day when Jesus was made "Lord," how can He be God? Acts 2:36

8 Since God is immortal and Jesus died on the cross, how can He be God? 1 Timothy 1:17; Luke 23:46

9 Is John 17:3 and 1 Corinthians 8:6 proof that God the Father is the one and only true God?

10 If Jesus is merely a "Word," according to John 1:1, how can an inanimate idea be God?

The Relationship of the Son to the Father

Introduction

This is a controversial point with many cults who deny the deity of Christ.

They say that Jesus, like us, is a son of God, but not God. They maintain that He is a son who is subservient to the Father and quote Scriptures to prove it.

How do we evangelicals answer their seemingly unanswerable arguments?

I believe that in brief the answer is this: As God, Jesus in His preincarnate state was, is, and always will be equal with God the Father.

However, in His incarnate state He is definitely subservient to the Father.

A study of the pre-incarnate Christ will help us to appreciate what the Son emptied Himself of in order to become our Savior, Philippians 2:5-8.

I Jesus Christ as God is Equal to the Father 1 John 2:23

John 5:18 "Therefore the Jews sought the more to kill Him, because He not only had broken the Sabbath, but said also that God was His Father, making Himself equal with God." The Jews who were strong believers in Deuteronomy 6:4, understood Christ's meaning.

The Jews recognized but one God, "The Lord our God is one Lord," and considered Christ's claims as blasphemous and worthy of death by stoning, Leviticus 24:12.

John 10:30 "I and My Father are one," is certainly a proof of His equality with God.

John 14:9 "He that hath seen Me hath seen the Father; and how sayest thou (Philip) then, Shew us the Father?" They are one and indivisible.

Colossians 1:15 "Who (Christ) is the image of the invisible God . . ." Jesus Christ is the visible reflection of the invisible God — invisible because He is a Spirit.

John 10:33 "For a good work we stone Thee not; but for blasphemy; and because that Thou being a man, makest Thyself God." Jesus was trying to prove to them that He was God but they stubbornly refused to believe.

Philippians 2:5,6 ". . . Christ Jesus: who, being in the form of God, thought it not robbery to be equal with God." Jesus was honestly equal with the Father God.

John 17:5 "And now, O Father, glorify Thou Me with Thine own self with the glory which I had with Thee before the world was." Jesus refers to His pre-incarnate glory.

John 1:1 "In the beginning was the Word (Christ), and the Word was with God, and the Word was God." This is a strong positive statement to open John's Gospel.

1 John 5:20 ". . .that we may know Him that is true, and we are in Him that is true, even in His Son Jesus Christ. This is the true God and eternal life."

John both in his Gospel and epistles states the fact repeatedly that Jesus is God.

Titus joins John in his testimony. Titus 2:13 "Looking for the blessed hope, and the glorious appearing of the great God and our Savior Jesus Christ." (One person only)

The One that we wait for is God the Savior who came the first time to Bethlehem.

The writer of Hebrew also adds his testimony. Hebrews 1:8, "But unto the Son He saith, Thy throne, O God, is for ever and ever." God the Father calls His Son "God."

Jude in his great benediction calls the Savior God. Jude 25, "To the only wise God our Savior." This refers to but one Person, the Lord Jesus Christ.

One of the difficult verses to understand is Colossians 2:9, "For in Him (Christ) dwelleth all the fulness of the Godhead bodily." This verse is too immense for mortal man.

To say the least, Christ is perfect and complete in deity — lacking not one thing.

To say that He is only "a" son of God is to insult and blaspheme the Savior.

At the Transfiguration in Matthew 17:2, we get a glimpse of the glory of the pre-incarnate Christ. "His face did shine as the sun."

Whoever refuses to accept Jesus as God, equal to the Father, is guilty of the enormous sin of rejecting the Word of God.

To question or deny the eternal pre-existence and glorious pre-incarnation of Christ does not lessen the fact that Jesus is and had always been God.

The one who questions these facts is guilty of awful slander against the Savior.

Let us rather glory in the fact that though He were true God, equal with the Father, that He emptied Himself of His majestic garments of Divinity for our sakes.

Let us fall before Him in worship, praise and adoration for His great sacrifice.

II Jesus Christ as Man is Subordinated to the Father

When Jesus Christ became man He voluntarily took the lower place — a place of humility and subordination to the Father God.

John 14:28 " Ye have heard how I said unto you, I go away, and come again unto you. If ye loved Me, ye would rejoice, because I said, I go unto the Father: for My Father is greater than I." Jesus the human, is speaking of the eternal God.

When Jesus was conceived of the Holy Spirit, then Christ entered into a new relationship with God. Hebrews 1:5 "For unto which of the angels said He (the Father) at any time, Thou art My Son, this day have I begotten Thee?" This occurred in Luke 1:35.

John 3:16 refers to Jesus as "only begotten Son." This was prophesied in Psalm 2:7

Does this begetting of the Son refer to the origin of the eternal God, the Lord Jesus?

Certainly not, for as God He was never born. He always existed, Isaiah 9:6,7.

The begetting refers to that which transpired in Luke 1:35, when the Holy Spirit came upon the Virgin Mary and the human Jesus was conceived, Luke 1:35.

A   Ways in which the Son was subordinated to the Father:

1   Jesus' earthly life was lived because of the Father: John 6:57 "As the living Father hath sent Me, I live by the Father." The Father sustained the Son.

2   Jesus could not do anything independently of the Father: John 5:19 "The Son can do nothing of Himself, but what He seeth the Father do: for what things soever He doeth, these also doeth the Son likewise."

3   Jesus Christ was sent to earth by the Father. John 6:29 "This is the work of God, that ye believe on Him whom He hath sent." Also John 8:29, 42.

4   The Father gave the Son authority and directions: John 10:18 " I lay it (My life) down of Myself. I have power to lay it down, and I have power to take it again. This commandment have I received of My Father." Also John 13:3.

5   Jesus Christ received His messages from the Father: John 8:26 "I speak to the world those things which I have heard of Him."

6   The Father gave to the Savior certain works to accomplish: John 5:36 "The works which the Father hath given Me to finish, the same works that I do, bear witness of Me, that the Father hath sent me." Also John 17:4.

7   The Father assigned a kingdom to the Son: Luke 22:29 "And I appoint unto you a kingdom, as My Father hath appointed unto Me."

8   During this present Church age Jesus is subjected to the head-ship of the Father: 1 Corinthians 11:3 "The head of the woman is the man; and the head of Christ is God."

9   Christ has become the way by which men are able to approach God: Hebrews 7:25 "Wherefore He is able also to save them to the uttermost that come unto God by Him, seeing He ever liveth to make intercession for them."

10   Jesus has become the way to God, the way of salvation. He is the only way: John 14:6.

11   Jesus referred to the Father as "My God." John 20:17 "Jesus saith unto her. . . I ascend unto. . .My God." Also in Matthew 27:46, the fourth saying from the cross.

B   The extent of this subordination — how long will it last?

Luke 22:29 says that the Father gave the Son a kingdom. The Son will return this to the Father. 1 Corinthians 15:24 "Then cometh the end, when He shall have delivered up the kingdom to God, even the Father."

The period of subordination to extends beyond this — beyond the consummation of this age, even beyond the Great White Throne judgment.

1 Corinthians 15:27,28 "For He hath put all things under His feet . . . then shall the Son also Himself be subject unto Him that put all things under Him, that God may be all in all."

Conclusion

If we understand the Scriptures aright there is no conflict here.

The pre-incarnate Christ is and always has been equal to the Father God Almighty.

The human incarnate Christ laid aside this position and in His self-humiliation chose a place of subordination to the Father as a child to his parent.

The more we study the sevenfold humbling of Christ (Philippians 2:5-8), the more we see manifested His tremendous love for us while we were still ugly sinners.

Let us hasten this wonderful message to all nations.

Review Questions

1   What were the five downward steps that Jesus took in Philippians 2:5-7?
2   Why did the Jews react so strongly in John 5:18?
3   How do you explain John 10:30?
4   What is the significance of John 1:1?
5   List four New Testament writers who speak of Christ as God.
6   In what way is Christ subordinated to the Father?
7   Explain John 14:28, "My Father is greater than I."
8   When was Jesus begotten? Psalm 2:7 and John 3:16.
9   Name seven ways in which the Son is subordinated to the Father.
10   How long will this period of subordination last?

11

The Humanity of Christ

Introduction

In order to be the Savior, Jesus had to be not only Divine and virgin-born, but He must also be a true man. He was like us in every respect except sinful.

1 Timothy 2:5 "For there is one God, and one mediator between God and men, the man (human) Christ Jesus."

Jesus had to be made like us in order to be a "faithful high priest in things pertaining to God," Hebrews 2:17.

Jesus was born under the law that He might redeem us from the law, Galatians 4:4,5.

The first Adam brought death. Christ, the second Adam, brought resurrection, 1 Corinthians 15:22.

In this lesson we present some of the proofs of the humanity of Christ.

I Jesus was Given Human Names

Matthew 1:21 "Thou shalt call His Name Jesus," — fulfilled in Matthew 1:23.

In 1 Timothy 2:5 (above) Jesus is distinctly called a man.

The phrase "Son of man"—which emphasizes His humanity—occurs 77 times, Luke 19:10.

Stephen, just before his death, saw Jesus and called Him "Son of man," Acts 7:56.

II Jesus had Human Ancestry

To get a kitten you must have cat parents. For Jesus to be human He must have a human parent, which He did in the person of His mother, Mary.

Luke 2:7 "And she (Mary) brought forth her firstborn Son."

Galatians 4:4 "But when the fullness of the time was come, God sent forth His Son, made of a woman, made under the law."

Jesus was born of the seed and lineage of David. Acts 13:23 "Of this man's seed (David) hath God according to His promise raised unto Israel a Savior, Jesus."

The genealogy in Matthew 1:1-16 traces the ancestry from Abraham to Christ.

Hebrews 7:14 "For it is evident that our Lord sprang out of Judah; of which tribe Moses spake nothing concerning priesthood."

III Jesus Possessed a Physical Nature

John 1:14 "And the Word was made flesh (human nature), and dwelt among us."

Hebrews 2:14 "Forasmuch then as the children are partakers of flesh and blood, He also Himself likewise took part of the same (i.e. flesh and blood)."

To not confess that Jesus Christ is a man is a mark of antichrist. 1 John 4:3 "And every spirit that confesseth not that Jesus Christ is come in the flesh is not of God: and this is that spirit of antichrist."

To test a demon-possessed person, ask this question: "Has Jesus Christ come in the flesh?" and they will answer with an emphatic "No."

IV Jesus was Subject to the Law

1 He grew. Luke 2:40 "And the Child (Jesus) grew, and waxed strong in spirit."

2 He asked questions. Luke 2:46 "And it came to pass that after three days they found Him (Jesus) in the temple, sitting in the midst of the doctors, both hearing them, and asking them questions."

3 He increased in wisdom. Luke 2:52 "And Jesus increased in wisdom and stature."

4 He learned obedience. Hebrews 5:8 "Though He (Jesus) were a Son, yet learned He obedience by the things which He suffered."

5 He suffered. Hebrews 2:18 "For in that He (Jesus) Himself hath suffered being tempted, He is able to succor them that are tempted." Hebrews 2:10 "For it became Him (Jesus), for whom are all things, and by whom are all things, in bringing many sons unto glory, to make the Captain of their salvation perfect through suffering."

6 He worked as a carpenter to the age of thirty: Mark 6:3 "Is not this the carpenter, the Son of Mary, the brother of James and Joses?"

Jesus' age is given in Luke 3:23.

Jesus was so human that He was mistaken for an ordinary carpenter.

7 He was tempted — the temptations in Matthew 4:1-11.

V Jesus was Moved by the Instincts of a Normal Human Being

1 He hungered: Matthew 4:2 "And when He had fasted forty days and forty nights, He was afterward hungry." See also Matthew 21:18.

2 He thirsted: John 4:7 "There cometh a woman of Samaria to draw water: Jesus saith unto her, give Me to drink."
   The fifth cry from the cross, "I thirst" — John 19:28.

3 He became weary: John 4:6 "Now Jacob's well was there. Jesus therefore, being wearied with His journey, sat thus on the well."

4 He slept: Matthew 8:24 "And behold there arose a great tempest in the sea, insomuch that the ship was covered with the waves: but He was asleep."

5 He loved: Mark 10:21 "Then Jesus beholding him loved him" — the rich young ruler.
   John 11:36 "Then said the Jews, Behold how He loved him" — Jesus loved Lazarus.

6 He had compassion: Matthew 9:36 "But when He saw the multitudes, He was moved with compassion on them, because they fainted."
   Matthew 23:37 "O Jerusalem, Jerusalem ... how often would I have gathered Thy children together, even as a hen gathereth her chickens under her wings . . ."

7 He was angry and grieved: Mark 3:4 "And He saith unto them, Is it lawful to do good on the sabbath days, or to do evil? to save life, or to kill?"
   John 2:16, righteous indignation was manifested in the cleansing of the temple.

8 He manifested reverential trust: Hebrews 5:7 "Who in the days of His flesh when He had offered up prayers and supplications with strong crying and tears unto Him that was able to save Him from death, and was heard in that He feared."

9 He groaned: John 11:33 "When Jesus therefore saw her weeping, and the Jews also weeping which came with her, He groaned in

and the Jews also weeping which came with her, He groaned
in the Spirit and was troubled."

10   He wept: John 11:35 "Jesus wept." Probably also in Gethsemane,
Matthew 26:38.
Luke 19:41, Jesus wept over the city of Jerusalem.
Hebrews 5:7 speaks of " ... supplications with strong crying and
tears ..."

11   He prayed: Matthew 14:23 "And when He had sent the multitudes away, He went up into a mountain apart to pray."

Doubtless He also possessed the sex instinct though this is not
referred to in Scripture, otherwise Hebrews 4:15 would not be true
(tempted in all points as we are).

VI Jesus Possessed Body, Soul and Spirit

1   Jesus had a body: John 1:14; Hebrews 2:14; Matthew 26:12, Jesus'
body was buried, Luke 23:52-56.

2   Jesus had a soul: Matthew 26:38 "My soul is exceeding sorrowful."
Jesus' soul went to Paradise at death, Luke 23:43.

3   Jesus had a spirit, which returned to the Father at death: Luke 23:46
"Father, into Thy hands I commend My spirit."

VII Jesus Died

The biological culmination of life is death. Man is born to die.

Hebrews 9:27 "And as it is appointed unto men once to die ..." Jesus
must keep this rule.

Jesus was in the prime of life when He was crucified on the cross of
Calvary.

Luke 23:33 "And when they were come to the place, which is called
Calvary, there they crucified Him, and the malefactors, one on the
right hand, and the other on the left."

Hebrews 2:9 "But we see Jesus, who was made a little lower than the
angels for the suffering of death, crowned with glory and honor;
that He by the grace of God should taste death for every man."

Jesus came to earth to die, and death was the major proof of His
humanity.

Conclusion

Jesus still possesses a body, even after His resurrection. Luke 24:39
"Behold My hands and My feet, that it is I Myself: handle Me and

see; for a spirit hath not flesh and bones, as ye see Me have."
John 20:27 "Reach hither thy finger and behold My hands."
In Acts 7:55, 56 Stephen at his martyrdom saw Jesus standing at God's
   right hand.
Jesus was human and like us in all but two points: 1) He did not
   possess a sin nature or original sin 2) He was sinless for He never
   committed one sin.

Review Questions

1   What are the six main proofs of the humanity of Christ?
2   What biblical phrase emphasizes Jesus' humanity?
3   What makes a baby human? Does Jesus qualify?
4   What does the expression "likeness of men" in Philippians 2:7
    mean?
5   List seven laws of human development that Jesus followed.
6   List seven normal human instincts that Jesus followed.
7   If Jesus had been only God could He have died? Why?
8   Does Jesus still have a body? Proof?
9   Name two major differences between Christ and us.
10 Why did Jesus become a man? (three reasons)

12

The Sinlessness of Christ

Introduction

We have learned that Jesus was born without original sin, without a sin nature, by virtue of the fact that He was virgin-born, without a human father.

In this lesson we go one step farther and show that Jesus lived His whole life without sin, without committing one sin. He lived and died without taint of sin.

It is true that Jesus Christ was not a hybrid, half God and half man. He was true man and true God, without being a mixture of the two natures.

The two natures of the Savior were separate and distinct in every respect.

The manhood of Jesus is essentially one with ours. It is a distinctive human phenomenon. He was an ideal man. He was a perfect and normal man.

Jesus is unique because of His life of sinlessness, a completely unspotted life.

I The Meaning of the Sinlessness of Christ

Sinfulness is failing to conform to the will of God. Sinlessness is complete conformity to the will of God. Hebrews 10:7 "Lo, I come . . . to do Thy will, O God."

John 17:4 "I have finished the work which Thou gavest Me to do."

Sinfulness is antagonism toward the will of God and deviating toward the path of sin.

Sin is external (lying, stealing, murder) but it is also internal. Matthew 15:19, the thoughts of the heart being the root of later evil actions.

Jesus was sinless both externally and internally.

He completely conformed at all times to that which is wholly good and holy.

Hebrews 7:26 describes the sinlessness of Christ as being "... holy, harmless (guileless), undefiled, separate from sinners." Holy means free from defilement.

Peter describes this sinlessness as being " ... as of a lamb without blemish and without spot," 1 Peter 1:19. This thought occurs in Hebrews 9:14, too.

II The Fact of the Sinlessness of Christ

In Acts 4:27,30 the expression, "Thy holy child Jesus" occurs twice, signifying that from birth He was holy, pure, sinless, and free from defilement.

The devils recognize Jesus as the "Holy One of God," Mark 1:24. The demons in Luke 4:34 cried out, "I know Thee who Thou art; the Holy One of God."

The strongest proof of the sinlessness of Christ is not the testimony of the devils but the plain, inspired Word of God. We believe God's Word is true.

1 Peter 2:21,22 "Christ ... did no sin, neither was guile found in His mouth."

1 John 3:5 "And ye know that He was manifested to take away our sins; in Him is no sin." Absolutely not a trace of sin in our Blessed Savior.

2 Corinthians 5:21 "For He hath made Him to be sin for us, who knew no sin," that is, He never became acquainted with sin. Jesus and sin were total strangers.

Hebrews 4:15 "For we have not an high priest which cannot be touched with the feeling of our infirmities; but was in all points tempted like as we are, yet without sin."

Everyone who has the hope of the Second Coming of Christ will " ... purify himself, even as He is pure," 1 John 3:3. Jesus Christ was perfect purity.

III Testimony regarding the Sinlessness of Christ

1 Jesus' own testimony: He saw sin in others but did not see sin in Himself.

John 8:46 "Which of you convinceth Me of sin?" He was without sin.

Christ was the only man that could ever make that claim honestly after Adam's fall.

Jesus never admitted a fault or ever asked for forgiveness of sins. No evil thought ever lodged in his perfect, holy mind.

2 Pontius Pilate, who was Jesus' judge, examined Him and said, "I find in Him no fault at all," John 18:38. What a clear testimony from a responsible judge under authority!

3 Mrs. Pontius Pilate was a woman, wife of the judge, and had no personal interest in Christ either favorably or otherwise. She had a dream and sent her husband the following message, "Have thou nothing to do with that just (pure, holy, righteous) man," Matthew 27:19.

4 The thief on the cross, Luke 23:41, referring to Jesus, said, "This man hath done nothing amiss."
   This is the testimony of a guilty murderer dying by crucifixion for his sin.

5 Judas Iscariot, a disciple of our Lord for His earthly ministry.
   Judas saw the miracles, heard His teaching, and observed Him closely, and finally betrayed Him for thirty pieces of silver.
   Judas testified, Matthew 27:4, after the condemnation, "I have sinned in that I have betrayed innocent blood." Yet if anyone could detect a flaw, a weakness, a sin in Jesus Christ it would have been one of the disciples who lived, ate, walked and talked with Him. Jesus was innocent of sin.

6 The Roman Centurion: Luke 23:47 "Certainly this was a righteous man."
   A wonderful testimony from a hardened Roman soldier.

IV Arguments against the Savior's Sinlessness

1 Some deny that sinlessness is possible. The fact that sinlessness is contrary to reason avails little in view of the stated facts of Scripture. He is sinless.

2 Some think that because of the fact that He was tempted He must have been susceptible to sin.
   Temptation in itself is not sin. It is yielding to temptation that is sin.
   Jesus was tempted by Satan, the world and circumstances, to sin, but He did not yield.

3 Some argue regarding the temptation in Matthew 4:1-11 that if Jesus were perfect the temptations would be unreal. How can a perfect person be tempted?
   Adam and Eve were created perfect without original sin. They were tempted and yielded, proving that temptation is real even to a perfect person.

4 Some say how could evil enter where there is neither bias toward
    evil or weakness toward sin? Adam and Eve sinned for they
    desired to become as gods, with the idea of maturity and
    development. The temptation was real and they sinned. We
    believe that Jesus was so constituted that He could have sinned
    if He desired for He was a perfect man, not a God-man (or
    mixture).
    Jesus' victory was absolute and complete for He did not once yield
    to sin.

V Consequences of Denying Christ's Sinlessness

If Jesus were sinful He had to die on Calvary for His own sin and we
are yet in our sins.

If Jesus were sinful, then He was neither the Son of God nor the Son
of man, the Savior.

If Jesus were sinful it would be impossible for Him to be a sacrifice on
Calvary.

If Christ were a sinner the Church is established on sinking sand, soon
to be destroyed.

To deny the sinlessness of Jesus Christ is to rob men of a Savior and
salvation.

Praise God that the Bible says He was sinless and today we have
salvation.

VI A Twofold Manifestation of
Christ's Sinlessness

1 Negatively — in never committing an act of sin or thinking or
    speaking a falsehood.
2 Positively — in always doing what was pleasing to God in thought,
    word and deed. Holiness is twofold: 1) a love of righteousness
    and 2) a hatred of iniquity.
    Jesus was perfectly balanced for He fulfilled every aspect of perfect
    sinlessness.

VII Consequences of Christ's Sinlessness

1 Being sinless He was the perfect revelation of God to mankind.
2 Being human and sinless it guarantees a perfect mediator. It shows
    that He came right down to the level of man, of being temptable
    yet resisting and overcoming.

3 Being human and sinless He became an acceptable sacrifice on Calvary for our sins.
4 He set before us a perfect example to follow, 1 Peter 2:21,22.
5 It points the way to a home in heaven opened to us by a sinless Savior.

Conclusion

Let us rise up and praise God that Jesus came without original sin and went back to heaven sinless for He lived a life of absolute moral perfection.

Let us bow down before Him in worship, praise, adoration for this wonderful victory.

What a wonderful message to take to people bound by the chains of sin, lust, habit, evil desires! There is liberty and victory through a perfectly victorious Savior.

Review Questions

1 Since Jesus had a human mother and a Divine Father, is He a mixture? Explain.
2 What is meant by the sinlessness of Christ?
3 What is the chief Scripture to prove the sinlessness of Christ?
4 Name five witnesses to Christ's sinlessness and their brief testimony.
5 Could Christ have sinned in the temptation in Matthew 4:1-11? Why?
6 Was Jesus the only perfect Being that was ever tempted? Who else?
7 Give four results if sin were found in Christ.
8 What is the twofold manifestation of Christ's sinlessness?
9 Name three consequences of Christ's sinlessness.
10 Is this a minor or major doctrine of Scripture? Why?

13

The Character of Christ

Introduction

This lesson is an attempt to tell what kind of person Jesus really was.

R. A. Torrey gives 56 pages to this subject in his book *What the Bible Teaches*.

We often sing or pray, "I want to be like Jesus." What do we mean by this?

This desire is most noble, but we need to emulate Him in more than one point.

He is our example, 1 Peter 2:21, not only in action but in character, too.

Romans 8:29, to be conformed to His image is basically being conformed to His character.

I Jesus Christ was Holy

This subject was covered in the lesson on the sinlessness of Christ.

Jesus Christ was holy, absolutely holy, for He was without a sin nature from birth.

Moreover, He did not commit any sin and always did that which was correct and pure.

In Acts 3:14 Peter refers to Jesus as "the Holy One and the Just (One)."

The Savior manifested His holiness in loving righteousness and hating iniquity. This is seen in His cleansing of the Temple and the denunciation of sin and hypocrisy.

Jesus hates sin so much that He was willing to die on Calvary to defeat sin and offer righteousness to all who will believe in Him.

Galatians 3:13 says Christ was a curse for us under the law. Romans 4:6 says God imputes righteousness to those who receive Jesus Christ as their Savior. See Revelation 19:8b.

II Jesus Christ was Loving

The Savior's love was manifested in two ways: 1) to His Father and 2) to mankind.

John 14:31 "But that the world may know that I love the Father."

Jesus manifested this love by obedience to the Father: John 6:38 "For I came down from heaven, not to do Mine own will but the will of Him that sent Me," also John 14:31b.

Jesus finished the work that the Father gave Him to do: John 17:4 and 19:30.

Christ especially loves the church: Ephesians 5:25 "Christ loved the church."

Jesus has a special love for His own: John 13:1 "Having loved His own..."

Jesus Christ also loves sinners. Luke 19:10 says He came to seek and save the lost. Matthew 9:13 shows Jesus obeyed His own teachings of Matthew 5:44 and loved His enemies, Luke 23:34.

Jesus loved children. The Bible gives this beautifully in the scenes in Mark 10:13-16.

He demonstrated His love by becoming poor that we might become rich: 2 Corinthians 8:9 (RV) "For ye know the grace of our Lord Jesus Christ, that though He was rich, yet for your sakes He became poor that ye through His poverty might become rich."

The supreme proof of His love was voluntarily dying for us: John 15:13 "Greater love hath no man than this, that a man lay down His life for His friends."

Jesus continues to manifest His love to us daily by daily care and sustenance: Matthew 6:33.

III Jesus Christ's Love for Souls

Let us follow our Savior in His never-dying love for the souls of men wandering in sin.

He came as the Good Shepherd to seek lost sheep both of the Jews and the Gentiles.

John 10:16 "And other sheep I have, which are not of this fold: them also I must bring ..."

Jesus loved the multitudes. He came to die for the world — all mankind: John 3:16.

But His ministry was mostly one of individual soul winning, reaching them one by one.

The first chapter of John records His dealings with two of John's disciples, Andrew and his friend, verses 37-40; Peter, verse 42; Philip, verse 43; Nathanael, verse 47.

John 3 with Nicodemus. John 4 with the woman at the well of Samaria. John 9 with the man born blind. Let's not be afraid to spend hours with a single soul.

In Luke 15:4 He bared His heart to go and search for the lost, "What man of you, having an hundred sheep, if he lose one of them, doth not leave the ninety and nine in the wilderness, and go after that which is lost, until he find it?"

Jesus entered into the joy of finding the lost sinner, Luke 15:5-7. In Luke 15:24 Jesus says when the prodigal returned home that they "began to be merry."

Likewise He was deeply grieved at every soul that rejected Him. Luke 19:41,42, Jesus wept over stiff-necked Jerusalem; not over the city, but their souls.

Let us pray that we will be conformed to this love for souls and individuals.

IV Jesus Christ was Compassionate

Jesus Christ was compassionate, for the Bible's shortest verse says, "Jesus wept" (John 11:35).

Jesus' compassion was manifested toward the multitudes: Mark 6:34 "And Jesus, when He came out, saw much people, and was moved with compassion toward them, because they were as sheep not having a shepherd." May we, too, have compassion like this.

Jesus' compassion caused Him to be concerned for the people's physical need: John 6:5.

Jesus' compassion forced Him to heal the blind: John 9:1-38; Matthew 20:34.

He had compassion on those possessed with demons: Mark 9:22, 25; Mark 5:1-13; Luke 4:41.

Jesus was compassionate towards the poor lepers: Mark 1:40-41; Luke 5:12-15.

Often we say we have compassion but Jesus *demonstrated* His compassion with actions.

He became a shepherd to the lost sheep. He became a Savior to the doomed. He healed the sick. He cast out demons. Let us love in both word and *in deed*.

V Jesus Christ was Prayerful

The four Gospels give us a glimpse into the great prayer life of the Savior, but none as strong as Hebrews 5:7, "Who in the days of His flesh, when He had offered up prayers and supplications with strong crying and tears unto Him that was able ..."

It was not uncommon for Jesus to pray all night: Luke 6:12; Mark 1:35.

Jesus prayed before great experiences like His Baptism, Temptation, etc. See Luke 3:21; John 6:15.

He prayed openly to the Father requesting miracles: Matthew 14:19; John 11:41,42.

Jesus ended His earthly life with a prayer on His lips to the Father: Luke 23:46.

Jesus often sought to be alone in prayer, in a solitary place or on the mountain side.

Sometimes He prayed alone, Matthew 14:13; sometimes with His disciples, Luke 9:28; Luke 22:39-46.

Jesus prayed for individuals: Peter in Luke 2:31,32; for "His own" in John 17:9,20.

He prayed in submission to the will of the Father in Gethsemane: Matthew 26:42.

Jesus taught His disciples to pray and told us to do likewise: Matthew 6:9-13.

By prayer He overcame temptation, wrought miracles, escaped death, glorified God.

VI Jesus Christ was Meek

Meekness is the attitude of mind that is opposed to harshness and contentiousness (Torrey).

Meekness manifests itself in gentleness and tenderness toward others.

Jesus Himself says that He is meek: Matthew 11:29 "Take My yoke upon you and learn of Me; for I am meek and lowly in heart ..." This is also stated in Matthew 12:20.

Paul asked the Corinthians this question: 1 Corinthians 4:21 "Shall I come unto you with a rod, or in love, and in the spirit of meekness?"

As Christians we are to learn meekness: Galatians 6:1 "Restore such an one in the spirit of meekness; considering thyself, lest thou also be tempted."

2 Timothy 2:24,25 "And the servant of the Lord must not strive; but

be gentle unto all men, apt to teach, patient, in meekness instructing ..."

Jesus manifested meekness in not breaking the bruised reed or quenching the smoking flax, Matthew 12:20. He dealt tenderly with the broken and fanned the dying fire.

VII Jesus Christ was Humble

Jesus was both meek and humble, "... lowly in heart," according to Matthew 11:29.

He was humble for He sought not His own glory but the Father's glory: John 8:50.

The Savior shunned publicity and fabulous advertising which caters to pride.

The humility of Jesus allowed Him to associate with publicans and sinners: Luke 15:1,2.

The humility of Jesus kept Him silent under outrageous charges: Isaiah 53:7; 1 Peter 2:23.

Jesus demonstrated His humility by washing the disciples' feet: John 13:4,5.

Philippians 2:8 "And being found in fashion as a man, He humbled Himself, and became obedient unto death, even the death of the cross."

Conclusion

Philippians 2:5 "Let this mind be in you, which was also in Christ Jesus."

Let us not imitate but reproduce the holiness, love, compassion, meekness and humility of the Savior, the Lord Jesus Christ. Let us be like Jesus — not only outwardly but inwardly — pure, true and prayerful as he is.

He longs to live this life of character again in us as we yield ourselves to Him.

Romans 6:19, let us yield our members to Him as "servants to righteousness unto holiness."

Review Questions

1 Tell seven things about the character of Christ.
2 In what two ways did the Savior manifest love?
3 List five different ones that Jesus loved.

4   What is the significance of John 10:16?
5   Did Jesus specialize in mass evangelism or personal evangelism?
6   List seven classes for whom Jesus had compassion.
7   What do you feel to be the greatest lesson on prayer that Jesus gave us?
8   What does the word "meek" mean?
9   Prove that Jesus was meek.
10 How did Jesus demonstrate His humility? (five ways)

14

The Teachings of Christ

Introduction

In this lesson we attempt to summarize the main teachings of Christ while on earth. Christ in His earthly ministry gave three long discourses: 1) The Sermon on the Mount, Matthew chapters 5-7; 2) Olivet Discourse, Matthew chapters 24-25; and 3) the Discourse in the Upper Room, John chapters 13-16, and probably 17; plus many other shorter messages.

Someone has said that Jesus touched on 18 subjects in the Sermon on the Mount.

Matthew 7:28,29 "The people were astonished at His doctrine, for He taught them as one having authority, and not as the scribes."

Luke 4:32 "And they were astonished at His doctrine: for His word was with power."

Luke 4:22 "And all bare Him witness, and wondered at the gracious words which proceeded out of His mouth."

In some ways His teachings were new, revolutionary and contrary to human reasoning.

I Jesus' Teaching about Salvation

In His conversation with Nicodemus He told him that he had to be born again, John 3:1-15.

In His talk with the Samaritan woman He made her thirsty for Himself, the living water.

In John 6, He revealed Himself as the true bread that could satisfy true soul-hunger.

In Luke 7:47,48 Jesus taught that He had the power to forgive sins of the penitent.

In John 10, the discourse on the Good Shepherd, Jesus revealed that He was the only door to salvation, and that no man could be saved except through Him.

In Matthew 11:28-30 Jesus gave an invitation for the laborers and weary-laden to come to Him for salvation and soul-rest.

This wonderful salvation invitation is further expanded in Luke
14:16-24 to include the wanderers on the highways and byways
— the poor, maimed, faltering and the blind.

The best loved of all salvation stories is the recovery of the Prodigal
in Luke 15.

II Jesus' Teaching about Daily Christian Living

In Matthew 5:33-48 we are taught 1) not to swear 2) to turn the other
cheek 3) to love enemies.

In Matthew 6:1-4; 19-21, about giving 1) to be done secretly
2) an eternal investment.

Jesus taught a great deal about prayer — Matthew 6:5-13,
Luke 11:1-13; John 14:13,14; 16:23-24. It was to be 1) done in secret
2) continuous 3) unlimited in scope and power.

Jesus taught that we must forgive others before He will forgive us:
Matthew 5:23,24; 6:14,15.

Jesus practiced fasting and taught it: Matthew 6:16-18; Luke 4:2,
before the Temptation.

Jesus cautioned against setting our affections on the necessities of life
but taught that these (daily needs of food, shelter and clothing)
would be provided by the Lord if we sought first the Kingdom of
God: Matthew 6:25-34.

Jesus taught that it was necessary to confess Christ as Lord openly:
Matthew 10:32,33; John 9:38.

Jesus instructed His converts to go home and witness to their relatives
first: Mark 5:19.

Jesus' teaching rang with assurance of salvation to the saved: John
3:16,18,36; John 5:24.

A great deal of the Upper Room discourse speaks of the ministry of
the indwelling Holy Spirit who guides, conducts, energizes and
strengthens the believer: John 14:16-26.

Jesus did not promise His believers and disciples an easy time but
mentioned persecution freely and promised help and grace for
every trial: John 16:1-6; Luke 12:11,12.

III Jesus' Teaching about Pharisees and False Teachers

Jesus was very loud in His denunciation of false teachers and hypocrites.

In Matthew 23:13-36 He says, "woe unto you, Scribes, Pharisees and hypocrites" eight times, verses 13,14,15,16,23,25,27 and 29, calling them blind guides and fools.

In John 8:44 Jesus told them that they were of their "father the devil" — strong language.

In Matthew 16:6 Jesus warned His disciples to "beware of the leaven of the Pharisees and of the Sadducees" who taught false doctrine denying the resurrection, etc.

Jesus taught that these false church leaders did their utmost to make converts but these were "twofold more the child of hell" than they were: Matthew 23:15.

Matthew 7:15-20 is a warning from the Savior to beware of false prophets that are ravening wolves dressed in sheep's clothing.

Luke 20:45-47 is a clear warning to the disciples to beware of the Scribes.

IV Jesus' Teaching about Stewardship

Jesus taught the right use of money and treasure in Luke 12:16-34. The treasure was not for the rich man's personal gratification for he was a "fool"; the true treasure (verses 33,34) was that which was sent to the Lord ahead of time.

When the woman gave two small coins in Mark 12:41-44, Jesus commended her very highly, because she was not rich: she had given inspite of being very very poor.

In Matthew 25:14-30, Jesus taught us to use our God-given talents for His glory.

In Luke 19:11-27, Jesus gave to His disciples the command to "occupy till I come"; we are to use the money that He gave us for the Lord's glory and extension of the kingdom.

Christians are stewards of their money, time, talents, gifts and opportunities.

V Jesus' Teaching about Heaven and Hell

Our Lord spoke of hell and eternal punishment at least 70 times in the Gospels.

Matthew 25:41 "Depart from Me, ye cursed, into everlasting fire, prepared for the devil and his angels." It was Jesus who gave us the clearest picture of torment in hell in Luke 16:19-31. Mark 9:42-48 is a solemn warning to avoid hell.

In the Upper Room discourse Jesus left the reassuring Word that He was going away for a little while to prepare the mansions and return to receive us, John 14:1-3.

To the dying repentant thief Jesus said, "Today shalt thou be with Me in paradise."

Jesus pictured heaven as a home with the Father God, Matthew 6:9; Luke 11:2.

Jesus came from heaven to die and bring many sons home to heaven, Hebrews 2:10.

VI Jesus' Teaching about Fruit Bearing

John 15:1-17, the heart of the Upper Room discourse, deals with the vine and the branches; with the desire that we should bear "fruit"; "more fruit"; "much fruit."

In the parable of the barren fig tree in Luke 13:6-9, the tree (Christian) that does not bear fruit was to be cut down, destroyed and cast into the fire.

In Matthew 7:16-20 Jesus teaches that "by their fruits ye shall know them."

In the Parable of the Sower and the Seed in Matthew 13:1-23, Jesus expresses His desire that each Christian should bear fruit — some thirtifold; others sixtifold; others one hundredfold.

As Christians we should be purged in order that we will bear more fruit, John 15:2.

The purging is a bitter experience of "digging and dunging," Luke 13:8, but essential.

Luke 6:43-46, we as Christians are to bear the fruit of the Spirit and win souls for Him

VII Jesus' Teaching on Prophecy

The Olivet discourse in Matthew 24 to 25 deals mostly with prophetical subjects.

Matthew 24:1-3 deals with the destruction of Jerusalem which took place in A.D. 70.

Matthew 24:4-14 deals with the deteriorating career of this age in which we live.

Matthew 24:15-26 deals with the Great Tribulation, the Time of Jacob's trouble.

Matthew 24:27-31 tells of the return of the Lord in glory. Further details are added in the parable of the fig tree, verses 32-51, and the Ten Virgins of Matthew 25:1-13.

Matthew 25:31-46 tells of the Judgment of the Nations, the separation of sheep and goats.

The seven mysteries of Matthew 13:1-52 are different views of the Kingdom of Heaven.

Conclusion

I suppose that the teachings of Christ could be summed up in one word — love.

He summarized the 600 commandments that the Orthodox Jew lived under to two commandments: 1) love God and 2) love your fellow-man, Matthew 22:37-39.

Love has become the supreme mark of a Christian: John 13:35 "By this shall all men know that ye are My disciples, if ye have love one to another."

In John 15:13 Jesus, referring to His substitutionary death on the cross, says that He was demonstrating the greatest love possible to an individual.

Jesus' prayer of intercession in John 17 is a plea for unity. See verses 11,21,22,23. Not necessarily organic union but unity of purpose in winning lost souls.

Jesus left the Church, His body, on earth to witness in His absence: Matthew 28:19; Mark 16:15.

Jesus' doctrine tells us not only to love the lovely but to love everyone, even our enemies, for He already loves them: Matthew 5:44; 1 John 4:19; Romans 5:8.

Review Questions

1 What were the three main discourses in the ministry of Christ?
2 Summarize in three points Jesus' teaching about salvation.
3 In what six ways would you consider the teachings of Jesus to be new and revolutionary?
4 Of whom did Jesus speak a great deal in the Upper Room discourse?
5 What passage of Scripture pronounces eight woes on Pharisees and hypocrites?
6 Are Christians stewards of money only? Explain.
7 Is it true that Jesus taught love and discarded hell? Explain.
8 Mention three Scripture portions that deal with fruitbearing.
9 What sermon of Christ deals with prophecy?
10 How can the commandments be summarized with the verb "love"?

15

The Commands of Christ

Introduction

The idea for this lesson came from an issue of the "Herald of His Coming" which lists 147 commandments, seven under each of the 21 headings.

(The Great Commission Prayer League lists 173 commandments of Christ taken from the Epistles and Revelation, whereas this lesson confines itself to the Gospels.)

This is a day of extreme lawlessness with many believing that Christ abolished or fulfilled the law and left us with one vague commandment — love.

I Repentance

Repentance is twofold: turning *from* sin and turning *to* God.

Matthew 4:17 "Repent: for the kingdom of heaven is at hand."

Luke 13:24 "Strive to enter in at the strait gate: for many ... shall not be able."

Matthew 6:33 "But seek ye first the kingdom of God, and His righteousness."

II Belief

We are to believe the Gospel; believe in Christ and in the Father.

Mark 1:15 "Repent ye, and believe the Gospel." This was spoken by Jesus, not John.

John 14:1 "Ye believe in God, believe also in Me." This is a definite command.

John 6:29 "This is the work of God, that ye believe on Him whom He hath sent."

III The New Birth

The new birth is the mysterious operation of the Spirit that converts.
John 3:7 "Marvel not that I said unto thee, Ye must be born again."
Luke 10:20 "Rejoice, because your names are written in heaven."
Matthew 12:33 "Either make the tree good, and his fruit good; or else make the tree corrupt, and his fruit corrupt: for the tree is known by his fruit." Conversion is the only solution.

IV Receiving the Holy Spirit

Each Christian is to be Spirit indwelt and empowered.
John 20:22 "He breathed on them and said unto them, Receive ye the Holy Ghost."
Luke 24:49 "Tarry ye in the city of Jerusalem, until ye be endued with power."

V Following Jesus

The believer has no choice but to follow Jesus implicitly.
John 12:26 "If any man serve Me, let him follow Me."
Luke 9:23 "If any man will come after Me let him deny himself, and take up his cross daily, and follow Me."
John 21:22 "Follow thou Me."
Luke 5:27 (Christ to Matthew) "Follow Me."

VI Prayer

The Christian's life is to be characterized by prayer.
Luke 21:36 "Watch ye therefore, and pray always."
Luke 22:40 "Pray that ye enter not into temptation."
Luke 10:2 "Pray ye therefore the Lord of the harvest, that He would send forth laborers into His harvest."
Luke 6:28 "Pray for them which despitefully use you."

VII Faith

The believer is made great because he has faith in a great God.
Mark 11:22 "Have faith in God." This is absolutely essential.
John 20:27 "Be not faithless, but believing." Away with unbelief.
Matthew 14:27 "Be of good cheer; it is I; be not afraid."

VIII Searching the Scriptures

This is a daily "must" in every believer's life.

John 5:39 "Search the Scriptures" — a plain command to every Christian.

John 15:20 "Remember the Word that I said unto you." Read, study and remember.

IX Letting your Light Shine

Each Christian must daily let his light shine brightly.

Matthew 5:16 "Let your light so shine before men, that they may see your good works."

John 15:16 " ... ye should go and bring forth fruit, and that your fruit should remain."

Mark 5:19 "Go home to thy friends, and tell them how great things the Lord hath done for thee."

X Supreme Love to God

Christians are to love and serve God completely.

Mark 12:30 "Thou shalt love the Lord thy God with all thy heart, and with all thy soul, and with all thy mind, and with all thy strength: this is the first commandment."

Matthew 4:10 "Thou shalt worship the Lord thy God, and Him only shalt thou serve."

XI Our Duty to Men in Authority

Christians are to love and obey them.

Mark 12:17 "Render to Caesar the things that are Caesar's"

XII Our Duty to our Neighbors

Our neighbor is the man in need.

Matthew 19:19 "Thou shalt love thy neighbor as thyself."

Luke 6:31 "As ye would that men should do to you, do ye also to them likewise."

XIII Covetousness

Our lives are to be heaven-centered and not earth-centered.

Luke 12:15 "Take heed, and beware of covetousness"; This is stronger than advice.

Matthew 5:42 "Give to him that asketh thee, and from him that would borrow of thee turn not thou away." This is difficult when so many beggars are present.

Matthew 6:19 "Lay not up for yourselves treasures upon earth."

XIV Hypocrisy

Beware of becoming a religious hypocrite.

Luke 12:1 "Beware ye of the leaven of the Pharisees, which is hypocrisy."

Matthew 23:2,3 " ... do not do according to their (Scribes' and Pharisees') works."

XV Meekness

Let's be like Christ in meekness, lowliness and humility.

Matthew 11:29 "Take My yoke upon you, and learn of Me; for I am meek and lowly in heart."

Mark 10:44 "And whosoever of you will be the chiefest, shall be servant of all."

Luke 17:10 "... say, We are unprofitable servants: we have done (only) our duty ..."

XVI Our Love to the Brethren

We are to love, forgive and forbear condemnation.

John 15:12 "... That ye love one another, as I have loved you" (fellow Christians).

Matthew 18:10 "Take heed that ye despise not one of these little ones" (children).

Matthew 5:24 "... first be reconciled to thy brother." Keep short accounts.

Luke 17:4 "And if he trespass against thee seven times in a day ... thou shalt forgive."

Luke 6:37 "Judge not ... condemn not ... forgive, and ye shall be forgiven."

XVII To be Perfect

Jesus could set no lower standard for believers.

Matthew 5:48 "Be ye therefore perfect, even as your Father which is

in heaven is perfect."
Luke 6:36 "Be ye therefore merciful, as your Father also is merciful."

XVIII Wisdom

This is not human wisdom but the wisdom from God.
Matthew 10:16 "Be ye therefore wise as serpents, and harmless as doves."
Matthew 7:6 "Give not that which is holy unto the dogs, neither cast ye your pearls before swine." This requires wisdom to know when to speak.

XIX Preaching the Gospel

Each believer is to preach the Gospel where he is.
Mark 16:15 "Go ye into all the world, and preach the Gospel to every creature."
Luke 24:47 "And that repentance and remission of sins should be preached in His Name among all nations, beginning at Jerusalem."
John 21:15,16,17 " ... Feed My lambs ... Feed My sheep ... Feed My sheep ..."

XX The Second Coming of Christ

We must be ready for this event at any moment.
Luke 12:40 "Be ye therefore ready also: for the Son of man cometh at an hour when ye think not."

XXI Faithful unto Death

True glory is a glorious finish.
Matthew 24:13 "But he that shall endure unto the end, the same shall be saved."

Conclusion

John 14:23 "If a man love Me, he will keep My words." This is the true motive. Use these commands as an inventory to check your personal lives before God. Jesus gives us these commands as a guide to follow to the strait gate.

Review Questions

1   How many commandments did Jesus give in the Gospels? In the Epistles and Revelation?
2   What are the purposes of these commandments?
3   What three things does Jesus ask us believers to believe in?
4   List five ways in which we can follow Jesus.
5   From Matthew 5:16, what "good works" are we to show to the world?
6   How am I to love God?
7   Quote the "Golden Rule."
8   Explain Luke 12:15, "A man's life consisteth not in the abundance of the things which he possesseth."
9   Why did Jesus tell us imperfect humans to be perfect in Matthew 5:48?
10 To whom are we to preach the Gospel?

16

The Miracles of Christ

Introduction

This subject has been for centuries a battleground on which men have fought.

The scientific mind of our twentieth century has attempted to solve the dispute.

Today there seem to be two schools of thought. Some accept miracles and others reject them.

The scientist rejects them because he can neither understand nor prove them.

The Christian accepts them because he has faith in a miracle-working God.

The word miracle is used very loosely today. Someone escapes death in car accident and states emphatically, "It was simply a miracle," when actually it was an act of Divine Providence — the protection of guardian angels. Or we might accidentally meet a desired person under the most unexpected circumstances. Again some would say it was a miracle. Actually it was Divine Providence.

Then let us begin with an acceptable definition of a miracle.

I Definition of the Word "Miracle"

A simple definition is that a miracle is the setting aside of a lower law by a higher law, the higher law being the law of God that superseded earth's laws.

For the apple to fall "up" instead of down would be a miracle. It would be the power of God superseding and changing the law of gravity and centrifugal force.

Here is a more scholarly definition: "An effect in nature not attributable to any of the recognized operations in nature, nor to the act of man, but indicative of superhuman power and serving as a sign or witness thereof." Lindsell and Woodbridge.

In Acts 4:16,22, both the Jewish Council and the Holy Spirit call the healing in Acts 3:1-11 "a miracle". Ordinarily a 40-year-old man who has never walked, doesn't walk.

II Uniqueness of Jesus' Miracles

The Lord's miracles were performed to prove His Deity and accredit His message.

John 2:11 "This beginning of miracles did Jesus in Cana of Galilee, and manifested forth His glory; and His disciples believed on Him."

The prophets (Moses, Aaron, Elijah, Peter and Paul) performed miracles by delegated power (power given them by God, specifically for the task), but Jesus performed His miracles by His own power to demonstrate His Deity.

In all, Jesus performed 35 to 40 miracles (recorded in the Gospels) of various types, because "all power" (Matthew 28:18) was His to use at His discretion.

Jesus in the Temptation, Luke 4:3,4, refused to perform a miracle to obey the devil or satisfy His hunger after 40 days and nights of fasting.

III The Scope of Jesus' Miracles

A **Over nature** Matthew 8:26-27 "Then He arose, and rebuked the winds and the sea; and there was a great calm. But the men marvelled, saying, What manner of man is this, that even the winds and the sea obey Him!"

B **Over devils** Jesus cast out devils in Mark 5:12-13 (demons went out into the swine); Also in Matthew 8:28-32; 9:32,33; 15:22-28; 17:14-18; Mark 1:23-27.

C **Over disease** Palsy, Matthew 8:13; 9:6; impotent man, John 5:9; curing a withered hand, Matthew 12:13; spirit of infirmity, Luke 13:12; stopped the flow of blood, Matthew 9:22; cured dropsy, Luke 14:2; healed fever, Matthew 8:15; speech to the dumb, Matthew 9:33; sight to the blind, John 9:1-38; hearing to the deaf, Matthew 11:5; cured leprosy, Matthew 8:3; Luke 17:19; Jesus healed at least ten different kinds of sicknesses.

D **Over death** He raised Lazarus from the dead, John 11:43,44; also Matthew 9:18-26; Jairus' daughter; Luke 7:12-15, the son of the widow of Nain.

E **Miscellaneous** Water to wine, John 2:1-11: feeding of the 5,000, John 6:1-14; walking on the sea, John 6:15-21; feeding of the 4,000, Matthew 15:32-39; the blasting of the fig tree, Matthew 21:18-22; finding of the coin in the fish's mouth, Matthew 17:27; miraculous draught of fishes, Luke 5:1-11; and again in John 21:6.

F **His own resurrection** was the greatest miracle of all, 1 Corinthians 15:4; Romans 1:4.

IV Credibility of Jesus' Miracles

Jesus' miracles are the very fabric of the Bible and cannot be separated from it.

The records of these miracles are not sensational, or even glowingly presented.

These miracles were performed openly in the presence of many witnesses for all to see.

The miracles of healing have never been disproved by scientists or doctors. Neither has anyone been able to reproduce any of them. Jesus' miracles were unique.

Jesus never performed a miracle for immoral or unworthy purposes. His motives were right.

Jesus' miracles were effected immediately. The healing was instantaneous and supernatural.

Jesus sought to prove to John the Baptist's enquiry that He was the Christ by His miracles that He had done, Matthew 11:3-6.

To attempt to explain the miracles is an insult to the power and integrity of Christ.

The miracles are true and we gladly affirm our belief in the recorded Word of God.

V Objections to Jesus' Miracles

1 Some say that Jesus' personality was so strong that His healings were by strong influences that could cure certain nervous disorders. This is entirely unsatisfactory.

2 Foolish suggestions to explain miracles only make the speaker ridiculous: The sea was shallow and Jesus really walked on the ground. When the lad gave the loaves and the fishes everybody dug into their lunches and gladly shared them. The dead were really not quite dead, just sleeping, etc.

3 Materialism refuses to recognize divine forces and acknowledges only physical forces, so rejects miracles outright.

4 To the Pantheist who recognizes the laws of nature only, miracles are impossible.

5 Agnosticism denies miracles for it denies the source of miracles — God Himself.

6 The naturalist says that the uniformity of nature excludes miracles.

7 Philosophy argues that miracles interrupt the continuity of thought, so are not desired.

8 To the optimist (or idealist) things are so good that miracles are not necessary.

9 Others reject the miracles simply "for insufficiency of evidence."

To us, the veracity of Scripture is such that we accept the Written Word without question.

VI Value of Jesus' Miracles

To us, the miracles are the credentials that identify Jesus as the Savior.

Jesus proved His Person and His Deity by the miracles that He performed.

Miracles are evidences of a superhuman power, 2 Thessalonians 2:9, (Antichrist's power is from Satan).

Jesus received His superhuman power from somewhere or someone. From whom? From God.

Miracles will not *save* anyone (John 12:37) but miracles should *lead one to faith*.

Matthew 8:27, miracles certainly strengthened the faith of those who already believed. Personally, I'm glad that Jesus performed miracles for it shatters any unbelief that I might have and teaches me to believe Him implicitly, without fear that He is too weak to complete the work of salvation that He has begun in me, Philippians 1:6.

VII The Possibility of Miracles Today

Miracles were performed in the Old Testament by men like Moses, Elijah and Elisha.

Jesus performed many miracles during the days of the Four Gospels.

After the ascension, miracles were performed by Peter, Paul and the other Apostles.

If miracles are wrought in the power of God, and they most certainly are, then as God never changes, miracles are still possible today, Hebrews 13:8.

In New Testament times miracles were often performed to accredit the messenger.

We do not need miracles to prove that Jesus is God, for the inspired Bible states it.

Conclusion

Let us honor the Lord by accepting the miracles at face value as they have been recorded in the Holy Word of God.

Let us not insult God with our puny intellect and question His statements in unbelief. Rather let us be like the Negro lady who said, "I believe the whale swallowed Jonah because the Bible says so. If the Bible said that Jonah swallowed the whale I'd believe that too!"

Review Questions

1　Why have scientists rejected the miracles?
2　Are all so-called miracles actually miracles?
3　What is a miracle?
4　In what three ways were Jesus' miracles unique?
5　List seven types of miracles that Jesus performed.
6　List eight diseases and physical defects that Jesus healed.
7　Why should we believe the miracles of Jesus Christ?
8　On what five grounds do some object to the miracles?
9　List three values of Jesus' miracles.
10　Are miracles possible today?

17

The Death of Christ

Introduction

The two doctrines most opposed by fallen man are Incarnation and Expiation.

"These two doctrines show the marvelous, inconceivable, infinite love of God to poor sinful humanity." — Dr. Adolph Saphir

Substitution is the great doctrine of Peter, Paul, James and Philip in Acts.

"There is not a ray of hope for man outside of substitution" — D. L. Moody

Death was the supreme work of the Lord Jesus here on earth. We come to live and death ends our work.

Jesus came to die. His purpose could be gained in no other way.

Sin involves the death penalty. Someone must bear it, either the sinner or a suitable substitute. There is no possibility of bribery at heaven's court.

The atonement is the heart of Christianity. Atonement settles the sin question.

It is said that C. H. Spurgeon, the "Prince of Preachers," would choose a text and from it preach on Calvary. Sin and the blood atonement is the central biblical issue.

The red line of blood passes right through the Bible from Genesis to Revelation.

I The Doctrine of His Death

1 Foretold by God

Isaiah 53:8 "He was cut off out of the land of the living."

Daniel 9:26 "After threescore and two weeks shall Messiah be cut off, but not for Himself." ("Cut off" here is a prophecy of death.)

Zechariah 13:7 "Smite the Shepherd, and the sheep shall be scattered."

2 His death was appointed by God

Isaiah 53:6 "The Lord hath laid on Him the iniquity of us all."

Isaiah 53:10 "Yet it pleased the Lord to bruise Him; He hath put Him to grief: when thou shalt make His soul an offering for sin ..."

Acts 2:23 "Him, being delivered by the determinate counsel and foreknowledge of God, ye have taken, and by wicked hands have crucified and slain."

3 The meaning of His death

a Atonement: Used 77 times, means a covering for sin. It is an Old Testament word that only occurs once in the New Testament and that is in Romans 5:11.

b Propitiation: This carries the thought of a mercy seat.
   1 John 2:2 "And He is the propitiation for our sins."

c Substitution: This is the idea of one taking the place of another. The innocent takes the punishment for the guilty.
   John 10:11 "The Good Shepherd giveth His life for the sheep."

d Redemption: The sinner in bondage is bought back by God with a certain purchase price.
   1 Peter 1:18,19 "Ye were not redeemed with corruptible things as silver and gold ... But with the precious Blood of Christ."

e Reconciliation: God and man were enemies but have now been made friends.
   Romans 5:10 "For if, when we were enemies, we were reconciled to God by the death of His Son ..." Jesus' death on Calvary reconciled God to man.

f Ransom. The price paid for the release of a prisoner (the one kidnapped by sin).
   Matthew 20:28 "The Son of man came not to be ministered unto, but to minister, and to give His life a ransom for many." See John 19:18.

4 The mode of His death

He died by crucifixion: Matthew 27:35; Mark 15:24; Luke 23:33.

It was prefigured to be on a pole — lifted up; Numbers 21:8; John 3:14.

It was an ignominious death. Hebrews 12:2 " ... endured the cross, despising the shame."

It was an accursed death. Galatians 3:13 "Christ hath redeemed us from the curse of the law, being made a curse for us: for it is written, Cursed is every one that hangeth on a tree."

5 His death was voluntary

He volunteered to die for us. He was not forced to do it.

John 10:18 "No man taketh it (My life) from Me, but I lay it down of Myself."

6   The reason for His death

Why did the Lord Jesus, the sinless One, have to die?

We can understand how a guilty person would have to die as a result of sin.

Jesus took our sin and died to satisfy the justice of a Holy God in heaven.

Sin demanded a payment — the death penalty. Only Christ could pay it in full.

All the attributes of God must be in harmony to make salvation possible.

God's loving nature could not forgive sin until His legal nature was satisfied.

In Calvary all the attributes of God found a perfect solution.

7   The result of His death

Salvation to all mankind that accepts Him as a substitute.

1 Timothy 4:10 "... who is the Savior of all men, specially of those that believe."

II   Objections to the Substitutionary Death of Christ

1   Cannot man suffer for his own sins? Yes, but the full penalty is eternal death and eternity will not be long enough to pay the complete debt.

2   Can man atone for his own sin? No. Eternal suffering is not enough. Hebrews 9:22 "Almost all things are by the law purged with blood: and without shedding of blood is no remission." Only death can satisfy the demands of God and the soul never succeeds in dying in hell. (Someone has defined hell as dying forever and never being able to die.)

3   The doctrine of the atonement was invented by Paul. No, it was preached by our Lord Jesus Christ Himself while He was still on the earth.

Matthew 16:21 "Jesus began to show to His disciples that He must go to Jerusalem, and suffer many things ... and be killed, and be raised again."

John 12:24 "Except a corn of wheat fall into the ground and die, it abideth alone: but if it die, it bringeth forth much fruit." Jesus was the corn about to die.

4 Will this doctrine not make men feel hopeless and sin even more? No. The cross teaches God's great hatred for sin. See Romans 6:1,2.

5 Is this not unfair to make the innocent suffer for our sins against His will? It *would* be unfair if Jesus were forced to suffer for our sins against His will. However, Jesus volunteered to die for us. It was His own desire to choose to do so.

6 Could God not just forgive the sinner without the terrible death on Calvary?

Sin has been committed against God. Why couldn't God just blot it out?

He could not, for the law of God must be satisfied.

Genesis 2:17 "In the day that thou eatest thereof thou shalt surely die."

Ezekiel 18:4 "The soul that sinneth it shall die."

Romans 6:23 "For the wages of sin is death."

Repentance does not remove the need for punishment for sin. Sin has been committed and sin must be dealt with according to God's own precepts.

The justice and honor of God are being challenged, and must be preserved. The holiness of God demands the death penalty for sin.

7 Is it not impossible to transfer guilt from a guilty one to an innocent one?

Human courts punish only the guilty one, but they could punish a substitute if such were desired, for the substitute voluntarily assumes the guilt of the other.

Isaiah 53:4 "Surely He hath borne our griefs, and carried our sorrows."

Isaiah 53:5 "But He was wounded for our transgressions, He was bruised for our iniquities: the chastisement of our peace was upon Him; and with His stripes we are healed."

1 Peter 2:24 "Who His own self bare our sins in His own body on the tree, that we, being dead to sins, should live unto righteousness: by whose stripes ye were healed."

8 If each sin requires eternal death, how could Christ suffer an innumerable number of deaths in the few short hours of Calvary?

It was not the amount of suffering that counted but the justice of

God that had to be satisfied. The fact that a holy sinless One suffered, made the difference.

The One who suffered was not a mere man. He was the God-man, 1 Timothy 2:5.

Isaiah 52:14 "His visage was so marred more than any man, and His form more than the sons of men." This verse suggests a death so horrible that God pulled down the curtain of darkness at Calvary lest men see that marred face, Luke 23:44.

Conclusion

The death of Jesus Christ is sufficient for every sinner. He died for the sins of the whole world. He died for your sins and particularly for *my* sins.

Review Questions

1   What must Jesus do in order to accomplish His mission on earth?
2   Give two Old Testament prophecies to prove your answer to question 1.
3   Give two Scriptures to show that God was willing to let Jesus die on earth.
4   Give five meanings of the death of Christ and an explanation of each.
5   Can man atone for his own sin? Why?
6   Why did Jesus die on Calvary?
7   What is the result of the death of Jesus Christ?
8   Couldn't God forgive sin without Jesus' dying? Why?
9   Is it possible to transfer guilt from a guilty person to an innocent one?
10   If the punishment for each sin is death, how could Jesus suffer innumerable deaths?

18

The Resurrection of Jesus Christ

Introduction

The doctrine of the resurrection is the foundation doctrine of the New Testament.

The resurrection is mentioned 104 times in the New Testament.

Christianity is the only religion with a living originator. Buddha is dead; Brahma (Hinduism) is dead; Mohammed is dead; Marx (Communism) is dead.

The boast and glory of Christianity is the empty tomb. Jesus is risen.

On the cross Jesus cried, "It is finished," and the Father said "Amen" by resurrecting the Son from the dead.

If Jesus did not rise from the grave, we are of all men most miserable, for we are yet in our sin; we are lost; eternally lost; 1 Corinthians 15:16-19.

Jesus said that He would die and rise again from the dead the third day, Matthew 16:21.

If the resurrection is true, then Jesus is indeed the Son of God.

This is the miracle on which all other miracles stand or fall.

If this, the greatest of miracles is true, then it is easy to believe all the rest.

I Evidence of the Resurrection

1 The empty tomb: Matthew 28:6 "He is not here: for He is risen, as He said. Come, see the place where the Lord lay."
   Luke 24:3 "And they entered in, and found not the body of the Lord Jesus."

2 The testimony of angels: Matthew 28: 5-6 ; also Luke 24:5-7
   "Why seek ye the living among the dead? He is not here, but is risen: remember how He spake unto you when He was yet in Galilee, saying, The Son of man must be delivered into the hands of sinful men, and be crucified, and the third day rise again."

3 People who talked to Him after the resurrection: Peter, Mary, Cleopas and Thomas.

4 Jesus ate and drank, showed His wounds, etc., to friends after the resurrection.

5 By the 500 who saw Him at one time, 1 Corinthians 15:6 "After that, He was seen of above five hundred brethren at once; of whom the greater part remain unto this present, but some are fallen asleep."

6 By His appearance to Stephen at his martyrdom, Acts 7:56 "And said, Behold, I see the heavens opened, and the Son of man standing on the right hand of God."

7 By His appearance to Paul on the Damascus road, Acts 9:5 "And he said, Who art Thou, Lord? And the Lord said, I am Jesus whom thou persecutest."

8 By the testimony of millions who have proved Him to be a living Savior.

9 By many infallible proofs, Acts 1:3.

II Explanations of Jesus' Resurrection

1 **The fraud theory** — that the whole story is a hoax; a deliberate imposture. History and the Scripture flatly deny such a ridiculous theory.

2 **The swoon theory** — that Jesus only fainted for the soldiers did not kill Him and that the cool tomb and spices caused Him to revive and come back to life.

   On the contrary, the spices were poisonous and would have killed Him instead.

3 **The hallucination theory** — the disciples wanted to see Jesus and thought that He would rise so they *imagined* that they saw Him.

   The Scriptures tell us that the disciples were steeped in unbelief and would scarcely believe after seeing Him. Thomas wouldn't believe without touching Him.

   The disciples were incredulously unbelieving, for which Jesus rebuked them, Luke 24:25.

4 **The ghost theory** — they only saw His ghost and thought that it was Jesus. A ghost does not have flesh and bones or eat and drink, Luke 24:39,43.

5 **The myth theory** — it was a wild story handed down by the ancients without truth. The whole canon of Scripture shows this

is a lie.

6 **The true explanation** — that Jesus Christ rose bodily from the grave as He said that He would. Acts 2:24 "Whom God hath raised up, having loosed the pains of death: because it was not possible that He should be holden of it."

III His Resurrection Body

1 It had flesh and bones: Luke 24:39 "Behold My hands and My feet, that it is I Myself; handle Me, and see; for a spirit hath not flesh and bones, as ye see Me have."
2 It was a glorious body: Philippians 3:21 "Who shall change our vile body, that it may be fashioned like unto His glorious body."
3 It was an immortal body — one that will never die: Romans 6:9 "Knowing that Christ being raised from the dead dieth no more; death hath no more dominion over Him."
4 It was a spiritual body: 1 Corinthians 15:44 "It is sown a natural body; it is raised a spiritual body."
5 The spirit body has the ability to pass through a solid wall, John 20:19 "Then the same day at evening, being the first day of the week, when the doors were shut where the disciples were assembled for fear of the Jews, came Jesus and stood in the midst, and saith unto them ..."

IV How did Jesus Rise from the Dead?

1 By the power of the Father: Acts 2:23,24 "... by wicked hands have crucified and slain: whom God hath raised up ..." Also Acts 3:15; 5:30.
2 By the power of Christ Himself: John 2:19 "Jesus answered and said unto them, Destroy this temple, and in three days I will raise it up." Also John 10:18.
3 By the power of the Holy Spirit: 1 Peter 3:18 "... being put to death in the flesh, but quickened by the Spirit."

V Results of the Resurrection

1 It proves the existence of God. If there is no God, how did Christ rise from the dead? He rose because a living God resurrected Him.
2 It proves the Deity of Christ. Romans 1:4 "And declared to be the

Son of God with power ... by the resurrection from the dead."

3 It means that salvation is an accomplished fact. Jesus said that salvation was completed when He died on the cross and the resurrection confirms it.

4 The resurrection guarantees that everyone else shall rise too:
a) The righteous unto life eternal,
b) The unrighteous to face an angry Judge and be condemned forever.

5 It prepares Him to fulfill His next promise, "I will come again."

6 The "power of His resurrection" (Philippians 3:10) is an experience that we may enjoy now. It means living in newness of life that comes to us by the resurrected Christ living His life anew through our bodies.

Conclusion

Resurrection is the greatest power in the world outside of the power of prayer.

Resurrection surpasses the power of the atom, hydrogen, cobalt or uranium (used in nuclear reactors).

These have the power to destroy; resurrection has the power to give life to the dead.

Story: Atheist dies and, to be sure that he will never rise, has in his will a clause, "My body is to be cremated and my ashes taken by plane and scattered in the seven seas." A thousand years later in the resurrection when the trumpet sounds, that body will come together and stand perfect in Christ's presence.

May this same mighty power of resurrection course through my body to keep me from sin.

The resurrection is the basis on which Christianity stands or falls.

The resurrection is the unshakable rock of Christian evidences. It is the Waterloo (utter defeat) of infidelity, agnosticism and atheism.

Because Christ rose, materialism, communism, atheism must fall.

Today the mightiest conqueror is death, who strides across the land, digging a trench across the hemispheres and filling it with the dead. (Talmage)

But resurrection is a greater power for it breaks the power of the grave.

Today we triumphantly say, "O death, where is thy sting? O grave, where is thy victory?" 1 Corinthians 15:55.

We serve a risen Savior. He is in the world today. Victory is ours as we march forward with the conquering Christ as the Head of the

Church militant.

May others be conscious that He is alive as He lives His life in our bodies.

Review Questions

1 What is the outstanding characteristic of Christianity?
2 Give six evidences of the resurrection.
3 What is the swoon theory regarding the resurrection? Is it true? Why?
4 How do we know that the hallucination theory is false?
5 What is the true explanation of Christ's resurrection?
6 Describe Christ's resurrection body.
7 How did Christ rise from the dead?
8 How does the resurrection of Christ prove the existence of God?
9 Why is the dogma of the resurrection denied by many?
10 What do you consider the greatest power in the world?

19

The Ascension of Christ

Introduction

The life of Jesus Christ can be told as four great miracles: Incarnation, resurrection, ascension and second coming. Today we study the third of these miracles.

The ascension is that event in which Christ departed visibly and returned to heaven.

He came to earth as a humble baby. He left the earth as the exalted conqueror.

When His earthly work was complete He entered into His heavenly ministry of preparing the Mansions and the High Priestly work of intercession.

I The Story of the Ascension

Acts 1:9-11 "And when He had spoken these things, while they beheld, He was taken up; and a cloud received Him out of their sight. And while they looked steadfastly toward heaven as He went up, behold two men stood by them in white apparel; which also said, Ye men of Galilee, why stand ye gazing up into heaven? This same Jesus, which is taken up from you into heaven, shall so come in like manner as ye have seen Him go into heaven."

The description can be summarized in two words: He ascended visibly and bodily.

II The Ascension was Prophesied and Taught in the Scriptures

Psalm 68:18 "Thou hast ascended on high, Thou hast led captivity captive."

Psalm 110:1 "The Lord said unto my Lord, Sit Thou at My right hand, until I make Thine enemies Thy footstool." After the ascension He sat at the Father's right hand.

Luke 9:51 "And it came to pass, when the time was come that He should be received up, He steadfastly set His face to go to Jerusalem." The ascension was in God's plan.

John 6:62 "What and if ye shall see the Son of man ascend up where He was before?"

John 14:28 "I go away ... I go unto the Father: for My Father is greater than I."

John 20:17 "Jesus saith unto her, Touch Me not; for I am not yet ascended to My Father; but go unto My brethren, and say unto them, I ascend unto My Father, and your Father."

The Old Testament spoke of it and Jesus taught freely of His ascension.

The disciples probably didn't understand it any more than they understood the precious truths of His death, burial and resurrection.

III The Ascension Occurred Forty Days after the Resurrection

Jesus delayed going back to His Father to remain on earth for several reasons.

1 To prove beyond the shadow of a doubt that He had actually risen from the dead.

   This was essential to establish the faith of the believers.

2 He tarried in order to give the disciples more instructions in the Christian faith.

   In the post-resurrection period Jesus was able to explain much of His past teaching in the light of that which occurred — His own death, burial and resurrection.

Acts 1:3 "To whom also He shewed Himself alive after His passion by many infallible proofs, being seen of them forty days, and speaking of the things pertaining to the kingdom of God."

IV The Manner of the Ascension

Luke 24:51 "And it came to pass, while He blessed them; He was parted from them, and carried up into heaven."

Jesus Christ is now seated at the right hand of the Father. Ephesians 1:20 "Which He wrought in Christ, when He raised Him from the dead, and set Him at His own right hand in the heavenly places."

Some think this expression, "God's right hand," is figurative, meaning power. However, I believe it is literally a geographical location, for Stephen saw Christ there.

Acts 7:56 "I see the heavens opened, and the Son of man standing on the right hand of God." True, it is difficult to localize the eternal God but it can be done.

The ascension was visible, not secret. It was seen and witnessed by the apostles.

Jesus Christ left personally, visibly and bodily and in like manner will He return in the Second Advent to this earth.

V The Necessity of the Ascension

Heaven was His home and it was logical that when His work was complete that He would return home again. John 14:28 "I go unto the Father."

Prophecy had to be fulfilled. He said that He would return to the Father and He did, John 16.

The Divine plan was that the Holy Spirit would not come to indwell believers until after the ascension of Christ. The ascension must precede Pentecost.

John 16:7 "It is expedient for you that I go away: for if I go not away, the Comforter will not come unto you; but if I depart, I will send Him unto you."

The ascension of Christ was a prerequisite to His further work of preparing mansions.

John 14:2,3 "I go to prepare a place for you. And if I go and prepare a place for you, I will come again, and receive you unto Myself."

It would have been wonderful if Jesus could have lived on earth forever in His post-resurrection power but that was not the plan of God for the Church.

1 Jesus ascended to complete the redemptive work that was required, John 20:16,17.

2 Jesus' ascension enabled His followers to do the promised greater works, John 14:12.

3 Jesus ascended to enter into the ministry of intercession at God's throne

4 Jesus' ascension makes His ministry worldwide, not localized in Palestine, Matthew 28:18.

5 The ascension becomes a strong proof and explanation of the resurrection body.

VI The Purpose of the Ascension

Jesus ascended to glorify the Father. John 17:1 "Father, the hour is come; glorify Thy Son, that Thy Son also may glorify Thee."

Jesus ascended to become a Prince and a Savior. Acts 5:31 "Him hath God exalted with His right hand to be a Prince and a Savior, for to give repentance."

Jesus ascended as a forerunner, opening the pathway for us. Hebrews 6:20 "Whither the forerunner is for us entered, even Jesus."

Jesus ascended to prepare our heavenly abode, John 14:2; to be our High Priest, Hebrews 9:21-24; and to take His appropriate seat, Hebrews 10:12,13.

VII The Results of the Ascension

He gave gifts to men. Ephesians 4:8 "When He ascended up on high, He led captivity captive, and gave gifts unto men." What gifts? Verse 11 says apostles, prophets, etc.

Because He ascended the Holy Spirit descended, John 16:7 and Acts 2:33.

He demonstrated that sins were purged by sitting down, showing completed action. Hebrews 1:3 "When He had by Himself purged our sins, sat down on the right hand."

Because of His ascension now we can come boldly to the Lord in prayer, Hebrews 4:14-16.

Because He has ascended He can now save to the uttermost, Hebrews 7:25. He can lift a sinner from the cesspool of sin to the highest heaven to be with Himself.

His presence in the heavenlies causes us to "draw near with a true heart in full assurance of faith, having our heart sprinkled from an evil conscience," Hebrews 10:22.

He stands now on the portals of heaven beckoning us to look "unto Jesus," Hebrews 12:2. He stands as the goal at the end of the journey.

Positionally we are seated with Him today in the heavenlies. Ephesians 2:6 "And hath raised us up together and made us sit together in heavenly places in Christ Jesus."

He ascended that He might fill all things. Ephesians 4:10 "He that descended is the same also that ascended up far above all heavens, that He might fill all things."

Now that He has ascended, angels, authorities and powers are subject to Him. 1 Peter 3:22 "Who is gone into heaven, and is on the right hand of God; angels and authorities and powers being made subject unto Him." His ascension became a coronation.

Ascension becomes one of the six articles of the mystery of godliness, 1 Timothy 3:16.

Conclusion

Because of the exaltation of Jesus Christ, one day every knee shall bow and every tongue shall confess that Jesus Christ is Lord to the glory of God the Father.

Philippians 2:9-11 "Wherefore God also hath highly exalted Him and given Him a Name which is above every name." Let's not wait until that day to glorify our Savior. Let's worship and serve this Christ who defied the laws of gravity and ascended bodily. Let's prepare to welcome Him soon as He returns bodily and visibly.

Review Questions

1   What are the four great miracles in the life of Christ?
2   Where is the story of the ascension recorded?
3   What was the prophecy of Christ's ascension?
4   Give two reasons why Jesus did not ascend immediately after the resurrection.
5   Describe the ascension.
6   List five reasons why it was necessary for Jesus to ascend.
7   Give four purposes of His ascension.
8   List seven results of the ascension.
9   What information about the ascension do we learn from 1 Peter 3:22?
10 What lesson would you learn linking Ephesians 4:10 with Matthew 18:20?

20

The Intercessory Work of Christ

Introduction

Is Christ idle today? What is He doing now? Does He spend all His time preparing mansions for the redeemed? This is one of His important tasks. John 14:2 "In My Father's house are many mansions: if it were not so, I would have told you. I go to prepare a place for you."

In addition to this ministry Jesus is actively engaged in the ministry of intercession.

Hebrews 7:25 "Seeing He ever liveth to make intercession for them."

Hebrews 9:24 "For Christ is not entered into the holy places made with hands, which are the figures of the true; but into heaven itself, now to appear in the presence of God for us."

A priest is a mediator, one who intercedes with a just God on behalf of guilty sinners.

Leviticus 4:16-18, the priest bears a bloody sacrifice or a sin offering to the Lord.

Job's desire was for a mediator, a daysman in his day. Job 9:33 "Neither is there any daysman between us, that might lay his hand upon us both."

We thank God often for Bethlehem and Calvary and we must also thank Him for His present advocacy at God's right hand on our behalf.

Day by day our High Priest pleads on our behalf to the Father God.

I Christ's Atoning Work was Finished on Earth

On the cross Jesus said, "It is finished," John 19:30. Salvation is perfectly complete.

Sin was righteously dealt with at the cross. Jesus will never die for sin again.

Hebrews 9:24-28 shows the sin and error of Romanism daily offering Mass, trying to re-enact Calvary each time a Mass is offered.

We consider this as blasphemy for it treats with contempt the Holy Scriptures.

II Christ Met the Conditions of Becoming a Priest

1 He was taken from among men. Hebrews 5:1 "For every high priest taken from among men is ordained for men in things pertaining to God, that he may offer both gifts and sacrifices for sins."

2 He was ordained or appointed to the task. Hebrews 3:2 "Christ Jesus ... who was faithful to Him that appointed Him (as High Priest)."

3 He was called of God to the task, Hebrews 5:4,5.

4 He served in things pertaining to God. Hebrews 2:17 "... that He might be a merciful and faithful high priest in things pertaining to God, to make reconciliation for the sins of the people."

5 He offered gifts and sacrifices for sins, Hebrews 5:1. Jesus Christ offered Himself.

III Christ was Made a Priest after the Aaronic Pattern

On earth Jesus never acted as a priest. He never entered the Holy of Holies.

1 Both offered sacrifice before the people. Jesus publicly offered Himself at Calvary.

2 Both appeared in God's presence for the people.

3 Both came out to bless the people.

However, Aaron as a man died. Jesus as God ever lives to intercede for us.

In this respect Jesus follows the Melchisedec pattern, a priest without end, Hebrews 5:6.

IV Christ Offered Himself as the Sacrifice on Calvary

While we were yet sinners the Savior died for us. He died at Jerusalem, without the gate upon that cross of shame.

His sacrifice was:

1) Voluntary, of a free will, Hebrews 10:5-10. He offered to die.
2) Substitutionary, Hebrews 7:24-28. He died instead of me.
3) Spotless, Hebrews 9:14. He was without spot, the perfect sinless Lamb.
4) With blood, Hebrews 9:12, His own blood, Divine blood, Acts 20:28.
5) Acceptable, Hebrews 13:20,21. The Father's justice was satisfied.
6) Final, Hebrews 7:27. There is no need for a re-enactment of Calvary.

V Christ now Appears in the Presence of God for Us

1 **The place** In heaven. Hebrews 9:1-8 tells of the responsibilities of the priest. Hebrews 9:11,12 "But Christ being come an high priest of good things to come, by a greater and more perfect tabernacle, not made with hands, that is to say, not of this building; neither by the blood of goats and calves, but by His own blood He entered in once into the holy place, having obtained eternal redemption." Hebrews 9:24 "Christ ... is entered into heaven itself ..." Acts 7:55.

2 **For whom?** His own. Hebrews 9:24, "... now to appear in the presence of God for us." See also Hebrews 7:24,25, interceding for those who come to God.

3 **Basis of His plea** is His own blood. Hebrews 9:12 "... by His own blood ..." In John 17:1-26 (His High Priestly Prayer), Jesus speaks of the finished work.

4 **His prayer**
  1 For grace to be given to the saints in need, 2 Corinthians 12:9.
  2 For strength to be given to the weak, John 17:11.
  3 That we may be kept from sin and temptation, John 17:15.
  4 That we shall be forgiven when we confess our sins, 1 John 1:9
  5 That we have power to witness for Christ, Acts 1:8.
  6 That we be conformed to the image of Christ, Romans 8:29.

5 **Purpose of the plea**
  1 To sustain life, Hebrews 9:24.
  2 To give cleansing, 1 John 2:1.

3 To give grace and help, Hebrews 4:15, 16.
4 To secure victory, Hebrews 2:17,18.

VI Christ is our Advocate now

Satan is the accuser of the brethren at the throne of God, Job 1:6-12.

To counteract the accusations of Satan we have a lawyer at the court of heaven.

Our lawyer-advocate is the Lord Jesus Christ Himself. 1 John 2:1 "My little children, these things I write unto you, that ye sin not. And if any man sin, we have an advocate with the Father, Jesus Christ the righteous: And He is the propitiation for our sins." The sacrifice becomes the lawyer.

When we sin He pleads for us on the ground of His finished work at Calvary.

The saint then receives the Father's forgiveness for the sake of the Savior, 1 John 1:9.

VII Christ Offers to be Your Intercessor Today

If we do not ask for forgiveness we will not receive it.

1 In times of severe trial we ought to be glad of a true friend at court.
2 The Savior stands ready at the court of heaven to assist us.
3 He is willing to be our personal representative to the Father.
4 As we pray we place our case in His hands for His divine care.
5 As a true man He was tempted in all points like as we are yet He was without sin. He overcame sin and now offers that overcoming power to us.
6 We do not know the accusations that Satan is constantly bringing to the Father against us. Some may be true but many, many may be false.
   Revelation 12:10 "The accuser of our brethren is cast down."
7 Our departed loved ones, saints or Mary cannot be our advocates.

Conclusion

Luke 22:31 "And the Lord said, Simon, Simon, behold, Satan hath desired to have you, that he may sift you as wheat: but I have prayed for thee that thy faith fail not."

This is Christ's present intercessory ministry on our behalf.

Since He knows all things He can pray about temptations even before they come.

Allow Him to plead your case to receive grace, strength and power for daily living.

Allow Him to plead your case to conform you to His blessed image, Romans 8:29.

The intercessory work of Christ has supplied strong motives for consistent and impressive Christian living. The resurrected Christ is watching over me.

The Christian soldier reckons on Jesus the Captain fighting the same battle but on a higher plane — fighting the battle in the heavenlies, Ephesians 6:12.

The humblest believer now rests in the love of that unseen Friend whose faithful care is unaffected by time or events.

Review Questions

1   What is Christ's present work?
2   Is Christ still engaged in the perfecting of salvation? Explain.
3   What five conditions did Christ meet in order to become a Priest?
4   After what pattern was Jesus made a Priest?
5   Describe Jesus' sacrifice on Calvary.
6   Where does Jesus perform His High Priestly duties?
7   Name five possible pleas of the High Priest.
8   Why is it necessary to have a High Priest in Heaven?
9   What comfort do we draw from Revelation 12:10?
10 Was Christ's prayer in Luke 22:31 an extraordinary event? Why?

21

The Second Coming of Christ

Introduction

There are three Greek words used to reveal this fact: 1) Parousia — personal presence 2) Apokalupsis — revelation and 3) Epiphaneia — appearing. These three words signify that there will come a time when Christ will return in a public, personal revelation of Himself to the world.

Some teach that the Second Coming is when at death "Jesus comes to receive the soul," but that would not be a public revelation visible to all the world.

Acts 1:10,11 describes the ascension which we studied in a previous lesson and described as being 1) personal 2) bodily 3) visible and 4) with power.

The Savior's first coming was in humiliation but the Second Advent will be glorious.

Actually there are three major viewpoints respecting His Second Coming:

1 Post millennial view: It teaches that the Second Coming will follow rather than precede the millennial age.

2 The A-millennial view: Supporters do not believe in a literal period of a thousand years but believe that when Christ comes everything ends quickly.

3 The pre-millennial view: The Lord comes and then the Millennium follows.

Another complication is that the Second Coming is in two stages:

1 The rapture which is secret (1 Thessalonians 4:15-17) when the Lord comes *for* His saints and we meet Him in the air.

2 The revelation which is public (Revelation 1:7), when the Lord comes *with* His saints to set up the Millennium, 1 Thessalonians 3:13.

An unsolved problem of pre-millennialists is whether the Church will go through the tribulation so there are the "pre-tribulation and mid-tribulation" debates.

I Prophecies of Christ's Second Coming

His first coming was prophesied and those prophecies came to pass literally.

This gives us great confidence that the prophecies of the Second Advent will also be fulfilled literally and not in a figurative or spiritual sense.

1 It was foretold by the prophets. Daniel 7:13 "I saw in the night visions, and, behold, one like the Son of man came with the clouds of heaven."

2 It was foretold by Jesus Himself. Matthew 25:31 "When the Son of man shall come in His glory, and all the holy angels with Him, then shall He sit upon the throne of His glory."

3 It was foretold by Paul. 1 Timothy 6:14 "Keep this commandment without spot, unrebukeable, until the appearing of our Lord Jesus Christ."

4 It was foretold by angels. Acts 1:10,11 when the Savior ascended from the earth.

None of these prophecies were fulfilled at His first coming.

II Time Of Christ's Coming

This is a secret that only the Lord knows. Matthew 24:36 "But of that day and hour knoweth no man, no, not the angels of heaven, but My Father only."

Jesus Christ as man did not know that date but Jesus Christ as God is omniscient and certainly knows the exact moment when it will occur.

I believe it is a movable date (2 Peter 3:12, R.V.) that can be advanced or retarded depending on the speed or slowness of taking the Gospel to every tribe, Matthew 24:14.

III Purpose of Christ's Coming

1 To complete the salvation of saints: He has delivered us from the power and penalty of sin but then He shall deliver us from the presence of sin, Hebrews 9:28.

2 To be glorified in His saints. 2 Thessalonians 1:10 "When He shall

come to be glorified in His saints, and to be admired in all them that believe."

3 To bring to light the hidden things of darkness. 1 Corinthians 4:5 "... who both will bring to light the hidden things of darkness, and make manifest the counsels of the hearts."

4 To judge. 2 Timothy 4:1 "... Christ, who shall judge the quick and the dead at His appearing."

5 To reign. Revelation 11:15 "... Christ; and He shall reign for ever and ever."

6 To receive us to be with Himself. John 14:3 "I will come again, and receive you unto Myself; that where I am, there ye may be also."

7 To destroy death. 1 Corinthians 15:25,26 "For He must reign, till He hath put all enemies under His feet. The last enemy that shall be destroyed is death."

IV How is Christ Coming?

A Secretly at the Rapture. 1 Thessalonians 5:2 "For yourselves know perfectly that the day of the Lord so cometh as a thief in the night." Matthew 24:44 "Therefore be ye also ready: for in such an hour as ye think not the Son of man cometh."
Matthew 24:50 "The lord of that servant shall come in a day when he looketh not for Him, and in an hour that he is not aware of." Be prepared to meet Him *today*.

B Publicly at the Revelation. Revelation 1:7 "Behold, He cometh with clouds; and every eye shall see Him, and they also which pierced Him." Matthew 24:30; Titus 2:13.

V Where is Christ Coming to?

A At the Rapture we will meet Him in the air, 1 Thessalonians 4:17.

B At the Revelation we will descend with Him to the earth. Probably He will land on the Mount of Olives, Zechariah 14:4.

VI Manner of His Coming

1 In the clouds. Matthew 24:30 "... see the Son of man coming in the clouds of heaven."

2 In the glory of His Father. Matthew 16:27 "For the Son of man shall come in the glory of His Father with His angels."

3 In His own glory. Matthew 25:31 "When the Son of man shall come

in His glory ..."

4 In flaming fire. 2 Thessalonians 1:8 "In flaming fire taking vengeance on them that know not God, and that obey not the
Gospel of our Lord Jesus Christ."

5 With power and great glory. Matthew 24:30 " ... clouds of heaven
with power and great glory."

6 As He ascended, in bodily form, Acts 1:9-11.

7 With a shout and the voice of the archangel. 1 Thessalonians 4:16
"For the Lord Himself shall descend ... with a shout, with the
voice of the archangel, and with the trump of God."

8 With His saints. 1 Thessalonians 3:13 " ... coming of ... Christ with
all His saints."

9 Accompanied by angels. Matthew 16:27 quoted above.

10 Suddenly. Mark 13:36 "Lest coming suddenly He find you
sleeping."

VII Signs of Christ's Coming

2 Timothy 3:1-7 lists 23 signs of His coming, most of which are very
evident today.

1 Perilous times	11 Trucebreakers (un-forgiving)	19 Lovers of pleasure more than lovers of God
2 Men loving themselves	12 False accusers	20 Having a *form* of godliness
3 Covetousness	13 Incontinent (with-out self-control)	21 Silly women laden with sins
4 Boasting	14 Fierce (brutal)	22 Divers lusts (all kinds of evil de-sires)
5 Proud	15 Despising good	
6 Blasphemy	16 Traitors	
7 Disobedient to parents	17 heady (rash)	23 Ever learning and never able to come to the knowledge of the truth
8 Unthankful	18 Highminded (con-ceited)	
9 Unholy		
10 Without natural affection		

Matthew 24:5-7, 12-38 list ten signs:

1 False Christs	5 Earthquakes	8 Eating
2 Wars and war rumors	6 Iniquity to abound	9 Drinking
3 Famines	7 Love of many waxes cold	10 Marrying
4 Pestilences		

Other signs include:
1 The destruction of Jerusalem, Luke 21:20,24
2 The completion of the Church, Romans 11:25
3 Gospel preached everywhere, Matthew 24:14
4 The coming of the antichrist, 2 Thessalonians 2:3-8.

Conclusion

Be not a scoffer like those in 2 Peter 3:3, for His coming is sure and certain.

Is it right to sell everything and sit on a hilltop waiting for Him? Definitely not.

We ought to plan and work as if He were not coming for another century but live a holy and pure life as if He were to return today. 1 Thessalonians 3:12,13.

This doctrine must affect our lives. It ought to keep us busy and *watching*.

Review Questions

1 Give the three Greek words and their meaning that are used in regard to His coming.
2 From Acts 1:10,11, what three words would describe His Second Coming?
3 List four people who prophesied of His Second Coming with Scripture references.
4 When will Christ return?
5 List seven purposes of Christ's Second Coming.
6 From 1 Thessalonians 5:2 and Matthew 24:44, what do you learn about the Second Coming?
7 Where is Christ coming to? Explain.
8 Tell twelve things about the manner of His coming.
9 Give ten signs of His coming: five from 2 Timothy 3:1-7 and five from Matthew 24.
10 What is the practical application of this doctrine?

22

The Results of His Return

Introduction

The Second Coming of Christ is said to be mentioned 318 times in the 260 chapters of the New Testament. It occupies one in every 25 verses of the New Testament.

From 1 Thessalonians 4:18, we learn that we are to comfort one another with the fact of the soon return of the Lord Jesus Christ. (So true of saints in Red countries)

The hope of the world for four millenniums was the coming of the promised Messiah; the hope of the New Testament is the imminent return of the Lord Jesus Christ.

The last prayer of the Bible, Revelation 22:20, is, "Even so, come, Lord Jesus."

This doctrine draws the wrath of Satan for he hates this final glorious event.

A worldly Church and carnal Christians also hate this purifying doctrine.

The fact of His return leads us to live a life of watchfulness, fidelity, wisdom, activity, simplicity, self restraint, prayer and abiding in Christ.

Disciples may disagree on doctrine but all ought to be occupied watching.

Special blessings are promised to those who watch faithfully. Luke 12:37 "Blessed are those servants, whom the Lord when He cometh shall find watching."

I With Regard to God

Isaiah 40:5 "And the glory of the Lord shall be revealed, and all flesh shall see it together: for the mouth of the Lord hath spoken it."

When Christ returns the glory of the Lord will be revealed. Everyone shall see it.

II With Regard to the Church

A   At the coming of Jesus Christ the dead in Christ shall rise. 1 Thessalonians 4:13-18 "The dead in Christ shall rise first" (verse 16).

B   At the coming of Christ the bodies of believers will be changed to be like His. Philippians 3:20,21 "... who shall change our vile body that it may be fashioned like unto His glorious body." See also 1 John 3:2.

   1 Corinthians 15:51-53 "We shall be changed, For this corruptible must put on incorruption, and this mortal must put on immortality."

C   At His coming the living believers and resurrected believers meet Him together, 1 Thessalonians 4:17, and continue to be with the Lord forever.

D   The *Bema* or judgment of believers will follow immediately, 2 Timothy 4:8; 1 Peter 5:4.

E   At the Revelation the Church will live and reign with Christ. Revelation 20:4 "They lived and reigned with Christ a thousand years."

III With Regard to Israel

The coming of Christ will be preceded by the re-gathering of Israel, Isaiah 11:11,12.

The prophecies of Ezekiel 36:24; 37:21; and Zephaniah 3:19,20, have largely been fulfilled.

Probably immediately after the Rapture there may be even a greater re-gathering.

At His coming, the nation of Israel, all 12 tribes, will be reunited, Ezekiel 37:19-24.

Jesus Christ, David's son, will reign as king as prophesied, Jeremiah 23:5,6.

Israel will doubtless be judged and cleansed at this time. Romans 11:26 "And so all Israel shall be saved: as it is written, there shall come out of Sion the Deliverer, and shall turn away ungodliness from Jacob." See Ezekiel 37:23 and 36:25-29.

Israel and Palestine shall prosper tremendously at this time, Jeremiah 31:31-34.

Ezekiel 36:37,38 "I will increase them with men like a flock. As the holy flock ..."

Ezekiel 36:33-37 "This land that was desolate is become like the garden of Eden."

Israel will then be the leading nation of the world, Zechariah 8:23; Isaiah 49:22,23.

At this time Israel will take the message of the kingdom to all nations; Isaiah 66:19, "They shall declare My glory among the Gentiles."

Many of the promises that Israel expected to be fulfilled at the first coming will actually be fulfilled when the Savior returns the second time.

IV With Regard to the Nations and Unregenerate Individuals

The coming is a happy day for the Church and Israel but a sad day for the rest.

Matthew 24:30 "And then shall appear the sign of the Son of man in heaven: and then shall all the tribes of the earth mourn," an unhappy day for the unconverted.

Revelation 1:7 "All the tribes of the earth shall mourn over Him."

The Judgment of the Nations will follow the Revelation of Christ. Matthew 25:31,32 "When the Son of man shall come in His glory ... then shall He sit upon the throne of His glory; and before Him shall be gathered all nations," sheep and goats divided.

It seems likely that the sheep nations will then follow the Lord, Isaiah 2:2,3.

The goat nations will be rendered vengeance in flaming fire, 2 Thessalonians 1:7-9.

Those remaining on earth will be forced to serve Christ for He will rule with a rod of iron, Psalm 2:9; Zechariah 9:10; Revelation 11:15.

These nations will cease war and live in peace, Micah 4:3,4; Isaiah 2:4.

V With Regard to Society as a Whole

The earth shall be full of the knowledge of the Lord, as the waters cover the sea.

Isaiah 11:9 "They shall not hurt nor destroy in all My holy mountain: for the earth shall be full of the knowledge of the Lord, as the waters cover the sea.'

VI With Regard to the Antichrist and the Devil

Antichrist will be revealed after the Rapture and his reign of terror will be culminated with the Revelation of our Lord Jesus Christ with His saints.

2 Thessalonians 2:8 "And then shall be revealed the lawless one [antichrist] whom the Lord Jesus shall stay with the breath of His mouth, and bring to naught the manifestation of his coming."

Revelation 19:20 tells of the final end when the antichrist is cast into the lake of fire.

The devil shall be chained and cast into the abyss for a thousand years beginning with the Revelation of the Lord Jesus Christ.

Revelation 20:1-3 "... the dragon, that old serpent, which is the Devil, and Satan, and bound him for a thousand years ... should deceive the nations no more, till the thousand years shall be fulfilled."

VII With Regard to the Physical Universe

Creation shall be delivered from the bondage of corruption. Romans 8:19-21 "For the earnest expectation of the creature waiteth for the manifestation of the sons of God ... itself also shall be delivered from the bondage of corruption."

The curse or at least part of it will be removed. Isaiah 55:13 "Instead of the thorn shall come up the fir tree, and instead of the brier shall come up the myrtle."

It will mean peace to the animal world. Isaiah 65:25 "The wolf and the lamb shall feed together, and the lion shall eat straw like the bullock ... They shall not hurt nor destroy in all My holy mountain, saith the Lord."

The wilderness will become fruitful. Isaiah 32:15 "Until the spirit be poured upon us from on high, and the wilderness be a fruitful field."

The desert shall blossom like the rose. Isaiah 35:1 "The wilderness and the solitary place shall be glad for them; and the desert shall rejoice and blossom as the rose.'

These things happen because the Second Coming ushers in the Millennium.

Conclusion

We are warned to watch and be ready. Mark 13:33 "Take ye heed, watch and pray: for ye know not when the time is."

Matthew 24:42 "Watch therefore: for ye know not what hour your Lord doth come."

We are warned that we have a stewardship given to us by our Lord and He requires that we be faithful in the discharge of that responsibility, Matthew 25:14-30.

We must be careful to maintain a worthy character, 1 John 3:1-3.

In view of His near return we must hasten to carry out the Great Commission of Matthew 28:18-20, the taking of the Gospel to every nation and every creature.

We must do our utmost to further the cause of missions and hasten the Lord's return.

Review Questions

1 How often is the doctrine of the Second Coming mentioned in the New Testament?
2 What and where is the last prayer of the Bible?
3 What is the result of the Second Coming in regard to God?
4 List five things that will happen in regard to the Church at His return.
5 What happens to Israel when the Lord returns?
6 What happens to the Gentile nations at His return?
7 Describe society during this glorious period.
8 What happens to the antichrist when Jesus returns?
9 To what extent will the curse be removed from the world after the Revelation of Christ?
10 What tasks must the Church accomplish in view of His soon return?

23

The Personality of the Holy Spirit

Introduction

With this lesson we begin our study of the Holy Spirit, the third Person of the Godhead.

The Holy Spirit has been sent by the Father and Son to indwell and guide believers.

Many people profess to believe in the Holy Spirit but actually they believe in God the Father, God the Son, and the Holy Spirit as the servant or errand boy.

This is false, for the Holy Spirit is equal to and in no way inferior to the other two.

Others reduce the Holy Spirit to an inanimate force such as electricity which is very powerful but completely devoid of any sort of life, certainly not Divine life!

In this lesson we attempt to prove His personality and His deity in the next lesson.

We believe that the Holy Spirit is a living Person for He can be approached or shunned, trusted or doubted, loved or hated, adored or insulted.

I The Importance of this Doctrine

A   If He is a living Person, the Holy God, equal to the Father and Son, then He ought to be worshipped as they are. Theoretically this is done in the Doxology and Gloria Patri.

His Name is linked with the Father and Son in the Benediction and baptismal formula, 2 Corinthians 13:14; Matthew 28:19.

B   If He is merely an influence or power we would refer to Him as "It" which is a heathenish conception which leads to the error, "I want to get more of 'it'."

If He is a Person then we must address Him with proper pronouns.

C   If He is a Person then we must get to know Him more intimately and personally.

II The Bible Uses Personal Pronouns in Referring to the Holy Spirit

John 15:26 "But when the Comforter is come ... He shall testify of Me."

John 16:8 "And when He is come, He will reprove the world ..."

John 16:13 "Howbeit when He, the Spirit of truth, is come, He will guide you."

John 16:14 "He shall glorify Me: for He shall receive of Mine ..."

In the Greek language the pronoun for "spirit" is ordinarily in the neuter gender.

The student of the Greek New Testament is startled at the masculine choice of pronouns.

In the passage, John 16:7,8, 13-15, twelve times the Greek masculine pronoun (skeinos) "He," is used of the Holy Spirit.

One notable exception is Romans 8:16, "The Spirit itself beareth witness with our spirit." This is an unfortunate mistake which is corrected in the Revised Version. The same mistake is made in Romans 8:26, but the Revised Version says, "... but the Spirit Himself maketh intercession for us with groanings that cannot be uttered."

III The Holy Spirit is a Person for He Possesses certain (Personal) Characteristics

A   **Will power** 1 Corinthians 12:11 "But all these worketh that one and the selfsame Spirit, dividing to every man severally as He will." The Holy Spirit makes decisions.

B   **Intelligence** Nehemiah 9:20 "Thou gavest also Thy good Spirit to instruct them."

A power or influence does not have knowledge with which to teach.

Romans 8:27 "And He that searcheth the hearts knoweth what is the mind of the Spirit, because He maketh intercession." He searches and has the ability to know things.

C   **Knowledge** 1 Corinthians 2:10-12 "What man knoweth the things of a man, save the spirit of man which is in him? even so the things of God knoweth no man, but the Spirit of God."

The Holy Spirit has knowledge and knows things.

D   **Power** Acts 1:8 "But ye shall receive power, after that the Holy Ghost is come upon you: and ye shall be witnesses unto Me." He powerfully changed Peter.

E   **Capacity for love** Romans 15:30 "... for the love of the Spirit ..."

F   **Capacity for grief** Ephesians 4:30 "And grieve not the Holy Spirit of God ..."

The Holy Spirit is a Person because He thinks, feels, purposes, knows, wills, loves and grieves.

The Spirit is certainly not merely an influence, for He has abilities of intelligence and emotions which are foreign to inanimate forces.

Let us never shun, doubt, hate or insult the Spirit. Let us continuously approach Him with faith, love and adoration.

IV The Holy Spirit Does Things that only a Person can Do

A   The Holy Spirit searches the deep things of God. 1 Corinthians 2:10 "The Spirit searcheth all things, yea, the deep things of God." Even the most modern computers would not be able to do this!

B   The Holy Spirit can speak. Revelation 2:7 "He that hath an ear, let him hear what the Spirit saith unto the churches."

C   The Holy Spirit can cry out. Galatians 4:6 "And because ye are sons, God hath sent forth the Spirit of His Son into your hearts, crying, Abba, Father."

D   The Holy Spirit intercedes. Romans 8:26 "The Spirit Himself maketh intercession for us with groanings which cannot be uttered."

E   The Holy Spirit testifies. John 15:26 "But when the Comforter is come ... He shall testify of Me."

F   The Holy Spirit teaches. John 14:26 "But the Comforter, which is the Holy Ghost, ... He shall teach you all things, and bring all things to your remembrance." This ability is also mentioned in John 16:12-14; Nehemiah 9:20.

G   The Holy Spirit leads and directs. Romans 8:14 "For as many as are led by the Spirit of God, they are the sons of God." Do I personally know of this leading?

H   The Holy Spirit commands. Acts 16:6,7 "... and were forbidden of the Holy Ghost to preach the Word in Asia ... but the Spirit suffered them not."

I   The Holy Spirit calls men to work and gives them tasks. Acts 13:2 "The Holy Ghost said, Separate Me Barnabas and Saul for the work whereunto I have called them." Also Acts 20:28 "The Holy Ghost hath made you overseers."

J   The Holy Spirit proceeds on the mission to which He is sent. John 15:26 "... whom I will send unto you from the Father, even the Spirit of truth, which proceedeth from the Father, He shall testify of Me."

V The Holy Spirit has been Assigned a Definite Office

He is the official Comforter. John 14:16 "He shall give you another Comforter."

The Greek word here, *Parakletos*, means "one alongside." He is a personal companion.

As a Person He becomes our best friend to guide us and comfort us. I strongly recommend that you read *The Holy Spirit*, by R. A. Torrey, pages 28 to 40.

He suggests that the application of this doctrine is most practical.

1 It is a cure for an abnormal fear of the dark. The Holy Spirit is with me.

2 It is a cure for insomnia. Try communing with the Spirit and you will fall asleep. 2 Corinthians 13:14 "... and the communion [talking together] of the Holy Ghost ..."

3 It is a cure for all loneliness. Develop this friendship with the Holy Spirit.

4 It is a cure for a broken heart. Let the Spirit occupy the aching void of the heart.

5 It is the greatest encouragement for power and a cure for helplessness.

6 It is an incentive in teaching and preaching. The Spirit is with me to guide me.

7 His presence is our authority in personal work — the living Spirit has directed me thus.

VI The Holy Spirit has Emotions

1 He can be grieved. Isaiah 63:10 "But they rebelled and vexed His Holy Spirit . . ."
2 He can be insulted. Hebrews 10:29 "And hath done despite unto the Spirit of grace."
3 He can be lied to. Acts 5:3 "Why hath Satan filled thine heart to lie to the Holy Ghost?"
4 He can be blasphemed. Matthew 12:31,32 "But the blasphemy against the Holy Ghost ..."

VII The Holy Spirit is a Person

We believe that He is a Person because He possesses all the necessary qualities of intellect, emotion, will, knowledge and actions.
Let us never insult Him by calling the Spirit "it" but always honor Him properly.

Conclusion

May we make much of the companionship of the living Person, the Holy Spirit.
Prayer: *"Lord teach me more of the communion of the Holy Spirit."*
Let the Holy Spirit be our companion, our partner and comrade with whom we have intimate fellowship moment by moment.

Review Questions

1 Give two wrong impressions of the Holy Spirit that people have.
2 Give three reasons why this subject is important.
3 Give three passages where the Bible (KJV) uses personal pronouns for the Holy Spirit.
4 Give two verses in the Bible (KJV) where the pronoun is mistranslated.
5 What is the meaning of the Greek word, "Parakletos"?
6 What six characteristics of a person does the Holy Spirit possess?
7 List ten things that the Holy Spirit does, proving that He is a Person.
8 What is the office of the Holy Spirit?
9 List seven practical applications of the "Parakletos."
10 Name four emotional qualities of the Holy Spirit.

24

The Deity and Names of the Holy Spirit

Introduction

In the last lesson we established the fact that the Holy Spirit is a Person. However He is not a human Person for He does not possess a human body as we do.

The Holy Spirit is not only a Person but we believe that He is a Divine Person.

The Holy Spirit is God Almighty, equal to the Father and the Son in every respect.

I The Deity of the Holy Spirit

We believe the Holy Spirit is divine because:

A The Holy Spirit possesses divine attributes

1 Eternal. Hebrews 9:14 "How much more shall the Blood of Christ, who through the eternal Spirit offered Himself without spot to God."

2 Omnipresent. Psalm 139:7-10 "Whither shall I go from Thy Spirit? or whither shall I flee from Thy presence? If I ascend up into heaven, Thou art there: if I make my bed in hell, behold Thou art there."

3 Omnipotent. Luke 1:35 the power of the Holy Spirit for the conception of the holy child.

Genesis 1:2 "The Spirit of God moved upon the face of the waters."

Job 26:13 "By His Spirit He hath garnished the heavens."

4 Omniscient. 1 Corinthians 2:10,11 "The Spirit searcheth all things, yea the deep things of God . . . knoweth no man, but the spirit of God."

John 14:26 "But the Comforter . . . He shall teach you all things."

John 16:12,13 ". . . the Spirit of truth, is come, He will guide you into all truth."

5   Holiness. Luke 11:13 ". . . the Holy Spirit . . ." The word holy is not a noun but an adjective describing His character.

6   Truth. 1 John 5:6 "It is the spirit that beareth witness, because the Spirit is truth."

7   Benevolent. Nehemiah 9:20 "Thou gavest also Thy good Spirit to instruct them."

8   Communion. 2 Corinthians 13:14 ". . . and the communion of the Holy Ghost . . ."

B   The Holy Spirit does things that only God could do

1   Creation. Job 33:4 "The Spirit of God hath made me."
    Psalm 104:30 "Thou sendest forth Thy Spirit, they are created . . ."

2   Salvation. 1 Corinthians 6:11 "Ye are justified in the Name of the Lord Jesus, and by the Spirit of our God." Also the sealing of the Spirit in Ephesians 1:13.

3   Giving life. John 6:63 "It is the Spirit that quickeneth; the flesh profiteth nothing: the words that I speak unto you, they are spirit and they are life.:

4   Author of the new birth. John 3:5,6 ". . . born of water and of the Spirit . . . that which is born of the Spirit is spirit."

5   Prophecy. 2 Peter 1:21 "For no prophecy ever came by the will of man; but holy men of God spake as they were moved by the Holy Ghost" (Bible inspiration)

6   Convincing men of righteousness and of judgment to come, John 16:8-11.

C   Scripture makes certain strong statements

1   In Isaiah 6:8-10, it says, " Also I heard the voice of the Lord, saying ..." and Paul referring to this passage in Acts 28:25-27, says, "Well spake the Holy Ghost by Esaias the prophet." This identifies "Lord" and "Holy Ghost."

2   In Acts 5:3-5, the Holy Spirit is called God, "Satan filled thine heart to lie to the Holy Ghost . . . thou hast not lied unto men but unto God."

D   Divine "formulae"

1   Matthew 28:19, the baptismal formula. "In the Name of the Father, and of the Son, and of the Holy Ghost."

2   2 Corinthians 13:14, the benediction, "The grace of the Lord Jesus Christ, and the love of God, and the communion of the Holy Ghost, be with you all."

3 John 14:16 "And I (Jesus Christ the Son) will pray the Father (God Himself) and He shall give you another Comforter (God the Holy Spirit)."

II The Holy Spirit is Distinct from the Father

Some people think that the Holy Spirit is the "Spirit of the Father" or the "Spirit of the Son" and not a separate distinct Person.

Luke 3:21,22 at the baptism of Jesus, three distinct Persons are in evidence:

1 God the Father said, "Thou art My beloved Son: in Thee I am well pleased."
2 God the Son was baptized by John the Baptist in the river Jordan.
3 God the Holy Spirit descended in bodily shape like a dove.

Matthew 28:19 the baptismal formula makes a clear distinction between the three Persons.

John 14:16, the Son prays; the Father sends; the Holy Spirit comes to abide.

Acts 2:33, the Son is exalted to the right hand of the Father; the Father is on His throne; the Holy Spirit is received by the Son and given to the Church.

The Father, Son, and Holy Spirit are three separate personalities, with mutual relations one to another, speaking to one another, recognizing each other (Torrey).

III The Subordination of the Spirit to the Father and the Son

John 14:26 the Father sends the Holy Spirit to earth and He obeys the command.

John 15:26 the Son sends the Holy Spirit to the believers and the Church.

Acts 16:7 RV, the Holy Spirit is referred to as "the Spirit of Jesus."

Romans 8:9 the Holy Spirit is referred to as "the Spirit of God."

The Holy Spirit speaks not from Himself but repeats that which He hears.

John 16:13 "He shall not speak of Himself; but whatsoever He shall hear, that shall He speak." This is true humiliation and condescension.

The Holy Spirit glorifies Christ. John 16:14 "He shall glorify Me: for He shall receive of Mine, and shall show it unto you."

The Name of the Holy Spirit follows that of the other two when the three are linked in one sentence: Matthew 28:19, Father, Son, Holy Spirit; 2 Corinthians 13:14, Son, Father, Spirit.

IV The Names of the Holy Spirit

1 The Holy Spirit	Luke 11:13 "Your heavenly Father gives the Holy Spirit."
2 The Spirit	John 3:6 "That which is born of the Spirit is spirit."
3 The Spirit of the Lord	Isaiah 11:2 "And the Spirit of the Lord shall rest upon Him."
4 The Spirit of Jehovah	Isaiah 61:1 "The Spirit of the Lord is upon Me."
5 The Spirit of the Living God	2 Corinthians 3:3 "... but with the Spirit of the Living God."
6 The Spirit of Christ	Romans 8:9 "Now if any man have not the Spirit of Christ."
7 The Spirit of His Son	Galatians 4:6 "God hath sent forth the Spirit of His Son into your hearts crying, Abba, Father."
8 The Spirit of Jesus Christ	Philippians 1:19 ". . . and the supply of the Spirit of Jesus . . ."
9 The Spirit of Jesus	Acts 16:7, RV "The Spirit of Jesus suffered them not."
10 The Spirit of Burning	Isaiah 4:4 "... purged the blood of Jerusalem from the midst thereof by the Spirit of Judgment and by the Spirit of burning." (Refining the dross)
11 The Spirit of Holiness	Romans 1:4 ". . . according to the Spirit of holiness . . ."
12 The Holy Spirit of Promise	Ephesians 1:13 ". . . sealed with that Holy Spirit of promise."
13 The Spirit of Truth	This is used in John 14:17; 15:26 and 16:13.
14 The Spirit of Life	Romans 8:2 "for the law of the Spirit of life in Christ Jesus . . ."

15	The Spirit of Wisdom and understanding; the Spirit of Counsel and Might; the Spirit of Knowledge	These thoughts and names occur Isaiah 11:2
16	The Spirit of Grace	Hebrews 10:29 ". . . done despite unto the Spirit of grace."
17	The Spirit of Glory	1 Peter 4:14 ". . . for the Spirit of glory and of God . . ."
18	The Eternal Spirit	Hebrews 9:14 ". . . who through the eternal Spirit offered Himself."
19	The Comforter	John 14:26; 15:26
20	The Oil of Gladness	Hebrews 1:9 ". . . anointed Thee with the oil of gladness . . ."

Conclusion

The Holy Spirit is also likened to a dove which is both timid and gentle.

He is likened to the wind, John 3:1-9, the unseen mysterious force in regeneration.

He is like a spring of water, the cleansing force in sanctification, John 4:14.

He is like an overflowing river of blessing in service, John 7:38,39.

He is the Comforter, consoling, guiding and directing in the Christian life, John 14:16.

Review Questions

1   What is the difference between us and the Holy Spirit if we are both "persons"?
2   List six attributes to prove the Deity of the Holy Spirit.
3   List six major works of the Spirit to show His Deity.
4   What do you learn by comparing Isaiah 6:8-10 with Acts 28:25-27?
5   What is the significance of Acts 5:3-5 with regard to this doctrine?
6   Why is the name of the Holy Spirit included in Matthew 28:19 and 2 Corinthians 13:14?
7   What do we learn about the Holy Spirit from Luke 3:21,22?
8   Give three verses to show the subordination of the Spirit to the

Father and Son.
9   List seven names of the Holy Spirit.
10   Name four things to which the Holy Spirit is likened.

25

The Work of the Holy Spirit

Introduction

The Holy Spirit is a Divine Personality who has a definite function in the world.

A study of the Scripture reveals that the Holy Spirit has been very active.

His activity has been shown in regard to the universe and the people on the earth.

Since Pentecost His ministry has changed somewhat with regard to believers.

In the Old Testament the Spirit had a "come and go" ministry. At Pentecost He came to indwell believers and abide in the living Church of Jesus Christ.

Judges 6:34 "But the Spirit of the Lord came upon Gideon."

1 Samuel 16:14 "But the Spirit of the Lord departed from Saul."

Judges 11:29 "Then the Spirit of the Lord came upon Jephtha."

Psalm 51:11 "Take not Thy Holy Spirit from me." This prayer of David is definitely inappropriate after Pentecost for the Spirit has now taken up residence permanently.

John 14:16 "... Comforter, that He may abide with you for ever."

I In Relation to Creation

The Holy Spirit was active in creation. Genesis 1:2 "The Spirit of God moved upon the face of the waters." See also Job 26:13, 14; Psalm 104:30; Job 33:4.

Psalm 33:6 "By the Word of the Lord were the heavens made; and all the host of them by the breath of His mouth." (breath of the Lord here being the Holy Spirit)

II In Relation to the Preservation
of the Universe

Isaiah 40:7 "The grass withereth, the flower fadeth: because the Spirit
of the Lord bloweth upon it." The Spirit creates and preserves. He
also destroys at will.

Psalm 104:30 "Thou sendest forth Thy Spirit, they are created: and
Thou renewest the face of the earth." By the Word of God and the
Spirit's power the world is renewed.

III In Relation to the Unbelievers

John 16:8-11 "And when He is come, He will reprove the world of sin,
and of righteousness, and of judgment."

He will convince the world of sin because they do not believe in Jesus
Christ.

He will convince the world of righteousness because Christ was
completely righteous.

He will convince the world of judgment for Christ has already been
judged (at Calvary).

It is the work of the Holy Spirit to constantly bear witness of Christ and
Calvary.

This He does largely though not exclusively through the testimony of
believers for He operates on the conscience of men through the
Word of God.

IV In Relation to the Scriptures

The Holy Spirit is the author of the Scriptures. 2 Peter 1:20,21 "Holy
men of God spake as they were moved by the Holy Ghost."

The Holy Spirit is also the interpreter of the Scriptures to us, John 16:14.

John 14:26 "He shall teach you all things and bring all things to your
remembrance, whatsoever I have said unto you."

O how faithful the Holy Spirit has been in my own life to bring back
to my memory verses of Scripture in the hour of need, particularly
in answering difficult questions.

V In Relation to Jesus Christ

A   Jesus was conceived by the Holy Spirit, literally born of the Spirit.
Luke 1:35.

B   He was led of the Spirit into the wilderness after the baptism to be tested, Matthew 4:1.

C Jesus was anointed by the Spirit for service, Acts 10:38.

D Jesus was crucified in the power of the Spirit, Hebrews 9:14.

E Jesus was resurrected from the grave by the power of the Holy Spirit, Romans 1:4; 8:11.

F Jesus instructed His disciples and Church through the Spirit, Acts 1:2.

G Jesus gave the Holy Spirit to the believers, Acts 2:33.

VI In Relation to the Believer

1 He assures the believer of sonship and makes him sonlike, Romans 8:16,17; Galatians 4:6.

2 He seals the believer as a pledge or earnest of future glory, 2 Corinthians 1:22; Ephesians 1:13,14.

3 He fills the believer with Himself, giving a victorious life, Acts 1:4-8; Ephesians 5:18.

4 He sanctifies the believer, sets him apart unto holiness, 2 Thessalonians 2:13; 1 Peter 1:2.

5 He abides continuously with the believer, John 14:16.

6 He takes the Word of God and teaches the believer, John 14:26 1 Corinthians 2:13.

7 He brings to remembrance the things that we have faithfully learned, John 14:26.

8 He testifies to us regarding the Savior. He constantly reveals Christ, John 15:26.

9 He guides the believer into all truth, John 16:13. This is the cure for error.

10 He takes our bodies and glorifies Christ in and through them, John 16:14.

11 He takes the things of Christ, spiritual things and reveals them to us, John 16:14.

12 He gives us power to obey God in the time of weakness and strengthens us, Ezekiel 36:27.

13 He gives the believer power to obey the truth irrespective of cost, 1 Peter 1:22.

14 He gives the believer freedom from the law of sin and death, Romans 8:2.

15 He takes the weak believer and fulfills the law of righteousness in him, Romans 8:3,4.

16 He gives the believer power to please God by granting victory over the flesh, Romans 8.

17 He will quicken this mortal body of ours, Romans 8:11.

18 He gives power to mortify the deeds of the body, Romans 8:13.

19 He directs the believer in his prayer life to pray in the will of God, Romans 8:26,27.

20 He gives the believer victory over the terrible desires of the flesh, Galatians 5:16,17.

21 He leads the believer out from under the law to liberty in Christ, Galatians 5:18.

22 He is the One that causes us to bear the fruit of the Spirit in Galatians 5:22,23.

23 He gives us a holy walk as we are led by the Holy Spirit, Galatians 5:25.

24 He assists us in putting away the things that displease our Father God, Ephesians 4:30-32.

25 He puts Satan to flight by lifting up a standard against him, James 4:7; Isaiah 59:19.

26 He gives rest to the soul that is trusting in the Lord, Isaiah 63:14.

27 He makes Jesus Christ Lord (master and King) in our private lives, 1 Corinthians 12:3.

28 He gives liberty, freedom to the child of God, 2 Corinthians 3:17.

29 He gives divine love to the children of God, Romans 5:5; Colossians 1:4,8.

30 He gives fullness of joy, complete happiness and satisfaction to the saints, Acts 13:52.

31 He strengthens the inward man with spiritual power — power to resist, Ephesians 3:16.

32 He gives righteousness, peace and joy to the Lord's children, Romans 14:17; 15:13.

33 He reveals, interprets and applies the deep things of God, 1 Corinthians 2:9-14; 1 Thessalonians 1:5.

34 He empowers us to impart truth to others, Acts 1:8; 1 Corinthians 2:1-4; 1 Thessalonians 1:5.

35 He inspires worship and adoration of God Himself, John 4:23,24; Philippians 3:3.

36 He comforts, Acts 9:31 "... and in the comfort of the Holy Ghost."

37 He calls men in Christ and directs them in their service, Acts 8:27-29; 13:2-4.

38 He leads in the details of the believer's life and service, Matthew

4:1; Romans 8:14; Acts 10.

39 He makes genuine our access to the Father in heaven, Ephesians 2:18.

40 He makes known our redemption rights, our possessions in Christ, 1 Corinthians 2:12.

(This list compiled by H. S. Miller in *The Christian Workers' Manual*. Though it is lengthy I doubt if it is complete, for it does not include the gifts of 1 Corinthians 12 that the Spirit gives to the Church.)

VII Other Works of the Holy Spirit

1 He strove with men in Genesis 6:3, attempting to turn them from sin to righteousness.

2 He enlightened men, Job 32:8; the Holy Spirit gave them understanding.

3 He endued men with skill. Exodus 31:2-5 "Bezaleel ... filled him with the Spirit of God in wisdom, and in understanding, and in knowledge, and in all manner of workmanship to devise cunning works."

4 He helped men do ordinary tasks like blowing a trumpet, Judges 6:34.

5 He gave physical strength to Samson, Judges 14:6.

I'm sure that this list too is far from complete, for the Spirit has been so active.

Conclusion

Let us praise the Lord for the faithful ministry of regeneration by the Spirit, John 3.

Let us praise the Lord for the gifts that He graciously gave us, 1 Corinthians 12:7-11.

Review Questions

1 Is it right to pray the prayer of Psalm 51:11b today? Why?

2 Give two verses that teach that the Holy Spirit was active in creation.

3 What verse teaches that the Holy Spirit renews and preserves the universe?

4 Of what three things does the Holy Spirit convict the world?

5 Name two ministries of the Holy Spirit in regard to the Scriptures.

6   List seven things that the Spirit did for the Savior.

7   Can you add one point to the list of forty things that the Spirit does for believers?

8   What are the five most precious works of the Spirit to you personally?

9   List five of the Spirit's works toward believers mentioned in the Book of Romans.

10   List five other works of the Holy Spirit.

26

Sins against the Holy Spirit

Introduction

In this fourth lesson on the Holy Spirit we study the sins against the Spirit.

The Holy Spirit is a Person that can be sinned against. Let us beware lest we sin against Him either consciously or unconsciously.

Some of these sins can probably only be committed by believers, others by unbelievers. However, these differences may be hard to prove.

Even Dr. Ironside who lists them separately admits that probably both believers and unbelievers are capable of doing the seven sins specifically listed as being against the Holy Spirit. (Outline from *Handfuls on Purpose*, James Smith).

I Blasphemed by the Presumption of Men

Blasphemy against the Holy Spirit is one sin for which there is no forgiveness.

Matthew 12:31,32 "Wherefore I say unto you, All manner of sin and blasphemy shall be forgiven unto men: but the blasphemy against the Holy Ghost shall not be forgiven."

It is called the unpardonable sin, the most awful sin that can be committed on earth.

Blasphemy against the Holy Spirit is ascribing to Satan the work of the Holy Spirit.

In Mark 3:22-30 Jesus cast out demons by the power of the Holy Spirit but the Scribes said that Jesus performed the miracles by Satan's power. This is blasphemy.

Beware of belittling the work of the Holy Spirit. This is a very serious matter.

Listen to Charles Finney, quoted in *Finney Lives On*, by Edman: "The Spirit is grieved by saying or publishing things that are calculated to undervalue the work of God. When a blessed work of God is spoken lightly of, not rendering to God the glory due to His Name, the Spirit is grieved. If anything is said about a revival, give only the plain and naked facts just as they are and let them pass for what they are worth." Psalm 78:41 is the sin of saved people.

II Insulted by the Pride of Men

Hebrews 10:29 "Of how much sorer punishment, suppose ye, shall he be thought worthy, who hath trodden under foot the Son of God, and hath counted the blood of the covenant, wherewith he was sanctified, an unholy thing, and hath done despite unto the Spirit of grace?"

The Holy Spirit presents the atoning work of Christ to the sinner. If the sinner refuses to believe or accept it, he is insulting the Holy Spirit.

In the rejection the sinner is saying to the Holy Spirit, "The whole work of Christ is a deception or lie and presents God with another plan of salvation (works)." It is counting the death of Christ as a common thing, the death of an ordinary man.

To deny the deity of Christ and the preciousness of the blood is to despise the witness of the Holy Spirit, 1 John 5:8.

III Vexed by the Disobedience of Men

Isaiah 63:9,10 "They rebelled, and vexed His Holy Spirit."

This portion refers to backslidden Israel but the principles of God never change and men today are as disobedient and rebellious against the Holy Spirit.

Think of the awfulness of redeemed ones rebelling and vexing the indwelling Spirit.

If we are honest with ourselves this has probably been our own hindrance, spiritually.

Sometimes the Spirit reveals ugliness within and instead of being thankful for the discovery, we rebel and our proud heart refuses to make the necessary confession.

The root of vexation is rebellion. It is caused by murmuring and complaining.

To refuse to accept the place in life and our assigned place in the Body of Christ that He gives, and to continuously complain, vexes Him to the point of righteous vexation.

After repeated warnings, multiplied blessings plus abundant light and knowledge, to persist in evil, to still ignore Him is surely vexing the Holy Spirit.

Let us listen, yield and obey but never vex the precious Holy Spirit. Let us cease our stubbornness of will and accept the blessing that He wants to give.

IV Resisted by the Unbelief of Men

Acts 7:51 "Ye do always resist the Holy Ghost: as your fathers did, so do ye."

We resist the Holy Spirit when we doubt the Word of God. Hebrews 3:19 "So we see that they could not enter in because of unbelief." Unbelief causes men to resist.

Often the Spirit quickens the conscience to do right but when we deliberately resist His pleading and leading we are actually manifesting unbelief.

Sometimes the Spirit quickens us to speak to a soul, to drop a sin, to become a missionary, to go to Bible school, to live a separated life, to give to the poor, but instead of obedience we resist His guidance.

Here is a warning: Genesis 6:3 "My Spirit shall not always strive with man." To resist too long God may turn us over to a reprobate mind, Romans 1:24.

If the Spirit is to have full possession of our heart we must cease all resistance and clean out all the evil that has so long polluted us — cast out unbelief.

V Tempted by the Insincerity of Men

Acts 5:1-9 "How is it that ye have agreed together to tempt the Spirit of the Lord?"

Ananias and Sapphira in seeking to deceive their brethren actually tempted and lied to the Holy Spirit. Rather than condemn others, let's examine ourselves.

A man is guilty of this when he pretends to his brethren that he is wholly devoted to God when he is actually indulging in secret sin, withholding from God.

Beware of a profession that is more holy before men than it is before the Lord.

Psalm 51:10 "Create in me a clean heart, O God." Do we stand in consecration and say, "I surrender all," when we know in our hearts that we are being hypocritical?

2 Kings 5:25-27, Gehazi lies, and becomes a leper as punishment. Never lie to the Spirit.

Every deception and exaggeration, every false impression intended to harm, and every lie to man is a lie to the Holy Ghost. — Oswald J. Smith.

VI Quenched by the Prejudice of Men

1 Thessalonians 5:19-20 "Quench not the Spirit." This is a solemn command.

The thought in quenching is the suffocation of a fire as in Isaiah 4:4, Spirit of burning.

Matthew 12:20 "A bruised reed shall He not break and smoking flax shall He not quench."

Ephesians 6:16 "Quench all the fiery darts of the wicked." Quench means to stifle, silence.

Do not quench, squash, put out, stifle, silence the pleading of the Holy Spirit.

When He speaks to us through the Word or conscience we must obey, irrespective of the cost.

If we allow the fire to be smothered in our lives, then only ashes will remain.

It is possible to quench the Spirit on one point but yield to Him on other issues.

When a person is first converted the Spirit speaks very loudly when he does wrong, but if the voice was ignored His influence becomes less and less until silenced.

Protests that go unheeded result in hardness of heart and lead to quenching.

Let us be careful in criticizing the manifestation of the Spirit in the testimony of some believer, or the sermon of some preacher, lest we be guilty of quenching *Him*.

VII Grieved by the Frivolity of Men

Ephesians 4:30 "And grieve not the Holy Spirit of God, whereby ye are sealed."

Parents have confidence in a child. Later the child steals and the parents are grieved.

The Spirit trusts us to resist sin and obey the Lord. If we fail He is made sad.

To refuse or fail undermines the confidence of the Spirit in us and disappoints Him.

The Spirit is pictured as a sensitive dove, one that is easily frightened away.

How often the Spirit is grieved by light and unprofitable conversation of saints.

The next verse (Ephesians 4:31) emphasizes this by saying, "Let all bitterness and wrath, and anger, and clamour, and evil speaking, be put away from you, with all malice."

The Spirit cannot join in the unprofitable talk, much less in the evil speaking.

Let us watch the door of our lips. We cannot afford to trifle with sin and grieve Him.

Men filled with the Holy Spirit are happy but solemn.

Conclusion

Resisting has to do basically with the regenerating work of the Spirit;
Grieving has to do with the indwelling of the Holy Spirit;
Quenching has to do with enduement for service.

Let us live in constant communion with the Spirit.

Review Questions

1   What are the seven sins against the Holy Spirit?
2   What is the unpardonable sin? Explain.
3   What is the warning regarding reporting news of a revival?
4   What is it to do "despite unto the Holy Ghost"? Hebrews 10:29.
5   How have men vexed the Holy Spirit?
6   What is the basic cause of resisting the Holy Spirit?
7   Give two illustrations of tempting the Holy Spirit.
8   What is the basic thought in quenching the Spirit?
9   Give an example of quenching the Spirit in one point but not in others.
10   What is the most common way of grieving the Holy Spirit?

27

The Spirit-Filled Life

Introduction

Outline from *The Holy Spirit in Evangelism*, J. B. Lawrence, chapter 3.

At conversion the believer receives the justified life. He is made righteous.

This is followed by a consecrated life when we acknowledge the Lord's ownership of our lives. 1 Corinthians 6:19,20 "Ye are not your own ... bought with a price."

At the altar of consecration we yield our lives and our wills to the Lord, Matthew 26:39.

This is followed by the emptied life when we cast aside evil and selfishness.

But we cannot live in a vacuum. Our lives must be filled with the Holy Spirit.

Ephesians 5:18 "And be not drunk with wine, wherein is excess; but be filled with the Spirit." This is a very strong New Testament command.

Someone told Billy Graham about a congregation that disciplined an elder for being drunk. Graham asked, "What would you do with an elder that is not Spirit-filled? Both things are mentioned in the same verse."

At conversion the believer is complete in Christ but generally does not enter into the fullness of his spiritual inheritance until much later.

By the fact of conversion every believer possesses the Holy Spirit, Romans 8:16.

Illustration of the occupancy of a house. The Spirit may be kept as a guest in the parlor *(sala)* but never given control of the kitchen, bedroom or storeroom.

The Spirit may reside but not preside, be simply a resident and not the president.

As we yield the control of our lives He fills us more and more with Himself.

Luke 11:13 "How much more shall your heavenly Father give the Holy Spirit to them that ask Him?" We are taught here to pray for the filling of the Spirit.

Note Dr. Scofield's unwise comment on this verse, "To go back to the promise of Luke 11:13 is to forget Pentecost and ignore the truth that every believer is indwelt by the Spirit" *(Scofield Bible)*.

Luke was written long after Pentecost. Pentecost speaks of the indwelling Christ while Luke 11:13 pleads for the filling and fullness of the Holy Spirit.

Is this a crisis experience separate from conversion? It need not be, but often it is harder for us to surrender *our wills* than it is to surrender our sins.

I The Holy Spirit and the Believer

The disciples were to tarry in Jerusalem waiting for Pentecost, Luke 24:49.

Acts 2:4 was the fulfillment of this promise when the Spirit came to abide.

Every believer has the Holy Spirit, but the Spirit does not control each believer.

The believer still has his stubborn rebellious will. He may pray or not, give or not, witness or not, surrender or not. He may obey or resist and grieve the Spirit.

The crowning act of faith is for the believer to abdicate his life to the Spirit.

This is not necessary for salvation, but it is necessary to be Spirit-filled.

The infilling is received when the believer consciously recognizes the Holy Spirit as being in full control of his life, completely governing every detail of life.

II Filling is a Command to be Obeyed

Is this wonderful experience a luxury for a few people like Apostles and Stephen?

It ought to be the experience of every believer. Ephesians 5:18 is not an optional command.

Saintly S. D. Gordon in *The Ministry of the Spirit* says, "Be God-intoxicated men!"

The picture in Ephesians 5:18 is a contrast between a man under the influence, completely directed by another power, either wine (earthly) or the Spirit, (heavenly).

Egypt always has the Nile but Egypt waits each year for its overflow. Having the Nile is one thing, but having the overflowing Nile is quite another. When the Nile overflows, Egypt is refreshed. Let us know the overflowing Spirit, John 7:38,39.

The original Greek language is in the imperative progressive — keep on being filled. Let the filling be constant and continuous.

The Apostle Peter was filled with the Spirit in Acts 2:4, and again in Acts 4:8, and again in Acts 4:31. Each day needs its own new fullness.

III Everyone Needs the Filling of the Spirit

Every believer in Jesus Christ needs the filling of the Holy Spirit.

The filling is for Apostles, preachers, fathers, mothers, young people and laborers.

We each need it for our own benefit in order to be the best possible Christian. Without it we cannot attain to the Lord's will for us regarding character and service.

The filling of the Spirit is an individual blessing. Men are saved and filled individually.

The filling must be individually received. I must personally do business with God.

The Spirit cannot illuminate our minds, warm our affections, purge our consciences or energize our wills until we surrender to Him and keep surrendered.

IV The Church Needs every Member to be Spirit-filled

Sometimes unwise, extravagant and fanatical things are done in the name of the filling of the Holy Spirit. Because of this many believers shun the filling.

Some say that the ability to speak in tongues is the proof of the Spirit-filling.

This is false. Tongues are a sign to the unbelievers of the reality of the Gospel to change lives, 1 Corinthians 14:22.

The Church needs Spirit-filled members. If the filling is lacking, the Church is plagued with disorders, dissensions, strife, backbiting, jealousy and scandal.

Let every member of the Church be Spirit-filled, the pastor, elders, deacons, Sunday School teachers, singers, choir members and ordinary members.

V The World Expects Believers to be Spirit-filled

Our Christian walk is twofold: 1) Godward and 2) outward to fellowmen.

The world expects every Christian to be almost perfect. To live up to the world's imaginary standard every believer desperately needs the Spirit's filling.

We cannot be effective witnesses if we are not Spirit-filled. To do the work of the Lord in the energy of the flesh can only lead to disappointment and failure.

Spirit-filled believers, living the crucified life in relation to the world, are an effective means in the Lord's hands to convict and convince sinners.

VI Conditions of Filling by the Holy Spirit

A   Forgiveness: Acts 2:38 "Repent and be baptized ... for the remission of sins, and ye shall receive the Holy Ghost." Psalm 66:18, the Holy Spirit cannot live with sin.

B   Sonship: Galatians 4:6 "Because ye are sons, God hath sent forth the Spirit of His Son into your hearts."

C   Desire: John 7:37-39 "*If* any man thirst ..." also Isaiah 44:3.

D   Faith: John 7:39, the Spirit given to those who believe; also Galatians 3:13,14.

E   Obedience: Acts 5:32, He gives the Holy Spirit to those who obey Him.

F   Waiting: Luke 24:49; Acts 1:4, "Wait for the promise of the Father." Be unhurried.

G   Prayer: Luke 11:13, The Holy Spirit given to those who ask Him. Also Acts 4:31.

H   Appropriate the truth, John 1:12. Ask and receive, Luke 11:9,10. Take the gift of the filling and live and act as if the transaction were real and genuine.

The secret of being filled with the Holy Spirit is surrender, surrendering our wills, bodies, possessions and every aspect of our lives to His control.

VII Results of Being Spirit-filled

A   Power to witness is one mighty manifestation of a Spirit-filled saint, Acts 1:8.

B   Power to live victorious Christian life, Acts 20:22-24, Paul speaking to Ephesians.

C   Glory will certainly accrue to the Lord, John 16:14, the Spirit's basic ministry.

The infilling of the Spirit is the indispensable qualification for all holy living.

The Holy Spirit quickens the intellect, affections, conscience, will and personality.

The filling is the secret of abiding, obeying and God-honoring trust in the Word.

Conclusion

We are not reservoirs but channels. We must overflow. Blessings must pour out.

Conversion first, then filling and overflowing. This is beautifully pictured in Bible pictures of the working of the Holy Spirit.

1   An overflowing spring, John 4:14
2   Overflowing fountain, John 7:37-39
3   An abundance of sap in the tree, Romans 8:11
4   As overflowing waters, Ephesians 5:18

Remember the filling is not a once-for-all experience. It must be repeated daily.

Review Questions

1   Give a negative and positive teaching from Ephesians 5:18.
2   Ought we to pray the prayer of Luke 11:13? Why?
3   Is the filling of the Holy Spirit simultaneous with conversion? Why?
4   What is the difference between being indwelt and filled with the Holy Spirit?
5   What is the mental picture received from Ephesians 5:18?
6   Does the filling of the Spirit come upon people by groups today? Why?
7   Is speaking in tongues proof of the filling of the Holy Spirit? Why?
8   How can saints live up to the expectations of unbelievers?

9 List nine conditions of filling by the Holy Spirit.
10 List six results of being Spirit-filled.

28

The Baptism of the Holy Spirit

Introduction

This is a highly controversial issue among evangelicals and theologians and it is not likely that this lesson will settle the issue!

I trust that this lesson will not confuse you, but rather that it will help to explain this most difficult and complex problem.

Notes from L. E. Maxwell, R. A. Torrey, E. W. Storie, Arthur Wallis, Ewan Harries, James Smith, J. O. Sanders, O. J. Smith and others.

This problem has been used by Satan to divide Christians while the ministry of the Spirit is actually to draw Christians together.

I Various Interpretations or Explanations of this Doctrine

A It is the first time that one is filled with the Holy Spirit

This interpretation feels that the terms "Baptism of the Spirit," "Filling of the Spirit," "the gift of the Holy Ghost," "endued with the Spirit," are similar.

However, we believe that they are not the same. The words baptism and filling are opposite in meaning. Baptism is immersion into something. Filling is putting something into the individual.

This theory stems from the story of Pentecost where in Acts 2:4 they were filled with the Holy Spirit and spoke in tongues, also Acts 10:44-46.

This can be explained by the fact that Pentecost was the opening of the dispensation of the Holy Spirit when everything occurred simultaneously.

B It is the experience of speaking in tongues

It is true that this did occur on four occasions. This was to publicly unify the various groups into one body.

In Acts 2, at Pentecost, those who spoke in tongues were Jewish believers.

In Acts 8:17, we have the acknowledging of the Samaritan believers.

In Acts 10:44, the "dogs of the Gentiles" are publicly accepted by the Spirit.

The fourth group was the disciples of John the Baptist, Acts 19:1-7.

The Gospel was to be preached in 1) Jerusalem 2) Judaea 3) Samaria and 4) to the world of Gentiles. The four experiences above correlate beautifully.

Pentecost was a transitional period that lasted several years from John the Baptist till at least Acts 19, when the 4 groups were properly assimilated.

We reject this explanation today for the transition was completed long ago.

C   It is a second work of grace (without tongues)

This stand is based mostly on the experiences of great men of God like Moody, Torrey, Finney, etc., when they had definite experiences apart from conversion.

Their proofs lie in such texts as Acts 8:15,16, which can be easily explained in the light of the transition period not being completed then, Acts 19:1,2.

However, now that the transition period from law to grace, from the dispensation of the Son to the dispensation of the Spirit is completed, this is not true.

It is very dangerous to attempt to build a doctrine on the experiences of men.

D   It referred to Pentecost only and is not applicable to us today

This is the attitude of many of the larger churches today, whereby they reject the doctrine and continue to ignore the teaching entirely.

They reject outward manifestations like tongues and go to the extreme of practically rejecting the entire doctrine. This, too, is entirely wrong.

It is true that the prophetical passages like Joel 2:28-32; Matthew 3:11; Mark 1:8; Luke 3:16; John 1:33 and Acts 1:5 were fulfilled at Pentecost.

However, we believe that in the light of verses like 1 Corinthians 12:13 and Ephesians 4:5, that the expression "baptism of the Holy Ghost" must have a present-day application to us, too.

E   It is the baptism referred to by John the Baptist in Matthew 3:11, and available today

This view confuses the "anointing of the Spirit" with "the baptism of the Spirit."

It says that in this special post-conversion experience that Jesus Himself will baptize the individual with the Holy Spirit.

It teaches that this baptism will occur when one has met the conditions of Psalm 45:7,8, which is loving righteousness and hating iniquity.

However, this passage refers to anointing and not baptism. Cf. Luke 4:18 and 1 Corinthians 12:13.

II The True or Correct Explanation of this Doctrine

I believe that the only doctrinal statement on this subject is 1 Corinthians 12:13, "For by one Spirit are we all baptized into one body, whether we be Jews or Gentiles, whether we be bond or free; and have been all made to drink into one Spirit."

The five prophecies of Matthew 3:11; Mark 1:8, Luke 3:16; John 1:33; Acts 1:5, were looking forward to Pentecost and were completely fulfilled "not many days" later.

The verb tense in 1 Corinthians 12:13 is in the past tense. It speaks of a completed experience. It is performed by the Holy Spirit at conversion.

The baptism of the Holy Spirit for us today is the placing of the new convert into the invisible Body of Christ by the Spirit at conversion.

Nowhere in the Epistles are we exhorted to seek the baptism of the Holy Spirit, for it was a completed experience. We need not worry or bother about it.

We are exhorted to be "filled with the Spirit," "grieve not," "quench not" the Spirit.

Acts 2:1-4, Pentecost was an experience to mark the initiation of a new dispensation.

J.O. Sanders points out four facts from 1 Corinthians 12:13:

1   Every believer has been baptized, "are we baptized ..."

2   The experience is in the past tense. It is a completed transaction.

3   The function of this baptism is to place the believer "into one body."

4 It unifies believers, cancelling all differences of race, color or politics.

III What is the "One Baptism" of Ephesians 4:5?

Ephesians 4:5 "One Lord, one faith, one baptism."

Some argue that there are at least two baptisms, water and spirit, and which is this?

In the mind of God, 1 Corinthians 12:13, the Spirit baptism must be the true baptism.

Water baptism, a required sacrament of the Church, is an earthly sign that the 1 Corinthians 12:13 baptism has already transpired.

True Spirit baptism causes Ephesians 5:30 to come into being, "For we are members of His body, of His flesh, and of His bones."

IV Outline on the Baptism of the Holy Ghost
(Mrs E. W. Weller)

It is an initial work taking place at the time of salvation.

"All are baptized into one body," 1 Corinthians 12:13; 1 Peter 3:20b,21; Titus 3:5.

Romans 6:3-11 is the only definition of baptism of the Spirit given in Scripture.

In the one act of living faith in Christ, believers are:

1 Born of the Spirit (the initiation into eternal life), John 3:3-8.
2 Receiving the earnest of the Spirit (pledge of its culmination), Ephesians 1:14; 2 Corinthians 1:22; 5:5.
3 Sealed with the Spirit (insurance of its continuance), Ephesians 1:13; Ephesians 4:30.
4 Indwelt by the Spirit (maintenance of eternal life in the soul), Romans 8:9.
5 Baptized into one body (a relational activity joining Christ and believers), 1 Corinthians 12:13.

V Definition of Baptism

1 Baptized into His death. Romans 6:3 "I am crucified with Christ," Galatians 2:20.
2 Baptized into His burial. Romans 6:4, complete identification into His body.

3 Baptized into His resurrection. Romans 6:5, complete entering into His new body.

4 Baptized into His resurrected life. Romans 6:8 "live with Him," live in His body.

The experience of 1 Corinthians 12:13 implies a complete identification with the Savior.

Conclusion

Colossians 2:10-12, by Spirit baptism we are complete in the new resurrected body.

At Pentecost, the day that the Holy Spirit came to abide, the disciples were filled, baptized and anointed with the Holy Spirit.

Pentecost was a definite historical event never to be repeated. It was the day of enthronement of the Spirit, when He assumed all His various offices.

We are baptized by the Spirit at conversion. We need the anointing with power of Acts 1:8 for service and we need to be constantly filled with the Spirit.

Review Questions

1 Give five interpretations of the baptism of the Holy Spirit.

2 What is the difference between the filling and the baptism of the Spirit?

3 Why is speaking in tongues not the baptism of the Holy Spirit?

4 Is the baptism of the Holy Spirit possible in this present generation? Why?

5 Does Psalm 45:7,8 specify the conditions of the baptism of the Holy Spirit?

6 What is the correct explanation of the baptism of the Holy Spirit?

7 Explain the "one baptism" of Ephesians 4:5.

8 What was Mrs. Weller's excellent explanation of the baptism of the Holy Spirit? (Section IV)

9 What all is included in being "baptized by the Spirit" into Jesus Christ?

10 Explain Colossians 2:10-12 in relation to the baptism of the Holy Spirit.

29

The Fruit and Gifts of the Holy Spirit

Introduction

There is an obvious difference between the work and fruit of the Holy Spirit.

The work of the Spirit is the direct result of the Spirit's active ministry.

The fruit of the Spirit is the outcome of His indwelling and our yielding to Him.

Galatians 5:17-23 is a sharp contrast between the works of the flesh and fruit of the Spirit.

The works of the flesh (17 of them) are the natural outcome of the Adamic nature.

The fruit of the Spirit is the result of the Holy Spirit operating on the new life.

The fruit of the Spirit (9 of them) is spoken of in the singular signifying the oneness of the fruit. It is not complete until all nine are present. The Christian is not complete until he manifests all nine graces.

I The Fruit of the Spirit

1 **Kinds of fruit** Galatians 5:22-23 lists the nine graces as a single unit, one fruit.

   a Love. This is divine love, an attribute of the indwelling God, 1 John 4:16; 1 Corinthians 13.

   b Joy, not the so-called happiness of the world but deep, deep gladness, Philippians 4:4.

   c Peace. This is the peace of God that satisfies the soul completely, Colossians 3:15.

   d Longsuffering (patience). The natural man is impatient. Saints are the opposite.

   e Gentleness (kindness or graciousness). Jesus was known by His graciousness.

f   Goodness (benevolence). This virtue makes the Christian full of good works.

g   Faith (faithfulness). He is dependable and can be relied on at all times.

h   Meekness (mildness of temper). He is humble, particularly true of us, 2 Timothy 2:25.

i   Temperance (self control), moderate in drink, appetite, dress, habit and fashion.

These nine are all opposite or contrary to the filthy natural works of the flesh.

These nine graces were beautifully portrayed in Christ for He was Spirit-filled.

2   **Fruit is an evidence of death** John 12:24 "Except a corn of wheat ... die, it abideth alone; but if it die, it bringeth forth much fruit."

If we are not dead we will merely bring forth the works of the flesh.

Fruit is the evidence because self has not been crucified as in the believer.

Many are fruitless because self has not been crucified so they continue to abide alone.

The new life alone is capable of bringing forth fruit to the glory of God.

3   **Fruit is necessary** John 15:2 "Every branch in Me that beareth not fruit He taketh away." Luke 13:9 "And if it bear fruit, well: and if not, then after that thou shalt cut it down." The only reason for our existence here after conversion is to bear fruit.

The fruitless cannot long enjoy the privileges of the fruitful. Fruitlessness and favor with God cannot live together. Away with barrenness.

Luke 13:7 "Behold these 3 years I [the husbandman representing God] come seeking fruit." He will not be satisfied with anything less than spiritual fruit.

James 5:7 "The husbandman waiteth for the precious fruit of the earth."

The Lord Jesus Christ is waiting for true fruit (Galatians 5:22,23) from our lives.

4   **Fruit affords identification** Matthew 12:33 "The tree is known by his fruit."

In Numbers 13:26, the spies showed the fruit of Canaan to prove that it was a good land.

In the New Testament the saint portrays the proper fruit, showing he is born again.

Appearance and profession are good but the vital evidence is the fruit to identify whether a tree is a mango or an apple, whether saint or hypocrite.

Matthew 7:16-20, grapes do not bear figs, thistles or thorns. Saints ought not to bear any of the works of the flesh, Galatians 5:17-21.

Very often our lives are a paradox of cursing and blessing, sweetness and bitterness, figs and olives, James 3:9-12. Is it any wonder that the world is perplexed?

5 **Purpose of the fruit** Matthew 21:34 "He sent His servants ... that they might receive the fruits." Fruit is not exclusively for the tree; others see our good works and glorify God. To produce sweet fruit for our own benefit alone is to dishonor the Father.

6 **Source of the fruit** Hosea 14:8 "From *Me* is thy fruit found." The source is in God. John 15:4 "As the branch cannot bear fruit of itself, except it abide in the vine; no more can ye except ye abide in Me." Natural fruit is wild fleshly works.

The saint abounds in fruit as he is rooted and grounded in Christ, Ephesians 3:17,18.

7 **Fruit is the source of propagation** Genesis 1:11 "And God said, Let the earth bring forth ... the fruit tree yielding fruit after his kind, whose seed is in itself."

The seed is the fruit. If there is no fruit there is no seed or reproduction.

If there is no spiritual fruit in our lives, then we cannot reproduce.

Rather than being a blessing, our lives become a hindrance to the Gospel.

Colossians 1:10 "... being fruitful in every good work, and increasing ..."

Have we reproduced? Is it because we have never borne fruit of the Spirit?

II The Gifts of the Spirit

1 **Kinds of gifts** 1 Corinthians 12:8-10, the gifts of wisdom, knowledge, faith, healing, miracles, prophecy, discernment, tongues, and the gift to interpret tongues.

1 Corinthians 12:28, the gifts that fit one to be an apostle, prophet, teacher, miracle-worker, healer, helper, administrator or linguist.

Ephesians 4:11-16 adds the following: gifts of evangelism, pastoral and gift of ministry.

Romans 12:6-8 adds: gifts of exhortation, gift of giving, gift of ruling, and the gift of showing mercy (probably about 24 different gifts)

2 **Gifts are sovereignly given** 1 Corinthians 12:11 "But all these worketh that one and the selfsame Spirit, dividing to every man severally as He will."

The Holy Spirit places the new convert in the Body of Christ and appropriately endows him for that particular location in the Body, Ephesians 2:21,22.

It is the prerogative of God to choose the location. It is His sovereign will alone.

As He chooses the location, so He continues to fashion and fit the new cell.

3 **Gifts are for profit** 1 Corinthians 12:7 "But the manifestation of the Spirit is given to every man to profit withal." It is given to make the cell more useful, profitable.

The whole Body profits because of the new gift that is added to a believer.

The human body does not have unnecessary parts (even the appendix has a function), and neither should the Body of Christ have useless drones in it.

Our conversion and baptism into the Body (1 Corinthians 12:13) was more than just so that we could escape hell; it was so that we would be a help and blessing to the Body.

The Body of Christ, the invisible Church, should be stronger because you have been placed in it and qualified by special gifts from the Holy Spirit.

4 **Gifts are to be desired** 1 Corinthians 12:31 "But covet earnestly the best gifts."

Don't be satisfied with just one or two gifts. Seek and pray for others that would help you in that particular position He has given you in the Body.

Paul mentions prophecy as the gift that is most desirable, 1 Corinthians 14:1,39.

In Matthew 25:14-30 some were given one talent (gift), others two and others five.

The man who received five gained five more and the one that was hidden in the earth in Matthew 25:28, was also given to him so that he eventually had eleven gifts.

At conversion we may have only one or two gifts but keep seeking more for His glory.

Personally I believe that when I graduated from Bible school I only had a couple of gifts, but I now see that He has given me several more in the past 20 years.

5 **Gifts are suited to each possessor** 1 Corinthians 7:7 "Every man hath his proper gift of God, one after this manner, and another after that."

Every believer in Jesus Christ has a gift. Not one person has been forgotten.

The administrator does not need the gift of preaching. The Holy Spirit gives the proper gift to each cell according to its functions.

6 **Gifts must be used** 1 Timothy 4:14 "Neglect not the gift that is in thee."

Some hide their gifts because they are not as spectacular as those of others.

The gift that is not used will rust and may even be taken away from us, Matthew 25:28.

I personally feel that I lost the gift of writing through being inactive for 18 months, while we lived under communism, and failing to use the talent.

7 **Gifts are to be improved** 2 Timothy 1:6 "Stir up the gift of God that is in thee."

The gift needs constant practice to be advantageous in the kingdom of God.

Let's concentrate on the constant improvement of these heavenly gifts — Colossians 1:29.

Conclusion

These are not natural talents. These are special gifts given by the Spirit. Let's consistently bear fruit as we are provided by the best possible gifts.

Review Questions

1 Why is the word "fruit" in the singular in Galatians 5:22?
2 List the nine graces that comprise the fruit of the Spirit.

3   List three reasons why some Christians do not bear the fruit of the Spirit.
4   List four paradoxes in James 3:9-12, regarding manifesting fruit.
5   List three purposes of fruitbearing.
6   List ten gifts of the Holy Spirit.
7   Who chooses the believer's place in the Body of Christ? Proof?
8   What evidence have we to signify that gifts can be increased after conversion?
9   Prove that every saint has at least one gift (three verses).
10 Give two things that must be done with spiritual gifts.

Further Teaching about the Holy Spirit

Introduction

This lesson is an attempt to cover other teaching about the Holy Spirit that is mentioned in Scripture but not included in previous lessons. This lesson does not intend to cover all that the Bible says on this subject.

I Emblems of the Holy Spirit
Dr. C. I. Scofield

A Water — John 3:5; John 7:38,39.
From water we learn five things about the Spirit.
1 Water fertilizes. The Spirit-filled Christians are like watered trees, Psalm 1:3.
2 Water refreshes — John 4:14; Psalm 46:4; Isaiah 41:17,18.
3 Water is freely given — Isaiah 55:1; John 4:14; Revelation 22:17.
4 Water cleanses. Ephesians 5:26, the Church washed and sanctified by the Spirit and the Word.
5 Water is abundant. John 7:37,38, not only water but "rivers" of water flowing.

B Fire
Matthew 3:11 "He shall baptize you with the Holy Ghost, and with fire."
1 Fire illuminates. John 5:35, John the Baptist, full of the Holy Spirit, was shining.
2 Fire burns. John 5:35, the Spirit of burning burned in John the Baptist.
3 Fire purifies. Malachi 3:2,3, the Holy Spirit purifies with a refiner's fire. Isaiah 4:4
4 Fire searches. The Holy Spirit, like fire, cannot be stationary, 1 Corinthians 2:10.

C   Wind — John 3:8.

   1   Wind is powerful. 1 Kings 19:11; Acts 2:2; His power is unsearchable.

   2   Wind is reviving. Ezekiel 37:9,10,14, the Spirit (wind) revives the dead bones.

   3   Wind is independent. John 3:8; 1 Corinthians 12:11; the Holy Spirit is sovereign.

   4   Wind is invisible but effective. John 3:8, we certainly see the Spirit's work.

D   Oil

Psalm 45:7 "Anointed Thee with the oil of gladness above Thy fellows."

   1   Oil consecrates. In the Old Testament oil consecrated, Exodus 29:7; cf. Luke 4:18.

   2   Oil comforts. Isaiah 61:3 "The oil of joy for mourning ..." cf. Hebrews 1:9.

   3   Oil illuminates. Matthew 25, the foolish virgins without oil couldn't shine.

   4   Oil heals. Luke 10:34, the Good Samaritan used oil picturing the Holy Spirit.

E   Rain and dew

Psalm 72:6 "He shall come down like rain upon the mown grass."

   1   Rain is imperceptible like the growth of a plant, Mark 4:26-29.

   2   Rain is refreshing. Psalm 68:9; Isaiah 18:4; the refreshing showers of revival.

   3   Rain is abundant. Psalm 133:3, who can measure the dew or the rain? or the Spirit?

   4   Rain fertilizes. Ezekiel 34:26,27, the showers of blessing can cause germination, growth.

F   Dove

Matthew 3:16, the Spirit descended as a dove at Jesus' baptism.

   1   The dove is very gentle. Matthew 10:16 "Harmless as doves" fruit of gentleness, Galatians 5:22.

G   Voice

Isaiah 6:8 "The voice of the Lord saying ..."

   1   The voice guides. Isaiah 30:21, the Spirit's voice guides us into truth. John 16:13.

   2   The voice speaks. Matthew 10:20 "The Spirit of your Father which speaketh in you."

   3   The voice warns. Hebrews 3:7-11; John 16:7-11, warning of sin,

righteousness and judgment.

H Seal

Revelation 7:2; Ephesians 4:30 "Whereby ye are sealed unto the day of redemption."

1 A seal authenticates. John 6:27; 2 Corinthians 1:22; we are marked, branded by the Spirit.

2 A seal secures. Ephesians 1:13,14, it is a down payment which secures the transaction.

II The Christian's Life is Lived in the Spirit

1 We worship God in the Spirit, John 4:24; Philippians 3:3. "Worship God in Spirit and in truth."

2 We understand things through the Spirit. Revelation 4:1,2; John understood, "in the Spirit."

3 Paul was bound "in the Spirit," Acts 20:22-24; a lovely description of a close union.

4 Being "in the Spirit" is proof that the Spirit is in us, Romans 8:9.

5 Christians live "in the Spirit," Galatians 5:25; our lives are so closely joined.

6 Christians walk "in the Spirit," Galatians 5:25; the Spirit guides the way that we take.

7 Christians' service is rendered "in the Spirit," Acts 6:3; 1 Corinthians 2:4.

8 We pray "in the Spirit," Ephesians 6:18; He guides us in this great exercise.

III The Power of the Holy Spirit
(Bible reading by James Smith)

1 It is needed. Luke 24:49 "Tarry until ye be endued with power"; it is useless to proceed in our Christian lives without the power of the Holy Spirit.

2 It is promised. Acts 1:8 "Ye shall receive power, after that the Holy Ghost is come upon you." 2 Timothy 1:7 "We have the Spirit of power."

3 It is life giving. The Spirit quickens and gives an abundance of life, 2 Corinthians 3:6.

4 It is sufficient. 1 Corinthians 2:3,4, Paul found the Spirit's power sufficient without oratory or gimmicks of any kind.

5 It cannot be purchased. Acts 8:18, Simon Magus tried it and was

soundly rebuked.

6 It cannot be imitated. Human zeal or fleshly effort must be rejected by the Lord; we may imitate Billy Sunday but we cannot imitate his power (Spirit's power).

7 It can be lost. Judges 16:20, Samson once knew the power of the Spirit and lost it. The Christian that loses spiritual power is like salt without savor, fit only to be cast out, Matthew 5:13.

IV The Holy Spirit as a Teacher
(notes from James Smith)

A **The characteristics of this teacher:**

1 Indispensable. 1 Corinthians 2:11,14; Romans 11:33; only the Spirit can search these things.

2 Infallible. 1 Corinthians 2:10 "The Spirit searcheth all things, yea, the deep things of God." The Spirit has the knowledge of God for He is God.

3 All-sufficient. 1 John 2:27 "Ye need not that any man teach you." John 14:26, the Holy Spirit will teach the things regarding Christ.

4 Unassuming. John 16:13 "He shall not speak of Himself."

B **The methods of His teaching:**

1 Enlightens the mind. Ephesians 1:17,18; He opens the eyes of the mind to the truth.

2 Points to the sufferings of Christ. John 16:11; Zechariah 12:10.

3 Quickens the understanding. Isaiah 11:2,3; He touches not only the mind but the brain.

4 Compares spiritual things. 1 Corinthians 2:13 "Comparing spiritual things with spiritual."

5 Reveals hidden things. Luke 2:26, revealed to Simeon by the Holy Spirit, John 16:14.

6 Recalls forgotten things. John 14:26 "He shall bring all things to your remembrance, whatsoever I have said unto you," Psalm 119:11.

7 Hindering selfish things. Acts 16:6,7, the Spirit forbade Paul and Silas, permitting them to go not their own way, but His way, a much better way.

C **When does He teach us:**

1 When we obey. Acts 8:26, Philip obeyed and then the Holy Spirit directed him.

2 When we meditate. Acts 10:19 "While Peter thought . . . the Spirit said . . ."

3 When we serve. Acts 13:2 "As they ministered to the Lord ... the Holy Ghost said ..."

4 When we wait. Luke 2:26, Simeon was waiting and then the Holy Spirit revealed it.

5 When we listen. Revelation 2:7 "He that hath an ear, let him hear."

V The Anointing of the Holy Spirit

The anointing is for power and for understanding of God's truth.

Our Lord was continually filled with the Spirit during His 30 pre-baptism years.

In Luke 3:21,22, Jesus was baptized in water and the Spirit descended in bodily form.

In Luke 4:1, Jesus full of the Holy Spirit was led out for the wilderness temptation.

In Luke 4:18, Jesus speaks of His anointing, reading from Isaiah 61:1 "The Spirit of the Lord is upon Me, because He hath anointed Me to preach the Gospel ..."

The prophecy of this anointing is found in Psalm 45:7,8 "Thou lovest righteousness, and hatest wickedness: therefore God, Thy God, hath anointed Thee with the oil of gladness above Thy fellows. All Thy garments smell of myrrh."

This anointing for powerful service is given after wickedness is burnt away by the fire of Matthew 3:11; and righteousness of Christ is manifested.

This anointing is likely a direct result of our surrender to the Lord and filling with the Holy Spirit.

There is but one anointing. Acts 1:8; 2 Corinthians 1:21,22; John 2:20,27; Acts 4:31.

The anointing of the Spirit is to be received by faith. John 7:37-39; 4:14.

Conclusion

Praise the Lord for the wonderful ministry of the Holy Spirit.

Review Questions

1 List seven emblems of the Holy Spirit.

2 Name five ways that water is a picture of the Holy Spirit.

3 How does fire demonstrate the work of the Spirit?

4 List five things that Christians should do in the Spirit.
5 Tell seven things about the power of the Holy Spirit.
6 Give four characteristics of the Spirit's teaching.
7 How does the Holy Spirit teach? (five things)
8 What are five conditions of being Spirit-taught?
9 What are the purposes of the anointing of the Spirit?
10 Give the prophecy and fulfillment of Christ's anointing.

31

The Inspiration of the Bible

Introduction

The author of the Bible is the Holy Spirit; the pages of the Bible are an authoritative revelation in written form of God's nature and purposes.

The Bible is the source book of our knowledge of God; it is the textbook of divine truth; the guide book to everlasting life.

The word "Bible" is derived from the Greek word "biblos" meaning "a book." The volume is known by other titles such as "the Scriptures"; "the Writings"; The Word of God; Luke 4:17; 2 Corinthians 3:14; Mark 12:10; Matthew 22:29; Hebrews 4:12.

The Bible is a library of 66 books, divided into two main sections; the Old Testament containing 39 books and the New Testament containing 27 books.

The Bible was written by 36-40 authors over a period of 1600 years and by different types of people in different parts of the world.

The unique design of the Bible is one of the best proofs of its divine inspiration. For so many different men to write a book without contradictions is a miracle.

The miracle can only be explained by the Master Author's guiding hand.

The cardinal theme of the Bible is Christ who becomes the key to understanding it.

The Old Testament was originally written in Hebrew, with parts of Daniel and Ezra being written in Aramaic; the New Testament was written in Greek.

I Meaning of Inspiration

"By inspiration we mean the supernatural control by God over the production of the Old and New Testament" — Robert Lee (author of *Doctrinal Outlines*.)

The Bible is *theopneustos* (God-breathed), 2 Timothy 3:16. "All Scripture is given by inspiration ... and is profitable ..."

"Inspiration is the strong conscious inbreathing of God into men, qualifying them to give utterance to truth. It is God speaking through men" — William Evans.

2 Peter 1:21, literal translation, "For not by the will of man was prophecy brought at any time, but being borne by the Holy Spirit, the holy men of God spoke."

The Holy Spirit was miraculously present, preserving accuracy in the writings.

Holy men of God, overshadowed by the Holy Spirit, wrote at His command; thus they were kept from all error as they recorded things known or unknown to them.

II Various Theories of Inspiration

We are curious to learn exactly how God the Holy Spirit gave the Scriptures. Some of the authors recorded history that they had witnessed; others wrote of things that had happened long ago (Moses and creation); others wrote prophecy.

A **Revelation** Some think the authors were in a trance and saw the Bible and simply copied it down word for word as it was revealed to them by the Lord.

We admit that many of the writers wrote prophecy but we reject this theory of inspiration for it would not allow the writer a choice of words at all.

The education and logical mind of Paul is evident in Romans and Galatians.

B **Illumination** The Holy Spirit illuminated them to see the events in a spiritual manner and then they wrote them down in their own words and style of writing.

We believe that not only the thoughts are inspired but also the words.

God allowed the writer to use his own words and education, revealing his personality.

However, we reject this theory as being not specific enough for Bible inspiration.

The Bible is not the result of godly men meditating on God, but God Himself inbreathing man to record the thoughts of God.

C   **Verbatim reporting** God dictated the Scriptures as an executive to a secretary.

This would reduce inspiration to a mere mechanical process. We reject this theory for the personalities or individualities of men like David, Moses and Peter are very evident in their writings.

Luke the doctor used a medical word in Luke 8:44 (staunched); David the shepherd wrote of sheep, sling shots, shepherd's equipment (rod and staff).

D   **Natural inspiration** This theory magnifies human genius, denying the supernatural, mysterious or peculiar in inspiration. This would reduce the Scriptures to special writings like those of Shakespeare, Milton, Confucius or Jose Rizal.

Inspiration is more than this; it is actually "thus saith the Lord"; God speaking.

We reject this theory for it caters to the doctrine that "the Bible contains the Word of God," whereas the Bible *is* the Word of God.

E   **Universal Christian inspiration** We are all sons of God and each at different times is inspired to write a book or poem; or inspired to do this or that. If this theory were true we could expect a new Bible at any time. Bible inspiration is more than this; it was a definite, special inspiration for the special task of writing the Bible, God's message to mankind.

F   **Mechanical inspiration** Men became machines and wrote under a strange compulsion, things that they likely did not understand or comprehend. We reject this for we see the loving nature of John in his epistles; the stern nature of James in his letter; the fiery emotional nature of Peter in his epistles.

G   **Thought inspiration** This theory says that God gave the main thought to the writer and they were free to express these in their own words as they thought best. We reject this for we believe that each word was scrutinized, censored and accepted by the Author, the Holy Spirit.

H   **Verbal inspiration** This theory claims that every word is inspired, some going so far as to say that even the punctuation marks were inspired by the Lord.

Actually there were no capitals or punctuation marks in the original languages.

I   **Partial inspiration** Parts of the Bible are inspired, suggesting that the Bible contains the Word of God; we reject this theory for 2 Timothy 3:16 says, "*All* Scripture."

This theory leaves each person free to choose and judge the "truly inspired portions."

This theory is rejected for it leads to doubt, uncertainty and utter confusion.

III The True Explanation — Plenary or Full Inspiration

We believe that all Scripture is equally inspired basing its claim on 2 Timothy 3:16.

(The Revised Version of 2 Timothy 3:16 says, "All Scripture that is divinely inspired is also profitable." This is incorrect, for it teaches partial inspiration.)

We do not actually know the "how" of inspiration but we believe that each writer had liberty to use his own personality, education, experience with certain limits.

The Holy Spirit guarded each thought, each phrase, each word to preserve accuracy.

IV The Bible Claims Inspiration

1 For the writers. 2 Peter 1:21 "Holy men of God spake as they were moved."

2 For the writings. 2 Timothy 3:16 "All Scripture is given by inspiration."

3 For the words. 1 Corinthians 2:13 "Which things also we speak, not in the words which man's wisdom teacheth, but which the Holy Ghost teacheth." 2 Peter 3:2 "That ye may be mindful of the words which were spoken before by the holy prophets, and of the commandment of us the apostles."

   Jude 17 "But, beloved, remember ye the words which were spoken before."

V Things to Remember about Inspiration

Translations are not inspired; there are copyist errors; none of the originals are in existence today; ancient copies being discovered are *almost identical*.

The Bible records facts as they are: Ananias told a lie and the lie is recorded; the Scribes said Jesus had a devil and was mad and their lie is recorded.

Conclusion

We accept the Scriptures as the infallible Word of God, the canon of 66 books as complete: we do not recognize the Apocrypha or any other books to be inspired.

The original Scriptures will be the standard of judgment in the last day, John 12:48.

Let us read the Bible daily and obey its message in our daily lives.

God's people must handle this book carefully and reverently; it is God's Book to us.

Let us rejoice that God hath spoken, and endeavor by the power of the Holy Spirit to walk in the light of its revelation.

Review Questions

1 Who is the master author of the Holy Bible?
2 Give two important texts that deal with Bible inspiration.
3 Tell something about the Bible: 1) Various names 2) sections 3) writers 4) length of time to write it 5) theme 6) languages.
4 What is meant by inspiration?
5 List eight incorrect theories of inspiration.
6 Tell in a sentence why we reject each theory presented in question 5.
7 Explain plenary or full inspiration.
8 Give a Scripture to show that the Bible claims inspiration for its writers; writings and its words.
9 Is the King James version inspired? Why?
10 Why do we reject the Apocrypha? Give one Scripture.

32

The Bible

Introduction

Next to the gift of Christ and the Holy Spirit, the Bible is the third greatest gift.

Sir Walter Scott, himself the author of many books and the possessor of a great library, said, "There is but one book, the Bible."

The Bible is the oldest book in existence. It required sixteen centuries to write it; the first writer died 1450 years before the last writer was born.

The Bible lends itself to translation and has been translated in whole or in part in more than a thousand languages and dialects.

I Seven Crowning Wonders of the Bible
(pamphlet, Rev. Dyson Hague)

1 The wonder of its formation; one book written in one place in one language, another book written in another country centuries later in another language.

2 The wonder of its unification; it is a library of 66 books, yet only one book, for it has but one author, the Holy Spirit. There are no contradictions.

3 The wonder of its age; it is the most ancient of all books.

4 The wonder of its sale; it is the best seller of all time.

5 The wonder of its interest; it is the only book that is read by all classes, and ages of mankind. It is read by sages and children; read by all nations.

6 The wonder of its language; it was written largely by uneducated men, yet it is considered a literary masterpiece.

7 The wonder of its preservation; it has been the most hated of all books. Time and again kings and governments have sought to burn and abolish it. Yet God has preserved it for us today and it can be found in almost every home.

II Seven Symbols used to Illustrate the Word of God

1 **A Sword:** The Bible is a pointed Word that convicts the hearer.
Hebrews 4:12 "For the Word of God is quick, and powerful, and sharper than any two-edged sword, piercing even to the dividing asunder of soul and spirit."

2 **A Hammer:** The Bible is powerful and breaks the resistance of the hearer.
Jeremiah 23:29 "Is not My Word ... saith the Lord ... like a hammer that breaketh the rock in pieces?"

3 **A Seed:** The Bible is a living Word regenerating the hearer.
1 Peter 1:23 "Being born again, not of corruptible seed, but of incorruptible (seed), by the Word of God, which liveth and abideth for ever."

4 **A Mirror:** The Bible is a faithful Word, revealing the individual to himself.
James 1:23-25 likens the Bible to a mirror, in which the sinner (or saint) looks and sees a true reflection of himself as portrayed by the Lord Himself.

5 **A Fire:** The Bible is a burning Word, consuming the dross in the hearer.
Jeremiah 23:29 "Is not My Word like as a fire? saith the Lord."
Jeremiah 20:9 "But His Word was in mine heart as a burning fire shut up in my bones."

6 **A Lamp:** The Bible is an illuminating Word guiding the believer day by day.
Psalm 119:105 "Thy Word is a lamp unto my feet, and a light unto my path."

7 **Food:** The Bible is nourishing food, feeding the soul (providing meat and drink).
1 Peter 2:2 "As newborn babes, desire the sincere milk of the Word, that ye may grow thereby." See also Hebrews 5:12-14.
1 Corinthians 3:2 "I have fed you with milk, and not with meat."
Romans 10:17 "So then faith cometh by hearing, and hearing by the Word of God."
The Word of God convicts, breaks, regenerates, reveals, consumes, illuminates and nourishes the individual.

III Seven Reasons for Preaching
the Word of God

In Mark 2:2, Jesus faced the multitude and made a tremendous decision; it was to preach the Word of God.

We are sent to preach not a new Church but Christ as He is revealed in the Bible.

We insist on preaching the Bible because it endures for time and eternity.

Isaiah 40:8 "The grass withereth, the flower fadeth: but the Word of our God shall stand for ever."

1 Conviction of sin comes through the preaching of the Word of God, Acts 2:14-37. In Peter's Pentecost sermon nine verses out of 23 are quotations from the Old Testament.

2 Faith comes by hearing the Word of God. Romans 10:17 "So then faith cometh by hearing, and hearing by the Word of God."

3 Cleansing comes from the Word of God. 2 Corinthians 7:1 "Having therefore these promises, dearly beloved, let us cleanse ourselves from all filthiness of the flesh and spirit, perfecting holiness in the fear of God." The promises are the words of God.

4 Assurance comes from the Word of God. 1 John 5:13 "These things have I written unto you that believe on the name of the Son of God; that ye may know that ye have eternal life."

5 Comfort comes from the Word of God. 1 Thessalonians 4:18 "Wherefore comfort one another with these words." (These words are the words recorded in the Bible)

6 Truth comes from the Word of God. Acts 17:11 "These were more noble than those in Thessalonica, in that they received the Word with all readiness of mind, and searched the Scriptures daily whether those things were so."

7 The new birth comes from the Word of God. 1 Peter 1:23 "Being born again, not of corruptible seed, but of incorruptible, by the Word of God."

IV Seven Reasons Why Some do not Read the
Word of God Jeremiah 15:16

1 Ignorant of its truths; ignorant of its formation and the information available.

2 Some have no hunger, they have eaten — feeding on ashes, Isaiah

44:20; feeding on politics, comics, etc.

3 Sickness; a sin-sick soul has no appetite for the Word of God.

4 Lunching between meals; living in the light, frivolous non-essentials of life.

5 The Book lacks flavor for some; business, sports, education have taken prime interest.

6 The Book is too sweet, Revelation 10:8-10; the Book was sweet as honey in the mouth. Some think the Bible is only for the sick, aged and the dying; too sweet and sentimental for practical, healthy people.

7 The Book is too bitter, Revelation 10:8-10; as soon as he had eaten the Book it became bitter in his belly. The truths of judgment, hell and sin are too bitter and some are afraid to read the Bible.

Let us say with Jeremiah in 15:16, "Thy words were found, and I did eat them; and Thy Word was unto me the joy and rejoicing of mine heart."

V Seven Points to Remember in Reading the Bible

1 Read it lovingly. The Bible is the Word of my Savior to me, Psalm 119:11.

2 Read it reverently. The Bible is the Word of God, the Almighty Savior and Judge.

3 Read it prayerfully. The Bible is God's message to me, to my own heart and life.

4 Read it meditatively. Be like Isaac of old and meditate on the Word of God.

5 Read it systematically. Read right through the Bible, not just selected portions.

6 Read it resolutely. I will obey that which my Father teaches me from His Book.

7 Read it daily. Not just on Sundays but every day of your life read a portion.

Conclusion

Make the Bible your constant guide and companion in life.

The Bible is the Word of God; it is worthy of being believed.

Breathe a prayer for the Holy Spirit to help you understand the sacred pages.

The Word of God, if neglected, will be our Judge at the last day, John 12:48.

Lord teach me to treasure this volume highly; to defend it when necessary and make me bold to proclaim the whole counsel of God.

Review Questions

1   Tell five things about the Bible.
2   List the seven crowning wonders of the Bible.
3   List seven symbols used to illustrate the Word of God.
4   Give seven things that the Word of God does for an individual.
5   What do we learn about the Bible from Hebrews 4:12? (5 things)
6   Give two reasons why Jesus preached the Word of God in Mark 2:2.
7   Give seven reasons why some do not read the Word of God.
8   How should one read the Bible?
9   Give seven reasons why Jesus preached the Word of God.
10   What is the solemn thought from John 12:48?

33

Further Studies about the Bible

Introduction

The Bible does not contain the Word of God; the Bible *is* the Word of God.

If the Bible were merely a human Book we could expect another very soon.

If the Bible were merely a human book why is it that man finds it so far beyond his grasp to master and understand every passage?

The reason that men deny the full inspiration of the Scriptures is the fact of sin and it is an attempt to minimize sin and its effects and final end.

The Bible contains truth hidden from man for ages and which he is just discovering now, Ephesians 3:5, RV.

The revelation made to the prophets was independent of their own thinking, 1 Peter 1:10-12; as they preached and wrote the facts were revealed to them.

No prophetical utterance was of the prophets' own will, 2 Peter 1:21, RV.

David claimed divine inspiration for his utterances, 2 Samuel 23:2, RV.

The writings of the apostles and prophets were the Word of God, 2 Peter 1:21.

The Bible is all pure gold, with nothing worthless mixed among its pages, 2 Timothy 3:16.

Nehemiah accepted the words of the prophets as God's Word, Nehemiah 9:13,30.

Jesus in Matthew 22:31, 32 quoted the Bible as the genuine Word of God to mankind.

In the Old Testament, 2600 times the prophets asserted that their words are the Word of God; a similar statement occurs 525 times in the New Testament.

I The Authority of the Bible

A few generations ago the Bible was accepted as the authoritative Word of God.

It is a very sad fact that this is no longer true; men today consider it smart or clever to challenge the authority of the Holy Scriptures.

We are living in a lawless age when men are rebelling against authority in every department of life — religious, political and intellectual.

By creation man has been made to crave authority and to worship a superior Being.

Many today admire the Bible as a wonderful Book but refuse to submit to its authority.

Even atheists will extol the Bible as literature far outdistancing all competitors.

Some Christians acknowledge Jesus Christ as supreme authority but refuse to yield to the authority of the Scriptures; this is an untenable position.

The Christ whom we accept as our authority is the Christ of the Holy Scriptures.

Reasons why some do not accept the Bible as final authority:

A   They think that the Bible and science disagree; it is true that many unproven unscientific theories disagree with the Bible; but it cannot be shown once where true proven science and the Bible disagree, 1 Timothy 6:20.

B   They think that the Bible and geology disagree;
Geologist Guyot affirms that true geology and the Bible agree perfectly.

C   They think that the Bible and general science disagree;
The late Sir G. G. Stokes, president of the Royal Society flatly refutes this.

D   They think that the Bible and chemistry disagree;
Radar, a great American chemist, refutes this error, too.

E   Some think that the Bible and geography disagree;
Dr. Christie, an eminent geographer, declares that there is not one geographical error in the Bible.

F   Some think that the Church is the final authority and not the Bible.
The Church antedates the New Testament but the Old Testament, the infallible Word of God, is much older and more authoritative than the Church.

G Possibly the true reason is "indifference," like that of Gallio in Acts 18:17.

II The Supremacy of the Bible

It is the supreme Book for it so far excels all other books ever written.

It has been the one Book that men turn to in the hour of tragedy and death.

It is supreme, for it has the answer to the questions of life and death.

It is the oldest Book; its influence upon nations and men is beyond computation.

It is a pure Book unmixed with myth and wild imaginings; it is the Word of God.

III Some Supposed Contradictions in the Bible

A   John 1:18 "No man hath seen God at any time." Exodus 24:10 "And they saw the God of Israel."

Actually both statements are correct.

They did not see God for He is a Spirit but they saw a physical reflection of God.

When I look in the mirror I see a reflection of my face but I've never seen my face as others see it.

B   Numbers 25:9 — 24,000 died in the plague; 1 Corinthians 10:8 — 23,000 fell in one day.

23,000 is the number that fell in one day and 24,000 the total number that died.

C   2 Samuel 24:24 David paid 50 shekels of silver for the threshing floor; 1 Chronicles 21:25, David paid 600 shekels of gold.

Answer: There are two distinct transactions; first David bought the threshing floor for 50 shekels and later bought the whole farm (estate) for 600 shekels.

D   1 Timothy 6:16 God dwells in light: 1 Kings 8:12, God dwells in thick darkness.

Answer: Both are true for God is omnipresent, dwelling everywhere.

E   Isaiah 40:28 God never gets tired and never needs rest; Exodus 31:17, God created the world in 6 days and rested and was refreshed on the seventh day.

It does not say that God rested because He was tired; God does not get tired. God rested the seventh day to appreciate that which He had created.

F   John 13:27, Satan entered into Judas during the Last Supper; Luke 22:3,4,7, it is obvious that Satan entered into Judas before the Last Supper.

Answer: Satan entered into Judas twice, the second time more completely.

G   Acts 1:9-12, Jesus ascended from Mount Olivet; Luke 24:50,51, Jesus ascended from Bethany.

Answer: Both are correct for Bethany is a place on the side of Mount Olivet.

H   Acts 9:7 Paul's companions heard the voice; Acts 22:9, 26:14, Paul's companions did not hear the voice.

Answer: The companions heard a sound like thunder but did not understand the words.

I   1 Kings 6 gives the period between Exodus and the beginning of building the Temple as 480 years; actually according to history it was 573 years.

Answer: The difference of 93 years is exactly the period of the Captivity under the Judges and not reckoned in Jewish history.

Years spent away from God are lost years, wasted, and not reckoned with the Lord.

J   1 Samuel 6:19 says God smote 50,070 for looking into the Ark of the Covenant;

Josephus the historian says that only 70 people were smitten.

Answer: Probably both are correct; God may have killed 70 people outright on the spot and the 50,000 later or as a consequence of this incident.

K   Luke 18:35,43, Jesus healed one blind man as they came near Jericho; Mark 10:46,52 Jesus healed one man as they departed from Jericho; Matthew 20:29-34, Jesus healed two unnamed men some distance from Jericho.

Answer: These are three separate, distinct instances and not 3 reports of one story.

L   Other apparent contradictions are as easily explained; the Bible is inerrant, or "free from error."

IV The Credibility of the Holy Bible

How do you know that the Bible is authentic? How do we know that the supposed authors actually wrote the books? Is the Bible worthy of belief? Yes.

Not one of the original manuscripts is still in existence — perhaps to prevent foolish men from worshipping them.

The oldest manuscripts in existence are 1) Vatican, at Rome, fourth century, 2) Siniatic, in Leningrad, Russia, fourth century, 3) Alexandrian, London, fifth century.

We accept the Bible as credible, for it was recognized as authentic by the Church in the year 180 AD.

External evidence of its acceptance can be gained from the Apostolic Fathers.

Even heretics and infidels have been forced to testify to its absolute credibility.

Notable among these are: Basilides, Caprocate, Celsus, Porphyry.

An examination of the 4,000 ancient manuscripts in existence confirms the credibility.

We believe the Bible is completely reliable and are willing to stake our lives on it.

Conclusion

Do not worship the Bible, but rather read it, believe it and obey it explicitly.

(Material from *Doctrinal Outlines*, R. Lee.)

Review Questions

1 About how many times do the speakers claim that their words are the words of God in the Bible?
2 Is there a disagreement between science and the Bible?
3 Why do you consider the Bible as the supreme book? (six reasons)
4 How do you reconcile John 1:18 and Exodus 24:10?
5 How do you reconcile Numbers 25:9 and 1 Corinthians 10:8?
6 How can we explain the discrepancy in 2 Samuel 24:24 and 1 Chronicles 21:25?
7 In the light of Isaiah 40:28, why did God rest in Exodus 31:17?
8 Explain the problem of 93 years difference between 1 Kings 6, reckoning of time from Exodus to the building of the Temple with historical records?
9 How can you reconcile the problem of the voice in Acts 9:7; Acts 22:9; and Acts 26:14?
10 Name the three oldest manuscripts in existence.

34

The Creation Story

Introduction

We believe that God is the Creator of all things.

Let's make a detailed study of this much accepted but little understood question that troubles many students today.

Some Bible teachers steer clear of this subject because of the bitter struggle between the theories of evolution and so-called science. 1 Timothy 6:20.

We gladly take our place with John in Revelation 4:11, "Thou art worthy, O Lord, to receive glory and honor and power: for Thou hast created all things, and for Thy pleasure they are and were created."

True, there may be many things that we do not understand, but that does not influence our decision or undermine our belief in God as our Creator.

I The Authority of Genesis and the Creation Story

Genesis 1:1 "In the beginning God created the heaven and the earth."

We accept the first verse and all succeeding verses of the Bible as the infallible, inspired Word of God.

Who wrote Genesis? Was the author present at creation? Who gave him the details?

We believe that Moses wrote this book; in fact he wrote the first five books of the Bible.

Genesis is accepted as the Word of God and is quoted more than sixty times in different books in the New Testament.

In Matthew 19:4-6 Jesus refers to the beginning of time and the creation of Adam and Eve.

In Matthew 24:37-39, Jesus refers to the details of the flood.

God gave the story of creation to Adam as a revelation of past history.

Just as God is capable of foretelling the future, He can accurately reveal the past. (Perhaps a playback of a *tape recording* for Moses to *hear!*)

We admire the beauty, brevity, logic and simpleness of the creation story, particularly as we contrast it with existing human accounts of creation.

The resurrected Christ, remonstrating with the disciples on the Emmaus road, began to teach them from the beginning — and so Luke 24:27 says He began at Moses. Cf. Luke 24:44.

II The Purpose of the Creation Story in Genesis

Some see only difficulties, contradictions and scientific puzzles here.

What do you see? I see God revealing Himself as the powerful Creator.

We see Him as a God of order, logic, reason and masterful planning.

The purpose of Genesis is not to answer all the questions of man.

The purpose is not to make us astronomers or geologists.

The purpose of this story is to lead us into worship of God Himself.

III The Date of Creation

Here is where the controversy rages between evangelicals and evolutionists.

The scientists maintain from the study of geology etc. that the earth is a few million years old and others say that it is only 6,000 years old.

Perhaps both sides are correct and a misunderstanding has arisen because of the unknown length of time between Genesis 1:2 and Genesis 1:3.

The figure 6,000 years is quite accurate as the length of man's existence on earth.

Genesis 1:1 refers to a date much earlier, maybe millions of years earlier, we do not know the time of the original creation of the world.

Reason demands that whatever God created would be perfect. Genesis 1:10,12,18,21,25.

We are assured that verse 2 does not refer to the original perfect creation but describes the desolation after some cataclysmal event after the original creation.

Genesis 1:2 infers that something terrible has happened; a great calamity; terrible punishment; "without form and void"; darkness describes the awful condition.

We believe that the events of Ezekiel 28:12-15 and Isaiah 14:9-14 fit in here; these passages describe the fall of Satan which was previous to the story of Genesis 3:1-7.

From Genesis 1:3 we have the story of the new beginning of the world.

Jeremiah 4:23-26 describes in greater detail the condition of Genesis 1:2.

IV Facts in Support of the Biblical Account of Creation

1 The Biblical account of all sacred books proclaims that there is but one God, who by a spoken Word created all things.

2 Note the wonderful design in division of the land and water, air and atmosphere.

  If the level of the ocean were to rise a few feet, large portions of land would be submerged. (The Sahara Desert would become a lake, etc.)

  Considering heat and evaporation of water, the balance is maintained.

  The air is perfectly balanced with oxygen and nitrogen (ratio 21:79).

  No physical or chemical law maintains this balance; kept by creative power of God.

  The lavishness of creation; hundreds of varieties of birds, flowers, animals, herbs, fruits, fish, trees and ferns. Evolution could not provide this.

3 A study of history and primitive man shows the savagery and natural brutality of man as mentioned in Genesis as a result of the fall.

  An isolated tribe, newly discovered will be an instance of degeneration.

  Animals are not brutal like man. The male of a beast does not maltreat his female; the animal does not continually eat foods that harm him; this is a mark of degenerate mankind. Brutality is the result of the fall.

V The Progression of Creation or Reconstruction

The Bible speaks of six creative days; some argue that each day was a Millennium (a thousand years long) in accordance with 2 Peter 3:8; I believe that they were days of 24 hours only.

Geologists tell us that the order of creation follows earth patterns — First day: night, with the division of light and darkness; day and night, Genesis 1:3-5.

Second day: firmament — division of atmosphere and water, Genesis 1:6-8.

Third day: dry land — division of land and water — grass, herbs, trees, Genesis 1;9-13.

Fourth day: sun, moon, stars, division of day and night rulers, Genesis 1:14-19.

Fifth day: life, fish, fowl, whales, Genesis 1:20-23.

Sixth day: creatures, cattle, creeping things, beasts, and lastly man, Genesis 1:24-31.

"And God saw that it was good" is the chorus that echoes day by day.

VI Man Created in the Image and after the Likeness of God

"Image" means the shadow or outline of a figure.

"Likeness" denotes the resemblance of that shadow to the figure.

"In the creation story the two words are practically synonymous" — Dr. William Evans

1 Corinthians 11:7 "He is the image and glory of God: but the woman is the glory of the man."

A free translation of Genesis 1:26 "Let us make man in Our image to be Our likeness."

1 The image of God does not denote physical likeness, for God is a spirit and a spirit does not have parts and passions as a man does.

2 The two expressions mean more than man having dominion over nature.

3 From Scripture we learn that it means knowledge, righteousness and holiness.

It refers to moral likeness not physical likeness.

Ephesians 4:23,24 "... and that ye put on the new man, which after God
is created in righteousness and true holiness."

Colossians 3:10 "And have put on the new man, which is renewed in
knowledge after the image of Him that created him."

Conclusion

Adam and Eve were created with intelligence, for Adam named the
animals.

The modern man, they say, started from ignorance and developed.

Man was created with moral and spiritual qualities and could have
resisted Satan.

The creation that came from God was pronounced "good" for no evil
comes from God.

"In the beginning God" — let God be in all our beginnings.

Let us recognize in our Creator His power, authority, method and
order.

Let us draw nigh to Him in reverence and worship, James 4:8.

Review Questions

1   What bearing does Matthew 19:4-6 have on the creation story?
2   What is the relationship between Genesis 1:1, Luke 24:44, and
    John 1:45?
3   List four outstanding literary qualities of the story of creation in
    Genesis 1.
4   Give two purposes of the creation story in Genesis.
5   What is the approximate date of the creation of the world?
6   What three passages give light on this perplexing problem of the
    creation date?
7   Give four facts in support of the biblical account of creation.
8   Trace the progress of the six days of reconstruction in Genesis.
9   Explain the meaning of man being created in the image of God.
    Give two Scriptures that help to clarify this point.
10 How can we best refute the claims of evolutionists?

35

Evolution

Introduction

In our last lesson we studied about the biblical account of creation.

Unfortunately this is not accepted as fact by many universities and seminaries today.

Evolution is not only taught as a possible theory but it is taught as a fact.

Maynard Shipley, head of the Science League of America, says, "Scientists the world over accept the general theory of evolution as valid and incontrovertible and regard the process of evolution as a fact."

Linville, Kelley and Cleave, in their textbook *General Zoology*, write, "all scientists at the present time agree that evolution is a fact."

As Christians we do not need to be unduly influenced by the opinions of majorities; majorities are often wrong; the crowd crucified Christ but the minority was right.

We believe that the Bible is true and that evolution is a false theory.

Dr. Arthur I. Brown, M.D., C.M., F.R.C.S.E, says, "Evolution (as a theory) has utterly collapsed from the weight of its own inherent absurdities and impossibilities."

I Evolution Defined

A concise definition by Herbert Spencer: "Evolution is always fundamentally an integration of matter and dissipation of motion."

A lengthy definition by the same writer: "Evolution is an integration of matter and concomitant dissipation of motion, during which the matter passes from an indefinite incoherent homogenity to a definite coherent heterogeneity, and during which the retained motion undergoes a paralleled transformation."

Mr. Spencer means that the process in nature is always from the simple to the complex; and from the complex to the more complex. He says this is true of both plants, animals and humans, too. The process was from non-living matter to plants, animals and then humans.

Briefly: Evolution is the gradual development of higher forms of life from a lower stage of living matter.

This theory seeks to explain the universe from a "primitive nebulosity" to a modern world.

II Claims of Evolution

It claims to include in its scope every atom of matter, even the most infinitesimal living thing.

It claims to include every living minute of time, past, present, or future.

It flatly rejects all other theories or explanations of the world and universe.

It emphasizes continuity but recognizes secondary causes like natural selection, heredity, adaptation to environment, physiological selection and the natural struggle for life and the survival of the fittest.

III Missing Links of Evolution

It fails to account for the first atom.

It fails to explain how the original matter changed from homogenous to a moving one.

It fails to explain how the present universe is a cosmos and not a chaos.

It fails to explain continuity — how does a horse produce a horse and not a further evolved animal.

It fails to explain how life came from the non-living original atom.

It fails to explain the introduction of animal sensation and consciousness.

It fails to explain the leap from the animal world to that of man.

It fails to explain the present distribution of matter on numberless stars and planets.

It fails to explain the changes from the psychic, social, moral and spiritual realms.

IV Theistic Evolution

To try to answer the first missing link, Theistic evolution says that somewhere in the dark misty past God created original matter and set the mass of atoms in motion.

Modern evolutionists are swinging more and more to *Theistic* evolution. Theistic evolution divides into two forms: one that God merely created the first atoms of matter and the other that God still assists in the emerging process.

V Attitudes towards Evolution

A   Some dogmatists hold the theory regardless of arguments presented against it.

B   Some hold evolution as a hypothesis possessing a high degree of probability but not yet established.

The marks of a legitimate hypothesis in science are:

1   It must not be inconsistent with facts already established as scientific.

2   It must be capable of verification or disproof by subsequent investigations.

3   It must be applicable to the description or explanation of the phenomena, and if it is, must assign a cause fully adequate to have produced them.

Evolution violates 1) and 3).

C   Some accept evolution in a modified form, i.e. Theistic evolution, etc.

D   Evangelicals reject the theory and accept God's story of creation in Genesis.

VI Some Famous Scientists do not Accept the Theory of Evolution

Notes from *In Green Pastures*, edited by T.R. Dunham.

Dr. Albert Flesschman, professor of Zoology in the University of Erlangen, Germany: "The Darwinian theory (of evolution) has not a single fact to confirm it in the realm of nature. It is not the result of scientific research but purely the product of the imagination . . . the doctrine of Descent has not been substantiated."

Sir John Ambrose Fleming, F.R.S., President of the Victoria Institute of London, England, published a book *Evolution or Creation* which is a crushing attack on evolution.

Douglas Dewar, distinguished naturalist of England and author of many books and an acknowledged authority, has written another book, *Difficulties of the Evolution Theory*, which is a complete and effective argument against evolution.

Dr. Clark Wissler, curator-in-chief, of the Anthropological section of the American Museum of Natural History, in his book *The Case Against Evolution* says, "As far as science has discovered there always was a man, some not so developed, but still human beings in all their functions, much as we are today . . . man came out of a blue sky as far as we have been able to delve back." (that means he was created)

Dr. Austin H. Clark, F.R.G.S., American Geophysical Union, an oceanographer, writes in *The New Evolution—Zoogenesis*, "The great groups of animal life do not merge into another. They are and have been fixed from the beginning."

Dr. Gerritt Miller, says, "We do not hesitate to confess that in place of demonstrable links between man and other mammals, we now possess nothing more than some fossils so fragmentary that they are susceptible of being interpreted as something else."

Professor L. T. More of Cincinnati University in *The Dogma of Evolution* writes, "unfortunate for Darwin's future reputation . . . every one of his arguments is contradicted by fact."

Douglas Dewar, in *Difficulties of the Evolution Theory*, writes, "The breeder, no matter on what plant or animal he experiments, after he has effected a number of minor changes in any given direction, is suddenly brought to a standstill; in a comparatively short time he reaches a stage at which he cannot accomplish more, no matter how much he try . . . this fact is fatal to the evolution theory."

Professor A. C. Seward of Cambridge wrote, "A student who takes an impartial retrospect soon discovers that the fossil record raises more problems than it solves."

Conclusion

The proofs of evolution from oceanography, botany, comparative anatomy, vestigial organs, embryology, geology and paleontology, etc. dissolve under true scientific investigation.

Evolution at best is but a system or fabric of hypothesis; much of it is pure fiction.

How much better to accept the Word of God and believe what true science proves, that man and everything were created perfect and each was created as it is now.

God's creation order was "after his kind," Genesis 1:24, to the living creatures; in verse 21 the command to the plant world was "after their kind" and this rule has been obeyed.

I take my stand with God and true science against the error of this venomous theory.

Lesson material from: *Why Christianity Is True*, E. Y. Mullins; *Heresies Exposed*, W. C. Irvine; and *In Green Pastures*, T. R. Dunham.

Review Questions

1   Why do you suppose evolution has such a hold on the universities of today?

2   What is the theory of evolution? (give a simple explanation in your own words)

3   What are the four claims of evolution?

4   Give six secondary causes recognized by evolution.

5   List the nine missing links of evolution.

6   What is the difference between atheistic and theistic evolution?

7   Is it wise to try to harmonize theistic evolution and the Bible account of creation?

8   Is it possible that the minority of scientists who reject evolution can be correct? Why?

9   Of the eight famous scientists quoted in this lesson which do you feel is the weightiest quotation? Why?

10   Give three verses from Genesis 1 to prove that evolution is wrong.

36

The Fall of Man

Introduction

The story of the fall of man is taught by religions other than Christianity.

Their stories may be distorted but they do recognize the awful fact.

Evolution creates problems rather than solves them; if Genesis is false, how do you account for the moral depravity and sinfulness of man?

Other religions do not hold such a high and lofty view of God as we do, thus the width between the sinner and God is much greater with us.

To some it is incompatible that a pure, holy, sinless God should have allowed sin and Satan to enter the Garden of Eden.

The answer to that question is locked in with the mysteries of God.

Genesis 3 gives a full account of this awful tragedy in the history of man.

This story does not tell of the advent of sin into the universe, for Satan had already sinned and been cast out of heaven. Ezekiel 28:12-15; Isaiah 14:9-14.

This story tells how sin entered into the human race and made us sinners.

Some look upon this story as an allegory; it is too simple for that.

Some look upon it as a myth; we accept the Bible as the infallible Word of God and we accept this portion too as an integral part of that revealed Word of God.

We look upon this as truth and we accept it literally; the curses are certainly literal for they are in evidence about us daily (weeds and perspiration).

I The Agent in the Fall

Genesis 3:1 Satan operating through the serpent.

It is a remarkable fact that serpents have been and still are objects of fear by man; man is afraid of snakes. A lover of snakes is looked at quizzically.

The pronoun "he" is used in Genesis 3:1, of Satan. The snake would have been "it." This is a case of demon possession.

II The Subtlety of Satan

Satan did not appear in his own person; he appeared as a beautiful serpent.

Some say that the serpent was the only creature that had the power of speech except man. (Josephus) If this is correct, Eve would think it was the serpent speaking.

Satan made the attack when Adam and Eve were apart. (There is strength in unity.)

Satan attacked the weaker vessel and he did it when she was near the tree.

Satan presented the temptation through legal appetites, inclinations and desires for food and knowledge.

Satan began his attack by casting doubt upon the Word of God, "Yea, hath God said?"

Satan said that the tree would cause her to know good and evil, but failed to tell her that she would lose the power to do good.

III The Test that God Set before Adam and Eve

Genesis 2:16,17 "And the Lord God commanded the man saying, Of every tree of the garden thou mayest freely eat: but of the tree of the knowledge of good and evil, thou shalt not eat of it: for in the day that thou eatest thereof thou shalt surely die."

IV Steps Leading to the Fall

Eve was too close to the tree; she should have fled from the place of temptation.

Perhaps she was standing admiring its beauty; admiring the forbidden thing soon leads to a covetous desire to possess or enjoy that thing.

She talked with the devil; never converse or argue with him, except as you quote Scripture to him.

She tampered with the Word of God; she added the phrase, "neither shall ye touch it." God had not said that in His command.

She subtracted the word "freely," from the original command.

She toned down the Word of God; God said, "Thou shalt surely die," and Eve said, "lest ye die."

Genesis 3:6, she looked at the tree and saw that it was good for food, pleasant to the eyes and one that could make her wise if she partook of it.

V The Actual Sin

Genesis 3:6 "And when the woman saw that the tree was good for food, and that it was pleasant to the eyes, and a tree to be desired to make one wise, she took of the fruit thereof, and did eat, and gave also unto her husband with her; and he did eat."

The immediate results:

1 They became sinners. Their spiritual life died, Ephesians 2:1
2 Their eyes were opened and they knew that they were naked.
3 They sewed fig leaves together to cover their nakedness.
4 They went and hid from the presence of God; sin divides man from God.

VI God Pronounces Curses Genesis 3:14-19

1 On the serpent: Cursed above all cattle and above every beast of the field. It was to crawl on its belly and eat dust all of its life.
2 On the woman: Pain and sorrow in childbirth. Her husband was to rule over her.
3 On the man: The ground to be cursed and to bring forth thorns and thistles. His life to be one of sorrow; to make a living with perspiration. To die and return to the dust from whence he came.

VII Results of the Fall

1 All men irrespective of condition or class are now sinners before God.
   Romans 3:9 "For we have before proved both Jews and Gentiles, that they are all under sin."
   Romans 3:10 "As it is written, there is none righteous, no, not one."
   Romans 3:23 "For all have sinned, and come short of the glory of God."
   Romans 5:12 "Wherefore, as by one man sin entered into the world, and death by sin; and so death passed upon all men, for that all have sinned."

There may be differences in degree but not in the fact of sin.

2   The whole world rests under condemnation, wrath, curse.

Romans 3:19 "That every mouth may be stopped, and all the world may become guilty before God."

Galatians 3:10 "Cursed is every one that continueth not in all things which are written in the book of the law to do them."

Ephesian 2:3 "And were by nature the children of wrath, even as others."

3   Unregenerate men are regarded as children of the devil, not sons of God.

John 8:44 "Ye are of your father the devil, and the lusts of your father ye will do."

By the new birth we become sons of God, John 1:12.

4   The whole human race is taken captive by Satan.

2 Corinthians 4:4 "In whom the god of this world hath blinded the minds of them which believe not, lest the light of the glorious Gospel . . ."

5   The entire nature of man, mentally, morally, spiritually and physically has been affected by sin.

a   The understanding is darkened, Ephesians 4:18, 1 Corinthians 2:14.

b   The heart is deceitful and wicked, Jeremiah 17:9,10.

c   The mind and conscience are defiled, Genesis 6:5, Titus 1:15.

d   The flesh and spirit are defiled, 2 Corinthians 7:5.

e   The will is enfeebled, Romans 7:18.

f   We are utterly destitute of any Godlike qualities, Romans 7:18.

Conclusion

Man is born a lost sinner, an enemy of God.

With the fall of man God promised a Redeemer and the plan of salvation.

This prophecy (Genesis 3:15) God fulfilled about 4,000 years later at Calvary.

God took the fig leaves and gave Adam and Eve coats of skins.

This is a picture of the blood redemption that is required to ransom a sinner.

Review Questions

1   Why did God allow sin and Satan to enter the Garden of Eden?

2   Who was the agent in the fall of man?

3   Give six points to show Satan's subtleness.
4   What was the test that God placed before mankind?
5   Give four mistakes that Eve made before sinning.
6   Give four immediate results of their partaking of the fruit.
7   What curses did God pronounce as a result of the fall of man?
8   List four results of the fall that are evident today with a Scripture for each.
9   Give six ways that each man is affected by sin.
10   Quote the first promise of a Savior.

37

Sin

Introduction

In our last lesson we learned about the fall of man because sin entered through Adam.

Today men mock at sin, considering it merely human weakness or tendency.

When a sense of sin falls upon mankind they will turn to God for mercy.

Not until we understand the awfulness of sin can we understand Calvary; only as we apprehend the meaning of Calvary do we see the exceeding sinfulness of sin as viewed by a holy, righteous God.

I Definition of Sin

The dictionary calls it transgression, evil, a violation of an accepted moral, religious or social code.

"Sin is any lack of conformity to the character of God whether in act or state."

"Sin is a hopelessly incurable disease of the soul" (the leprosy or cancer of sin).

"Sin is characteristic of the old nature, the flesh, and finds expression daily."

1 John 3:4 "For sin is the transgression of the law."

  1 Sin is an act — the breaking of a law or commandment is sin.
  2 Sin is a state — the fallen state of man without righteousness.
  3 Sin is a nature — the nature of fallen man at enmity against God.

II Origin of Sin

1 Sin originated with Satan, Isaiah 14:12-14. This is explained in James 1:14,15, "But every man is tempted, when he is drawn away of his own lust, and enticed. Then when lust hath conceived, it bringeth forth sin: and sin, when it is finished, bringeth

forth death."

2   Sin entered the world through Adam. Romans 5:12 "Wherefore, as
by one man sin entered into the world, and death by sin ..."
3   The fact of the fall of man, Genesis 3:1-6.
Man — a) listened to the slanders against God
b) doubted God's love and His Word
c) looked at what God had forbidden
d) lusted for what God had prohibited
e) absolute disobedience to God's commands

III The Manifestations of Sin

1   Transgression — the overstepping of the law.
Psalm 51:1 "Blot out my transgressions."
2   Iniquity — an act inherently wrong or forbidden, as breaking a
commandment.
3   Error — the departure from right.
Psalm 51:9 "... and blot out all mine iniquities."
4   Missing the mark — the failure to meet the divine standard.
1 John 5:17; Romans 3:23.
5   Trespass — the intrusion of the self-will into the sphere of God's
authority
6   Lawlessness — this is spiritual anarchy.
1 Timothy 1:9 "... for the lawless and disobedient."
7   Debt — a failure in duty, the sin of omission, the things that we
leave undone
8   Unbelief — an insult to the divine veracity of God.
Hebrews 3:12 "... evil heart of unbelief"

IV Lists of Sins

1   Exodus 20:3-17 (The ten commandments): idolatry, cursing, Sabbath breaking, disrespect to parents, murder, adultery, stealing,
lying, covetousness (nine sins)
2   1 Corinthians 6:9,10: effeminacy, masturbation, drunkenness,
slander, extortion (five sins)
3   Romans 1:29-31: unrighteousness, fornication, wickedness, mali-
ciousness, envy, debate, deceit, malignity, whisperers, back-
biters, haters of God, despiteful, proud, boasters, inventors of
evil things, covenant breakers, without natural affection, impla-
cable, unmerciful (19 sins)

4 1 Timothy 1:9-11: lawlessness, disobedience, unholiness, profanity, whoremonger, kidnapping (six sins)

5 Colossians 3:5-8: inordinate affection, evil sexual desire, anger, wrath, malice, blasphemy, filthy communication (seven sins)

6 Galatians 5:19-21: lustfulness, witchcraft, hatred, variance, emulations, strife, seditions, heresies, revellings (nine sins)

7 Mark 7:20-23: evil thoughts, an evil eye, foolishness (three sins)

A total of over fifty different sins with many variations of each one.

V Sin cannot be Hidden

Numbers 32:23 "But if ye will not do so, behold, ye have sinned against the Lord: and be sure your sin will find you out."

Proverbs 28:13 "He that covereth his sins shall not prosper: but whoso confesseth and forsaketh them shall have mercy."

It is not only the sin that will be discovered but the sinner will be revealed, too. God sees and uncovers hidden sins — Adam, Cain, Achan, Ananias and Sapphira tried to hide things from God but failed to do so.

VI The Results of Sin

1 Death—a word signifying separation. Romans 6:23 "For the wages of sin is death; but the gift of God is eternal life through Jesus Christ our Lord."

2 Lost — man is lost to God, and man is lost from heaven. Luke 15:24 "For this my son was dead, and is alive again; he was lost, and is found."

3 Condemnation — this is a judicial word signifying God's judgment. John 3:18 "... but he that believeth not is condemned already, because he hath not believed in the name of the only begotten Son of God."

4 Guilt — an indicative word signifying being conscience-stricken. Genesis 26:10 "...one of the people might have lien (slept) with thy wife, and thou shouldest have brought guiltiness upon us.'

5 Perdition — a prospective word signifying destruction and damnation. 1 Timothy 6:9 "... which drown men in destruction and perdition."

6 Punishment — a conscious word signifying penal infliction. Matthew 25:46 "And these shall go away into everlasting punishment."

7   Eternal fire — a durative word signifying the length of punishment. Jude 7 "...are set forth for an example, suffering the
vengeance of eternal fire."
8   Hell — the abode of the devil and those who follow him. Matthew
25:41 "Then shall He say also unto them on the left hand, Depart
from Me, ye cursed, into everlasting fire, prepared for the devil
and his angels."
9   Lake of fire — the second death. Revelation 20:14 "And death and
hell were cast into the lake of fire. This is the second death."

VII The Remedy for Sin

Christ in His atonement and resurrection is the only remedy for sin.
John 1:29 "Behold the Lamb of God, which taketh away the sin of the
world."
1 John 3:5 "And ye know that He was manifested to take away our sins;
and in Him is no sin."
No man can cleanse himself from sin. Job 9:30,31 "If I wash myself
with snow water, and make my hands never so clean; yet shalt
Thou plunge me in the ditch."
Jeremiah 2:22 "For though thou wash thee with nitre, and take thee
much soap, yet thine iniquity is marked before Me, saith the Lord
God."
The remedy for sin is forgiveness through the Blood of Christ.
Ephesians 1:7 "In whom we have redemption through His Blood,
the forgiveness of sins."
1 John 1:7 "... and the Blood of Jesus Christ His Son cleanseth us from
all sin."
No man is without sin, therefore we all need a Savior. Galatians 3:22
"But the Scripture hath concluded *all* under sin." Romans 3:23 "For
all have sinned, and come short of the glory of God."

Conclusion

Christ is the required Savior for He alone was without sin.
2 Corinthians 5:21 "For He hath made Him to be sin for us, who knew
no sin; that we might be made the righteousness of God in Him."
Hebrews 4:15 "For we have not an High Priest which cannot be
touched with the feeling of our infirmities; but was in all points
tempted like as we are, yet *without* sin."
1 John 3:5 "... and in Him is no sin." 1 Peter 2:22 "Who did no sin ..."

God is too holy to condone or look at sin, Habakkuk 1:13 "Thou art of purer eyes than to behold evil, and canst not look on iniquity."

A prayer: *"Lord, teach me to see the exceeding sinfulness of sin (Romans 7:13), and teach me to hate sin (Psalm 97:10, Ye that love the Lord, hate evil); Lord, teach me to confess my sin (1 John 1:9); Lord, teach me to forsake sin (Proverbs 28:13)."*

Review Questions

1   What is the key to understanding Calvary?
2   Define sin.
3   List and define the three aspects of sin.
4   Give four Scriptures that deal with the origin of sin.
5   Give eight manifestations of sin and a short explanation of each.
6   List two passages (one from the O.T. and one from the N.T.) that give lists of sins.
7   What major truths about sin do we learn from Numbers 32:23 and Proverbs 28:13?
8   Give nine results of sin with a short explanation of each.
9   What is the remedy for sin?
10   Give a fourfold prayer of a Christian regarding sin.

38

Man a Tripartite Being

Introduction

In the conclusion of Lesson 4, on the Trinity, we said that man was a tripartite being; man consists of three component parts: body, soul and spirit.

There are two passages that clearly teach that man has three parts.

1 Thessalonians 5:23 "And the very God of peace sanctify you wholly; and I pray to God, your whole spirit and soul and body be preserved blameless unto the coming of our Lord Jesus Christ."

This verse clearly states that man has three separate, distinct parts; the distinctions may be slight but they exist, nevertheless.

Hebrews 4:12 "For the Word of God is quick, and powerful, and sharper than any two-edged sword, piercing even to the dividing asunder of soul and spirit, and of the joints and marrow, and is a discerner of the thoughts ..."

Some people teach that the soul and spirit are two words but meaning the same thing; this verse definitely tells us that they are divisible.

It is true that in many passages of Scripture it seems that the terms soul and spirit are used interchangeably, but there are other passages where this is impossible.

Let us study the Scriptures for the answer.

Briefly, then, this is the distinction:

1 Spirit gives man "God-consciousness" — the ability to communicate with God.

2 Soul gives man "self-consciousness" — the ability to be a person, personality.

3 Body gives man "world-consciousness" — the ability through the senses to understand.

I The Origin of Man

Genesis 1:1 tells us that God existed in the beginning; He always existed; He is eternal.

Genesis 1:26,27, records the fact chronologically that man was created on the sixth day.

Genesis 2:7 gives the details of how it was done, "And the Lord God formed man of the dust of the ground, and breathed into his nostrils the breath of life; and man became a living soul."

The three parts of man are referred to in this verse:

1   The body of man — our flesh, bones, blood were made of the dust of the ground.

2   The spirit — breathed into man's nostrils by the Lord God.

3   "And man became a living soul"; this is the union of the other two. It is the part of man above the body but beneath the spirit and acts as a medium between the two. (Baxson)

II The Body of Man

This is the part of man with which we are most familiar — the physical part of man.

Psalm 139:14 "I will praise Thee; for I am fearfully and wonderfully made."

The Bible tells us that the body of man was formed from the dust of the earth.

Dust is analyzed as containing 96 elements and man also contains 96 elements, and they are identically the same ones — a wonderful proof of creation.

To mention some of the 96: calcium, carbon, chlorine, fluorine, hydrogen, iodine, iron, magnesium, nitrogen, oxygen, phosphorus, potassium, silicon and sodium.

Genesis 3:19, God in pronouncing the curse upon man after the fall, says, "In the sweat of thy face shalt thou eat bread, till thou return unto the ground; for out of it was thou taken: for dust thou art, and unto dust shalt thou return."

The body of man has five senses: sight, hearing, taste, touch and smell.

All ecstasy, pain, sensation or ability is expressed in and through the physical body.

After the fall the body became a dying, death-doomed body. (Chafer)

Hebrews 9:27 "And as it is appointed unto men once to die ..." Ever since the fall into sin in the Garden of Eden, man is born with an appointment with death.

III The Spirit of Man

The spirit gives man God-consciousness, the ability to communicate with God.

God breathed into the nostrils of Adam, giving him the spirit (wind, breath).

Someone has said that man is "dust inbreathed by Deity."

"The spirit receives impressions of outward and material things through the soul and the body, but it belongs to a higher level and is capable of a direct knowledge of God by relation to its own higher senses and faculties. The spirit is the capital city of the human personality." (A. T. Pierson)

God is a Spirit, John 4:24, and the spirit of man is the part that resembles God most.

This is manifested in our assurance of salvation. Romans 8:16 "The Spirit Himself beareth witness with our spirit, that we are the children of God."

Ecclesiastes 12:7 teaches that at death the body goes to the dust and the spirit back to God; "Then shall the dust return to the earth as it was: and the spirit shall return unto God who gave it."

Ecclesiastes 3:21 "Who knoweth the spirit of man that goeth upward, and the spirit of the beast that goeth downward to the earth?"

The spirit of man at death goes upward to God; spirit of the beast goes downward.

Luke 12:20 "But God said unto him, Thou fool, this night thy soul shall be required of thee."

The soul of the beggar went to Abraham's bosom, Luke 16:22; the soul of the rich man was taken to hell, Luke 16:23.

IV The Soul of Man

The soul is self-consciousness; it stands for the individual, personal life.

The Bible speaks of a hungry soul, a weary soul, Jeremiah 31:25; a thirsty soul, Psalm 42:2; a grieved soul, Job 30:25; a loving soul, Song of Solomon 1:7.

The soul seems to be the part of man midway between the body and the spirit, yet it is not a mixture of the two, though at times it seems to take on characteristics of one or the other.

The soul joins two worlds, the physical and the spiritual.

The work of the soul is to coordinate the activities of the two diverse parts.

The soul is to keep the body, as the lowest in subjection to the spirit the highest.

"God designed that the human spirit indwelt and ruled by the Holy Spirit, should keep man in constant touch with Himself, and maintain in everything its proper pre-eminence, ruling soul and body." (A. T. Pierson)

It is the soul of man that Jesus died to redeem on the cross. Hebrews 10:39 "... but of them that believe to the saving of the soul."

James 1:21 "... receive ... which is able to save your souls."

Psalm 49:8 "For the redemption of their soul is precious."

Luke 16:23 tells us that the soul can be lost in the place of punishment.

Revelation 18:12, 13 lists commodities in which merchants deal: gold, silver, precious stones, ivory, wood, ointment, wine, oil, animals and the souls of men.

Men gamble their souls for a moment of pleasure.

Conclusion

God created man a tripartite being to love the Lord and to enjoy life and nature.

Man was created with the ability to think, love and make decisions, Isaiah 1:18.

Man was made for God; the spirit of man was made to commune with God.

"And they heard the voice of the Lord God walking in the garden in the cool of the day," Genesis 3:8 is a beautiful picture of this fellowship.

You must prepare for the day of resurrection when your component parts will be reunited and you will stand before the Judge of all the earth.

Jesus died on the cross to save our souls from the terrors of hell.

Review Questions

1   What do we mean by the expression, "Man is a tripartite being"?
2   Give two passages of Scripture to prove that man has three component parts.
3   Briefly, what is the distinction between these three parts?
4   Tell the story of the creation of man.
5   In what way are we fearfully and wonderfully made? Psalm 139:14

6   What is the relationship of Genesis 3:19 to an analysis of dust?
7   Distinguish between soul and spirit.
8   How does God communicate with an individual?
9   List six adjectives used in the Bible to describe the soul.
10   Give three verses to show which part of man Jesus came to save.

39

Angels

Introduction

Little attention is paid to this doctrine today, for men consider it
  almost valueless except as angels occur in bedtime stories.

However, we should not underestimate the ministry of angels,
  particularly that of guardian angels; we certainly do not know how
  much we owe to them.

Story of missionary who was forced to sleep outside one night and
  robbers were planning to steal from him but were frightened away
  by the presence of 16 soldiers with swords. The missionary
  laughed at such a story but later on furlough found that a group of
  16 people had prayed specially for him on that particular night.
  Praise the Lord for the ministry of angels.

I The Existence of Angels

The word "angel" first occurs in Genesis 16:7, where the angel of the
  Lord ministered to Hagar after Sarah had mistreated her (1913 BC).

The angels were created by God but the time of that creation is not
  revealed.

Colossians 1:16 "For by Him were all things created, that are in
  heaven, and that are in earth, visible and invisible."

Matthew 4:11 angels came to minister to Jesus at the great temptation.

In Matthew 18:10 Jesus said, speaking of guardian angels, "Take heed
  that ye despise not one of these little ones; for I say unto you, That
  in heaven their angels do always behold the face of My Father
  which is in heaven."

Jesus believed in angels and so did Paul, Colossians 2:18; 2 Thessalonians 1:7.

II The Nature of Angels

Angels are spirit beings. Hebrews 1:14 "Are they (angels) not all ministering spirits ...?

Psalm 104:4 "Who maketh His angels spirits; His ministers a flaming fire."

As spirits, angels are not bound by natural human laws; angels can enter locked prisons — Acts 12:7; open prison doors — Acts 5:19; ascend in a flame — Judges 13:19,20.

Angels are able to travel great distances very quickly (heaven to earth, which may be many light years apart). Compare Daniel 10:12,13, angel apologized for being 21 days late.

Angels are wiser than men. 2 Samuel 14:20 "My lord is wise, according to the wisdom of an angel of God, to know all things that are in the earth."

Angels are strong. Psalm 103:20 "Bless the Lord, ye His angels, that excel in strength."

  a One angel killed 185,000 Assyrian soldiers in one night, 2 Kings 19:35.

  b One angel slew 70,000 Israelites following David's sin in 2 Samuel 24:15,16.

  c One angel thwarted the power of Rome, broke the seal and rolled away the stone from the tomb, Matthew 28:2,4.

  d One angel will one day bind the devil and imprison him for a thousand years.

There are various ranks and orders of angels: Michael is called an archangel, Jude 9. The Bible speaks of archangels, angels, principalities, powers, dominions and thrones — Colossians 1:16; Daniel 10:12-21; 1 Thessalonians 4:16: 1 Peter 3:22.

Angels are immortal, Luke 20:35,36, without material bodies, knowing nothing of decay and death; if Jesus had become an angel he could not have died.

Angels neither marry nor are given in marriage — Matthew 22:30; Luke 20:35,36.

III The Number of Angels

Angels seem to be innumerable. Revelation 5:11 "And I beheld, and I heard the voice of many angels round about the throne and the beasts and the elders: and the number of them was ten thousand times ten thousand, and thousands of thousands."

Hebrews 12:22 "... unto the city of the living God, the heavenly Jerusalem, and to an innumerable company of angels."

Matthew 26:53, Jesus spoke of being able to call for twelve legions of angels (3,000 to 6,000 each).

2 Kings 6:17 the servant of Elisha saw the mountains full of chariots of fire round about Elisha and these doubtless were angels.

IV The Fall of Angels

Angels are described by our Lord as being holy (sinless and pure). Mark 8:38 "... when He cometh in the glory of His Father with the holy angels."

Angels as created beings were created holy — Luke 9:26; 2 Peter 2:4; Jude 6.

On the basis of 1 Timothy 5:21, (elect angels, inferring that these are now confirmed in holiness) we gather that God placed the angels on probation for a time.

When the test came some defected and some maintained their innocence and were confirmed in their goodness, Psalm 89:7, RV.

2 Peter 2:4, speaks of the fall of angels, ".... the angels that sinned."

The actual test and time of the fall of angels is uncertain; however, there are several guesses which are only theories:

    1 That they rebelled when Satan tried to become like God — Isaiah 14; Ezekiel 28; Revelation 12:7.

    2 That it was the sin of pride and disobedience.

    3 That it was the sin of cohabitation with women on earth, Genesis 6:1-4.

On the basis of Matthew 25:41 "... the devil and his angels," I would be inclined to believe that the first, number 1, is the most likely answer.

As a result of their fall they are awaiting judgment. Jude 6 "And the angels which kept not their first estate but left their own habitation, He hath reserved in everlasting chains under darkness unto the judgment of the great day."

V The Works of Angels

1 In heaven — to honor, worship and serve the Lord God, Revelation 5:11-12; 8:3,4.

2 On earth — running errands for the Lord: a) showing Hagar a

fountain b) appearing before Joshua with a drawn sword c) releasing chains from Peter d) opening prison doors e) feeding, stengthening and defending God's children, etc.

3 To exercise God's judgments and purposes: a) to block Balaam's pathway, Numbers 22:22 b) to kill Herod, Acts 12:23 c) to gather the sinful tares at the last judgment and burn them, Matthew 13:41.

4 To guide believers: An angel guided Philip to meet the Ethiopian eunuch, Acts 8:26.

5 To assist, protect and strengthen saints: a) Elijah in 1 Kings 19 b) Daniel in the lions' den, Daniel 6:22 c) Jesus in Matthew 4:11; Luke 22:43 (Gethsemane).

6 They will accompany our Lord when He returns, Matthew 25:31; 2 Thessalonians 1:7-8.

7 They take the Lord's children to heaven at death, Luke 16:22.

8 The angels had a part in the giving of the law, Hebrews 2:2, RV; Acts 7:53; Galatians 3:19.

VI The Abode of Angels

The present abode of the angels is in heaven. Matthew 22:30 "For in the resurrection they neither marry, nor are given in marriage, but are as the angels of God in heaven." Also Ephesians 3:10; John 1:51; Luke 2:13,15.

VII The Superiority of Men over Angels

Angels and our first parents were both created perfect, angels as spirit beings and Adam and Eve as human fleshly beings.

However, in other ways we today are superior to angels:

1 Angels are not allowed to preach the Gospel — this ministry has been given to us.

"When I sing redemption story, angels will fold their wings, for they never knew the glory that my salvation brings."

2 Men will one day judge angels. 1 Corinthians 6:3 "Know ye not that we shall judge angels?"

Perhaps we will only judge the fallen angels referred to in Jude 6.

This great honor is indeed a glorious yet humbling thought for the redeemed.

Though we fell into sin, yet God has raised us up higher than angels in Christ.

Conclusion

When the angels sinned the Lord did not provide a Savior for them. How wonderful that He deigned to die for the likes of us.

Let us constantly thank God for the faithful, untiring ministry of guardian angels.

Matthew 18:10 infers that there are angels assigned to children. "That in heaven their (these little ones) angels do always behold the face of My Father ..."

Wonderful as angels are we must never worship them, Revelation 22:8,9.

Angels can become visible and eat human food: Luke 2:9; Genesis 32:1,2; 18:5.

Review Questions

1 When and how did angels begin?
2 Give three references to prove the existence of angels.
3 Tell six things about the nature of angels.
4 List four outstanding feats of angels to demonstrate their strength.
5 What verse gives some idea of the number of angels?
6 Give three possible causes of the downfall of angels.
7 Name seven things included in the work of angels.
8 Give seven ways that men are superior to angels.
9 What lesson do we learn about angels from Revelation 22:8,9?
10 What comforting lesson do we learn from Luke 16:22 regarding angels?

Satan

Introduction

The Christian life is a battle against our great foe, Satan, called the devil.

By virtue of the fall of man we became the devil's possession, his pawns.

We share the same fate — cursed by God and destined to hell.

When we receive Jesus Christ as our Savior this relationship of Satan and sinner is broken, but Satan does not give us up easily; he fights desperately to regain us.

The Bible tells us to resist Satan, fight him, give him no place in our lives.

I Satan's Origin

Satan is a created being according to the Lord in Colossians 1:16; the time is unknown.

Satan is described in Ezekiel 28:12-19:

Verse 12 — Satan was full of wisdom and perfect in beauty.

Verse 13 — He was covered with precious stones, sardius, topaz, diamond, beryl, onyx, jasper, sapphire, emerald, carbuncle and gold.

He was capable of using tabrets and pipes for he was musical.

Verse 14 — he was the anointed cherub, perhaps the chiefest, highest angel.

Verse 17 — his heart was lifted up because of his beauty and wisdom.

Verse 15 — he was created perfect and remained perfect until sin entered him.

Verse 16 — sin and iniquity were discovered in Satan.

Verses 16-18—Satan was cast out from the presence of God in heaven.

Satan is also described in Isaiah 14:12-17:

Verse 12 — he was called Lucifer, the son of the morning.

Verse 13,14 — his pride led him to desire to be like the most High God.

Verse 15 — his destiny is mentioned as being hell, down to the sides of the pit. ·

Since Satan has been cast out of heaven he now makes his abode in the air, Ephesians 2:2.

Satan still has a limited access to heaven to accuse the brethren: Job 1:6-12; Zechariah 3:1.

This power may continue until the fulfillment of Revelation 12:10.

II Satan's Personality

Many today do not believe in a personal devil, recognizing only the evil tendencies of the flesh or vices as human weaknesses.

Jesus speaking in John 8:44 said to the unbelieving Jews, "Ye are of your father the devil, and the lusts of your father ye will do." He must be a person to be a father.

In Job 1:6-12, Satan talks to God accusing Job of evil; an influence cannot talk.

In the account of the Temptation of Christ, in Matthew 4:1-11, Jesus was dealing with a real person, a real enemy, a tricky, subtle foe.

Satan is a real person, possessing life, intelligence, will power and feelings.

Satan, however, is a spirit being and does not possess a human body (neither tail or horn.)

III Satan's Character

1 He is a thief. Matthew 13:19, the devil steals the Word of God from the hearts of hearers: "When any one heareth the word of the kingdom, and understandeth it not, then cometh the wicked one, and catcheth away that which was sown in his heart."

2 He is subtle. 2 Corinthians 11:3, Satan beguiled Eve: "... as the serpent beguiled Eve through his subtlety." See Lesson 36.

3 He is a murderer. John 8:44 "Ye are of your father the devil, and the lusts of your father ye will do. He was a murderer from the beginning."

4 He is a liar. John 8:44 "When he (Satan) speaketh a lie, he speaketh of his own: for he is a liar, and the father of it."

5. He is a deceiver. Revelation 12:9 "...and Satan, which deceiveth the whole world. . ."

IV Satan's Titles

1 He is an **angel of light.** 2 Corinthians 11:13-15 "For Satan himself is transformed into an angel of light."

2 He is a **roaring lion.** 1 Peter 5:8 "... your adversary the devil, as a roaring lion, walketh about, seeking whom he may devour."

3 He is **the prince of the power of the air.** Ephesians 2:2 "... according to the prince of the power of the air, the spirit that now worketh in the children of disobedience."

4 He is **the power of darkness.** Colossians 1:13 "... delivered us from the power of darkness, and hath translated us into the kingdom of His dear Son."

5 He is **the great dragon, the serpent, the devil, Satan.** Revelation 12:9 "And the great dragon was cast out, that old serpent, called the Devil, and Satan, which deceiveth the whole world": he was cast out into the earth, and his angels."

6 He is **the prince of this world.** John 14:30 "For the prince of this world cometh, and hath nothing in Me."

7 He is **the god of this world.** 2 Corinthians 4:4 "In whom the god of this world hath blinded the minds of them which believe not."

8 He is **king of the bottomless pit, whose name in the Hebrew is Abaddon,** Revelation 9:11.

V Satan's Work

1 To seek whom he may devour. 1 Peter 5:8 "The devil, as a roaring lion, walketh about, seeking whom he may devour."

2 To sow tares and evil doctrine. Matthew 13:25,30 "His enemy came and sowed tares among the wheat and went his way."

3 To blind the minds of men. 2 Corinthians 4:4 "In whom the god of this world hath blinded the minds of them which believe not."

4 To accuse the brethren. Revelation 12:10 "For the accuser of our brethren is cast down, which accused them before our God day and night."

5 To sift (test) the Christians. Luke 22:31 "And the Lord said, Simon, Simon, behold, Satan hath desired to have you, that he may sift you as wheat: but I have prayed."

6 To destroy the flesh (lives) of men. 1 Corinthians 5:5 "To deliver such an one unto Satan for the destruction of the flesh, that the spirit may be saved in the day."

VI Satan's Subordinates

1 Satan's angels, evil spirits, unclean spirits and devils. 2 Peter 2:4 "For if God spared not the angels that sinned, but cast them down to hell, and delivered them into chains of darkness ..."

   Jude 6 "And the angels which kept not their first estate ... reserved in everlasting chains under darkness unto the judgment of the great day."

2 Principalities, powers, world rulers and spiritual hosts. Ephesians 6:12 'For we wrestle not against flesh and blood, but against principalities, against powers, against the rulers of the darkness of this world, against spiritual wickedness in high places."

3 Sinners who do his will. John 8:44 "Ye are of your father the devil, and the lusts of your father ye will do."

4 Saints sometimes inadvertently allow Satan to use them as Peter did in Matthew 16:22, 23. Jesus looked at Peter but rebuked Satan who had spoken through Peter's lips.

VII Satan's Destiny

1 At a future date he will be cast out of heaven. Revelation 12:7 "And there was war in heaven: Michael and his angels fought against the dragon; and the dragon fought and his angels, and prevailed not; neither was their place found any more in heaven."

   Satan still has access to heaven today.

2 Then Satan will begin to stir up men against God. Revelation 12:12 "Woe to the inhabiters of the earth and of the sea! for the devil is come down unto you, having great wrath, because he knoweth that he hath but a short time."

3 Then he will be chained by an angel. Revelation 20:1-3 "And I saw an angel come down from heaven, having the key of the bottomless pit and a great chain in his hand. And he laid hold on the dragon, that old serpent, which is the Devil, and Satan, and bound him a thousand years."

4 Satan will be cast into the bottomless pit for the thousand years, Revelation 20:3.

5 After this he will be loosed for a little season and go out to deceive men and attempt to revolt against God. Revelation 20:7,8 "And when the thousand years are expired, Satan shall be loosed out of his prison, and shall go out to deceive the nations which are in the four quarters of the earth, Gog and Magog, to gather them

together to battle: the number of whom is as the sand of the sea."
6   Satan is defeated and cast into the lake of fire forever, Revelation
20:7-10.

Conclusion

Satan is mighty but God is Almighty; Satan was forever defeated at
Calvary. Let us constantly claim victory over Satan through the
Blood of Calvary, Revelation 12:11.

Review Questions

1   Tell seven things about Satan before his fall.
2   Show that Satan is a person (Five points).
3   Give a five-fold character sketch of Satan.
4   Which one of the characteristics listed in question 3 do you
consider to be the most terrifying? Why?
5   Name eight titles ascribed to Satan.
6   Name five things that Satan does.
7   Who are Satan's subordinates or assistants?
8   Give one illustration from the life of Christ where Satan was able
to speak through the lips of a disciple.
9   On the basis of Revelation 12:7-12, and 20:1-10, trace the destiny
of Satan.
10   What sin caused Lucifer the cherub to become Satan the devil?

41

Demonology

Introduction

Notes from *Essentials of Demonology*, Langton; *Biblical Demonology*, Unger; and *Angels and Demons*, Needham.

Belief in the existence of evil spirits has prevailed among all the known peoples of the world from the earliest times of which we have knowledge. These spirits are often thought to be the departed ghosts which have come back to annoy the living.

Those professing to see demons have seen them in human forms, as well as animal and hybrid forms of various sorts; ordinarily demons are invisible spirits.

Jesus accepted without demur belief in the existence of demons, and the Gospel of Mark tells many stories of Jesus casting out demons.

Some people question whether demons and spirits exist today; I strongly believe they exist.

I The Origin of Demons

The Bible is rather hazy in answering this question, and several answers are presented for our consideration; the first of the following theories is generally accepted now.

1 When Satan sinned against God in Isaiah 14;12-20; Ezekiel 28:11-19; some say that he did not sin alone but was the leader of a group of angels. When Satan fell he and his angels were cast out, and these fallen angels have become demons.

In Matthew 12:26 Satan is presented as a king over a kingdom of lesser devils.

2 Some see in Genesis 6:1-6 angels coming to earth and co-habiting with women. The offspring were giants and some say that these became demons after death.

Others explain this passage as the intermarriage of the godly line of Seth and the ungodly line of Cain. If this were so, what would cause the children to be giants, superhuman beings? Genesis 6:4.

The same expression, "sons of God" occurs in Job 1:6 where the "sons of God" came to present themselves before the Lord. The sons of Seth certainly did not have access to the heavenlies, inferring thereby that these were angelic beings.

3   A third explanation is that demons are the spirits of a pre-Adamite race that perished between the first two verses of Genesis 1; and is described in Jeremiah 4:23-26 where it says, "...there was no man...," inferring that there had been men there at one time.

II   The Existence of Demons Today

Scriptural testimony is clear that there was an abundance of demons at the time the Savior was here on earth.

Man today boasts of an age of science and enlightenment and dismisses the biblical claim as a mere remnant of medieval superstition or an amusing joke.

New Testament writers firmly believed in demons and John in Revelation 9:20 speaks of a future time (the time of the Great Tribulation) when men will continue to worship devils; many pagan peoples today are ardent spirit worshippers.

Several of us living in Manila can testify today to having seen demon possessed people and having heard the demons speak through the lips of these people.

III   The Nature of Demons

Demons are spirit beings; in Matthew 8:16 Jesus cast out the spirits.

In Mark 1:23 the demon is called an "unclean spirit"; demons and evil spirits are one and the same thing.

Paul says that we wrestle not against "flesh and blood" Ephesians 6:12, but against the non-material, the incorporeal, the unseen powers of the air.

Demons, though spirits, have personalities and are represented as intelligent beings: Mark 5:10; Luke 4:34; Genesis 3:1; 2 Corinthians 11:14.

Because of their supernatural knowledge men have attempted to get advance information from them about coming events; people consult evil spirits in fortune telling.

Demons are represented as being morally unclean: Matthew 10:1; Mark 1:27; Romans 6:13; Luke 8:27.

They seem to have superhuman strength requiring several people to hold the demonized person.

They cause dumbness, blindness, insanity, suicidal mania, etc.

IV The Activity of Demons

1 They oppose God and seek to defeat His will. Satan is the accuser of the brethren. Satan is limited to one place at a time, his servants the demons are the active force that gathers the information for Satan. Revelation 12:10; 2:13.

2 They oppress man and seek to hinder his welfare: Job 1:12; Luke 13:16, the woman was oppressed by Satan for 18 years (that is Satan or his servant the demon).

Satan is not omnipresent, omnipotent nor omniscient, so the greater part of his colossal activity must be relegated to demons.

Demons distress mankind by deranging both body and mind, Mark 1:23-27; 5:1-20.

3 Demons nevertheless accomplish God's purposes.

God used a lying spirit to punish wicked King Ahab, 1 Kings 22:23; Revelation 16:13-16, demons will lure the God-resisting armies to Armageddon.

V The Organization of Demons

Satan is ubiquitous for he seems to be present everywhere at the same time, but actually he is limited to one geographical location at a time.

Satan's seat was Pergamos in Revelation 2:13, but he has likely moved it several times since then.

Satan operates a well organized multitude of demons: Daniel 7:19,20; Revelation 12:4,7.

Satan's kingdom is not merely an uncoordinated mob, Matthew 12:26, but it is revealed as a highly systematized empire of evil, elaborately organized.

Satan rules over fallen man with his government of pride, ambition, selfishness, force, greed, and pleasure. John 14:30; 18:36; Ephesians 2:2; 6:12; 1 John 2:15-17.

Satan similarly holds sway over the fallen spirits as an organized kingdom of evil. Some of the fallen angels are even now reserved in chains under darkness, Jude 6.

VI The Doom of Demons

The doom of all demons, like that of Satan, was sealed by Christ on Calvary.

The abyss is the intermediate place of punishment of demons, Revelation 9:11.

The demons know that their doom is coming. Matthew 8:29 "What have we to do with Thee, Jesus, Thou Son of God? Art thou come hither to torment us before the time?"

The eternal doom of demons will be with Satan in eternal fire. Matthew 25:41 "...everlasting fire, prepared for the devil and his angels."

VII Forms of Demon Practice

1 **Divination** — the ability with the aid of familiar spirits to foresee or to foretell the future. Leviticus 20:27, the one with a familiar spirit was to be put to death.

2 **Necromancy** — this is contacting a dead body as Saul did in contacting Samuel, 1 Samuel 28:8. This is a heinous sin in God's sight: 2 Chronicles 33:6; Leviticus 20:6.

3 **Prognostication** — this is illustrated in Ezekiel 21:21, and includes divination, idols and the inspection of the entrails of fowls and animals.

4 **Magic** — this was a great science in Egypt, Genesis 41:8, entailing a mixture of science (astronomy, astrology) and familiar spirits. This is practiced today in hypnotism, mind cures and fortune telling; do not seek healing in a mysterious way.

5 **Sorcery** — this involved strange formulas relating to astronomy, chemistry and familiar spirits, Isaiah 47:9-13; it is referred to in Acts 19:18,19, where all were burnt.

6 **Witchcraft** — a conscious complicity with evil spirits. This is condemned in Galatians 5:20. It is essentially devil worship and counted as rebellion, 1 Samuel 15:23.

For more details on this subject consult *Between Christ and Satan*, by Kurt Koch, who is a specialist on these matters.

Conclusion

Four tests will assist in the recognition of demon possession or demon influence.

1 Those connected with evil spirits always work in darkness.

2　The spirits deny the personality of Satan as an evil being.

3　They hate the name of the Lord Jesus Christ and the expression, "The Blood of Christ."

4　They deny that Jesus Christ has come in the flesh, 1 John 4:3.

Some suggestions to help in casting out demons:

1　Resist Satan in the name of the Lord Jesus Christ; it is best to use the Savior's full title.

2　Pray in faith believing and get as many others as possible to pray with you; never work alone except under an extreme emergency.

3　Fast if the demon is stubborn. Mark 9:29 "...come forth ... by prayer and fasting."

4　Speak and sing much about the Blood of Christ. Revelation 12:11 "... overcame .... by the Blood of the Lamb."

5　Quote or read Scripture showing that Christ triumphed over all powers of evil.

Review Questions

1　What is the common thought regarding spirits?

2　Give three possible explanations as to the origin of demons.

3　Has education and science eradicated spirits and demons? Why?

4　Tell six things about demons and evil spirits.

5　Describe the activity of demons.

6　Elaborate on Satan's organization through demonic powers.

7　What is the final destiny of evil spirits?

8　List six form of demonic practices.

9　Give four tests to assist in recognizing demon possession or influence.

10　Give five suggestions about casting out demons.

42

Satan's Attacks Against Christians

Introduction

Notes from the booklet *How to Resist the Devil*, F. J. Perryman.

In a previous lesson we learned that Satan was a real, living, active enemy.

1 Peter 5:8,9 "Be sober, be vigilant; because your adversary the devil, as a roaring lion, walketh about, seeking whom he may devour; whom resist steadfast in the faith, knowing that the same afflictions are accomplished in your brethren that are in the world."

Ephesians 4:27 "Neither give place to the devil."

If we do not resist the devil, things will go wrong for we are disobeying God.

Satan attacks every true child of God, and you and I are no exceptions to the rule.

Resist means to withstand; to be firm against; to fight against if necessary.

Be sober means to be sane, to be mentally self-controlled; to be on guard.

Be vigilant means to be awake, to be watchful like a sentry on guard duty, ever watching and listening for the approach of the enemy.

Satan is a liar, murderer, divider, counterfeiter, roaring lion or an angel of light.

Many try to fight a passive fight by saying, "I just trust the Lord and ignore Satan."

God says, "Be strong, stand up, draw the sword, resist, withstand, and overcome."

Not only the heroes of faith are to fight but each individual Christian, too.

The war between God and Satan began in Isaiah 14 and Ezekiel 28, and continues today.

Genesis 3:15, speaks of the continuous enmity between Satan and mankind.

"I was born from above, not to go under in defeat, but born to triumph." — Perryman

I Ways in which Satan Attacks Christians
2 Corinthians 2:11

1 **The devil makes us lazy** A spirit of lethargy, heaviness comes over us; the brain becomes abnormally dull, tired and ambition-less.

Perhaps we blame sleeplessness, the weather, diet or pressure of duties.

Check each point: Have I had sufficient sleep? Is the weather hotter now than before? Is my diet sufficient? Am I busier than I should be?

If the answers are negative then recognize the thing as an attack of Satan and rebuke him in the Name of the Lord; Satan will be forced to flee from you.

James 4:7 "Resist the devil, and he will flee from you."

2 **Sleeplessness** If Satan succeeds in making us lose sleep, then our senses will be dulled; our activities are arrested and weakened; normal operations of life are undermined.

3 **Pressure of duties** This makes us tired, overwhelmed and irritable; if we are too busy, too active, delays can frustrate us and Satan gets an advantage of us.

Satan can cause traffic jams to delay us to attempt to exasperate us.

Beware of the time when unexpected callers or the children annoy us.

4 **Nerves** Satan tries to attack the body and cause us to become nervous wrecks. If he succeeds in this then the devil gets us to sin easily in our weakened position.

5 **Satan wrecks minds** 2 Corinthians 4:4, Satan blinds the minds of the unsaved. And Satan is striving today to regain control of the minds of Christians. Satan attempts to enter the mind through a wrong thought, impression or idea lodged in the realm of the thought life. Scripture says a man is, as his thoughts make him.

Satan may enter our mind through a root of bitterness, a grudge, a disappointment (in love, school or business), pride, etc.

6 **By death** Satan is a murderer and seeks by accidents to claim the lives of mankind.

God holds the keys of life and death, yet God gives this power to Satan at times; in Job 1:12 God gave Satan the power to destroy Job's family and consequently in Job 1:18,19 his seven sons and three daughters were killed by a collapsing building.

7   **By suicide** Satan tried to get Christ to commit suicide by jumping off the pinnacle of the Temple in the great temptation of Matthew 4:6.

Perryman tells the story of a man who couldn't shave himself because the temptation to cut his own throat was so great.

Doubtless this is the explanation of most suicides; Satan has gained an entrance.

8   **By moods** These are common to man but the devil must not be allowed to take advantage of them for his own pernicious plottings.

Watch your moods closely and seek victory through Christ over them quickly and constantly.

9   **Money spending habits** Many of us succumb to "impulse buying," or have bought items we could not afford. The devil often takes advantage of a weakness and makes us sin by overdoing it.

10   **Fashion craze or habit:** God says that women are to dress modestly.

Many err in dress by following modern fashions without considering the effects that it might have on the opposite sex.

Some men have committed terrible sins but confessed later, "I had no intention of doing it but because of her immodest dress I was tempted beyond the power of my resistance."

11   **Improper use of tongues** opens the door to evil spirits. Some individuals seeking special "Spirit-blessings" try to consciously empty their minds, and Satan is glad to fill the vacuum. (Some tongues are doubtless genuine.)

12   **Confusing believers regarding guidance** Satan comes to the seeking soul with many suggestions; he makes a fog in the mind by creating a great uncertainty.

Recognize the difference: God's voice is specific while Satan's is indecisive.

13   **Daydreaming** This is one of the devil's most fruitful fields. There are good and bad day dreams; watch your passive, uncontrolled mental musings.

Flagrant sin is often the outworkings of accomplished daydreams.

14   **Feelings** These, like thoughts and moods must be watched; don't be touchy; don't say "I wonder if he meant to insult me? Why did he say that?"

Live by the faith of the Son of God and not by feelings.

15 **Criticism** We must be prepared to receive it; we may be misinterpreted, misunderstood.

This could overwhelm us and lead us to introspection and discouragement.

16 **Discouragement** is one of the major weapons utilized by the devil.

17 **Old age** You have served the Lord faithfully; Satan will say "Now you are too old to resist; just relax and take life a lot easier." This is the devil's lie.

18 **Preachers have many temptations,** so pray much for them.

a Satan tempts us to be flippant during the worship, and the tangible presence of the Lord is lost from the meeting.

b Temptation to spiritual pride: "A fine prayer"; "good sermon"; excessive compliments.

c Vision of great results - seeing "myself" as the center of a great revival; great crowds; much publicity; hundreds of decisions. (Pray for famous evangelists like Dr. Billy Graham.)

A missionary under attack experiences "perplexing situations," stress of conflicts, disappointments, discouragements, "mental breakdown," "blow upon blow," "baffled," and as a result the missionary is seemingly enveloped in darkness.

II How to Resist the Devil

1 Recognize these as attacks of the devil. James 4:7 "Resist the devil."

2 Resist, fight, draw the sword, Ephesians 6:11, "...that ye may be able to stand against the wiles of the devil."

3 Use the armor provided for the saint and listed in Ephesians 6:10-18.

Verse 14 — loins girt about with truth.

Verse 14 — chest protected by the breastplate of righteousness.

Verse 15 — feet shod with the preparation of the Gospel of peace.

Verse 16 — body protected with the shield of faith, to turn aside Satan's fiery darts.

Verse 17 — head protected with the helmet of salvation.

Verse 17 — offensive warfare engaged with the sword of the Spirit, the Word of God.

4 Put on Christ. Romans 13:14 "But put ye on the Lord Jesus Christ,

and make not provision for the flesh, to fulfill the lusts thereof." Christ in me must be the Victor.

5   Use the Word. Christ in the great temptation in Matthew 4:1-11, did not pray or call for angels to protect Him, but three times He quoted Scripture to Satan, verses 4, 7, and 10.

6   Take the offensive; display the triumphant life.

7   Use your will or willpower by saying, "I will not sin"; "I resolve by the power of the indwelling Christ and His grace to overcome and be victor over sin."

8   Seek the guidance of the Holy Spirit: the Spirit will guide us as to whether or not the temptation is of the devil (for example in the matter of guidance).

9   Prayer. Ephesians 6:18 "Praying always with all prayer and supplication in the Spirit, and watching thereunto with all perseverance and supplication for all saints."

10   Plead the Blood of Christ to cover you. Satan will always flee from the presence of the Blood. Revelation 12:11 "And they overcame him (Satan) by the Blood of the Lamb."

Conclusion

If you sin, confess it immediately and claim forgiveness on the basis of 1 John 1:9. Rise up and take the sword and fight more diligently.

Review Questions

1   What five lessons can we learn from 1 Peter 5:8,9 about Christian warfare?

2   Is it profitable to fight a passive fight against Satan? Why?

3   List a dozen methods that Satan uses to attack Christians.

4   Check the nineteen methods of Satan mentioned in this lesson and list those that the enemy has never used against you personally.

5   What is the precious promise of James 4:7?

6   Is it wrong to be moody? Why?

7   Mention three special temptations of Christian workers.

8   List seven things to remember in resisting the devil.

9   In Ephesians 6:10-18, identify the pieces of armor and the parts of the body they protect.

10   Quote Revelation 12:11.

43

Justification

Introduction

One of the modern errors of today is to identify justification with pardon. Justification is more than pardon; to justify means to declare righteous.

God's problem in redeeming man was to justify the sinner without condoning or justifying his sin. God could not compromise in judgment and treat sin lightly. Law and justice demanded the death penalty for every sin.

Ezekiel 18:4 "The soul that sinneth, it shall die." See also Ezekiel 18:20.

The mercy of God yearned to rescue the offender in the interests of love.

In a human court the judge justifies the righteous and condemns the wicked.

Deuteronomy 25:1 "Then they shall justify the righteous and condemn the wicked."

God refuses to justify the guilty. Exodus 23:7 "I will not justify the wicked."

God pronounces judgment on human judges that pervert judgment. Isaiah 5:22-23 "Woe unto them ... which justify the wicked for reward, and take away the righteousness of the righteous from him!"

Luke 16:15, Jesus condemns the Pharisees for justifying themselves before God.

The law, Romans 2:13, said, "But the doers of the law shall be justified."

But the question facing the Triune God was: "What man could keep the law perfectly?"

Romans 3:23 "For all have sinned, and come short of the glory of God."

The problem was so perplexing that only infinite wisdom and the grace of God were equal to the task of solving it.

God's solution: Jesus volunteered to be the Man to live the perfect life according to the law, gain the righteousness and then give it as a gift to the believing.

I Definition

What is justification? It is being accounted righteous before God; the sinner puts on the righteousness of Jesus Christ and God sees him perfect in the righteousness of Christ.

Henceforth God sees the sinner righteous in the Savior — hidden in His wonderful Person.

Justification is the judicial act of God whereby those who put faith in Christ are declared righteous in His eyes, and free from guilt and punishment.

Romans 4:3 "Abraham believed God, and it was counted unto him for righteousness."

Romans 4:5 "But to him that worketh not, but believeth on Him that justified the ungodly, his faith is counted for righteousness."

II The Contents of Justification

1 The forgiveness of sin and the removal of its guilt and punishment

For a holy and righteous God to forgive sin is not a small matter; the truth is that God actually delights in forgiving and cleansing iniquity.

Micah 7:18,19 "Who is a God like unto Thee, that pardoneth iniquity, and passeth by the transgression of the remnant of His heritage? He retaineth not His anger forever, because He delighteth in mercy ... He will subdue our iniquities; and Thou wilt cast all their sins into the depths of the sea."

In justification all our sins are forgiven and the guilt and punishment thereof removed.

Acts 13:38,39 "Be it known unto you therefore, men and brethren, that through this Man is preached unto you the forgiveness of sins: and by Him all that believe are justified from all things, from which ye could not be justified by the law of Moses."

2 The imputation of Christ's righteousness

The forgiven sinner is not like a discharged prisoner who has served his term and is discharged from further punishment, but with no rights of citizenship.

In Christ Jesus the sinner receives the full rights of citizenship.

Romans 3:22 "Even the righteousness of God which is by faith of Jesus Christ unto all and upon all them that believe."

The perfect, holy righteousness of Jesus Christ is imputed to the sinner.

III The Condition of Forgiveness - Faith

The sinner calls out, "How can I receive this gift of righteousness?"

The answer is, "By believing" on the Lord Jesus Christ as Savior and Lord.

Galatians 2:16 "Knowing that a man is not justified by the works of the law, but by the faith of Jesus Christ, even we have believed in Jesus Christ, that we might be justified by the faith of Christ, and not by the works of the law."

Romans 3:26 "To declare, I say, at this time His righteousness: that He might be just, and the justifier of him which believeth in Jesus."

Romans 4:5 "But to him that worketh not, but believeth on Him that justifieth."

The best of men need to be saved by faith in Jesus Christ and wicked sinners can also be justified in the same way.

IV The Means of Justification

1 By God. He is the author or donor of justification. Romans 8:33 "Who shall lay any thing to the charge of God's elect? It is God that justifieth."

   Justification is a judicial act performed by God, the Father Almighty.

2 By grace. Grace is the foundation or source of justification. Romans 3:24

   "Being justified freely by His grace through the redemption that is in Christ Jesus."

   Titus 3:7 "That being justified by His grace, we should be made heirs according to the hope of eternal life."

3 By Blood. Blood is the foundation or ground of justification. Romans 5:9 "Much more then, being now justified by His Blood, we shall be saved from wrath through Him."

4 By resurrection. Resurrection is the acknowledgment or proclamation of justification.

   Romans 4:25 ' Who was delivered for our offenses, and was raised again for our justification."

V The Evidence of Justification - Works

The one who is truly justified will manifest this fact in good works.
James 2:21-23 "Was not Abraham our father justified by works, when
he had offered Isaac his son upon the altar? Seest thou how faith
wrought with his works, and by works was faith made perfect?
And the Scripture was fulfilled which saith, Abraham believed
God, and it was imputed unto him for righteousness."
This passage shows the proper relationship between faith and works.
By faith we are justified but after that we will live a righteous life
which manifests good works.

VI The Results of Justification

1 Peace. Romans 5:1, "Therefore being justified by faith, we have
    peace with God."
    Peace of conscience through the mercy of God.
    Peace of heart through the love of God.
    Peace of mind through the truth of God.
    Peace of soul through the presence of God.
2 Access into the presence of God for worship, praise and petition.
    Romans 5:2 "By whom also we have access by faith into this grace."
    Access into favor with God — a new standing through justification.
3 Tribulation. Rev. Samuel Matthew of Madras, India, very carefully
    pointed out what he considered the two great results of justifi-
    cation: peace with God and tribulation in this world, Romans
    5:3. Compare 2 Timothy 3:12, "Yea, and all that will live godly
    in Christ Jesus shall suffer persecution."

Conclusion

We are justified judicially by God. Romans 8:33 "It is God that
    justifieth." We are justified meritoriously by Christ. Isaiah 53:11
    "He shall see of the travail of His soul, and shall be satisfied: for by
    His knowledge shall My righteous Servant justify many; for He
    shall bear their iniquities."
We are justified meditatively by faith. Romans 5:1 "Therefore being
    justified by faith."
We are justified evidentially by works. James 2:14 "What doth it profit,
    my brethren, though a man say he hath faith, and have not works?"
In Luke 8:13,14, the sinner that prayed, "God be merciful to me a
    sinner," went home justified, said the Lord Jesus Christ.

Review Questions

1   What is the difference between justification and pardon?
2   Define justification.
3   State the two items contained in justification with a Scripture for each.
4   How can you reconcile Exodus 23:7 and 1 Corinthians 6:11?
5   What is the condition of justification? (3 Scriptures)
6   List the three means of justification (one Scripture for each).
7   What is the connection between resurrection and justification?
8   How can you reconcile James 2:21-23 and Romans 4:3-5?
9   List five results of justification from Romans 5:1-3.
10 How is Romans 5:1 a fulfillment of Isaiah 53:11?

44

The New Birth or Regeneration

Introduction

Conversion and regeneration are inseparable; conversion is the act of turning from sin to Christ; regeneration is being made a new creature by the Spirit's power.

Regeneration or the new birth is the instrument that brings us into the family of God; into the kingdom of the Son of God.

The only way to become a Christian is by being born again; born by the power of the Holy Spirit.

The new birth is the door to salvation and consequently to heaven.

I Definition

What is regeneration? It means a rebirth or a re-creation — a new birth, a second birth, a new creation.

Regeneration is the creation by the Holy Spirit of a new life in man called the "new creation", or the "new man."

Like the first birth it is an event and not a process, though from the first conviction of sin to regeneration may cover many days, weeks, months or even years.

Yet, the actual birth takes place in a second, as one passes from darkness to light.

The person has a second birthday and begins a new life.

II Necessity of Regeneration

Who needs to be born again? Only the very good like Nicodemus? Only the very bad like the persecutor Paul? Is it a matter of opinion and choice?

The Scriptures plainly teach that all need to be born again; the language of the Savior is imperative.

John 3:3 "Verily, verily I say unto thee, Except a man be born again, he cannot see the kingdom of God." John 3:7 "Ye must be born again."

There are no exceptions to this rule (outside of the Savior); neither sex, age, position or condition exempts anyone from the necessity of the new birth.

There is no substitute for the new birth; to fail to be born again is to be lost.

Galatians 6:15 "For in Christ Jesus neither circumcision availeth any thing, nor uncircumcision, but a new creature." To become a new creature is to be born again.

Jeremiah 13:23 "Can the Ethiopian change his skin, or the leopard his spots? then may ye also do good, that are accustomed to do evil"; it is impossible without a re-birth.

Jeremiah 17:9 "The heart is deceitful above all things, and desperately wicked: who can know it?" Only God can give a new, clean pure heart; this is the new birth.

The universal sinful condition of man demands a change, the new birth for salvation.

The holiness of God demands that men be born again. Hebrews 12:14 "Follow peace with all men, and holiness, without which no man shall see the Lord."

Holiness is foreign to natural man; it can only be obtained through the new birth.

To live the life of God we must have the nature of God — God's own holy nature.

III Nature of Regeneration

1 It is not baptism. Baptism is a Church ordinance signifying that one is a Christian and has died with Christ, been buried, has risen, and is now living with Christ, daily.

It is not reformation. Reformation is the act of the old nature of turning from certain evils while regeneration is the supernatural act of God; it is a spiritual crisis; it is a revolution; it is a complete right-about-face.

2 Regeneration is a spiritual quickening, a new birth, a new creation. From creation everything has brought forth "after his kind" — sinners beget sinners.

We cannot alter the old nature, or reform it or re-invigorate it but we need a new birth, the impartation of a different "kind"

— God's holy nature.

2 Corinthians 5:17 "Therefore if any man be in Christ, he is a new creature: old things are passed away; behold, all things are become new."

Ephesians 2:1 "And you hath He quickened, who were dead in trespasses and sins." A change from death to life; this is not reformation — this is a spiritual resurrection.

We were born the first time physically and the second birth is a spiritual birth.

IV The Agents Used in the New Birth

1 **The Word of God** James 1:18 "Of His own will begat He us with the Word of Truth."

1 Peter 1:23 "Being born again, not of corruptible seed, but of incorruptible, by the Word of God, which liveth and abideth for ever."

One reason that so few people are born again today through modern preaching is that there isn't enough of the Word of God in modern sermons.

Galatians 3:2 "Received ye the Spirit by the works of the law, or by the hearing of faith?"

It is faith generated by the hearing of the Word of God that saves a soul.

2 **The Spirit of God** — The Holy Spirit.

John 3:5 "Except a man be born of water and of the Spirit, he cannot enter ..."

John 3:6 "That which is born of the flesh is flesh; and that which is born of the Spirit is spirit." Spiritual life is begotten by the Holy Spirit.

John 3:8 ". . . so is every one that is born of the Spirit." The ministry of the Holy Spirit is first to convict the sinner and then to convert him — to do the actual work of bringing him into the kingdom of God.

V The Method of Regeneration

1 **The Divine side** John 1:13 "Which were born, not of blood, nor of the will of the flesh, nor of the will of man, but of God."

We were begotten by the will of God — James 1:18, quoted in IV above.

Regeneration is a creative act on the part of God — not reformation by man.

2 **The human side** John 1:12 "But as many as received Him, to them gave He power to become the sons of God, even to them that believe on His name."

The human part is to believe and receive Jesus Christ as our personal Savior.

1 Corinthians 4:15 "... for in Christ Jesus have I begotten you through the Gospel."

The Gospel is the power of God (Romans 1:16) that is capable of changing men's lives.

To be born again, believe and receive the Gospel, the Word of God. 1 Peter 1:25 "And this is the Word which by the Gospel is preached unto you."

The author of regeneration is God; the channel of regeneration is Christ; the executive of regeneration is the Holy Spirit; the medium of regeneration is through receiving Christ by believing the Word of God.

VI The Evidence of Regeneration

1 The one who is born again lives a righteous life. 1 John 2:29 "If ye know that He is righteous, ye know that every one that doeth righteousness is born of Him."

2 The born again one does not live a life of sin. 1 John 3:9 "Whosoever is born of God doth not commit sin." The new nature of God in us cannot sin.

John 5:18 "We know that whosoever is born of God sinneth not."

3 The born again individual will fulfill the commands to love. Luke 10:27; 1 John 4:7"... and every one that loveth is born of God, and knoweth God."

4 The born again individual lives an overcoming life. 1 John 5:4 "For whatsoever is born of God overcometh the world."

5 The born again one believes that Jesus is the Christ. 1 John 5:1 "Whosoever believeth that Jesus is the Christ is born of God."

VII The Results of Regeneration

The heart is changed; sin is hated; Christ is loved; the life is changed. New and holy desires spring up like a well of living water, John 4:14. The new life overflows in love and good works to others.

John 7:38 "He that believeth on Me, as the Scripture hath said, out of his inmost being shall flow rivers of living water."

Conclusion

The new birth is a sovereign work of the Holy Spirit, for, "The Spirit bloweth where he listeth." John 3:8 RV

The new birth is a secret work, for man, "... can not tell," John 3:8, but evidences will come later and manifest themselves in many ways to their fellow man.

Pray that each one of us will manifest these evidences daily in our lives.

Review Questions

1 Define regeneration.
2 List three possible exceptions to the rule of John 3:3.
3 What is the difference between baptism and the new birth?
4 Explain 2 Corinthians 5:17 in the light of John 3:3.
5 Give four Scriptures (two each) to show that there are two agents at work in regeneration.
6 From John 1:12,13, show the two sides of the new birth.
7 Give five evidences of a changed life.
8 Give five results of regeneration.
9 Why did Jesus use the symbol of wind to explain the new birth in John 3:8?
10 Write a paragraph of 50-100 words on John 3:3.

45

Adoption

Introduction

Regeneration begins the new life in the soul when it is born again by the Spirit.

Justification deals with the new attitude of God towards that soul.

Adoption admits man into the family of God with filial joy to our Father God.

Regeneration is a changed *nature*; justification is a changed *standing*; sanctification is a changed *character*; while adoption is a changed *position*.

In regeneration the believer becomes a child of God; in adoption that child receives the position of an adult son; the baby or minor becomes an adult.

Galatians 4:5 "To redeem them that were under the law, that we might receive the adoption of sons."

Galatians 4:7 "Wherefore thou art no more a servant, but a son; and if a son, then an heir of God through Christ."

Adoption is our growing up into Christ and occupying our new position.

Here are two questions for each of us to ponder:

1 Is this standing instantaneous with conversion?
2 Can the adopted son be disinherited and cast away for being a prodigal?

I The Meaning of Adoption

Adoption is a Greek word which means, "the placing of a son."

Romans 8:15 "But ye have received the Spirit of adoption, whereby we cry, Abba, Father."

Ephesians 1:5 "Having predestinated us unto the adoption of children by Jesus Christ."

In Bible times the word had a twofold meaning:

1 The private act of receiving a stranger into the family as a son.

2 The public, legal ceremonial act of recognizing the son as the heir
   — something like a "coming out", or "coming of age" party.

Until this ceremony was performed the child actually differed little
from servants in the home.

The word deals not with our relationship with God but our position
before Him.

Adoption is the act of God whereby He places the justified believer as
an adult son to enjoy the privileges and responsibilities of the
position.

In Exodus 2, Moses became the adopted son of Pharaoh's daughter
with all the rights and privileges of that position when he came of
age.

In Hebrews 11:24, Moses rejected his Egyptian position for something
better, for, "By faith Moses, when he was come to years, refused to
be called the son of Pharaoh's daughter."

II The Condition of Adoption

Adoption has only one condition and that is to abide in Christ — union
with Him.

Galatians 3:26 "For ye are all the children of God by faith in Christ
Jesus."

We do not have to wait until we have been a saint for one year or ten
years: we immediately enter into all the blessings of a fully
recognized heir of God.

III The Time of Adoption

1 It occurred before the foundation of the world. Romans 9:11 "For
   the children being not yet born, neither having done any good
   or evil, that the purpose of God according to election might
   stand, not of works, but of Him that calleth."

   Adoption is a gracious act on the part of God entirely of mercy, we
   do not deserve or merit this loving favor from a holy God.

2 It actually occurs the moment that one believes in Jesus Christ.

   1 John 3:2 "Beloved, now are we the sons of God . . ." Sonship is a
   present possession.

   We can truthfully say, "I'm a child of the King," not His slave but
   His son and heir.

   We are not mere children under maids and tutors but adult
   members of the family.

3   Adoption will be completed at the resurrection when we enter His
        presence.
        Romans 8:23 "... waiting for the adoption, . . . the redemption of our
        body."
        Often in this world we are not recognized as sons of God. On that
        day we will occupy our rightful positions. Today we may be con-
        sidered the outcasts of society.
        Then we will throw off the disguise (this body) and put on the new
        body.

IV The Sign of Adoption

The sign of adoption is to be led by the Holy Spirit. Romans 8:14 "For
    as many as are led by the Spirit of God, they are the sons of God."
Guidance by the Holy Spirit is the path to sonship and the proof of
    sonship.
The Holy Spirit guides the believer into the truth of God. John 16:13
    "When He, the Spirit of truth, is come, He will guide you into all
    truth."
Galatians 5:18 "But if ye be led of the Spirit, ye are not under the law";
    that is, you are delivered from the tutor and schoolmaster; you are
    free.

V The Cry of Adoption "Abba Father"

Romans 8:15 "But ye have received the Spirit of adoption, whereby we
    cry, Abba, Father."
Galatians 4:6 "And because ye are sons, God hath sent forth the Spirit
    of His Son into your hearts, crying, Abba, Father."
Mark 14:36, Jesus in Gethsemane prays, "Abba, Father." This is a
    special word of endearment, of close relationship. "Abba," is
    Aramaic, the language of Christ's childhood. "Father" is a Greek
    word, the language of the educated and learned of His day. A slave
    was never allowed to address his master as, "Abba."

VI The Blessings of Adoption

1   They become objects of God's peculiar love. John 17:23 "... and
        hast loved them, as Thou hast loved Me." — the intimate love
        relationship of Father and Son.
2   They become objects of the Father's fatherly care. Luke 12:27-33,

the Father God looks after their livelihood as to what they will eat and wear; their occupation and health.

3   They have the family name. 1 John 3:1 ". . . should be called the sons of God."

4   They have the family likeness. Romans 8:29 ". . . conformed to the image of His Son."

5   They have the family love. 1 John 3:14 "We know that we have passed from death unto life, because we love the brethren." (and they love us too)

6   They have the filial spirit, Romans 8:15 "Abba, Father", the parent, child relationship.

7   They have the family gathering. John 14:23 "We will come unto Him."

8   They receive fatherly chastisement. Hebrews 12:5-11 which proves that they are true sons.

9   They receive fatherly comfort. 2 Corinthians 1:4 "Who comforteth us in all our tribulation."

10   They receive the Father's inheritance. 1 Peter 1:4 "To an inheritance, incorruptible."

VII The Responsibility of Adoption

Members of the royal family of heaven must behave with becoming dignity. We are to walk worthy of this high honor in keeping with our position. We must love and serve one another as brothers and sisters in the same family.

John 13:14 "If I then, your Lord and master, have washed your feet; ye also ought to wash one another's feet."

John 15:17 "These things I command you, that ye love one another."

Conclusion

As a child enjoys the free run of the house and the privileges of running into the father's presence at any time, so does the believer approach God's presence.

Those who are adopted into the family of God are led by the Spirit of God.

Am I led by the Holy Spirit? Do I have a childlike confidence in my Father?

Do I avail myself of this liberty of access into His very own presence?

Do I love the brethren, the family of God, as I ought to?

Am I a filial son? Am I obedient to the commands that He has given me?

Let us leave our spiritual babyhood and assume our position of manhood in Christ.

We ought to possess our possessions and live as sons of God; heirs of God.

Sometimes when parents adopt a child they try to keep that fact a secret from their child lest he or she feels less than a full son or daughter.

The story is told of one child, who knew that he was adopted, and was being teased by another child, "You're just an adopted child," with the inference that probably he was illegitimate or something. However, the child was proud of being adopted and replied, "Yes, I'm adopted. My parents chose me, picked me out of many babies. Your parents had to take what they got."

It is true that we are adopted into God's family; He chose us, praise His name!

Review Questions

1 Distinguish between regeneration, justification and adoption.
2 Give the two Palestinian meanings of adoption and its present Scriptural meaning.
3 What is the condition of adoption?
4 Give the three tenses of adoption with one Scripture for each.
5 What is the sign that an individual is adopted into the family of God?
6 Explain, "Abba, Father."
7 List seven blessings of adoption.
8 What is the relationship between Hebrews 12:5-11 and adoption?
9 What is the responsibility of an adopted son (or daughter) to God?
10 What is the blessed privilege of an adopted son?

46

Faith

Introduction

Faith is fundamental to Christian creed and conduct for we are saved by faith, Ephesians 2:8. As Christ conversed with people and healed them He looked for the characteristic of faith in each one.

1 The Syrophoenician woman showed persevering faith, Mark 7:26.
2 The centurion manifested a humble faith, Matthew 8:8-10.
3 The blind man showed an earnest faith, Mark 10:51.
4 Daniel manifested a daring faith, Daniel 6:10-23.

Faith is confidence in God that leads us to believe His Word, the Holy Bible.

By faith we receive Jesus Christ as our Savior and confess Him to the world.

I Definition of Faith

Dictionary: Faith is belief, trust, fidelity, or loyalty to a creed or religion.

Bible: Hebrews 11:1 "Now faith is the substance of things hoped for, the evidence of things not seen."

We relax and, without looking, place our whole weight on a chair; faith says we will not fall.

Faith is simple enough for the child to fulfill but too sublime for the sage to comprehend fully or explain satisfactorily.

Faith is not the blind act of the soul; faith in God rests upon the best of evidence, the infallible Word of God.

Faith is trust in the God of the Scriptures and in Jesus Christ whom He hath sent, which receives Him as Savior and Lord and impels loving obedience and good works.

The faith that saves is a personal trust in the Lord Jesus Christ.

II Necessity of Faith

Hebrews 11:6 "But without faith it is impossible to please Him: for he that cometh to God must believe that He is, and that He is a rewarder of them that diligently seek Him."

There can be no dealings with the invisible God without faith in His existence.

We must believe that He exists; that He rewards men; this confidence is called faith.

Faith is necessary to salvation. Acts 16:31 "Believe ... and be saved." Exercise faith.

III Nature of Faith

There are two kinds of faith in regard to salvation:

1 Head belief — a knowledge of the historical Christ and a general acceptance of the Bible.
2 Heart belief — faith from the heart that causes the person to act on his faith.

Acts 16:31 "And they said, Believe on the Lord Jesus Christ ..."; "on" not "in"; for example, a sick man has a bottle of medicine. He believes *in* the medicine, that if taken he would recover. But if he believes *on* the medicine, he will act on his belief and actually swallow the medicine.

Caution: We must base our faith on Christ and not faith in our own faith.

True faith in Christ is believing to the extent of receiving Christ, John 1:12; Colossians 2:6.

Neither knowledge nor assent is true faith; true faith involves appropriation.

Faith is the soul leaping forth to embrace the Christ in whom it believes.

IV Source of Faith

1 The Divine side

Faith is the work of the Triune God.

a) God the Father. Romans 12:3 "... according as God hath dealt to every man the measure of faith;" Every man, therefore, has the inward potential of faith.

1 Corinthians 12:9 "To another faith by the same Spirit..." Some

have more faith than others for faith is one of the gifts of the Holy Spirit.

b) God the Son. Hebrews 12:2 "Looking unto Jesus, the author and finisher of our faith..."

Luke 17:5 "And the apostles said unto the Lord, Increase our faith."

We all have faith but as we exercise it and pray our faith grows and increases.

c) God the Spirit. Galatians 5:22 "But the fruit of the Spirit is love, joy ... faith ..."

2   The human side

Romans 10:17 "So then faith cometh by hearing, and hearing by the Word of God."

As we read stories of the Bible our faith grows greater and greater. As we listen to God's Word preached our faith grows stronger and stronger.

Acts 4:4, the people heard the Word of God (spoken Word) and believed — had faith.

Mark 9:24 "Lord, I believe; help Thou mine unbelief." Let this be our constant confession and prayer; Luke 17:5, disciples prayed, "Increase our faith."

Matthew 17:19-21, Jesus tells His disciples that certain demons can only be cast out by prayer and fasting accompanied by a living, vital faith in the Lord.

V   Object of Faith

1   **The Word of God** Faith must never be faith in a nebulous thing called "faith."

It must be faith in the Word of God; faith accepts the statements of the Bible as the revealed Word of God, as the very Word of God, true and genuine.

2   **The Person of Christ** Faith in itself is not a Savior; it is faith in a Person — the Divine Person called the Lord Jesus Christ.

Faith is not a meritorious thing in itself, but the medium by which I receive the Lord Jesus Christ as my personal Savior and Lord.

VI   Principle of Faith

The principle of faith is the same as that which we act on in everyday life; we ask the grocer for milk and accept the tin without looking into the tin to see whether or not there is milk inside; we believe the label and act accordingly.

All business is carried on by the principle of faith and confidence in others by relying on the testimony of others.

The taxi driver doesn't ask to see your money first; by faith he believes that you have money and will pay him at the end of the route.

Faith in God is putting confidence in Him and in His Word; it is resting on the testimony of the individual involved, be he merchant, salesman, or the Lord Himself.

VII Results of Faith

1 We are saved by faith. Genesis 15:6 "And he (Abraham) believed in the Lord; and He counted it to him for righteousness." Compare Romans 4:3.

2 We receive Christ by faith. John 1:12 "...even to them that believe on His name."

3 We are justified by faith. Romans 5:1 "Therefore being justified by faith ..."

4 We become children of God by faith. Galatians 3:26 "For ye are all the children of God by faith in Christ Jesus."

5 We are sanctified by faith. Acts 26:18 "...which are sanctified by faith..."

6 We are kept by faith. 1 Peter 1:5 "We are kept by the power of God through faith..."

7 Faith brings rest. Hebrews 4:3 "For we which have believed do enter into rest."

8 All the exploits recorded in Hebrews 11 are possible to those who have faith.

9 Our eternal destiny is determined by our faith or the lack of it (unbelief).

By faith we can be saved and spend eternity in heaven with our Lord Jesus Christ.

By unbelief we will be found yet in our sins and finally cast into hell forever.

Conclusion

Matthew 17:20 "I (Jesus) say unto you, If ye have faith as a grain of mustard seed, ye shall say unto this mountain, Remove hence to yonder place; and it shall remove; and nothing shall be impossible unto you."

Jesus attributes a kind of omnipotence to faith; the disciple by faith will do greater things than his Master; here is a Niagara of power for you and me.

Hebrews 4:2 "For unto us was the Gospel preached, as well as unto them: but the Word preached did not profit them, not being mixed with faith in them that heard it."

Pray that the word we give in sermons, Sunday School lessons and in conversation will be mixed with faith on the part of them that hear; ask God to give them faith.

The great question for the Christian to answer is not, "What can I do?" but "How much can I believe (how big is my faith)?"

Mark 9:23 "Jesus said unto him, *if* thou canst believe, all things are possible to him that believeth." Lord, I want to believe, help my unbelief and increase my faith.

Review Questions

1   Give examples of four kinds of faith. (one example for each kind)
2   Define faith in two ways: 1) dictionary and 2) biblical
3   How essential is faith?
4   Distinguish between head and heart belief.
5   Give three verses to show the divine side of faith.
6   Give two verses that emphasize the human side of faith.
7   Explain: "Saving faith is not faith in a nebulous thing called 'faith'."
8   What is the principle of faith?
9   Give five major results of faith.
10   What lesson do we learn about faith from Matthew 17:20?

47

Repentance

Introduction

Under the Old Testament order of law and sacrifices the people confessed their sin, offered a sacrifice and then often returned to repeat the sin.

Gospel repentance is turning from sin and turning unto God. Acts 20:21 "Testifying both to the Jews, and also to the Greeks, repentance toward God, and faith toward our Lord."

It is called "repentance unto life," because the new mind is not merely to depart from evil, but to obtain the life that is found in Christ. Acts 11:18 "Then hath God also to the Gentiles granted repentance unto life."

It is also called repentance unto salvation, as that is its object. 2 Corinthians 7:10 "For godly sorrow worketh repentance to salvation not to be repented of."

As it is not to be repented of again it means that one is not to return again to that sin; it infers a changed attitude toward sin; not going back to iniquity.

I Definition of Repentance

1   Repentance is not merely sorrow for sin; there are many who weep over sin but, without repentance, immediately return to the same sin.

Doing penance is not repentance, for it gives the sinner some merit to earn in order to gain salvation and often hinders true repentance.

Judas Iscariot and Esau showed sorrow for sin but they did not repent.

Hebrews 12:17 "He (Esau) found no place of repentance, though he sought it carefully with tears." Remorse and tears often accompany repentance, but they are not repentance in themselves.

2 Repentance is a change of mind that leads to a change of conduct. Matthew 21:28-32, the boy at first refused to work in the vineyard but later repented, changed his mind and then went and actually worked in the vineyard.

II Necessity of Repentance

1 All need to repent because all are guilty in God's sight.
Jesus' first sermon after the baptism and testing in the wilderness was on repentance.
Matthew 4:17 "From that time Jesus began to preach, and to say, Repent: for the kingdom of heaven is at hand."
Luke 13:3, Jesus preaching said, "Except ye repent, ye shall all likewise perish."
2 Repentance comes before believing. Mark 1:15 "Repent ye, and believe the Gospel."
3 Repentance comes before forgiveness. Luke 24:47 "And that repentance and remission of sins should be preached in His name among all nations."
4 Repentance comes before conversion. Acts 3:19 "Repent ye therefore, and be converted."
5 God commands repentance. Acts 17:30 "In the past God overlooked such ignorance, but now He commands people everywhere to repent." NIV

III Importance of Repentance

Repentance is a very prominent subject in the Scriptures, being mentioned over one hundred times in the Bible.
Repentance was the theme of John the Baptist. Matthew 3:1,2 "In those days came John the Baptist, preaching in the wilderness of Judea, and saying, Repent ye."
When Jesus sent forth His disciples to preach, He commanded them to preach repentance. Mark 6:12 "And they went out, and preached that men should repent."
After Pentecost the disciples preached repentance. Acts 2:38 "Then Peter said unto them, Repent, and be baptized every one of you."
This was the message of the Apostle Paul, too. See Acts 20:21, quoted in the introduction.
The burden of the heart of God is that all should repent. 2 Peter 3:9 "... not willing that any should perish, but that all should come to

repentance."

Failure to obey God here will lead to eternal damnation. Luke 13:3 "Except ye repent, ye shall all likewise perish."

IV The Nature of Repentance

1 As touching the intellect Matthew 21:29 "He answered and said, I will not: but afterward he repented, and went." The lad changed his mind, thoughts and views.

Repentance is a revolution touching our attitude and views toward sin and righteousness.

Repentance teaches us to hate sin and learn to love holiness and purity.

The prodigal son repented; he changed his mind about living in a far country and decided to return to his father's household as a servant.

When Peter at Pentecost asked the Jews to repent, he meant for them to change their minds about the Person of Christ. From considering Jesus a mere man, a blasphemer or an impostor, to recognizing Him as the Son of God, the Messiah, the Redeemer of the world.

2 As touching the emotions 2 Corinthians 7:9 "Now I rejoice, not that ye were made sorry, but that ye sorrowed to repentance."

Very often feelings play a great part in repentance; repentance is a hard battle.

Luke 10:13 "They (Tyre and Sidon) had a great while ago repented, sitting in sackcloth and ashes."

Luke 7:44 "...but she hath washed My feet with tears..." (demonstrating repentance).

The publican in Luke 18:13 smote upon his breast, indicating sorrow of heart.

The Greek word for repentance means to cause one great concern.

The Hebrew word for repentance means to pant, sigh, or moan (expressing grief).

Psalm 38:18 "For I will declare mine iniquity; I will be sorry for my sin."

3 As touching the will The Hebrew word for repent also means to "turn".

Luke 15:18,20, the prodigal said, "I will arise ... and he arose."

Repentance is a crisis with a changed experience in view.

Paul taught repentance as an experience rather than a single act (rising and going).

Repentance is a two fold act: 1) Turning from sin and 2) turning unto God.

Turning from sin without turning to God is reformation without regeneration.

1 Thessalonians 1:9 "...how ye turned to God from idols to serve the living and true God."

Acts 26:18 "...and from the power of Satan unto God."

V How is Repentance Produced?

Basically it is a gift of God. Acts 11:18 "...saying, Then hath God also to the Gentiles granted repentance unto life."

2 Timothy 2:25 "If God peradventure will give them repentance to the acknowledging of the truth." Repentance is a privilege granted to us by God the Father.

As people hear the message of the Gospel, the Holy Spirit convicts them of their sin and a great desire to repent comes over the individual as a result.

Jonah preached repentance to Nineveh; they believed the message and turned to God.

Romans 2:4 "...not knowing that the goodness of God leadeth thee to repentance?"

Revelation 3:19 "As many as I love, I rebuke and chasten: be zealous therefore, and repent."

God often uses chastisements or rebukes to cause us to repent of our sins.

VI The Results of Repentance

1 **All heaven is made glad** Luke 15:7,10 "I say unto you, that likewise joy shall be in heaven over one sinner that repenteth."

2 **It brings pardon and forgiveness of sins** Isaiah 55:7 "Let the wicked forsake his way, and the unrighteous man his thoughts: and let him return unto the Lord, and He will have mercy upon him; and to our God, for He will abundantly pardon."

Acts 3:19 "Repent ye therefore, and be converted, that your sins may be blotted out, when the times of refreshing shall come from the presence of the Lord."

Repentance does not cause one to merit forgiveness; repentance is merely a condition.

Repentance prepares a man for pardon but it does not entitle him to it. (After repentance we are still unworthy of the Lord's love and forgiveness.)

3 **The Holy Spirit is poured out upon the penitent.** Acts 2:38 "Repent ... and ye shall receive the gift of the Holy Ghost."

Conclusion

All the blessings of Lesson 49 follow the true believer's initial repentance Godward. A redeemed sinner should never cease to be penitent.

Review Questions

1   What is the difference between Old and New Testament repentance?
2   What is the object of repentance according to 2 Corinthians 7:10?
3   Define repentance.
4   What are the two aspects of repentance according to 1 Thessalonians 1:9 and Acts 26:18?
5   Give five points proving the necessity of repentance.
6   How does repentance affect the intellect?
7   How does repentance affect the emotions?
8   How does repentance affect the will?
9   How is repentance produced?
10   What are the results of repentance?

48

Forgiveness

Introduction

By virtue of the fall of man all men have become sinners.

Sin is the one thing that will keep men out of heaven; heaven is a holy place and nothing evil shall ever enter there.

The keynote to getting to heaven is forgiveness; if God forgives us our sins then no one will be able to prevent us from entering heaven.

To sinful man, forgiveness becomes the most important problem in his life.

In the Old Testament there are three words for forgiveness: One means "to cover"; another means "to lift away"; and the third means "to send away".

"In the New Testament forgiveness is the separation of the sinner from his sins through the sacrifice of Christ and upon the ground of pure grace." — R. Lee

I The Author of Forgiveness
God Alone

Since the sinner has broken the law of God, only God can forgive him that sin.

If you steal my hammer I can forgive you for that, but if you break one of the laws of the Philippines I cannot forgive you for that.

When you break the law of God no man can forgive; only God can forgive you.

Luke 7:49 "...began to say within themselves, who is this that forgiveth sins also?"

Mark 2:7 "Why doth this man thus speak blasphemies? Who can forgive sins but God only?"

The Jews in both cases were correct for only God can forgive sin.

Never go to a human being for forgiveness; go directly to the One sinned against.

1 John 1:9 "If we confess our sins, He is faithful and just to forgive..."

He, the Lord God, the holy One, the giver of the law, is willing to forgive sinners.

Because Jesus is both God and the Son of God, He has been appointed to forgive sin.

Acts 5:31 "Him hath God exalted with His right hand to be a Prince and a Savior, for to give repentance to Israel, and forgiveness of sins."

II The Channel of Forgiveness
Jesus Christ

Acts 13:38 "Be it known unto you therefore, men and brethren, that through this Man (Jesus Christ) is preached unto you the forgiveness of sins."

This is the wonderful message of salvation to sin-burdened souls.

In Luke 7:48, the Savior personally forgave the woman, "Thy sins are forgiven."

In Mark 2:9, Jesus personally forgave the palsied man, "Thy sins be forgiven thee."

Jesus is not here bodily today but He is here invisibly ready to forgive each one of us.

We can close our eyes right now and tell Him all about our sins and He will forgive.

Forgiveness cannot be found in any Church, sacrament or ordinance but is found in Christ alone.

III The Foundation of Forgiveness

1 Forgiveness is bestowed on the ground of the Lord's compassion. Psalm 78:38

"But He being full of compassion, forgave their iniquity, and destroyed them not."

2 Forgiveness is bestowed on the ground of divine justice. 1 John 1:9 "...faithful and just to forgive ..."; God can forgive sin and yet remain holy and just.

3 Forgiveness is bestowed on the basis of the Blood of Christ. Ephesians 1:7 "In whom we have redemption through His Blood, the forgiveness of sins..."

By Blood is meant the propitiatory work of Christ. On the cross He shed His blood as a ransom and complete payment for our eternal redemption.

God has decreed that, "The soul that sinneth, it shall die," Ezekiel 18:4.

Sin brought death, and because man sinned, as a consequence he must die.

Genesis 2:17 "In the day that thou eatest thereof thou shalt surely die."

God has always required blood, symbolical of death as payment for sin.

To cover the nakedness of Adam and Eve, blood was shed to get the coats of skin, Genesis 3:21.

Abel's offering was accepted because it contained blood, and Cain's offering was rejected because it did not have blood, Genesis 4:3-5.

Leviticus 17:11 "For the life of the flesh is in the blood: and I have given it to you upon the altar to make an atonement for your souls."

IV The Completeness of Forgiveness
All Sin

When Jesus forgives sin, He forgives *all* of it, not one quarter or one half or 499/500, but *all*.

Luke 7:47 "Wherefore I say unto thee, Her sins which are many, are forgiven."

Psalm 103:3 "Who forgiveth *all* thine iniquities . . ."

Psalm 32:1,2 The Lord forgives the transgression, sin, iniquity — everything, *all* forgiven.

Colossians 2:13 "...having forgiven you *all* trespasses."

Matthew 12:31 "Wherefore I say unto you, *all* manner of sin and blasphemy shall be forgiven unto men."

This is a most important point.

If one sin remained unforgiven that individual could not go to heaven, but would be forced to spend eternity in hell.

Revelation 21:27 "And there shall in no wise enter into it anything that defileth."

One sin can contaminate you and heaven forever; one sin brought death on all men.

V The Possession of Forgiveness
"We have," a present possession

Many expect to wait until after death to know whether or not they have been forgiven.

The Gospel brings the glad news of a forgiveness that is a present possession.

Ephesians 1:7 "In whom we have redemption through His Blood, the forgiveness of sins."

The woman in Luke 7:36-50 received forgiveness immediately.

1 John 2:12 "I write unto you, little children, because your sins are forgiven you for His Name's sake."

We present a positive Gospel message that men might know assuredly here and now that their sins have been forgiven beyond the shadow of a doubt.

VI The Conditions of Forgiveness

1 Repentance Acts 5:31 "...to give repentance to Israel and forgiveness of sins."

Repentance comes before forgiveness; repentance is turning from sin unto God.

Acts 2:38 "Then Peter said unto them, Repent and be baptized every one of you in the name of Jesus Christ for the remission of sins."

In the story in Luke 7:36-50, the woman expressed her repentance in tears and humility.

2 Faith Luke 7:50 "Thy faith hath saved thee"; repentance led to faith and forgiveness.

3 Confession 1 John 1:9 "If we confess our sins, He is faithful and just to forgive us our sins, and to cleanse us from all unrighteousness."

The unconfessed sin cannot be forgiven; let us pray that the Holy Spirit will reveal the sins to us and give us grace to confess every one.

Psalm 32:5 "I acknowledged my sin unto Thee, and mine iniquity have I not hid. I said, I will confess my transgressions unto the Lord; and Thou forgavest the iniquity of my sin."

This was David's experience and it can be our experience, too.

4 Forgiving others Matthew 6:15 "But if ye forgive not men their trespasses, neither will your Father forgive your trespasses." See also Luke 6:37.

Let us remember the exhortation of Ephesians 4:32, "And be ye kind one to another, tenderhearted, forgiving one another, even as God for Christ's sake hath forgiven you."

Forgiveness should be easy for a Christian as pictured in Matthew 18:21-35.

VII The Frequency of Forgiveness
How often can we be forgiven?

As often as we sin and confess our sins, the Blood of Jesus Christ is available to forgive us, if we meet the conditions as set forth above.

Repentance involves forsaking the sin and promising by God's strength not to repeat it.

Shall we continue in sin then, that grace may abound, because God will readily forgive us, anyway?

This question was propounded in Romans 6:1, and answered by the Lord through Paul in Romans 6:2, "God forbid", for such a thought is anathema to the Lord.

How often should we forgive someone who sins against us? The Savior answered this question in Matthew 18:21-35, not till seventy times, but continuously.

Conclusion

The three messages that have been written personally by God:

1 The ten commandments in Exodus 20. The law is God's standard of behavior for man.

2 Daniel 5:27, "Thou art weighed in the balances, and art found wanting" — *guilty*. Romans 3:23.

3 John 8:1-11, Jesus wrote with His finger in the sand. What did he write? We do not know, but I think that He wrote the word, "Forgiven."

Come today and receive the full forgiveness for *all* your sins and then, "go and sin no more."

Review Questions

1 Why were the devout Jews so puzzled and righteously indignant in Luke 7:49 and Mark 2:7?

2 What is the significance of the word "just" in 1 John 1:9?

3 State the three facts on which forgiveness is based with one Scripture for each.

4 What is the significance of the word "man" in Acts 13:38?

5 In what way is Ephesians 1:7 the fulfillment of Leviticus 17:11?
6 Give three verses to show that God forgives all of our sins.
7 On the basis of Revelation 21:27, how many sins would it take to keep one out of heaven?
8 How would you prove that it is possible to have complete assurance of forgiveness *today* ?
9 List four conditions of receiving forgiveness from the Lord (one Scripture for each).
10 How often do we need forgiveness? How often must we forgive others?

49

What Happens When One Believes on the Lord

Introduction

My theology teacher taught that the moment a sinner accepted Christ 38 things happen, though he may not be conscious of more than "sins forgiven" or "peace" or "happiness."

Take the illustration of a car with the motor running. When the gear is engaged, the moment the driver releases the clutch many, many things happen! But perhaps all the driver knows is that the car is in motion.

When the sinner accepts Christ perhaps a hundred things happen, but the new Christian learns only gradually about what has taken place.

Rev. Ray Frame has divided these various things into several neat categories.

I In Relation to God the Father

1 **Access to God's grace** Ephesians 2:18 "For through Him (Christ) we both have access by one Spirit unto the Father." We have access first to salvation, then to prayer.

Ephesians 3:12, "In whom we have boldness and access with confidence by the faith of Him."

2 **Adoption as a son into God's family** Galatians 4:5 "To redeem them that were under the law, that we might receive the adoption of sons."

Ephesians 1:5, "Having predestinated us unto the adoption of children by Jesus Christ."

3 **Inheritance** Acts 26:18 "...that they may receive forgiveness of sins, and inheritance among them which are sanctified."

4 **Elected** 1 Peter 1:2 "Elect according to the foreknowledge of God the Father."

Ephesians 1:4 "...chosen in Him before the foundation of the world."

John 15:16, "Ye have not chosen Me, but I have chosen (elected, election) you."

5 **Child of God** John 1:12 "But as many as received Him, to them gave He power to become the sons of God, even to them that believe on His Name."

1 John 3:1 "Behold what manner of love the Father hath bestowed upon us, that we should be called the sons of God."

6 **Heavenly Citizenship** Philippians 3:20 "For our conversation (citizenship) is in heaven; from whence also we look for the Savior."

7 **Heir of God** Romans 8:17, "And if children, then heirs; heirs of God, and joint-heirs with Christ."

Galatians 3:29, "And if ye be Christ's, then are ye Abraham's seed, and heirs according to the promise."

8 **New Creation** 2 Corinthians 5:17 "Therefore if any man be in Christ, he is a new creature (creation): old things are passed away; behold, all things are become new."

We were born with the old nature, the fallen Adamic nature; now we have God's nature.

9 **Servant of God** Romans 6:22, "But now being made free from sin, and become servants to God." Romans 1:1, "Paul, a servant of Jesus Christ..."

10 **Priest of God** 1 Peter 2:9, "But ye are a chosen generation, a royal priesthood."

1 Peter 2:5, "Ye also, as lively stones, are built up a spiritual house, an holy priesthood, to offer up spiritual sacrifices, acceptable to God."

11 **Reconciliation with God** Romans 5:10 "We were reconciled to God by the death of His Son, much more, being reconciled, we shall be saved by His life."

Ephesians 2:12,13, "Ye were without Christ . . . aliens . . . strangers . . . without God . . . but now in Christ Jesus . . . made nigh (reconciled) by the Blood of Christ."

12 **Sanctification** 1 Corinthians 6:11 "And such were some of you: but ye are washed, but ye are sanctified ... in the name of the Lord Jesus."

Acts 26:18 lists sanctification as a direct result of conversion.

II In Relation to God the Son

13   Accepted in the Beloved Ephesians 1:6 "To the praise of the glory of His grace, wherein He hath made us accepted in the Beloved."

For Jesus' sake we are granted full welcome into God's family, presence and possessions.

14   Baptized into Christ's Body 1 Corinthians 12:13 "For by one Spirit are we all baptized into one body (the invisible Body of Christ)."

Galatians 3:27 "For as many of you as have been baptized into Christ have put on Christ."

15   Buried with Christ Romans 6:4, "Therefore we are buried with Him by baptism into death." Colossians 3:3 "For ye are dead, and your life is hid with Christ in God."

16   Love Gift to the Son from the Father John 17:9 "I pray for them . . . which Thou hast given Me; for they are Thine."

We are a special love gift from the Father to the Son, Christ Jesus.

17   Saved by Christ Acts 16:31 "Believe on the Lord Jesus Christ, and thou shalt be saved, and thy house."

Acts 4:12 ". . . for there is none other name under heaven given among men, whereby we must be saved." (the precious name of the Lord Jesus Christ)

18   Indwelt by Christ Revelation 3:20 "Behold, I stand at the door, and knock: if any man hear My voice, and open the door, I will come in to him, and will sup with him."

John 14:23 "And We (Christ and the Holy Spirit) will come unto him, and make Our abode with him."

19   Possesses Eternal Life John 10:28 "And I give unto them eternal life; and they shall never perish."

1 John 5:13 ". . . that ye may know that ye have eternal life, and that ye may believe."

20   Peace John 14:27 "Peace I leave with you, My peace I give unto you."

Philippians 4:7 "And the peace of God, which passeth all understanding, shall keep your hearts and minds through Christ Jesus."

21   Friend of God John 15:15 "Henceforth I call you not servants; for the servant knoweth not what his Lord doeth: but I have called you friends."

22   Name recorded in heaven Luke 10:20 "Rejoice, because your names are written in heaven."

Philippians 4:3 ". . . fellow laborers, whose names are in the book of life." Compare Revelation 13:8.

23   **Seated with Christ in the heavenlies** Ephesians 2:6 "And hath raised us up together, and made us (Christ and believer) sit together in heavenly places . . ."

24   **Receives a blessed hope** Titus 2:13 "Looking for that blessed hope, and the glorious appearing of the great God and our Savior Jesus Christ."

Revelation 22:20 "He which testifieth these things saith, Surely I come quickly. Amen. Even so, come Lord Jesus."

25   **Fellowship with the Trinity** 1 John 1:3 ". . . that ye also may have fellowship with us: and truly our fellowship is with the Father, and with His Son Jesus Christ."

26   **Mansion of Glory becomes His** John 14:2 "In My Father's house are many mansions: if it were not so, I would have told you. I go to prepare a place for you."

III   In Relation to God the Holy Spirit

27   **Born again** John 3:3,7 ". . . be born again . . ."; John 3:5 "Except a man be born of water and of the Spirit, he cannot enter into the kingdom of God."

1 Peter 1:23, the Holy Spirit takes the Word of God and re-creates the individual.

28   **Anointed by the Holy Spirit** 1 John 2:27 "But the anointing which ye have received of Him abideth in you, and ye need not that any man teach you." John 14:26; 16:13.

29   **Temple of the Holy Spirit** 1 Corinthians 6:19 "What? know ye not that your body is the temple of the Holy Ghost which is in you."

30   **Given a Spiritual Gift by the Holy Spirit** 1 Corinthians 12:11 "But all these worketh that one and the selfsame Spirit, dividing to every man severally as He will."

31   **Indwelt by the Holy Spirit** Romans 8:16 "The Spirit Himself beareth witness with our spirit, that we are the children of God."

32   **Sealed by the Holy Spirit** Ephesians 1:13 ". . . in whom also after that ye believed, ye were sealed with that Holy Spirit of promise."

IV In Relation to Sin

33   Forgiven Luke 7:48 "And He said unto her, Thy sins are for-given." (also verse 47)

Ephesians 1:7 "In whom we have redemption through His Blood, the forgiveness of sins."

34   Justified Romans 5:1 "Therefore being justified by faith, we have peace with God." Romans 4:5 "believeth on Him that justifieth the ungodly." . . .

35   Redeemed Revelation 5:9 "...and hast redeemed us to God by the Blood."

1 Peter 1:18,19 ". . . not redeemed with corruptible things, as silver and gold."

V In Relation to Satan

36   Christ becomes our Advocate 1 John 2:1 "We have an advocate (defence lawyer) with the Father, Jesus Christ the righteous."

37   Victory over sin John 5:4 "For whatsoever is born of God overcometh the world: and this is the victory that overcometh the world, even our faith."

VI In Relation to Others

38   Ambassadors 2 Corinthians 5:20 "Now then we are ambassa-dors for Christ."

He automatically has a responsibility to the outside world as a witness.

Conclusion

He receives *all spiritual blessings.* Ephesians 1:3 "Blessed be the God and Father of our Lord Jesus Christ, who hath blessed us with all spiritual blessings in heavenly places in Christ."

Psalm 23:6 "Surely goodness and mercy shall follow me all the days of my life: and I will dwell in the house of the Lord for ever."

Review Questions

1   Is it possible that many more things happen than we realize at conversion? Give an illustration.

2   Is it true that only thirty-eight things happen when a person receives Christ as Savior?

3 Of the twelve things listed in relation to God the Father, how many did you realize the day that you were saved?

4 Of the thirty-eight things listed which one has meant the most to you? Why?

5 List seven things that happen when one believes in relation to God the Father.

6 List seven things that happen when one believes in relation to God the Son.

7 List five things that happen when one believes in relation to God the Spirit.

8 List three things that happen when one believes in relation to sin.

9 List two things that happen when one believes in relation to Satan.

10 State one thing that happens when one believes in relation to our fellow men.

50

Sanctification

Introduction

This is a very important subject, for Hebrews 12:14 says, "Follow peace with all men, and holiness, without which no man shall see the Lord."

In regeneration our nature is changed: in justification our standing is changed; in adoption our position is changed; in sanctification our character is changed.

Sanctification shows the fruit of a justified life: we need to be sanctified for our Savior was sanctified —

1 By His Father. John 10:36 "Say ye of Him, whom the Father hath sanctified..."
2 By Himself. John 17:19 "And for their sakes I sanctify Myself."
3 By His people. 1 Peter 3:15 "But sanctify the Lord God in your hearts."

Sanctification is the will of God for every believer. 1 Thessalonians 4:3 "For this is the will of God, even your sanctification."

The subject of holiness and sanctification is mentioned 1066 times in the Bible.

I The Meaning of Sanctification

Sanctification is the work of the Holy Spirit; sanctification and holiness are the same in essence. The basic meaning of sanctification is separation.

Psalm 4:3 "But know that the Lord hath set apart him that is godly for himself."

Believers have been set apart by God for the Lord to use as He desires.

The Bible meaning of sanctification is to be set apart 1) by God 2) for God 3) from sin 4) unto a holy life — Hebrews 12:14.

2 Timothy 2:21 "If a man therefore purge himself from these, he shall be a vessel unto honour, sanctified, and meet for the Master's use, and prepared unto every good work."

The Bible speaks of sanctifying the Tabernacle and its contents: men, buildings, fields, firstborn, temple, priests and a nation —Exodus 40:9-11; Leviticus 27:14-16: Numbers 8:17.

However, for believers it carried a two-fold meaning:
1 separation *from* evil (2 Chronicles 29:5, 15-18)
2 separation *unto* God (Leviticus 27:16).

II The Author of Sanctification
(the Trinity)

1 **By God the Father** 1 Thessalonians 5:23,24 "And the very God of peace sanctify you wholly; and I pray God that your whole spirit and soul and body be preserved blameless unto the coming of our Lord Jesus Christ."
2 **By God the Son** Ephesians 5:26 "That he (Christ) might sanctify and cleanse it (the Church of which believers are a part) with the washing of water by the Word."
3 **By God the Holy Spirit** 2 Thessalonians 2:13 "...because God hath from the beginning chosen you to salvation through sanctification of the Spirit."

Dr. Griffith Thomas said, "holiness is not an achievement to be accomplished, but a gift to be accepted." The constant use of this gift will increase our sanctification.

III The Means of Sanctification

How are we sanctified?
1 **By the Word of God** John 17:17 "Sanctify them (the believers) through Thy truth."

To be sanctified, spend much time with the Word of God; it purifies and cleanses.

It is the Word that reveals sin; in the New Testament there are 21 lists of sins with a total of 202 sins of which 103 are different.
2 **By blood** Hebrews 13:12 "Wherefore Jesus also, that He might sanctify the people with His own Blood, suffered without the gate."

The Word reveals the sin; the Blood cleanses it away; Result is sanctification.
3 **By chastisement** Hebrews 12:10,11 "For they verily for a few days chastened us after their own pleasure; but he for our profit, that we might be partakers of His holiness... afterward it yieldeth the peaceable fruit of righteousness."

4 By yielding to God Romans 6:19 "... iniquity unto iniquity; even so now yield your members servants to righteousness unto holiness." (holiness — sanctification)

5 By ourselves 2 Corinthians 7:1 "Having therefore these promises, dearly beloved, let us cleanse ourselves from all filthiness of the flesh and spirit, perfecting holiness in the fear of God."

We, too, have a part in sanctification; our part is seeking out the sin: judging it; casting it away; praying for cleansing; praying for strength to live a holy life.

Daily we must appropriate Christ as our sanctification; daily we must claim His holiness, His faith, His love and His grace.

The secret of a holy life is the continuous appropriation of the Savior's holy life.

Our degree of sanctification is in relation to our appropriation of the Lord.

IV Time of our Sanctification

There are great diversities of opinion here. Some say that it was completed the moment we believed, being synonymous with conversion.

Others stress the need of a second work of grace; an experience quite separate from conversion; some treat it as a crisis experience that eradicates the old nature.

Others teach that sanctification is both instantaneous and progressive.

Personally, I believe from a study of Scripture that a combination of those is true:

1 Instantaneous with conversion 1 Corinthians 6:11 "But such were some of you: but ye are washed, but ye are sanctified, but ye are justified in the name of the Lord."

It speaks of sanctification as a past experience with washing and justification.

2 Progressive James 1:22-25 is the illustration of a man who looks into a mirror and, seeing a spot of dirt, goes and washes it away.

The mirror is the Word of God which reveals sin and then we ought to confess it.

The Holy Spirit does not reveal all of our unchristianlikeness at one time, that would be too discouraging and would lead to despair.

The moment that something is revealed we should seek cleansing and continuously pursue a path of progressive sanctification.

3 **Complete and final** 1 Thessalonians 5:23 "... sanctify you wholly... unto the coming of our Lord Jesus Christ." Completely holy in every part — body, soul, and spirit.

Some day we will be completely holy without one grace missing; mature and perfect.

This wonderful experience will be ours when Christ comes and our bodies are changed.

Then we shall be like Him, 1 John 3:2, perfect and holy! O marvelous day!

Paul in Philippians 3:12-14, was *pressing on* towards that future perfection, while daily perfecting his earthly progressive sanctification.

V The Reason for our Sanctification

John 17:19 "And for their sakes I sanctify Myself, that they also may be sanctified."

If Jesus Christ needed to be sanctified then I certainly need to be sanctified, too.

How could He, the Holy Son of God be made *more* holy? A possible answer is found in Romans 15:3 "For even Christ pleased not Himself," — always pressing for something better.

It behooves us as disciples to press on, ever on, ever upward, to be more like Him.

VI The Results of Sanctification

1 Perfection through Christ. Hebrews 10:14 "For by one offering He hath perfected for ever them that are sanctified."

2 The fruit of Holiness. Romans 6:22 "But now being made free from sin, and become servants to God, ye have your fruit unto holiness."

Is there a longing in your soul for holiness? for sanctification? for purity? for Christ-likeness? for a greater conformity to the image of God's Son?

Confess to Him your sin, and your need, and He will satisfy the deepest longings of your soul. The price is to be willing to part with sin and uncleanness.

VII How to Retain a Sanctified Walk

1   Live a life of implicit obedience to the light given to you by the Holy Spirit.
2   If you fail, immediately confess it to God and He will instantly restore you.
3   Resist the devil and he will flee from you, James 4:7.
4   Be faithful in regular seasons of Bible reading, prayer, witnessing, and living for others.

Conclusion

Sanctification guarantees us an inheritance beyond the grave. Acts 26:18 "To open their eyes, and to turn them from darkness to light, and from the power of Satan unto God, that they may receive forgiveness of sins, and inheritance among them which are sanctified."

Do not look within and be discouraged; look up and be encouraged. 1 Thessalonians 5:24 "Faithful is he that calleth you, who also will *do it.*"

Review Questions

1   Define sanctification.
2   What do we learn of sanctification from 1 Thessalonians 4:3 and Hebrews 12:14?
3   Give one verse each to show that the Trinity is involved in sanctification.
4   State the four instruments of sanctification and one verse for each.
5   Give the tenses of sanctification with one Scripture for each.
6   Can you find a reason for our sanctification in John 17:19?
7   List six results of sanctification.
8   How can we retain a sanctified walk?
9   What is the nature of sanctification according to John 17:17?
10   What is the difference between sanctification and holiness?

51

Assurance of Salvation

Introduction

Assurance of salvation is necessary if a believer is to help others spiritually.

"In my church some *think* that they are Christians, most of them *hope* so, some *say* so, and a few *know* that they are saved." — Rev. H. Hildebrand

Are you married? Are you sure? You are either married or not. There is no halfway place. A person is either saved or lost. Either "in Christ" or outside.

Salvation is a miracle change. Has the miracle taken place? Yes, or no?

If we are "in Christ" then we ought to have the full assurance of salvation. Many church people do not believe that it is possible to be sure of salvation now. They feel that it is sacrilegious to make such a statement. Faith believes God.

If we were saved by works then they would be correct, for one would need to keep working and furthermore, the quality of the works would need to meet a standard.

But salvation is a gift (Ephesians 2:8) which we receive and then we possess salvation.

I Definition of "Assurance of Salvation"

To have assurance of salvation is to be absolutely confident that we are saved and that if we die suddenly, we would go immediately to heaven.

Assurance of salvation is possessing salvation — possessing the Lord Jesus Christ.

Salvation is eternal life; it is the life of God; it is Divine life.

If I possess eternal life, then I am saved — saved for time and eternity.

John 10:28,29 "And I give unto them eternal life; and they shall never perish, neither shall any man pluck them out of My hand."

II Who May Have Assurance of Salvation?

1 Those who have received Jesus Christ as their personal Savior. John 1:12 "But as many as received Him, to them gave He power (authority) to become the sons of God."

2 Those who believe in Jesus Christ. John 3:16 ". . . whosoever (ex. Alban Douglas) believeth in Him should not perish, but have everlasting life..."

John 3:36 "He that believeth on the Son hath everlasting life."

III Basis of Assurance of Salvation

Can assurance be based on feelings? No, never. Satan might control or influence our feelings. Health, weather, circumstances and environment affect feelings.

To some entering salvation it is a real emotional thrill. No feelings at all to others, so feelings cannot be our guide.

God has given us three things upon which to base our assurance:

1 **The witness of the Holy Spirit** Romans 8:16 "The Spirit Himself beareth witness with our spirit, that we are the children of God."

Previous to conversion, the Spirit will have been convicting of sin, righteousness and judgment to come. Now His gracious ministry is changed.

In a believer, the Holy Spirit speaks peace to the soul and grants an inner rest that confirms to the individual that he really belongs to Jesus now.

Galatians 4:6 "And because ye are sons, God hath sent forth the Spirit of His Son into your hearts, crying, Abba, Father." "Abba" is a term of close relationship.

The Holy Spirit gently whispers to my spirit, "You are a child of God now."

2 **The Word of God** Very often, the Holy Spirit witnesses through the written Word.

1 John 5:10 "He that believeth on the Son of God hath the witness in himself."

1 John 5:13 "These things have I written unto you that believe on the name of the Son of God; that ye may *know* that ye have eternal life, and that ye *may believe* on the name of the Son of God." Condition, "believe"; result, "know."

If the devil comes and tempts you to doubt your salvation, put your finger on this verse and rebuke the devil in the name of the Lord and Satan will flee from you. Say to Satan: "The Word of God says that if I believe on Jesus Christ I have eternal life. On (give the date) I believed on Jesus, therefore I have eternal life. I am saved. My sins are forgiven. I am on my way to heaven."

Let the Word of God be the foundation on which you build a strong assurance. Then others will come to you seeking one who speaks with authority of eternal things.

Other verses of Scripture upon which to base assurance of salvation:

John 5:24 "Verily, verily, I say unto you, He that heareth My Word, and believeth on Him that sent Me, *hath* everlasting life, and shall not come into condemnation; but is passed from death unto life." (Believeth — Hath)

Acts 13:39 "And by Him all that believe are justified from all things." (those who meet the condition of believing are justified)

Luke 7:48 "And he (Jesus) said unto her, Thy sins are forgiven." (When the sins are removed, the path to heaven is open and clear.)

Romans 10:13 "For whosoever shall call upon the Name of the Lord shall be saved." (If I have called on the Lord Jesus, then I am saved.)

3 **The changed life** Everyone around sees the change in us and assures our own heart that we are saved — truly a child of God — truly born again.

1 John 3:14 "We know that we have passed from death unto life, because we love the brethren." This is a positive sign, exemplifying salvation.

The Christian is a new creature in Christ (2 Corinthians 5:17) and this is manifested in new affections, new likes, new dislikes, new loves and new hatreds. The power and presence of evil habits are gone, confirming that I am truly saved.

IV The Problem of Assurance of Salvation

Since the Word of God and the Holy Spirit are so clear that it is possible to have the assurance, why do so few have assurance?

With some it is because they have listened to the devil's accusations. The acid test boils down to answering two questions:

1 Have I received Jesus Christ as my personal Savior?
2 Do I truly believe on the Lord Jesus Christ?

If I can answer a definite "yes" to both questions then, on the basis of the Word of God, I am saved.

To doubt the Word of God is a terrible sin casting shame on God's

Holy Bible.

It is not presumption to believe the Word of God. It is faith that honors and pleases God that rejoices His heart, Hebrews 11:6.

V Hindrances to an Assurance of Salvation

1 Failure to trust the Word of God. If I am truly saved, then I must pray that God will increase my faith and help me to believe what the Bible says.

A liberal education often undermines faith in the Bible. Pray that such effects of liberal teaching will be removed, and that God will give us an old-fashioned faith in the Word.

2 Spiritual drowsiness. In the *Pilgrim's Progress* by John Bunyan, Christian fell asleep and lost his scroll. Often Christians fall asleep and lose both their joy and assurance of salvation. If this has happened to you, you must confess your sins according to 1 John 1:9, and start again.

3 Worldliness. The love of the world chokes out desires for God, the Word and prayer.

4 Lack of the fullness of the Holy Spirit, John 7:37-39. This is often caused by lack of surrender to the control of the Spirit in my life. The cure — do not try to serve two masters. Yield your will to Him and He will guide.

5 Over emphasis on doctrines like predestination, election, or carnal or eternal security.

6 Sin and backsliding: The cure — 1 John 1:9.

Conclusion

Lord, search my heart and see if I possess salvation — if Jesus truly lives within.

If I am truly saved, help me never to doubt the plain statements of the Bible.

If I am not saved, O Lord, take away a false security. I want to know the truth.

Caution: Be careful in persuading people that they are saved. This is the work of the Holy Spirit and He is the one that knows and searches the heart.

Assurance of salvation made me a much stronger Christian. Assurance is not presumption or pride, it is simple trust in God's Word.

To say "I know I'm saved" requires humility, for it can only be done by His grace and mercy; He saves me; He keeps me; He will bring me to heaven.

Review Questions

1   Define assurance of salvation.
2   What is salvation?
3   Who may have assurance of salvation?
4   On what three things is assurance of salvation based?
5   List five verses that teach assurance of salvation.
6   What is the biggest change that comes in the life when Christ enters that person?
7   Why do many people lack assurance of salvation? (five reasons)
8   Is it presumptous to say, "I'm saved"? Why?
9   List five hindrances to full assurance of salvation.
10   Should a personal worker persuade a new convert that he is saved? Why?

52

Confession of Christ

Introduction

Notes from Moody Colportage booklet, *On Being a Real Christian*, G. C. Weiss.

Matthew 10:32,33 "Whosoever therefore shall confess Me before men, him will I confess also before My Father which is in heaven. But whosoever shall deny Me before men, him will I also deny before My Father which is in heaven."

Romans 10:9 "That if thou shalt confess with thy mouth the Lord Jesus, and shalt believe in thine heart that God hath raised Him from the dead, thou shalt be saved."

Is it possible to be a secret believer? (one that does not confess Christ openly)

Yes, apparently, for a short time. In John 19:38 Joseph of Arimathaea was a secret believer, but later openly confessed Christ in asking for the body of Jesus.

It is impossible to *remain* a secret believer, for Matthew 10:32,33 and Romans 10:9 are essential.

These share two parts to salvation:

1 Believing in the heart, which is receiving the Lord Jesus as Savior.

2 Confessing with the mouth that Jesus Christ is Lord.

The penitent thief on the cross confessed Jesus as Lord, Luke 23:42 "Lord, remember me when Thou comest into Thy kingdom."

Paul on the Damascus road, Acts 9:5 "Who art Thou, Lord?"

1 Corinthians 12:3 "...and that no man can say that Jesus is the Lord, but by the Holy Ghost."

I The Necessity of Confessing Christ Audibly

1 We must confess Christ audibly because Christ commanded it. (Matthew 10:32,33)

2 It is a source of help and strength in our own lives. In confessing Christ, very often the greatest blessing is the joy in our own heart. It strengthens our faith and gives us greater courage to do exploits for Him.

A witnessing Christian is not liable to backslide. Conversely, many backsliders can trace their downfall to their failure to confess Christ publicly.

3 Confession of Christ brings real joy to the convert. Joy comes from obedience to Him. My first testimony, though very short, brought great joy.

4 Confession of Christ solves many problems. Others know who you are and what you stand for and respect you for a clear-cut stand. The world despises a weak, cowardly, secret Christian.

Temptations to wordly places of amusements are halted and invitations to Church activities are multiplied. It automatically puts you in a different group.

5 Because of what Christ has done for you. If someone did a great thing for you, you would tell everyone about it. Suppose you were rescued from death in some way.

We are saved by a great Savior and we surely must tell the news to everyone.

II Methods of Confessing Christ

1 Publicly in a church assembly, prayer meeting, Young People's Meeting, Testimony meeting.

2 Privately to your friends, relatives and neighbors, in daily conversation.

3 Confess Christ publicly, in public baptism, in association with a good church.

4 Confess Christ by joining a true, spiritual, active Christian church.

5 Confess Christ by constant attendance at church services and the communion table.

Perhaps the most difficult, yet most essential, is the simple relating of our testimony to friends, relatives, and strangers.

III Frequency of Confessing Christ

Is one public confession enough for life? No, it is something that we must do repeatedly.

The Christian life that is not confessed (made known) will starve and die.

Jeremiah 20:9 "Then I said, I will not make mention of Him, nor speak any more in His name. But His Word was in mine heart as a burning fire shut up in my bones, and I was weary with forbearing, and I could not stay."

This is the experience of every true Christian that attempts to limit his testimony.

A fire cannot be hid. It must reveal itself. A Christian must confess (or witness) repeatedly.

IV To Whom should we Witness?

Acts 1:8 "But ye shall receive power, after that the Holy Ghost is come upon you: and ye shall be witnesses unto Me both in Jerusalem, and in all Judea, and in Samaria, and unto the uttermost part of the earth."

The disciples were to witness to everyone. Jerusalem was their home town, Judea the province, Samaria the neighboring country, and then on to the heathen.

Acts 5:20 "Go, stand and speak in the Temple to the people all the words of this life." They were to witness and testify to all the people.

Our chief responsibility is to witness to our relatives and friends. Then later our circle of influence will grow and we will reach more and more people.

V What should we Say in Confessing Christ?

A confession of Christ is a declaration that the speaker is a Christian.

A witness is one that knows something. Witnessing is not necessarily preaching sermons, but telling the simple story of actual facts that we know.

A witness' knowledge must be positive, definite, personal, not hear-say or imagination.

It must be something that has affected one of his five senses — heard, felt, tasted, saw, touched.

1 A witness for Christ must be saved himself. His testimony must be capable of enduring under cross-examination.

2 Tell the simple facts of your conversion and the change in your own life.

3 Tell about answers to prayer that you have received. Psalm 50:15

"And call upon Me in the day of trouble: I will deliver thee, and thou shalt glorify Me."

4 Tell how Christ satisfied you completely. If you say, "I'm saved and really happy since Jesus took my sins away," people will listen to your sincerity. Don't say that you are happy and look as miserable as death.

5 Tell about personal victory over sin and temptations. This interests people and is glorifying to the Savior that gives you the victory. Of course, your personal life must be clean before you can say this.

6 Tell about your favorite verses in the Bible; about how God speaks to you this morning from a particular passage of Scripture.

7 Give your friends the Gospel of Christ. Speak of the Savior's perfect life, death, burial, resurrection, ascension and second coming, and of future judgment.

VI Hindrances to Confessing Christ

There ought not to be any, for we ought to obey the plain commands of Scripture.

1 **Fear of man** Afraid of repercussions. Afraid of what people say. 2 Timothy 1:7 "For God hath not given us the spirit of fear; but of power and of love..."

1 John 4:18 "There is no fear in love; but perfect love casteth out fear."
Philippians 4:13 "I can do all things through Christ which strengtheneth me," even witnessing for Christ.

2 **Shame** 2 Timothy 1:8 "Be not thou therefore ashamed of the testimony of our Lord ... but be thou partaker of the afflictions of the Gospel."

3 **Impure life** Fear that the spoken testimony will not be in agreement with the actual life lived. Begin at the beginning. Confess your sins according to 1 John 1:9 and ask the Lord to give you a new, fresh beginning with Him.

A public confession of failure is a good starting point of a reconsecrated life.

VII Danger of Not Witnessing

Ezekiel 33:8 "When I say unto the wicked, O wicked man, thou shalt surely die; if thou dost not speak to warn the wicked from his way, that wicked man shall die in his iniquity; but his blood will I require at thine hand."

This is a solemn warning to the silent believer on the Lord Jesus Christ. We are not necessarily responsible for the results. If they refuse to accept our witness and earnest pleading that is their responsibility.

Conclusion

Have you ever confessed Christ as Savior? as Lord? Revelation 2:10.

Review Questions

1   What is the basic requirement for every believer according to Matthew 10:32,33 and Romans 10:9?
2   Is it possible to be a secret believer? Explain.
3   List five reasons for confessing Christ audibly.
4   Name five methods of confessing Christ.
5   Is one public confession of Christ sufficient for life? Why?
6   To whom should a believer witness?
7   Tell some things to mention in an acceptable testimony. (seven things)
8   Why don't Christians confess Christ?
9   What is the danger of not witnessing?
10   When did you last confess Christ? What did you say?

53

Soul Winning

Introduction

Notes from *The Divine Art of Soul Winning*, J. O. Sanders; *The Soul Winner's Fire*, John R. Rice; also notes from L. E. Maxwell's messages.

Proverbs 11:30 "He that winneth souls is wise." See also Daniel 12:3.

Psalm 126:5,6 "They that sow in tears shall reap in joy. He that goeth forth and weepeth, bearing precious seed, shall doubtless come again with rejoicing, bringing his sheaves with him."

Few are called to be preachers, but every born again Christian is called to be a soul winner — one who deals individually and personally with souls.

Preachers and missionaries often get so busy with meetings and classes that they forget the private touch of personal soul winning.

Story of pastor's bad dream: He stood at the judgment bar and God asked, "Where are the souls of your friends and servants?" "I don't know, Lord," he said, and sank into hell. As he finished relating the story to his wife he fell over dead.

Soul winning is a definite effort to lead a definite person to accept a definite Savior at a definite time (Billy Sunday).

Small caliber men won Moody and Spurgeon. Andrew brought Peter to Christ.

"If I were utterly selfish and had no care for anything but my own happiness, I would choose, if I might under God, to be a soul winner, for never did I know perfect overflowing, unutterable happiness of the purest and most ennobling order till I first heard of one who had sought and found the Savior through my means."

Charles Haddon Spurgeon.

I Reasons for Being a Soul Winner

1 The worth of a soul. We may be the only one who can make an impression on that particular soul, and his soul is worth more than

all the world, Mark 8:35-38.

2 The fact of hell. If we truly believed that souls were headed for a lost eternity of hell fire, brimstone, torture, darkness, anguish and pain forever, we would surely do all in our power to persuade men to turn from sin to Jesus Christ.

3 The sufferings of Christ on the cross for each sinner. Did He suffer in vain?

4 The emptiness, folly and vanity of this world. In Christ we have found something and we have something positive and enduring to present to our friends.

5 The desire to have the family circle complete in heaven. Wouldn't it be sad to know that one relative was missing because we were lazy or careless?

6 The glories of heaven drive the soul winner on to have others share these.

7 The personal rewards that are offered to faithful soul winners — crowns, etc.

II Needs of a Personal Worker

1 He must be saved himself and be sure of his own salvation (Lesson 51).

2 He must live a pure life, inside and outside — a life surrendered to Jesus Christ.

3 He must work in a spirit of love and perseverance, not be arrogant or overbearing.

4 He must have a fair knowledge of the Bible and know how to use the Bible. Many shy away from personal work, excusing themselves with their ignorance of the Bible. Actually, ignorance is no excuse. Study the Bible diligently. God says in James 1:5. "If any of you lack wisdom, let him ask of God, that giveth to all men liberally, and upbraideth not; and it shall be given him."

5 He must be a man of prayer, relying on the Lord to convert the sinner

6 His life must be powerful in that it is filled with the Holy Spirit. Ephesians 5:18 "And be not drunk with wine, wherein is excess; but be filled with the Spirit."

7 He must have a compassion for lost souls — a passion for the lost. If he does not, he will work with a dead, mechanical, dispassionate concern, and the individual will respond accordingly.

III God's Way in Soul Winning
Psalm 126:5,6

1 The "GO" in soul winning *"He that goeth forth . . ."*

Do not wait for the sinner to speak to you or open the conversation. God's order is that we go to him and maneuver the conversation to salvation.

2 The broken heart in soul winning *". . . weepeth . . ."*

Jesus wept over Jerusalem. His heart was full of compassion for the lost.

Jeremiah wishes that he might weep day and night for Israel, Jeremiah 9:1.

Paul wept for souls. Acts 20:19 ". . . with many tears and temptations. . ."

Acts 20:31 "I ceased not to warn every one night and day with tears."

3 The Word of God *". . . bearing precious seed . . ."*

Do not expect people to be converted by your rhetoric, logic or arguments.

Peter tells us that men are born again by the Word of God. 1 Peter 1:23

Jesus exhorts us in the parable of the Sower and the Seed to use good seed.

One verse might be sufficient and generally a mass of verses only confuses.

Learn verses by memory. At least. Learn the reference so that you can find it.

Depend on the Word of God for conviction of sin and renewing in faith.

4 The certainty of results *". . . shall doubtless come again, . . . bringing his sheaves . . ."*

You will not win every one that you talk to. But you will win some. Would it not be wonderful if we won 2% of them to the Lord. Also, we may talk to the same person ten times and then win him the eleventh time.

Each conversation is perhaps a link in the chain drawing others to Christ. (One seed for the crow, one for the cutworm, one that doesn't sprout, one to grow.)

5 The soul winner's joy *". . . shall come again with rejoicing . . ."* *"reap in joy . . ."*

The Bible speaks of rejoicing in heaven over one sinner that repents, Luke 15:7-10.

Isaiah 53:11 "He shall see of the travail of His soul, and shall be satisfied."

The joy of personal salvation is often superseded by the joy of soul winning.

IV   Procedure and General Rules

1   **Seek and pray for opportunities,** and then use them. Don't wait for a more convenient season.

2   **Lead directly to a definite acceptance of Christ.** It is quite possible to talk about Christ, the Bible, and related subjects, but never face the main issue.

3   **Deal with your own age and sex if possible.** However, if the Spirit (not self) prompts you to speak to someone else, don't hesitate; proceed at once.

4   **Be courteous.** Don't be overbearing or too talkative. Let them speak, too. Don't argue.

5   **Avoid familiarities.** Some might appreciate it but the most people resent it.

6   **Deal with the person alone if at all possible.** In a crowd he will "save face" with excuses, but alone he is more apt to open up to you, heart to heart.

7   **Always keep confidences.** If he confesses sins, etc., remember the Bible says. "He which converteth the sinner from the error of his way, shall save a soul from death, and shall hide a multitude of sins," James 5:20.

8   **Don't be drawn into an argument.** The devil uses this as a sidetrack from conversion.

9   **Don't rely on your own ability or experience.** Keep silently praying for guidance.

10   **Don't become impatient.** It is a tremendous decision — the greatest decision in life — and it is only right that people consider well before taking the step.

11   **Deal with sinners as if you are a fellow sinner** — not a superior being.

Conclusion

When the person is ready to make the decision, get him to kneel if possible.

Pray for him and with him, but get him to pray audibly too if possible.

After prayer give him some verse of the Bible for assurance of
   salvation.
If possible, keep in contact with him and continue to instruct the
   convert.
Get him to witness and work for Christ at once.
If your attempts fail, keep praying, keep trying, and God will give
   grace and fruit.

Review Questions

1   List four passages of Scripture that emphasize soul winning.
2   Give seven reasons for being a soul winner.
3   What are the seven requirements of being a soul winner?
4   Quote James 1:5, as it is an encouragement to the soul winner.
5   Comment on the part that tears have in soul winning.
6   On what two things can the soul winner rely very heavily for
    positive results?
7   What is the threefold joy when a person is converted?
8   List the eleven general rules in soul winning.
9   Which point in question 8 do you consider most important?
    Why?
10 How do you actually lead a soul to Jesus Christ?

54

Consecration

Introduction

The word "consecration" is an Old Testament word meaning to devote, separate, dedicate or set apart for the service or glory of God. The word occurs twice in the New Testament, Hebrews 7:28 and Hebrews 10:20.

Hebrews 7:28 ". . . maketh the Son (Jesus), who is consecrated for evermore."

Hebrews 10:20 "By a new and living way, which He hath consecrated for us, through the veil."

Consecration does not mean conversion or a state of sinless perfection.

Consecration is not necessarily a sudden impulse or emotion developed in excitement.

Consecration is simply the soul trusting wholly in Jesus — no holding back in reserve. It is giving ourselves up to Christ forever as bought with a price — no longer my own.

It is not necessarily volunteering for full time service, though that might develop.

1 Chronicles 29:5 "...who then is willing to consecrate his service this day unto the Lord?"

Service is definitely one aspect of consecration. Basically, it should be worship.

"Who is willing?" — God presents an opportunity to use to offer ourselves to Him.

God will never cross the threshold of human responsibility.

"Willing to consecrate" — consecration is an act of the will. I must make a decision.

Consecration is abdicating the rulership of our lives in favor of King Jesus.

The "I" yields to the authority of Christ as Master. Who is boss in your life?

My personal consecration came as a result of four sermons on the four surrenders of Abraham:

1 Leaving country and kindred, Genesis 12:1
2 Separation from Lot, Genesis 13:9
3 Casting out Hagar and Ishmael, Genesis 21:10
4 Offering of Isaac, Genesis 22

I What is Consecration?

Consecration involves two acts:

1 Yielding my will to God — the presentation of myself to Christ for His glory.
2 Consecration is the act of God when He accepts the sacrifice that I make.

The priests did not *consecrate* themselves. Aaron and his sons merely yielded.

Consecration involves devoting myself to God (Micah 4:13); it involves separation unto God (Numbers 6:12); it involves filling (Exodus 29:33) — be filled with the Spirit; it also involves being set apart for God's service (Exodus 28:3).

II Who can be Consecrated?

Those that are cleansed by the blood of Christ may be eligible for consecration.

Those who are members of God's family are invited to consecrate themselves.

Consecration is not exclusive to the great, mighty or talented, but open to every believer.

Paul says, "I beseech you therefore, brethren, by the mercies of God, that ye present your bodies . . ." Romans 12:1.

III The Appeal to Consecration
Romans 12:1 "By the mercies of God."

We are not commanded to come by force or authority but by His mercies.

Our consecration is not prompted by fear, but by love and mercy.

Some of God's mercies; justification, identification, sanctification, indwelling of the Holy Spirit, no condemnation, daily help, heaven after death, health, friends, church.

IV The Act of Consecration
Romans 12:1 "Present your bodies."

1 It is voluntary. Paul makes a beseeching, pleading call or invitation. It is like giving a present. We are not forced to do it.
2 It is personal, "Your bodies" — This means our lives, everything that we have.
3 It is sacrificial, "a living sacrifice."
It is putting our lives on the altar, as Abraham presented Isaac.

This presentation of ourselves to God surely delights the heart of our Father.

The earthly father is hurt if the child draws back from him.

The child accepts the father's protection, food and clothes, but the father also desires the child's intimate fellowship.

I believe this act is a supreme act of worship. Genesis 22:5 "I and the lad will go yonder and worship, and come again to you."

V The Argument for Consecration
Romans 12:1 "Reasonable service."

If we have been truly redeemed, then it is only reasonable that we give Him our puny service.

Intelligent Christianity lends itself to service, gladly and unreservedly.

Billy Sunday said, "God's service is not unreasonable. It is the only sensible thing to do." If we consider it for a moment, there can be no other conclusion.

Maybe we say that it is too hard. It was hard for the Father to part with the Son. It was hard for Abraham to offer Isaac. The life of Joseph was hard. It was hard for Moses to leave the comforts of Pharaoh's palace. It was hard for Job to lose all. It was hard for Paul to witness at Rome and Ephesus, but it was the will of God, and they accepted it.

VI What am I to Consecrate?
Romans 12:1 "Your bodies."

1 My body must be given to Him to use as He desires, whereby He may get more glory.

Our bodies are not our own. They have been redeemed by Christ with His blood.

a Give Him our physical strength.
   Praise God for health and use it for Him.
b Give Him our feet to run errands of mercy — to take the Gospel to someone.
c Give Him our hands to do works of benevolence and lift the fallen.
d Give Him our eyes to seek out the needy and the perishing.
e Give Him our ears to hear the cry of the distressed and seek them for Him.

2 Give Him my time. He must govern the use of my time. Let Him arrange the program. Interruptions then will come from Him. My study time, my work time, my play time, must be counted as sacred. Let Him guide you moment by moment in this matter. Ephesians 5:16, Colossians 4:5 "redeeming the time."

3 Give Him my talents. Whether I have one or two or five or ten talents, let them all be for *Him*.

a Ability to speak, to preach, to teach, to minister the Word of God.
b Ability to sing, play an instrument, lead a choir or orchestra for His Glory.
c Ability to write books, poems, articles, Christian stories. Write for *Him*.
d Ability to pray, to be an intercessor, a prayer warrior. One of the greatest talents.
e Ability in leadership and organization. This is much needed in the church today.
f Ability to be a good follower, to assist others, to carry out programs.
g Ability as manifested in my vocation: nurse, teacher, electrician, shopkeeper.

4 Give Him my possessions. We gladly present to Him our gold, silver, all that we possess.
Not only give Him the tithe but give Him everything.

5 Give Him my heart. This is what He wants more than anything else.
The heart is symbolical of the inner man, the real self.
2 Corinthians 8:5 ". . . but first gave their own selves to the Lord . . ."
Consecration means giving everything that I have to the Lord, but giving myself first.

VII The Results of Consecration
Romans 12:2

1 A life that is not conformed to this world. It is not a worldly, selfish life.

2 A life that is transformed by the renewed mind. The renewed man thinks as God thinks, with eternity and eternal values in view.

3 A life lived harmoniously in the will of God — happily following His plan for me.

4 A life that is acceptable. God's will is never obnoxious. This life will surely be acceptable both by God and by man.

5 A life that is good. It will be beneficial. Never fear the consequences of consecration. Men and women will rise up and call you blessed because you obeyed God.

6 A life that is happy, joyous, victorious, because it was lived in the perfect will of God, the One who created me and redeemed me with His precious Blood.

Conclusion

Consecration is a process. It is daily, and moment by moment yielding in the daily crisis.

The daily renewal of our consecration is not by the flesh but by the indwelling Spirit as a supreme act of worship. Even now, consecrate your all to the Savior.

Caution: Never take it back. A gift is given to be reclaimed no more.

Review Questions

1 What do we learn about consecration from 1 Chronicles 29:5?

2 What is the basic purpose of consecration?

3 Name the two acts involved in consecration.

4 Who is eligible to make an acceptable consecration?

5 What is the New Testament appeal to consecration based on?

6 What three things do we learn about consecration from Romans 12:1?

7 If consecration is difficult does that mean that it is unreasonable? Why?

8 How does God propose to use the consecrated bodies of saints?

9 List some things that might be included under the general topic of presenting our bodies to Him?

10 Name five results of consecration.

55

Finding the Lord's Will

Introduction

Notes from *God's Will For Your Life*, S. M. Goder; *The Perfect Will of God*, G. Christian Weiss; and others.

The Christian is one who has renounced his own will and submits to the will of God for his life in all that he does (Goodman).

The problem that faces every Christian is how to ascertain the will of God.

The life of Jesus Christ on earth is a perfect illustration of absolute conformity to the will of God.

Hebrews 10:7 "Then said I, Lo, I come . . . to do Thy will, O God." Jesus Christ came to earth to fulfill God's will.

Jesus actually finished the work that the Father gave him to do on earth. John 17:4 "I have finished the work which Thou gavest Me to do."

As Jesus was assigned a specific task to perform on earth, so similarly, each Christian is assigned a special task. It is your responsibility and mine to learn form the Lord the plan for our lives.

I God has a Plan for Every Life

There is a divine blueprint for each one of God's people. This plan is suited to our personalities, talents, needs, potentialities and environment.

Ephesians 2:10 "For we are His workmanship, created in Christ Jesus unto good works, which God hath before ordained that we should walk in them."

Go has ordained certain specific tasks, works for each individual Christian.

Hebrews 12:1 " . . . run with patience the race that is set before us." There is a different race for each one of us. Paul could say, "I have finished my course." He fulfilled his ministry and his work was completed. 2 Timothy 4:7

Acts 22:14 "And he said, The God of our fathers hath chosen thee, that thou shouldest know His will." God wanted Paul to know the Lord's will.

God's plan for you is very personal. It is just for you. Psalm 32:8 "I will instruct thee and teach thee in the way which thou shalt go: I will guide thee with Mine eye."

God's plan is very detailed. Psalm 37:23 "The steps of a good man are ordered by the Lord." God doesn''t always reveal the distant future, but step by step.

God's plan is continuous. Isaiah 58:11 "And the Lord shall guide thee continually."

God's plan is definite and specific. Isaiah 30:21 "And thine ears shall hear a word behind thee, saying, "This is the way, walk ye in it, when ye turn to the right hand, and when ye turn to the left." The Lord guides by His Spirit through the Word.

God wants us to enquire about His plan. Psalm 143:8 "Cause me to know the way wherein I should walk." God wants us to be much in prayer for daily details.

The will of God is always good, acceptable and perfect for that particular believer. Romans 12:2 ". . . that ye may prove what is that good, and acceptable, and perfect, will of God."

II God's Plan is very Important for Every Life

It is a sad fact that it is possible to miss the plan of God in our selfish and stubborn ways to do our own planning. This is a tragic mistake and to be avoided.

We are incapable of planning our own lives. Jeremiah 10:23 "O Lord, I know that the way of man is not in himself: it is not in man that walketh to direct his steps."

Only God knows the future and He is the One capable of choosing our vocation or path.

III God's Plan always Includes Certain Features

Separation from sin unto holiness. 1 Thessalonians 4:3 "For this is the will of God, even your sanctification." God is holy and it is His will that we be like Him.

Prayer and thanksgiving are always God's will for us. 1 Thessalonians 5:17,18 "Pray without ceasing. In every thing give thanks: for this is the will of God in Christ . . ."

Doing good deeds is always God's will. 1 Peter 2:15 "For so is the will of God, that with well doing ye may put to silence the ignorance of foolish men."

IV Conditions of Guidance

1 Trust in the Lord, Psalm 37:3; Psalm 32:8. Guidance is only for the believer.
   God's plan for the unsaved consists of one point — believe and be saved.
2 Delight thyself also in the Lord, Psalm 37:4 — be eager, willing to know His will and obey.
3 Commit thy way unto the Lord, Psalm 37:5. We must have complete, explicit faith in Him.
4 Rest in the Lord and wait patiently for Him, Psalm 37:7. God promises to guide, but not necessarily to reveal his will the same day that you request it.
5 Surrender to the will of God. We must be willing to obey His will, Romans 12:1,2.
6 Separation from the world and all known sin. Romans 12:2 "And be not conformed to this world . . . that ye may prove . . . " Separation, then, the revealing of His will.
7 Spiritual mindedness, Romans 12:2 "Renewing of your mind" Your mind in tune with the Lord, His Spirit, His Book, to hear His still, small voice.

V Methods of Guidance

The question then comes, How does God reveal His will to the seeking individual?

The truth is that God is sovereign and does not work according to a set pattern, for He deals with each person differently.

Sometimes God reveals His will through opportunities, circumstances, the wish of parents, the advice of friends, the evaluation of one's own abilities, personal inclination, the needs of the day and conscience. (Drummond)

1 God often guides through verses of Scripture that speak loudly to you. Caution: Don't close your eyes and point at a random verse. God does not act haphazardly.

Saturate yourself with the Word of God that the Lord can bring various portions to your mind. God's will is never contrary to the

Bible. Therefore, know the Word.

2   Inner conviction that is given by the Spirit of God. Romans 8:16 "The Spirit Himself beareth witness with our spirit," — that a certain course of action is good, right, or wrong.

Caution: Is it the voice of my own desires or is it what God wants me to do?

Acts 13:2 "The Holy Spirit said, 'Separate me Barnabas and Saul'" The Holy Spirit has been given for the purpose of guidance. John 16:13 "But when He, the Spirit of truth, is come, He will guide you into all truth."

3   Circumstances. God may close one door and open another.

Nothing happens to the child of God by accident. Each item is planned by the Father.

We accept the circumstances as guideposts in the direction of His leading.

In driving, the red lights are just as important for guidance as the green lights.

In "guidance," a mitigating circumstance may be a stop light, while we "wait patiently" for Him.

4   God sometimes guides by a vision. Paul in Acts 16:9,10 "Come over into Macedonia and help us."

5   By putting out a fleece, Judges 6:37-39. Gideon prayed that if certain things happened this way or that, then the Lord's will would be accordingly.

Caution: Be careful and do not arrange the conditioning circumstances in such a way that our own will would almost inevitably win. Don't say in a rainy season, "If it rains tomorrow I will go to town; if it doesn't rain I will stay home," when you really want to go to town very badly.

VI George Mueller's Formula for Finding Guidance

1   Surrender your own will. Have no definite choice in the matter. Be absolutely neutral.
2   Seek the Spirit's will through God's Word.
3   Note providential circumstances.
4   Pray for guidance.
5   Wait on God.

VII F. B. Meyer's Formula for Guidance

"When the Word of God, the impulse of the Holy Spirit in my heart, and the outward circumstances are in harmony, then I am convinced that I am acting in accordance with the will of God."

Conclusion

Often guidance is a combination of several factors.

You only need light for one step at a time. Obey the light that God has already given you and then He will give you further light.

Remember that God *wants* to give you both the master plan and minute details of your life. Wait patiently on Him and he will reveal them day by day.

Review Questions

1 What do we learn about the life of Jesus Christ from Hebrews 10:7 and John 17:4?

2 When were the plans for your life drawn up?

3 What do we learn about the will of God from Acts 22:14 and Psalm 32:8?

4 List six general principles about the will of God.

5 Mention three features that the will of God include.

6 Give seven conditions of guidance into the will of God.

7 Have you ever been conscious of the leading of the Holy Spirit as mentioned in Acts 13:2; Romans 8:16; and John 16:13? Explain.

8 What was George Mueller's formula for seeking guidance?

9 Of the five methods listed in section V (methods of guidance), which is the most dangerous to use? Why?

10 Mention the three guiding lights of guidance followed by Rev. F. B. Meyer.

56

Prayer

Introduction

"Prayer is talking with Jesus."

"Prayer is an offering up of our desires to God for all things lawful and needful, with humble confidence that we shall obtain them through the mediation of our Lord and Savior Jesus Christ."

"Prayer is worship addressed to the Father, in the name of Christ, and the power of the Holy Spirit" — Dr. H. W. Frost.

"Prayer is the soul of man talking to God."

"Prayer should consist of at least four parts — ACTS — remember the word ACTS.

Adoration — praise and worship of the soul to God, Psalm 95:6.

Confession — repentance from every known sin, Psalm 32:5.

Thanksgiving — Philippians 4:6 — be thankful for anything, everything.

Supplication — intercession, requests, petitions and desires, 1 Timothy 2:1."

Our prayers should be directed to God the Father, Acts 12:5, in the name of Jesus Christ, John 14:13, through the power of the Holy Spirit, Ephesians 6:18.

I Where to Pray

1 Everywhere. 1 Timothy 2:8 "I will therefore that men pray every where."

2 In the closet. Matthew 6:6 "But thou, when thou prayest, enter into thy closet, and when thou hast shut thy door, pray to thy Father which is in secret."

3 In the Temple (church). Luke 18:10 "Two men went up into the temple to pray."

Psalm 26:12, praying before the great congregation. Solomon in 1 Kings 8:22-53.

Private prayer will be made in the secret place.

Family prayer will be made with a small group.
Public prayer will be made before the congregation.

II When to Pray

1 Always Luke 18:1 "Men ought always to pray, and not to faint."
1 Thessalonians 5:17 "Pray without ceasing."
2 In the morning Psalm 5:3 "My voice shalt Thou hear in the morning, O Lord; in the morning will I direct my prayer unto Thee, and will look up."
3 At noon and in the evening Psalm 55:17 "Evening, and morning, and at noon, will I pray, and cry aloud: and He shall hear my voice."
4 Daily Psalm 86:3 "Be merciful unto me, O Lord: for I cry unto Thee daily."
5 Day and night Psalm 88:1 "O Lord God . . . I have cried day and night before Thee."
Daniel prayed three times a day, Daniel 6:10.

III Subjects for Prayer

1. Matthew 6:9-13 (the Lord's prayer) — the second coming of Christ, the will of the Lord, daily bread, forgiveness, guidance, victory over temptation and sin.
2. James 5:13-16 — pray for the sick.
3. 1 Timothy 2:1-4 — pray for all men, for kings, for all in authority, for our own personal lives — and for the salvation of sinners.
4. Isaiah 38:1-5 — pray for a longer life.
5. Daniel 6:18-23 — pray for personal safety and the safety of others.
6. 1 Kings 3:5-9 — pray for wisdom and understanding.
7. Matthew 6:25-34 — pray for clothing, shelter and food.
8. Romans 1:10 — pray for a prosperous journey.
9. Colossians 1:28 — pray for every Christian to be made perfect in Christ Jesus.
10. Matthew 5:38-48 — pray for them that despitefully use you and persecute you, pray for your enemies.
11. 1 Timothy 5:17 — pray for those over you in the church.

IV How to Pray

1 We should be guided by the Holy Spirit in our praying. Romans 8:26,27 ". . . for we know not what we should pray for as we ought: but the Spirit Himself maketh intercession for us with groanings which cannot be uttered. And He that searcheth the hearts knoweth what is the mind of the Spirit, because he maketh intercession for the saints according to the will of God."

2 We must pray with faith in the existence of God. Hebrews 11:6 "But without faith it is impossible to please Him: for he that cometh to God must believe that He is (exists)."

3 We must believe that God rewards faithful intercession. Hebrews 11:6 ". . . and that He is a rewarder of them that diligently seek Him."

4 There must be persistence in prayer. Luke 18:1-8, the persistent widow got the request. Luke 11:1-13, the persistent knocker received the bread.

5 We must pray with humility. 2 Chronicles 7:14 "If My people, which are called by My name, shall humble themselves, and pray, and seek My face . . ."

6 We must be prepared to repent of our sins. 2 Chronicles 7:14 ". . . and turn from their wicked ways."

V Conditions of Prayer

1 We must pray in the will of God. Romans 8:27 (quoted in point IV); Matthew 26:39, Jesus prayed, ". . . not as I will, but as Thou wilt."

2 We must forgive others before God will hear and answer our prayers. Mark 11:25 "And when ye stand praying, forgive, if ye have ought against any."

3 We must pray in faith believing. Mark 11:24 "What things soever ye desire when ye pray, believe that ye receive them, and ye shall have them." James 1:6,7 "But let him ask in faith, nothing wavering. For he that wavereth is like a wave of the sea driven with the wind and tossed. For let not that man think that he shall receive anything of the Lord."

4 We must keep His commandments. 1 John 3:22 "And whatsoever we ask, we receive of Him, because we keep His commandments, and do those things that are pleasing in His sight."

5 We must abide in Christ. John 15:7 "If ye abide in Me, and My words abide in you, ye shall ask what ye will, and it shall be done unto you."

6 We must pray in the Holy Spirit, Jude 20 " . . . praying in the Holy Ghost."

7 We must pray in Jesus' name. John 16:24 "Hitherto have ye asked nothing in My name: ask, and ye shall receive, that your joy may be full."

VI Hindrances to Prayer

1 Unbelief, James 1:6,7 quoted above.

2 An unforgiving spirit, Mark 11:25, quoted above.

3 Iniquity, Psalm 66:18 "If I regard iniquity in my heart, the Lord will not hear me."

4 Asking amiss. (Asking with wrong motives or out of the will of God) James 4:3 "Ye ask, and receive not, because ye ask amiss, that ye may consume it upon your lusts."

VII Some Prayer Promises

Matthew 7:7,8; Mark 11:24; Luke 11:9-13; John 15:7;
Ephesians 3:12,20; Philippians 4:6, 19; Hebrews 4:16; 1 John 5:14,15.

Conclusion

What answers does God give to prayer? God gives one of three answers: 1) Yes 2) No 3) Wait

Isaiah 65:24 "And it shall come to pass, that before they call, I will answer; and while they are yet speaking, I will hear."

2 Corinthians 12:7-10, Paul prayed for healing and God said, "No."

I prayed for my father's conversion for 17 years — God answered in His own scheduled time. We must wait for God's will and God's time.

The one prayer of a sinner that God promises to hear is Luke 18:13 "God be merciful to me a sinner." See also 2 Peter 3:9.

We will never learn to pray by reading books on the subject. We must pray.

Be sure to thank Him constantly for answered prayer.

Review Questions

1 Define prayer.

2 What four things should prayer include?

3 List three places where prayer ought to be made.

4 Give two illustrations to prove that it is possible to obey

Luke 18:1.

5   List fifteen things for which we should pray.
6   What three things do we learn about prayer from Romans 8:26,27?
7   Name one absolute essential before prayer becomes effective.
8   List seven conditions of prayer.
9   Give four hindrances to prayer.
10   Mention four possible answers to a single prayer.

57

The Quiet Time

Introduction

Notes from an Inter-Varsity-Fellowship booklet on prayer by Bishop Frank Houghton et al., and other sources.

I believe that the Quiet Time is the secret of a Christian's daily life.

Observations show that Christians who fail here soon grow cold and backslide.

D. E. Hoste said that they never knew which new workers that arrived in China would do well in the years to come, for it all depended on how well they guarded the Quiet Time.

The Christian that perseveres in the Quiet Time grows steadily day by day with the Lord.

Genesis 19:27 "And Abraham woke up early in the morning to the place where he stood before the Lord."

Abraham is an excellent example for the morning Quiet Time. Notice:

1 He got up early in the morning. This is an excellent Christian practice.
2 He had a special place to meet God. We ought to, too.
3 He did this daily, not spasmodically.
4 He stood before the Lord, waiting for the Lord to speak to him.

2 Peter 3:18 "But grow in grace, and in the knowledge of our Lord and Savior . . ."

The plant requires air, sunshine, and food to grow.

Our physical bodies require food, sunshine and exercise. Our spiritual lives also need nourishment, not spasmodically, but every day of our Christian lives.

David says in Psalm 5:3 "My voice shalt Thou hear in the morning, O Lord; in the morning will I direct my prayer unto Thee, and will look up."

Jesus not only prayed in the morning but sometimes prayed all night.

Luke 6:12 ". . . He . . . continued all night in prayer." See also Matthew 14:23.

Jesus' example and the experience of older Christians become our authority for observing a daily Quiet Time with the Lord and His precious Word.

This is the message that I need most in my own personal Christian life.

I Purpose of the Quiet Time

I believe that the basic purpose of the Quiet Time is fellowship with God. He desires this communion even more than you do. The Father desires our daily worship.

I've observed how lovers like to be together. "I'm in love with the Lover of my soul."

A second purpose might be strength for the day. The Christian life is a battle against sin, the world and the devil. Ephesians 6:12 "We wrestle . . ." against spiritual foes.

The Quiet Time also affords an opportunity for systematic Bible Study and prayer.

II Preparation for the Quiet Time

Go to bed on time. Avoid late nights and strong coffee if it keeps you awake.

Maintain a stern discipline here and God will bless you abundantly for it.

Get wide awake before reading or praying. Wash in cold water or take a hot drink.

A friend says, "A cup of tea or coffee helps me to have an intelligent Quiet Time."

If you get sleepy on your knees, change your position. Abraham "stood." You can walk and pray out loud if that helps you to concentrate.

In reading the Scriptures put away distracting objects (letters, mail, pictures).

Don't do all the talking in your devotions. Psalm 46:10 "Be still, and know that I am God."

Stop talking and listen to His voice. Job's friends sat down with Job for seven days and "none spake a word," Job 2:13, We have lost this wonderful art today.

Seek the leading, guidance and blessing of the Holy Spirit in your Quiet Time.

Be willing to obey that which you read in the Word of God, John 2:5.
Come before Him with a cleansed heart. Psalm 51:17 "The sacrifices
of God are a broken spirit: a broken and a contrite heart, O God,
Thou wilt not despise."

III Material for the Quiet Time

1 Bible. Make time for regular Bible reading in the Quiet Time.
Claim a quiet place for reading and meditating. Expect His presence. Let your heart be still. Have an object in view — not sermons
but devotions.
Read the Bible faithfully according to a set plan.
2 Notebook and pen to record something from the Word. Navigator
system, etc.
3 A book with prayer requests and space to record the answers.

IV The Navigator System of Bible Study
in the Quiet Time

In Bible Study, choose a plan. Read by chapters, books or by subjects.
After Bible reading, record the answers to these questions.

1 What new thing have I learned today?
2 Is there a command for me to obey?
3 Is there an example for me to follow?
4 Is there an error for me to avoid?
5 Is there a sin for me to forsake?
6 Is there a promise for me to claim?
7 Is there a new thought about God Himself?

V A Plan for the Quiet Time

Try to prevent your Quiet Time from becoming mechanical. Where
the Spirit of the Lord is, there is liberty.
Have your Quiet Time at the same time each day if possible.
Aim at a systematic plan, probably half time reading and half time
praying.
Don't be rigid. If the Spirit of prayer descends, continue praying. If the
Word shines with new light, read on in His blessed Book, and be
filled.
A suggested order: A brief prayer, Bible reading and then prayer.
Learn to pray out the Scripture passage that you have just read. This

keeps the prayer from being the same every day.
Use the Word as a basis for praise and petition.

VI Prayer in the Quiet Time

Real prayer requires much time and discipline. Perseverance day by
day is the real test.

Check the prayer list booklet and notice prayer answers. Don't forget
to thank the Lord for answered prayer.

Psalm 50:15 "Call upon me in the day of trouble: I will deliver thee, and
thou shalt glorify me." Do it by praising the Lord.

In praying let the prayer be simple but very sincere. Just talk to the
Father God as a child to his father.

Let the prayer contain four basic elements: A-C-T-S.

1 **Adoration** — praise and worship of the soul to God. Psalm 95:6
"O come, let us worship and bow down: let us kneel before the Lord
our Maker."

2 **Confession** — repentance and turning from every known sin.
Psalm 32:5 "I acknowledge my sin unto Thee, and mine iniquity have
I not hid. I said, I will confess my transgressions unto the Lord; and
Thou forgavest the iniquity of my sin."

3 **Thanksgiving** — thankful for anything, everything, joys and sorrows, Philippians 4:6.

4 **Supplication** — intercession, petitions, requests and desires,
1 Timothy 2:1.

VII Problems of the Quiet Time

Satan will see to it that your Quiet Time is opposed every day. It will
be a daily battle.

If you miss a morning it is not necessarily a failure. Confess the error
and be forgiven the moment that the Holy Spirit reminds you of
your inconsistency.

Concentration will be a real problem. Ephesians 6:12 — It is a battle
of the mind.

To get victory meditate on the cross, the Blood and the mighty power
of the resurrection.

Small children may be a problem, and parents will need to work out
a plan.

Review Questions

1 What is the major secret of a successful Christian life?
2 Give four good lessons that we can learn about the Quiet Time from Abraham.
3 Give three purposes of the Quiet Time.
4 List five hints to remember in preparing for the Quiet Time.
5 What lesson about the Quiet Time do we learn from Psalm 46:10?
6 Name three things to take with you in your Quiet Time.
7 What seven questions do the Navigators ask about each Bible passage?
8 Describe the division of time in your private Quiet Time.
9 How can one prevent the prayer from being the same each day?
10 What do you find to be the greatest hindrance to your Quiet Time?

58

The Victorious Christian Life

Introduction

Notes from *How to Live the Victorious Life,* by an Unknown Christian, also *The Victorious Life,* by J. Irvin Overholtzer.

After conversion my heart cry was for holiness, to be like Christ, to overcome sin and to live above the world.

God took me to Bible School to teach me this precious lesson. Do you desire it?

Sometimes one hears testimonies of missionaries and preachers who after years of failure attend a Keswick meeting and suddenly come into blessing.

Some Christians try and try and when they don't succeed, sink down to a lower level of Christian experience, living on a standard lower than they desire, but helpless to advance and fearful lest they make fools of themselves by trying.

Other Christians have never heard of the victorious life and continue sinning and confessing, sinning and confessing. Is this all that Christ has to offer?

I Possibility of the Victorious Life

The Bible teaches glorious victory over sin for every believer. 1 John 5:4 "For whatsoever is born of God overcometh the world: and this is the victory that overcometh the world, even our faith."

John isn't speaking about victory in heaven but victory on earth — daily victory.

If this verse is not true in a believer's life, then there is something wrong.

Satan will do his utmost to keep this knowledge from a Christian.

The devil does not mind a religious person or a powerless Christian, but he surely fears the power of a triumphant life.

I would add my testimony to many others that this victorious life is possible, not only for the sanctified few but for every one born into the family of God.

II Promises of the Victorious Life

John 7:37,38 "Jesus stood and cried . . . out of his inmost being shall flow rivers of living water." This is Jesus' own promise to you, a believer.

John 10:10 "I am come that they might have life, and . . . have it more abundantly." Jesus doesn't want us to have just a little bit of life and victory, but abundantly.

Romans 6:14 "For sin shall not have dominion over you." This is strong language.

2 Corinthians 2:14 "Now thanks be unto God, which always causeth us to triumph in Christ." "Always," not just sometimes, but always. Ours is the victory through Christ.

1 Corinthians 10:13 promises victory over every temptation for every believer.

Romans 8:37 "Nay, in all these things we are more than conquerors through Him." Not just victory, but abundant, super-abounding victory over our enemies.

Galatians 5:16, The Christian life does not fulfill the lust (will or desire) of the flesh.

III Principle of the Victorious Life
"By Faith"

The principle is that the victorious life is a gift received from God by faith.

Our salvation was a gift. We did not deserve it or earn it in the least.

Victory is also a gift. We cannot attain it in our own strength. That is impossible.

Romans 1:17 "The just (the ones justified) shall live by faith." See also Galatians 3:11; Hebrews 10:38.

The believer is saved and begins a new life in the Spirit. Most Christians are like the foolish Galatians that tried to continue in the flesh by works.

Victory is the work of the Savior in us, not our accomplishment in the least.

Our "strength is made perfect in weakness," 2 Corinthians 12:9. As we confess our inability to gain victory and yield to the mighty power of Christ, He gains the victory.

The drunkard is converted and immediately gets victory over liquor. That is the victorious life. Respectable people need victory over themselves and pet sins.

"Faith does nothing; faith lets God do it all," Dr. C. G. Trumbull.

"One qualification that you must have for the victorious life is the broken pinion,* the broken nature, uttermost weakness," Dr. C. G. Trumbull. Surely we can qualify.

The secret of victory is in the indwelling Christ. Victory is in trusting, not trying.

* *flight feathers of bird's wing*

IV The Secret of the Victorious Life
Identification

I believe that the secret of the victorious life is our identification with Christ.

Romans 6:4-22 is generally accepted as the victory chapter.

In the cross of Christ two important truths are taught — substitution and identification.

To the sinner we teach substitution. "Look and live." To the saint it is "Look and die."

1 Identification with Christ's death — I died with Christ

Romans 6:5 "Planted together (Christ and I) in the likeness of His death."

Romans 6:6 "Our old man (the Adamic sin nature) is crucified *with Him*."

Galatians 2:20 "I am crucified *with Christ*." Absolute identification.

Death frees a man once and forever from the power and dominion of sin, Romans 6:7.

2 Identification with Christ's burial — I was buried with Him

Romans 6:4 "Therefore we are buried *with Him*." Dead things ought to be buried.

3 Identification with Christ's resurrection — I rose with Christ

Romans 6:5 "*We* (Christ rist and believer) shall be also in the likeness of His resurrection."

4 Identification with Christ's present triumphant life

Romans 6:4 ". . . even so we also should walk in newness of life."

Romans 6:6 ". . . that henceforth we should not serve sin."

Romans 6:8 ". . . we believe that we shall also live *with Him.*

Romans 6:10 ". . . in that He liveth, He liveth unto God." By life lived only for Him.

The secret is that the indwelling Christ lives in the heart and life of each believer for the purpose of becoming Lord and Master of that life.

Colossians 1:27 ". . . Christ in you, the hope of glory . . ." "I am dead and the living Christ lives and rules in my yielded body and gains constant triumphant victory for me."

V What is Needed in a Victorious Life
To Yield

If it is true that I am dead to sin with Christ, then there is only one thing for me to do and that is to yield myself to God.

Romans 6:13 "Neither yield ye your members as instruments of unrighteousness unto sin: but yield yourselves unto God, as those that are alive from the dead."

Assume your new position by faith — "alive from the dead." You are now living on resurrection ground — on the victory side of the cross.

Sin and the world have no hold on you. Don't fight sin. You can't. Instead, yield to a more powerful force — the power of the resurrected Christ.

VI The Choice of a Victorious Life
Victory or Defeat

As a Christian I still have my own free will. If I choose victory I certainly may have it as a gift from the Lord.

If I reject this gift of victory I will continue to live a defeated Christian life.

Romans 6:16 "Know ye not, that to whom ye yield yourselves servants to obey, his servants ye are to whom ye obey; whether of sin unto death, or of obedience unto righteousness?" The choice is mine: righteousness or sin.

Romans 6:18 "Being then made free from sin . . ." Freedom is ours for the taking.

Warning from verse 19: If I choose uncleanness it will lead down from iniquity to iniquity.

Exhortation from verse 22: Since you are free from sin become a bondslave to Jesus.

The choice then is to whom will I surrender myself and my members?

Conclusion

What shall we do if we try this and fail? Remember that 1 John 1:9 is still true.

He has not failed. Your fall does not weaken Christ. He will forgive you and cause that this fall will be used to strengthen you against a similar failure.

Do not rely on past victories for future victory. Always rely on Christ alone.

Memorize the promises. Quote them to the devil. Rest in the Lord constantly.

Victory can only be ours as we obey all the commands of the Spirit to us personally.

The only time that you can live the victorious life is *now*. Begin today.

Let us not only know this truth doctrinally, but also know it experimentally in our lives.

Hudson Taylor came into victory through this sentence: " . . . not a striving to have faith, but a looking off to the faithful One seems all that we need."

My desire, "I live; yet not I, but Christ liveth in me," Galatians 2:20.

Review Questions

1   What should be the natural heart cry of a new convert?

2   What is the glorious promise of 1 John 5:4?

3   List five promises of the victorious Christian life.

4   What is the principle of victorious living based on 1 John 5:4 and Romans 1:17?

5   Show the difference between substitution and identification.

6   Trace our identification with Christ from Romans 6:4-22.

7   What is the Christian's practical part in overcoming sin?

8   If Christian victory is possible why do so many Christians miss it?

9   If a Christian tries to get victory and fails miserably, does that necessarily mean lifelong defeat? Explain.

10   Quote the sentence that taught Dr. J. Hudson Taylor the secret of victory.

59

Separation

Introduction

Notes from *The Victorious or Spirit-Filled Life*, J. Irvin Overholtzer, and
  other sources.

1 John 2:15 "Love not the world, neither the things that are in the
  world. If any man love the world, the love of the Father is not in
  him."

These are hard words, yet as Christians we must face them daily.
  Some extremists trying to obey them go away in seclusion and live
  in monasteries. We realize that this is wrong, but do we know
  where to draw the line?

I The Meaning of the Word "World" in Scripture

In John 3:16 we are told that God loved the world and gave His Son
  to save it.

Here the word "world" refers to the people — the sinners that inhabit
  the world.

Jesus loved the world of sinners and we Christians are also to love the
  sinners.

The Apostle John explains the meaning of the word "world" in 1 John
  2:16, the very next verse after telling us not to love it.

"World" means "the lust of the flesh" and the "lust of the eyes" and the
  "pride of life."

The word "world" means this present world system which is controlled by Satan.

There is no allusion to leaving the material blessings of this life.

These blessings God give liberally and richly for all to enjoy.
  1 Timothy 6:17 " . . . but in the living God, who giveth us richly all
  things to enjoy."

This would include innocent laughter, the play of children, clean
  social life, healthful recreation, the beauty of nature and the love of

flowers. These cannot be unscriptural, worldly or sinful. To consider these wrong would make one an ascetic.

Jesus enjoyed nature. He spoke of plants, seeds and trees.

Jesus' social contracts were broad — with the family at Bethany; eating in the Pharisee's home, Luke 7:36; the marriage in Cana, John 2; resting in a quiet place, Mark 6:31.

In fact, the Savior was accused of being a gluttonous person, Matthew 11:16-19 "The Son of man came eating and drinking, and they say, Behold a man gluttonous, and a winebibber, a friend of publicans and sinners. . . "

The problem of where to draw rules on what is right and wrong is very, very difficult.

II Matters in which we Can be Definite

1 Marriage between a believer and an unbeliever is forbidden, 2 Corinthians 6:14-17 "Be ye not unequally yoked together with unbelievers."

Amos 3:3 "Can two walk together, except they be agreed?" This is a definite Scriptural principle that does not change with the passing ages.

2 Separate from all unrighteousness, 2 Corinthians 6:14 ". . . for what fellowship hath righteousness with unrighteousness?"

Some believe business partnership between believers and unbelievers is forbidden by this verse.

3 Separate from all works of darkness, 2 Corinthians 6:14 ". . . and what communion hath light with darkness?" The Christian is indwelt by Christ, the Light of the World.

4 Separate from Belial, the old devil, 2 Corinthians 6:15 "And what concord hath Christ with Belial?" The Christian is indwelt by the Son of God.

5 Separate from infidels, 2 Corinthians 6:15 ". . . or what part hath he that believeth with an infidel?" We must separate for we can have no fellowship.

6 Separate from idols, 2 Corinthians 6:16 "And what agreement hath the temple of God with idols?" A Christian is God's temple, indwelt by the Lord Himself.

7 Separate from false teachers that dispute about primary doctrines, 1 Timothy 6:5 ". . . from such withdraw thyself." See 1 Timothy 1:4; 4:7; Galatians 3:2.

8 Separate from heretics, 2 John 9-11. Do not allow such in the home.
9 Separate from all known forms of sin and immorality (liquor, etc.) 1 Peter 1:16.

III Matters in which we Cannot be Definite

1 Time How much time ought we to give to worship, business, study, family and pleasure? To give excess time to any one field could be entirely wrong in relation to the entire day or life for which we are responsible.

2 Pleasure Pleasure are generally innocent and enjoyable, but some types are harmful.

3 Sport Most sports are beneficial and healthful, but one must keep balanced here.

4 Worldly amusements — dancing, cards, theater, magazines, betel nut, smoking, make-up, modern styles of dress and hairdo, hobbies, television, fiestas, clubs, dating. These things are not mentioned in the Scriptures, so there are no specific instructions.

IV Three basic Rules to Follow

If a certain point is troubling us, apply these three rules. Let it be very personal.

1 I must separate from anything that is designed to overthrow my faith in God, such as infidel or atheistic clubs, Communist organizations, etc.

2 I must separate from anything that would destroy my testimony. My testimony is one of the most priceless things that I possess here on earth.

3 I must separate from anything that would debase my morals and lead me to sin. If cards lead me to gambling, then I must leave them. If dancing causes me to have impure and unholy desires, then to me that thing becomes sinful.

V Some general Rules to Follow

1 If my action causes my brother to stumble, then I must not do it. 1 Corinthians 8:13 "Wherefore, it meat make my brother to offend, I will eat no flesh while the world standeth, lest I make my brother to offend."

Paul was willing to deny himself the harmful pleasure if it hindered his testimony.

2   Seek guidance from God by prayer and Bible study regarding a particular issue. Strive always to have a clear conscience before God and man, Acts 24:16.

3   Whatsoever ye do, do all to the glory of God, Colossians 3:17 "And whatsoever ye do in word or deed, do all in the name of the Lord Jesus, giving thanks to God." Can I do this thing (chew betel nut, dress like a star or celebrity) to God's glory? If the answer after prayer is "No," then that thing becomes sin to me, James 4:17.

4   In all things use sanctified common sense. God is a reasonable Being and desires to reason with you on the matter. Isaiah 1:18 "Come now, and let us reason together."

5   I must separate from anything that harms my body — physically, mentally or emotionally. 1 Corinthians 6:19,20, "What know ye not that your body is the temple of the Holy Ghost which is in you, which ye have of God, and ye are not your own? For ye are bought with a price: therefore glorify God in your body, and in your spirit, which are God's."

6   Is it pleasing to Jesus Christ? Would Jesus do this thing?
If He would not do it, then I must not do it.
1 Peter 2:21 ". . . Christ . . . leaving us an example, that ye should follow His steps."

7   Will it strengthen my testimony? Will it weaken my testimony?

VI Some Helpful Scriptures

Romans 12:2 "And be not conformed to this world: but be ye transformed by the renewing of your mind." This is the plain command of Scripture.

James 4:4 "Ye adulterers and adulteresses, know ye not that the friendship of the world is enmity with God? whosoever therefore will be a friend of the world is the enemy of God."

Hebrews 11:13 "Confessed that they were strangers and pilgrims on the earth."

Think of Moses, Hebrews 11:25 "Choosing rather to suffer affliction with the people of God, than to enjoy the pleasures of sin for a season."

Think of Demas, 2 Timothy 4:10 "For Demas hath forsaken me, having loved this present world, and is departed."

2 Corinthians 6:17 "Wherefore come out from among them, and be ye

separate, saith the Lord, and touch not the unclean thing; and I will receive you."

Conclusion

Let us be reasonable and not judge others harshly. To his own master he standeth. Let us not separate with an air of superiority. Let us separate with meekness.

Remember, separation is twofold: 1) from sin, and 2) unto God.

Review Questions

1 Explain the conflict between John 3:16 and 1 John 2:15 (re: loving the world).
2 Are there certain aspects of the world that we may love? Explain.
3 List the eight things from which saints are to separate.
4 Give four illustrations of unequal yokes.
5 Suggest a balanced schedule of time for a father of a family for one week covering such items as worship, business, study, family, pleasure, eating and sleeping.
6 Give three basic rules to follow in deciding whether a thing is permissible or not.
7 What does 1 Corinthians 8:13, teach about innocent or doubtful pleasures?
8 What can we learn about separation from 1 Corinthians 6:19,20?
9 Contrasting Hebrews 11:25, and 2 Timothy 4:10, what do we learn about separation?
10 What are the two parts to remember in separation?

60

Backsliding

Introduction

Often we find someone that is a strong Christian today but is backslidden later.

Sometimes we ask the question: Who will be the next to leave the Lord? and the inevitable answer is "not me."

Remember the solemn warning of 1 Corinthians 10:12, "Wherefore let him that thinketh he standeth take heed lest he fall."

Proverbs 16:18 "Pride goeth before destruction, and an haughty spirit before a fall."

We are all kept by the grace and strength of the Lord. He is able to keep us. However, if we deliberately refuse His grace and assistance, we will fall.

2 Timothy 1:12 "I . . . am persuaded that he is able to keep . . ." He surely is!

I Definition of Backsliding

Backsliding is turning away from God. 1 Kings 11:9 "And the Lord was angry with Solomon, because his heart was turned from the Lord God."

Backsliding is growing cold and leaving the first love. Revelation 2:4 "Nevertheless I have somewhat against thee, because thou hast left thy first love."

Backsliding is turning from the simplicity of the Gospel to salvation by law.

Galatians 5:4 ". . . whosoever of you are justified by the law; ye are fallen from grace."

Some define backsliding as one sin that separates a believer from the Lord.

Isaiah 59:2 "But your iniquities have separated between you and your God."

Speaking generally, backsliding is growing cold and losing interest in the Lord, the Bible, prayer, church attendance and witnessing, and turning toward the world.

II Backsliding is a Gradual Process

I do not believe that anyone backslides suddenly. It is true that we may be shocked by the sudden outward manifestation of terrible sin. But the truth is that many little things have entered in and undermined the life.

The story of Lot's backsliding illustrates this point of seven downward steps.

1 **Covetousness** Genesis 13:10 "And Lot lifted up his eyes, and beheld all the plain."

Often the eyes are the first to leave the Savior. They see something attractive.

Many a man has made the mistake of fixing his eyes on the wrong object.

2 **Choosing too low** Lot chose the plain instead of the mountain, Genesis 13:11.

See also Genesis 19:17. Friends, lift up your sights. Aim high. Keep looking to the Savior, Hebrews 12:1.

3 **Compromise** Lot pitched his tent toward Sodom, Genesis 13:12,13. Lot compromised and lived near the place of sin. Abraham prospered up there on the mountain with God. The Bible says, "Flee also youthful lusts," 2 Timothy 2:22. Don't live near Sodom (sin).

4 **Captured by the enemy** Genesis 14:11,12 If one lives near sin one will be captured.

Let the converted drunkard leave the pub. Let the thief be removed from the place of temptation. If you flirt with the world you will get burned.

If you give sin your finger, it will soon take your hand, arm, body and then soul.

5 **Carnal living** "Lot sat in the gate of Sodom", Genesis 19:1, a member of the town council. Lot has gained worldly influence but lost his spiritual influence. Genesis 19:16, "And while he lingered . . ." Lot loved Sodom. Lot loved the thing that God hated, and was about to destroy. Do we love sin?

6 **Criminal weakness** Genesis 19:8 Lot was willing to give his two daughters into sin.

When a man goes down he takes others with him. Romans 14:7 is very
very true.

Lot was as one that mocked (an old joker) to his sons-in-law, Genesis
19:14.

7 **Carousing** Genesis 19:33-38 Here we find Lot drinking wine and
engaged in immorality.

Lot loved sin. Lot lingered in sin. Wine always leads to immorality.
Let us not condemn Lot. 2 Peter 2:6-8 is still true. Let us observe and
beware.

III Outward Causes of Backsliding

1   **Covetousness** Genesis 13:10. Lot lusting for something that was
not God's will for him.

2   **Society** Genesis 19:26. Lot's wife looked to the things that she
loved and became a pillar of salt.

3   **Fear** Matthew 26:70-74. Peter denied the Savior because he
feared man.

4   **Haughty spirit** Proverbs 16:18 ". . . and an haughty spirit before
a fall."

5   **Selfishness** Proverbs 14:14 "The backslider in heart shall be
filled with his own ways: . . ." He ought to be concerned with the Lord's
will and ways.

6   **Idolatry** Exodus 32:8, Israel constantly went away from the
Lord after false gods.

7   **Disobedience** Saul in 1 Samuel 15:11, "Saul . . . is turned back
from following Me, and hath not performed My commandments."

8   **Love of gold, silver and garments** Achan in Joshua 7:1-24.

9   **Love of money** Judas Iscariot in John 13:29.

10   **Outlandish women** Solomon in Nehemiah 13:26.

11   **Ambition for power** Simon Magus in Acts 8:19. He tried to buy
it with money.

12   **Love of the world** Demas in 2 Timothy 4:10.

IV The True Cause of Backsliding

1 **Failure to maintain the Quiet Time** Many a person has come back
to the Lord and sometimes through bitter tears said, "I lost out with
God in my Quiet Time."

2 **Failure to pray.** We need prayers to intercede to God for strength. To fail to pray is a form of pride, and Proverbs 16:18 goes into effect. Often the thing that crowds out prayer time will eventually cause the fall.

3 **Failure to read the Bible** 2 Timothy 2:15 "Study to shew thyself approved. . ." It is disobedience to God and will surely bring repercussions.

We need to pray to be informed about the will and plan of God for us.

4 **Failure to attend church** Hebrews 10:25 "Not forsaking the assembling of ourselves together, as the manner of some is . . ."

Be-sure to attend church once a week plus Bible Study, Young People's and prayer meetings.

5 **Failure to obey the Holy Spirit** Ephesians 4:30 "And grieve not the Holy Spirit of God, whereby ye are sealed unto the day of redemption."

6 **Failure to confess Christ** Matthew 10:33 "But whosoever shall deny Me before men, him will I also deny before My Father which is in heaven." See Romans 10:9.

7 **Failure to walk in the light** 1 John 1:7 "But if we walk in the light, as He is in the light . . ." We ought to obey the light He gives us and follow quickly.

V The Results of Backsliding

There will be a loss of power, a loss of peace, a loss of joy and happiness.

Murmuring and darkness will begin to cloud the daily pathway.

Backsliding will lead to the loss of rewards and the person will "suffer loss," 1 Corinthians 3:15. Some teach that it may even lead to the loss of the soul.

VI God's Invitation to Return

Jeremiah 3:22 "Return, ye backsliding children, and I will heal your backslidings.

Behold, we come unto Thee; for Thou art the Lord our God."

VII God's Promise of Pardon for Backsliding

Hosea 14:4 "I will heal their backsliding, I will love them freely: for Mine anger is turned away from him."

Conclusion

May I exhort you in the name of the Lord and by His strength never to backslide.

Revelation 2:10 "Be thou faithful unto death, and I will give thee a crown of life."

The true Christian hates backsliding. Psalm 101:3 "I will set no wicked thing before mine eyes: I hate the work of them that turn aside."

" . . . before mine eyes:" — be very, very careful what is set before thine eyes.

This is the true Object to set the gaze on: Hebrews 12:2, "Looking unto Jesus. . ."

Paul's goal was Christ. Philippians 3:14 "I press toward the mark for the prize of the high calling of God in Christ Jesus."

Review Questions

1   What is the solemn warning of 1 Corinthians 10:12, and Proverbs 16:18?
2   Give four definitions of backsliding.
3   Trace the seven downward steps in Lot's backsliding.
4   List ten causes of backsliding.
5   Give seven possible causes of backsliding.
6   List six results of backsliding.
7   What is the connection between Genesis 3:22 and 1 John 1:9?
8   What helpful lesson regarding backsliding do we learn from Psalm 101:3?
9   How can Hebrews 12:2, and Philippians 3:4, keep us from backsliding?
10 Quote Hosea 14:4.

61

Worship

Introduction

Notes from *Worship*, Alfred P. Gibbs.

Worship is different from prayer and praise. "Lord save my soul" is prayer; "Lord, thank you for saving my soul" is praise; "Thank you, Lord, for what Thou art" is worship.

The first mention of worship in the Bible is in Genesis 22:5, Abraham says to the men, "I and the lad will go yonder and worship, and come again to you."

Matthew 2:2,11, the wise men came to worship the newborn King, Jesus Christ.

Matthew 4:10, Jesus quotes the commandment, "Thou shalt worship the Lord thy God."

John 4:24 "God is a Spirit: and they that worship Him must worship Him in Spirit and in truth."

I The Meaning of Worship

The word *worship*, like *grace* and *love*, is indefinable.

It means to do reverence or homage to a superior being. Man ought to worship God.

"The overflow of a grateful heart, under a sense of Divine favor," Psalm 23:5.

"The outpouring of a soul at rest in the presence of God," Song of Solomon 2:3,4.

"Worship is the upspring of a heart that has known the Father as a Giver, the Son as a Savior, and the Holy Spirit as the indwelling Spirit."

"Worship is the occupation of the heart, not with its needs, or even with its blessings, but with God Himself," 2 Samuel 7:18-22.

II The Importance of Worship

1 It is the first commandment of the law, Exodus 20:1,2. Exodus 34:14, "For thou shalt worship no other god: for the Lord, whose name is Jealous, is a jealous God."
2 God caused the erection of the Tabernacle and Temple for the purpose of worship. There is a great deal of instruction in Leviticus regarding worship of the true God.
3 God taught men like Abraham, Moses, Isaiah, David and others the art of worship.
4 Worship will be our occupation for eternity, Revelation, chapters 4 and 5.

III The Object of Worship

The Scripture is very clear in Luke 4:8, "Thou shalt worship the Lord thy God." Psalm 45:11 "... for He is thy Lord; and worship thou Him."

We are not to worship idols. Exodus 20:3 "Thou shalt have no other gods before Me."

Many in the world worship dead idols of wood and stone.

Many others worship idols of self, money, business, pleasure, recreation, family, possessions, power, science.

Neither are we to worship men. Acts 10:25,26, the story of Cornelius kneeling before Peter.

We are not to worship angels. Revelation 19:10 and 22:8,9 state that this is forbidden.

We are not to worship nature, Deuteronomy 4:14-20; Job 31:24-28. We may admire nature, but we must not engage in worship of the sun, moon, stars, trees, etc.

1 We are to worship the Father God. John 4:23 "The Father seeketh such to worship Him." We are to worship Him because of what He has done, loving us and giving His Son for us.
2 We are to worship the Son Jesus Christ our Lord and Savior, John 9:38.
   We are to worship Him because of what He has done, His incarnation, life and sacrifice.
   We are to worship Him because of His present work, as our Intercessor and High Priest.
3 We are not instructed to worship the Holy Spirit, though it may not be wrong.

IV The Basis for Worship

How can a sinner acceptably worship a holy God? The only basis is by the Blood of Jesus Christ as a sacrifice accepted by the righteous Father, Hebrews 10:19.

We must worship remembering our relationship with the "Father," Matthew 6:9; Romans 8:15.

V The Holy Spirit Leads a Believer into Worship

The power for worship is the Holy Spirit who guides and directs our worship of the Lord.

The Holy Spirit teaches one to worship, appreciate and apprehend Him in Bible reading.

Worship is not primarily something that is to be stored up and released at a meeting, but it is something which should rise continually from the believer's soul.

For a full worship of God we must not possess a grieved Holy Spirit, or a quenched One.

Allow the Holy Spirit to teach and guide you into acceptable worship of the Father and Son.

VI The Manner of Worship

1 Worship must be spiritual, that is, in the spirit, John 4:24 ". . . worship Him in Spirit . . ."

2 Worship must be sincere, that is, in truth. God looks at the heart to see whether or not the words of our lips are true, sincere and genuine expressions of our inmost being.

3 Worship must be intelligent. God does not put a premium on ignorance, but He desires that we have a knowledge of what the Bible teaches. Some attempt to worship God by bowing in church and reciting prayers that they don't understand.

Following through a church service is not necessarily worshipping God. Some minds may be miles away, preparing meals or catching fish or making money.

Each Christian is duty bound to see to it that the worship he presents to God through Christ is spiritual, sincere and intelligent.

Worship in church or in private is a heart exercise that cannot be defined by rules.

We may worship in each part of the service: singing, praying, preaching, offering, etc.

The Lord greatly longs for the worship of our hearts, but He is often disappointed.

It delights the heart of the Father to find true worshippers of Himself.

VII Hindrances to Worship

Worship is the Christian's highest occupation, and is therefore contested by Satan.

1 **Self-will** Nadab and Abihu, Leviticus 10:1-11, died for attempting to offer strange fire.

The believer in worship proposes and seconds a motion of nonconfidence in himself.

2 **Worldliness** The believer is in the world but definitely not *of* the world, John 17:11-15. Christ becomes the center and circumference of the Christian life. Worship is the person, mind and body concentrating on the Lord Himself.

3 **A critical spirit** Those who go to church and then "roast the preacher" by their criticism of him over dinner, have not worshipped God. True worship goes beyond the preacher, church and choir.

Galatians 5:15. Realize that others are human and prone to err too. Look on the commendable and pour out your heart in love and adoration to God for the help received.

Do not look for something to criticize. Look rather for something to commend.

4 **Slothfulness** Those who are just too lazy to exert the energy needed to worship God, Proverbs 24:30-34.

Many, in attempting to worship God fall asleep mentally if not physically and fail in their basic desire to meet the Lord and praise Him.

Spiritual laziness must be viewed as a thief, and spiritual lethargy must therefore give place to spiritual alertness.

5 **Impatience** The Lord says, "Wait," Isaiah 40:31, but our speeded up generation has failed to learn to sit quietly in His presence in meditation of His goodness and works.

6 **Formalism**, substituting a ritual or set order for the free heart worship of God.

7 **An unforgiving spirit** Matthew 5:23,24. Grudges etc. must be

forgiven and restitution made.

8 **Pride** of person, race, education or accomplishments will deter from true worship, James 4:6.

Conclusion

Where are we to worship God? In Mount Gerizim or Jerusalem? John 4:20. The Lord answers that the place is immaterial. It is the spiritual condition of the person, not the geographical location of the believer. We can worship in church, at home, etc.

We worship God when we enter into His presence and engage in worship, the highest occupation.

There are two main results of true worship:

1 God shall be glorified, for then He receives the praise, honor and glory due Him.

2 The believer will be blest. God will fill the worshipper's heart with joy and peace.

May there constantly rise from your heart and mine a constant flow of adoring worship which will delight His heart and bring glory to His Holy Name.

Review Questions

1 Show the difference between worship, prayer and praise.

2 Define worship.

3 Give the fourfold importance of worship.

4 Contrasting Exodus 20:3 and Luke 4:8, what do we learn?

5 Comparing Hebrews 10:9; Matthew 6:9; and Romans 8:15, what is the basis for worship?

6 What part does the Holy Spirit have in worship?

7 Describe the manner of worship.

8 In what part of the Sunday worship service do you find it easiest to worship God? (Processional, invocation, prayer, hymn singing, choral anthem, Scripture reading, sermon, offering, benediction or recessional?)

9 List seven hindrances to worship.

10 What are the two main results of true worship?

62

Christian Suffering

Introduction

Notes from *Christ, Indwelling and Enthroned*, O.J. Sanders; *The Discipline of Life*, V. Raymond Edman; *Why do Christians Suffer?*, Rev. T. Epp.

Often Christians have severe and fiery trials. Some are affected bodily, others mentally, some financially and others in direct or indirect attacks of Satan.

Many are calling out to God, "Why? Why do I have to suffer like this?"

Philippians 1:29 "For unto you it is given in the behalf of Christ, not only to believe on Him, but also to suffer for His sake."

This text states a plain fact. You and I have a double opportunity:

1　to believe on the Lord Jesus Christ, and
2　to suffer for His sake.

We surely want to believe on the Lord Jesus Christ and be saved. We want salvation, forgiveness, heaven, love, the Lord Jesus.

With this comes the privilege to suffer. Philippians 3:10 "That I may know Him and the power of His resurrection, and the fellowship of His sufferings. . ."

This was the prayer of the Apostle Paul.

Jesus suffered. In Bethlehem He was misunderstood, cursed, blasphemed. In Gethsemane was the bitter trial. He was smitten, lashed, crucified, etc.

Our sufferings are very light in comparison. 2 Corinthians 4:17 "For our light affliction, which is but for a moment, worketh for us a far more exceeding and eternal weight of glory."

To some, life is meaningless, for it consists only of turmoil, trouble, pain and tears. To the true Christian, life has a plan, for God has a purpose for each life.

"And we know that all things work together for good to them that love God, to them who are the called according to *His* purpose," Romans 8:28.

I How does Suffering come?

1 **Through our own mistakes and sin** Galatians 6:7 "Be not deceived; God is not mocked: for whatsoever a man soweth, that shall he also reap." The man who has committed murder can be forgiven by God, but he must still suffer prison for his crime.

The man that ruins his body with liquor must still reap the effects of a body that has been weakened or wrecked by sin.

We accept even these as from Him and search our hearts fully to repent and seek grace not to repeat these terrible things.

2 **The mistakes and sins of others** "Why did God allow him to say that terrible thing?"

No trial or affliction can reach you without His permission.

3 **Through temptations** 1 Corinthians 10:13 "There hath no temptation taken you but such as is common to man: but God is faithful, who will not suffer you to be tempted above that ye are able; but will with the temptation also make a way to escape, that ye may be able to bear it."

God knows your "load limit" — the amount that you can endure.

4 **Through God's providential dealings** These can be incomprehensible to the troubled soul and in desperation he calls out, "Why, why?"

God does not promise to give us the reason for His actions. He is sovereign.

Even in deepest affliction, rest assured that He is the loving heavenly Father.

John the Baptist was mightily used, but was later imprisoned. Jesus was nearby, but made no visit or answer to his query. Jesus says, "Trust Me in prison, John."

II Why do Sufferings come?

1 **As a result of sin**
   a John 5:14 "Afterward Jesus findeth him in the temple, and saith unto him, Behold, thou art made whole: sin no more, lest a worse thing come unto thee." This would infer that his sickness was the result of sin. He had been sick 38 years.
   b Miriam, Numbers 12:10. She was white with leprosy for the sin of murmuring against Moses, the servant of the Lord.
   c King Asa, 2 Chronicles 16:12. In his youth he trusted God, but in his old age he refused the leadings of the Lord and was

punished with a foot disease.

2 That the works of God might be made manifest John 9:2,3.

The disciples ask: Who sinned, this man or his parents, that he has been born blind?

Jesus gave the startling answer, "Neither one, for this happened that Jesus could heal him."

When others are ill, do not cruelly judge them and say, "What sin has he committed this time?"

The Lord may make him sick to get more fellowship with him.

3 For the glory of God John 11:4 "This sickness is not unto death, but for the glory of God," and Lazarus was raised from the dead and many believed.

Surely God has derived a great deal of glory from this story all through the years.

Whatever our trial might be, we should take this sweet attitude. If this thing delights the heart of the Father, then I am happy.

4 The work of the enemy — with God's permissive will

a This was the experience of Job in the book of Job.

b The outcast of Gadara was mentally ill because of the indwelling demons, Mark 5:1-5.

c The woman was bound by Satan for 18 years in Luke 13:16.

d Acts 10:38 speaks of those that are oppressed of the devil.

5 Chastisement (child training) Hebrews 12:5-13

a The parent cannot let the child have its own way always. Neither can God with us.

b The parent gladly yields if the child chooses wisely. God is trying to teach us to make wise and right decisions.

c The goal of chastisement is a trained child who makes good decisions even when far away from parental authority.

Suffering is often a part of His plan to train us.

III The Purpose of Suffering

1 To prove our sonship Hebrews 12:8 "But if ye be without chastisement, whereof all are partakers, then are ye bastards, and not sons."

2 Timothy 3:12 "Yea, and all that will live godly in Christ Jesus shall suffer persecution."

If I do not suffer, then I am not a true Christian. The parent that really loves a child must punish him. Suffering is a proof of

God's special love.

2 **To profit us** Hebrews 12:10 "... for our profit ..." Suffering is for our good.

Take a bar of steel that is worth ₱100. If it yields to pounding, it can become much more valuable. Horseshoes, ₱300; needles, ₱700; knives, ₱65,000; watch springs, ₱500,000. Why the difference? Beaten, pounded, fire and pain.

3 **To produce holiness** Hebrews 12:10 "... partakers of *His* holiness." He wants to make us more holy, more godlike, more like Himself. This takes the fire of suffering.

4 **To test us** Are we genuine Christians? Can we trust Him in pain and suffering? It takes the fire to take away the dross and leave the pure gold.

5 **To produce a harvest** Hebrews 12:11 "... nevertheless afterward it yieldeth the peaceable fruit." Will our lives be "nothing but leaves" or will they bear fruit? Galatians 5:22,23.

Suffering is one of God's choicest fertilizers to increase the harvest.

IV Our Response to Suffering

1 We may despise it, rebelling instead of submitting. This attitude leads to hardness.

2 We may faint under it. We need not, though, for the Lord says, 2 Corinthians 12:9 "My grace is sufficient for thee." There is grace to bear the thorn, the trial and the suffering.

3 We may acquiesce and bear it. This is the lowest form of victory.

4 We may happily yield to the will of God — embrace the will of God and pray for progress in the Christian life. This is the highest form of victory.

Conclusion

If I stand in the center of the circle of the will of God, then all that comes to me, sickness, suffering, trials, pain, misunderstanding, envy, neglect, loss, darkness, etc., will be from His dear hand, and I will know that it is good for me.

Review Questions

1 What is the double privilege of each person according to Philippians 1:29?

2 List some of the sufferings of Jesus Christ.

3   How will our earthly sufferings finally be adjudged? (2 Corinthians 4:17)
4   What does Galatians 6:7 teach us about suffering?
5   List four ways in which suffering may come.
6   Why do sufferings come? (Five things)
7   Name three people who suffered because of sin.
8   What are the six purposes of suffering?
9   Mention four possible responses to suffering.
10 Where is the safest place to be at all times?

63

Water Baptism

Introduction

Baptism is a controversial subject, but nevertheless it is one that must be taught.

In Acts 8:26-40, Philip taught the Eunuch beyond conversion to the deeper truths of the Word of God. It was the Eunuch who cried out, "See, here is water."

We do well to lead souls to Christ, but we should also teach assurance of salvation, Acts 8:39.

Baptism is a New Testament doctrine, but the word "baptize" is found in 1 Corinthians 10:2, referring to Israel passing through the Red Sea, overshadowed by the cloud.

John the Baptist, the forerunner of Christ, came preaching and baptizing.

John's message was, Mark 1:4, "John did baptize in the wilderness, and preached the baptism of repentance for the remission of sins."

John's baptism was not his own innovation but it came from heaven, Mark 11:30.

Multitudes came to be baptized by John, Luke 3:7.

The intelligentsia rejected John's baptism and consequently suffered spiritually.

Luke 7:30 "... rejected the counsel of God against themselves, being not baptized."

John only baptized those who brought forth fruit worthy of repentance, Luke 3:8.

Luke 3:8-14 lists the fruit required: benevolence, kindness, love, generosity, honesty, justice, faithfulness, meekness, quietness, temperance, contentment.

This list bears a striking resemblance to the fruit of the Spirit listed in Galatians 5:22.

I The Meaning of Baptism

Baptism does not mean regeneration or forgiveness of sins. See Lesson 27.

Baptism states the fact of an event that has already transpired beforehand.

Baptism is an outward symbol of an inward reality — a genuine conversion.

1 It means obedience to the command of Christ, Mark 16:16 "He that believeth and is baptized shall be saved." Note that believing comes before baptism.

2 It means following Christ's example. 1 Peter 2:21 "... because Christ also suffered for us, leaving us an example, that ye should follow His steps." See also John 13:15.

3 It means fulfilling all righteousness. Matthew 3:15 "Suffer it to be so now: for thus it becometh us to fulfill all righteousness." If Jesus needed it, I certainly do, too.

4 It means separation by death from sin.
Colossians 3:3 "For ye are dead, and your life is hid with Christ in God." See also Galatians 6:14.

5 It means identification with Christ, Romans 6:4-13.
   a Identification in His death. Romans 6:5 "... planted together in the likeness of His death."
   b Identification in His burial. Romans 6:4 "... buried *with Him* by baptism into death."
   c Identification in His resurrection. Romans 6:4 "... like as Christ was raised up from the dead by the glory of the Father, Even so we also should walk in newness of life."

6 It means association with Christ's body. 1 Corinthians 12:13 "For by one Spirit are we all baptized into one body." One body, the church, visible and invisible.

II Who may be Baptized?

1 Those who have heard the Gospel and believed it, Mark 16:16, quoted above.

2 Those whose eyes are opened. Acts 9:18 "And immediately there fell from his eyes as it had been scales: and he received sight forthwith, and arose, and was baptized."

3 Those who have repented. Acts 2:38 "Repent, and be baptized every one of you in the name of Jesus." Repentance is twofold:

Turning from sin and turning to serve God.

4 Those who bring forth fruit worthy of repentance. Luke 3:8 and Matthew 3:8.

5 Those who have received the Holy Spirit. Acts 10:47 "Can any man forbid water, that these should not be baptized, which have received the Holy Ghost as well as we?"

6 Those who have been taught the Word of God. Matthew 28:19,20 "Go ye therefore, and teach all nations, baptizing them . . . teaching them to observe all things whatsoever I have commanded you." This would involve teaching the New Testament.

7 Those who have died, and who now live a new spiritual life in Christ. This is the basic teaching of Romans 6:1-13, that every believer ought to understand well.

III How should One be Baptized?

1 **In what name?**
   a Of the Father, Son and Holy Spirit, Matthew 28:19, the Great Commission.
   b In the Name of the Lord Jesus, Acts 8:16; Acts 19:5, Paul at Ephesus.
   c In the Name of the Lord, Acts 10:48. Peter referring to Gentiles.

2 **What substance is used?** Water only, Acts 8:36 "See, here is water." John 3:23 "And John also was baptizing in Aenon. . . because there was much water there"

3 **By whom should baptism be performed?** By one or more representatives of the Church. Examples, John the Baptist, Philip, Peter, Paul and Silas, Ananias, etc.

4 **Where was baptism performed?**
   a Generally in a river. Jesus, Matthew 3:13-17; John the Baptist's work, John 3:22,23.
   b Sometimes in a building or under conditions not specified. Lydia, Acts 16:13-15; the jailor and his household, Acts 16:33; Simon the sorcerer, Acts 8:12,13.

5 **Mode of baptism:**
   a By pouring, perhaps a carry-over from the Old Testament anointing, 1 Samuel 10:1.
   b By sprinkling, perhaps a carry-over from Old Testament circumcision.

Evangelicals who practice baptism of infants by sprinkling believe:
  i They are not doing it to save the child.
  ii Children of believing parents, before they have wilfully sinned against their conscience, are in a state of salvation, 1 Corinthians 7:14; Matthew 18:10.
  iii Baptism takes the place of circumcision. Children were circumcised on the eighth day.
  iv Parents make promises to the Lord and to the church on behalf of the children.
  v This baptism is not valid for church membership until the full implications are understood and then they are received by confirmation or other service.
  vi This baptism is denied to children of unbelieving parents.
  c By immersion. The original meaning of "baptize" is to immerse. Immersion was the commonly accepted mode of baptism in the New Testament according to history.
Matthew 3:16, the Savior "went up straightway out of the water."
Acts 8:38,39, the Eunuch and Philip, "went down both into the water" and "they were come up out of the water."
According to Romans 6:1-13, immersion is certainly a more complete picture of death, burial and resurrection than either pouring or sprinkling.
Sprinkling and pouring could illustrate cleansing and consecration.
The believer immersed in water is a sign to the world that he has died, been buried, and resurrected and is now living for Jesus.
Colossians 2:12 "Buried with Him in baptism, wherein also ye are risen with him."
The important thing is not the mode but the inner spiritual meaning.

IV When Should One be Baptized?

Not when I want to have my sins forgiven. Not when I decide to become a Protestant.
Not to advance myself socially or for business or matrimonial purposes.
1 When one is old enough to understand and meet the conditions of Section II above.
Were children baptized in the New Testament? There are records of three households being baptized:

Philippian Jailor, Acts 16; Stephanas, 1 Corinthians 1:16: Lydia, Acts 16:15, but there is no mention of children. Acts 8:12, "They were baptized, both men and women."

Some prefer to dedicate children to the Lord rather than baptize them.

If a child dies unbaptized will it be lost? No. Baptism will neither save nor condemn the child. Salvation is through Christ, not through baptism, Acts 4:12.

David's child in 2 Samuel 12:15-23 died uncircumcised and unbaptized, yet David says, "I shall go to him." And surely David went to heaven where he expected to meet him.

Conclusion

In baptism I take a public stand with God and righteousness against the devil and sin.

Baptism is a challenge to the powers of darkness. I'm living for the Lord Jesus.

Baptism is an act of faith calling on the grace of God for strength to overcome.

Baptism is a command. It is not optional. It is for me to obey and submit.

If Jesus needed to be baptized to fulfill all righteousness, I surely need to be also.

Let us prayerfully and perseveringly press on to baptism and the overcoming life.

Review Questions

1   Why did the Eunuch desire to be baptized in Acts 8:36?
2   Who suffered when the intelligentsia refused the baptism of John the Baptist? Luke 7:30.
3   Give six meanings of baptism.
4   What is the threefold identification of a believer with Christ in Romans 6:4, 5?
5   List the seven requirements of those seeking baptism.
6   How should one be baptized — in what name? With what substance?
7   Where was baptism generally performed in the New Testament times? Give two illustrations.
8   Give the three modes of baptism practiced today. Which is the most Scriptural? Why?

9   When should a Christian be baptized?
10   If a child dies unbaptized will it be lost? Why?

64

Holy Communion

Introduction

Holy Communion is one of the Sacraments instituted by Christ Himself, Matthew 26:26-29.

Christ only celebrated this once with His disciples — on the eve of Gethsemane.

The story of the first Communion is told in the Gospels, and by running the narratives together this seems to be the correct order.

1 The disciples gather at the table but their fellowship was marred by an argument as to who was the greatest among them, Luke 22:24-30.

2 As a rebuke Jesus washed their feet, John 13:1-20.

3 Jesus declares that one of them would betray Him, Matthew 26:21-25.

4 This arouses great excitement and each one asks, "Lord, is it I?" Matthew 26:21-23.

5 Jesus says that the traitor is eating with them, John 13:21,22.

6 Peter makes a sign for John to ask the question, John 13:23-25.

7 Jesus gives the sign. The one that receives the sop, Matthew 26:23.

8 Judas leaves to the surprise of all, John 13:26-30.

9 Jesus took bread, blessed, broke it and gave it to them, Luke 22:19.

10 Jesus took the cup, blessed it and gave it to them. Luke 22:20.

11 They sang a hymn and went out to the Garden of Gethsemane, Matthew 26:30-36.

I Is it Possible to Conduct a Communion Today exactly as the First?

If we were to follow the pattern of the first Communion these would be necessary:

1 It was evening. Matthew 26:20 "Now when the even was come,

He sat down with the twelve."

2 It was held in the Upper Room. Luke 22:12 ". . . he shall show you a large upper room."

3 They ate unleavened bread. Matthew 26:17 ". . . the feast of unleavened bread. . ."

4 The bread must be broken. Luke 22:19 "And He took bread. . . and brake it."

5 They used only one loaf and one cup, Matthew 26:26,27. Common Oriental practice.

6 They were in a reclining position, John 13:23-26. John was leaning on Jesus' breast.

7 It was held after the meal. Matthew 26:26 "And as they were eating. . ."

8 No women were present, only the Lord Jesus and His disciples.

II Purpose of a Communion Service

We do not partake of Communion to receive forgiveness of sins. There is no power in the Sacrament to give the recipient forgiveness.

We partake of Communion in obedience to the command of Christ, 1 Corinthians 11:24.

We partake in anticipation of His soon return, 1 Corinthians 11:26.

We partake to show forth the Lord's death, 1 Corinthians 11:26.

No one partakes of this meal because he is worthy. It is all of His grace that we have been born into the family of God. No one sits in pride at this table.

Our coming merges two things, our unworthiness and our confidence. If we are true children of God we come boldly for fellowship and strength.

Let us not draw back in fear from a loving Heavenly Father's table. He bids us to come and we ought not to deny Him the pleasure of our fellowship.

At the Communion He would draw near to commune with us as on the Emmaus Road.

III Who may Partake of Communion?

Only those who have been born into the family of God have the right to sit at His table in fellowship with the Lord.

The unbeliever and natural man belong at the "table of devils"

1 Corinthians 10:21.

Some churches make the rule that only baptized believers may partake.

Most evangelical churches welcome members in good standing in other evangelical churches to partake of the Communion with them.

Some strict churches will give Communion only to members of their own Assembly.

Members that are being disciplined and barred from the Lord's Table should refrain from partaking in that or any other church until the proper time.

IV Self Examination is Essential before Partaking of Communion

1 Corinthians 11:28 "But let a man examine himself, and so let him eat of that bread, and drink of that cup."

2 Corinthians 13:5 "Examine yourselves, whether ye be in the faith; prove your own selves."

Psalm 26:2 "Examine me, O Lord, and prove me; try my reins and my heart."

Psalm 139:23 "Search me, O God, and know my heart: try me, and know my thoughts."

The candidate should pray, "Lord turn the searchlight of Thy Word on me."

To examine oneself means to scrutinize, investigate carefully, search and test.

1 Whom am I to examine? The preacher? My wife? Elders? Neighbours? *No!* Myself.

2 Why must we examine ourselves?
   a Because it is the direct command of the Scriptures.
   b To eat unworthily brings judgment, weakness, sickness and an early death.

   It must be an examination that finds sin and then casts it away in contrition.

3 How am I to examine myself? By asking myself certain pertinent questions.
   a Do I really and truly believe on the Lord Jesus Christ? Acts 16:31.
   b Am I really born again in the family of God? John 3:3-7.

c Is there any unconfessed sin in my life? Self-pity? Pride? Covetousness? Laziness? Disobedience? Love of sin? Love of the world? Has my thought life been clean? Have I consistently witnessed for Christ? Have I been faithful in Bible reading and prayer? Have I kept my promise to pray for individuals?

d Do I heartily repent of my sins? Confession without repentance is mockery.

e Do I promise in my heart to live a more holy life?

f Do I love God with all my heart, soul, strength and mind? Luke 10:27a.

g Do I love my neighbour as myself? Luke 10:27b.

h Have I forgiven those who have sinned against me? Matthew 6:14,15; 5:23,24.

i Am I obedient in my heart to the commands of Christ to me personally? To preach? To sing? To give to the poor? To teach Sunday School? To witness? To tithe?

j Have I been obedient in my preparation for this Communion?

V Requirements for a Communion Service

Bread and wine are the two substances used as symbols of the Body and Blood.

We teach neither transubstantiation nor consubstantiation, but believe that the elements continue to remain merely elements, symbols or pictures.

We flatly deny any mystical power or change in the elements.

The bread is unleavened, signifying that sin is put away. From this we infer that after Communion we ought to live clean, holy lives.

VI Results

The believer is cleansed and purified as he has examined himself and claimed the Blood to remove not only the sin but the desire to sin.

The believer is strengthened by the fellowship with the Lord and fellow believers.

The believer is edified as he has meditated on the death and return of Christ.

Conclusion

Where do we go from the Communion Table?

Some go to market, to cockpit or gambling table. This is entirely wrong.

The disciples went out and denied and forsook the Savior after the first Communion.

We ought to go from Communion to the place of prayer. Let the blessing go deeper.

We ought to advance in our Christian lives to a place of daily victory in Christ.

Every believer ought to come humbly, yet boldly and often to the Communion table.

Let us partake of this Supper with an air of expectancy, "Till he come."

Remember Jesus' words, "This do in remembrance of Me." As we partake, let us think of His incarnation, birth, baptism, ministry, transfiguration, temptation, miracles, teaching, hardships, Gethsemane, trials, mockings, scourgings, death, resurrection, ascension and second coming. Fill your mind at the Communion with *Him*.

Review Questions

1 List the eleven parts to the first Lord's Supper.
2 Mention some things about the first Communion that are not ordinarily practiced now.
3 Is there forgiveness of sins in the Communion? Explain.
4 Why do we partake of Communion? (Three reasons)
5 Who may partake of Holy Communion?
6 What is the one essential of every believer before partaking of Communion?
7 How are we to examine ourselves? (Six questions to ask ourselves)
8 What are the two requirements for a Communion service? Do they remain as such throughout the service?
9 List three results of partaking of Communion.
10 Jesus said, "This do in remembrance of Me" — What should we remember about Him?

65

Christian Fellowship

Introduction

1 John 1:7 "But if we walk in the light, as He is in the light, we have fellowship one with another."

1 John 1:3 ". . . that ye also may have fellowship with us: and truly our fellowship is with the Father, and with His Son Jesus Christ."

The secular meaning of fellowship is association of a friendly character: comradeship: common interest of those in fraternal orders: friendly companionship.

Some say "fellowship" is "two fellows in the same ship"; this is false, for passengers on the same boat can avoid speaking to each other if they have nothing in common.

Christian fellowship is much deeper, sweeter than secular fellowship; Bible fellowship means spiritual communion, a joint partnership, a joint sharing, mutual partakers.

College fellowships have little in common (same school) (same hobby) but Christian fellowship is far more inclusive; it involves much more; it encircles whole life

All born of the same Father (John 1:13); bought with the same price (1 Corinthians 6:20); members of the same Body (Colossians 1:18); taught by the same Spirit (John 16;13): walking in the same path (2 Corinthians 5:7); serving the same Master (Matthew 23:8): heirs of the same inheritance (Romans 8:17).

I Basis of Fellowship

Fellowship is conditional upon our walking in the light, 1 John 1:7 (quoted above).

Sin breaks fellowship; broken fellowship can be restored by repentance and confession.

Isaiah 59:2 "But your iniquities have separated between you and your God."

1 John 1:7 provides the formula for restored fellowship — cleansing

in the Blood of Christ.

This Blood application is not automatic; it comes as we confess our sins, 1 John 1:9.

Walking in the light means walking in obedience to the will of God; following His footsteps daily; following His footsteps we do no sin, 1 Peter 2:21,22.

Fellowship is based on an intimate family relationship to Christ and His family.

Can two walk together except they be agreed? Amos 3:3. Certainly not! They must be agreed on 1) place of meeting — the cross; 2) the direction to go — heaven-ward; 3) goal — holiness with Christ; 4) pace or speed — He sets the pace and we must follow.

We have fellowship, for our status has changed from that of an enemy to a fellow citizen of that heavenly land.

II With Whom do we have Fellowship?

1 With the Father and the Son — 1 John 1:3 (quoted in introduction), we are born into God's family and now as real members of the family we have heart-to-heart fellowship.

1 Corinthians 1:9 ". . . called unto the fellowship of His Son, Jesus Christ our Lord"; the basic call is fellowship rather than sacrifice or service.

2 With fellow Christians — 1 John 1:3,7, fellowship with the apostles, disciples, believers.

Christians love to be together; to talk together; to pray together; to sing together; to laugh together; to weep together; just to be together.

Christians love to come together to speak of the things of the Lord and to share experiences and testimonies.

We need this fellowship for mutual strengthening and encouragement; the isolated Christian may be starved and lose out spiritually.

First seek fellowship with the Lord in prayer and Bible reading and then with His other sons and daughters; fellowship radiates in the face of the saint.

III   Why must we have Fellowship with others?

Hebrews 10:25 "Not forsaking the assembling of ourselves together, as the manner of some is."

Fellowship is God's ordained order for mankind; God created man to labor six days and be free to rest, fellowship and worship on the seventh day.

God recognized this principle in creation for He said, Genesis 2:18 "It is not good that the man should be alone; I will make him an helpmeet for him"; this refers to marriage but it is equally true in Christian growth as well.

Jesus recognized this principle when He sent out His disciples two by two, Mark 6:7.

It is true that some Christians have matured while living in isolation in prison but they are the exception to the rule.

IV   How do we have Fellowship?

Ordinarily by getting together for Church worship; but there is also fellowship in prayer meetings, testimony meetings and street meetings.

Students in colleges have fellowship in group Bible study and small prayer cells.

Fellowship is often sweetest where two or three meet informally as Jesus says in Matthew 18:20.

Two riding together in a jeep or bus can have excellent fellowship; sweet communion.

Two Christian on a work-gang may fellowship together; Jesus and the two disciples had excellent fellowship on the Emmaus Road, Luke 24:32.

Jesus drew near and their hearts were strangely warmed; this is a spiritual fellowship.

Acts 2:42 "And they (the saints in the Jerusalem Church) continued steadfastly in the apostles' doctrine and fellowship and in breaking of bread, and in prayers."

The early Church thrived on fellowship; they considered it absolutely essential.

Fellowship is not a passive thing; it isn't just attending a meeting; fellowship is when we contribute something to the meeting; it is a "give and take process."

V The Purposes of Fellowship

1 To strengthen one another; even if we do not need fellowship we owe it to others to give fellowship to them; in the process we too will be blessed.

2 To encourage one another in the hard places of life; many with smiling faces are covering aching hearts and burdened souls; let's make their load a bit easier.

3 To share experiences for the mutual benefit of all; our testimony may prevent someone else from making a similar error and suffering as we have done in our ignorance.

4 To manifest our joys that all may rejoice with us; Psalm 50:15, the fellowship of the thrill of answered prayer; this will surely encourage others to keep praying.

5 To weep with them that weep — Romans 12:15: the fellowship of tears, of sorrow and suffering.

6 To enlighten the weaker brother in the mysteries of the Word of God; as you learn, share it and it will be impressed on your mind and you will be ready to learn more.

7 To exhort the backslider to return to the Lord; your offer of fellowship may remind him or happier days and create a longing to return to the Savior and blessing.

VI With Whom is Fellowship Denied?

1 Devils. 1 Corinthians 10:20 "I would not that ye should have fellowship with devils." This would include witch doctors, necromancers, spirit mediums, all forms of demonism or spiritism.

2 The unfruitful works of darkness. Ephesians 5:11 "And have no fellowship with the unfruitful works of darkness, but rather reprove them." This would include night clubs, liquor outlets, criminal gangs, atheist clubs, communists, cells, etc. See John 3:19.

3 Unbelievers, unrighteousness, darkness, Belial and infidels — this list is found in 2 Corinthians 6:14-16; we may have business relations with unsaved people but not spiritual fellowship; we must witness to the unsaved but not enter into their wicked deeds.

With whom then may I have fellowship? Fellowship is best and sweetest with those who share our evangelical Christian faith.

VII Results of Christian Fellowship

1 We learn to walk in the light in obedience to the Lord's will, 1 John 1:7.
2 We learn to suffer together, Philippians 3:10; this fellowship can be very meaningful.
3 We learn to serve together, Colossians 4:7; fellow servants of the blessed Lord Jesus.
4 We learn to comfort one another, 1 Thessalonians 4:18; by sharing the Word and experiences.
5 We learn to pray for one another, 1 Thessalonians 5:25; fellowship in sharing requests.
6 We learn to bear one another's burdens, Galatians 6:2; sharing joys and sorrows.
7 We learn to rejoice with the joyful, Romans 12:15; joy is happily contagious and invigorating.
8 We grow and glow for the Lord, 2 Peter 3:18; we give and receive reciprocal blessings.

Conclusion

Begin the day with fellowship, Godward, in the Quiet Time, prayer and Bible study.

Meditate much on the Word of God during the day; let the Lord be our predominant thought.

Keep company with believers of like faith but constantly make contacts with the unsaved waiting for opportunities to witness to them and invite them to be saved.

What is the difference between listening to a great radio sermon and being in a Church? Basically, the difference is one of fellowship; it is good to listen to great radio preachers but on Sunday morning we ought to be in our own Church, exuding fellowship.

Review Questions

1 What is the difference between secular and Christian fellowship?
2 Mention seven things that believers have in common.
3 List four things on which fellowship is based.
4 With whom do we have fellowship?
5 Why must we have fellowship with other Christians?
6 How can believers have fellowship together?

7 List seven purposes of fellowship.
8 On the basis of passages like 1 Corinthians 10:20; Ephesians 5:11; John 3:19; 2 Corinthians 6:14-16, with whom is fellowship denied?
9 List seven results of fellowship.
10 Is fellowship a command, a privilege, an optional responsibility, or merely a spiritual exercise?

66

The Church

Introduction

The Bible does not recognize any one visible church on earth as "the Church."

The Church which is His body consists of all regenerated souls, each one redeemed by the Blood of Christ and transformed by the Holy Spirit.

Only a small part of the Church is on earth for a great part have already gone to be with the Lord.

The Church has no visible head on earth but an unseen Head (Christ) in heaven.

Christ gave His life that He might found the Church. Ephesians 5:25 ". . . as Christ also loved the Church, and gave Himself for it."

The supreme work of God in this age is the gathering of the Church. Acts 15:14 ". . . God at the first did visit the Gentiles, to take out of them a people for His name." These chosen people are baptized into Christ's body (Church).

I Definition of the Church

The Christian Church is a New Testament institution beginning with Pentecost and ending probably with the rapture, the Second Coming of Christ.

The word "Church" comes from the Greek word *Ecclesia* meaning "to call out from." Christians are called out from the world system to be "in Christ."

1 Corinthians 1:2 "Unto the Church of God which is at Corinth . . . called to be saints."

The word Church can refer to a local group of believers. Philemon 2 ". . . and to the church in thy house." Colossians 4:15 ". . . and the church which is in his house."

The word Church can also mean the Church universal. 1 Corinthians 15:9 "I. . . am not meet to be called an apostle, because I persecuted the church of God."

1 Distinction between the Church and the Kingdom

The kingdom, according to the parables in Matthew 13, is comprised of both good and bad. The Church is therefore a part of the Kingdom. The Kingdom which was once rejected by the Jews will be constituted when the Messiah comes.

2 Distinction between the visible Church and the invisible

The visible Church consists of those whose names are on local Church rolls, all earthly denominations and sects, good, bad and indifferent would be included in the visible Church.

The invisible Church is made up of those whose names are written in the Lamb's Book of life, Revelation 21:27.

3 Distinction between the local Church and the universal Church

By the local Church is meant any local congregation in a given location.

The Church universal is a term which includes all Churches everywhere.

4 Distinction between the Church actual and ideal

The actual Church includes those who are imperfect yet striving after perfection through Christ.

The ideal Church is made up of those who have already gone to heaven and are perfect now.

5 Distinction between the Church militant and the Church triumphant

The Church militant refers to the true Church on earth.

The Church triumphant refers to the section of the Church already in heaven.

II The Foundation of the Church

Matthew 16:16-18 ". . . upon this rock I will build My Church . . ."

The Church was founded by Jesus Christ on Peter's confession that Jesus Christ was (and is) the Son of God, the Messiah, the Christ, God incarnate in humanity.

Our Savior did not build the Church on Peter, but on Peter's words.

A study of Matthew 16:16-18; John 20:19-23; Matthew 18:18 will show one that Peter did not receive a higher position than the other disciples (all could bind).

Historically the Church was founded at Pentecost, Acts 2, when the Spirit descended.

Acts 2:47 "The Lord added to the Church daily such as should be saved." They had stated places of meeting, Acts 1:13; 5:12; 2:46; 12:12. They had stated times of meeting — daily — Acts 2:46, each Lord's Day, Acts 20:7.

III Conditions of Membership in the Church

1 Repentance, Acts 2:38, "Then Peter said unto them, Repent," at Pentecost.
2 Faith in the Lord Jesus Christ as Savior, Lord and Son of God, Matthew 16:16-18.
3 Salvation, regeneration, the new birth, Acts 2:47, the saved added to the Church. They were not added to the Church in order to be saved but added to the church because they were saved already. (A member of the invisible Church becoming a member of the earthly visible Church.)
4 Baptism in the Name of the Trinity, Acts 2:38, ". . . repent and be baptized . . ." Matthew 28:19: Acts 10:47,48; Acts 22:16.
5 Continuance in the Apostles' doctrine. Acts 2:42 "And they continued stedfastly in the Apostles' doctrine." They lived according to the Scripture.

IV Biblical Symbols of the Church

1 Body Christ is the Head of the body and we are members of His body. Colossians 1:18 "And He is the Head of the body, the Church . . ." Ephesians 1:22,23; Colossians 2:19 ". . . the Head, from which all the body by joints and bands having nourishment ministered, and knit together, increaseth with the increase of God."
2 A temple, building, habitation or dwelling place for God's Spirit. Ephesians 2:20,21. Of this building, Christ is the chief cornerstone and we are different parts of the building.
3 Bride of Christ. 2 Corinthians 11:2 "For I have espoused you to one husband, that I may present you as a chaste virgin to Christ." Christ is the bridegroom, John 3:29. The wedding will take place in Revelation 19:7, "let us be glad and rejoice, and give honour to Him: for the marriage of the Lamb is come, and His wife hath made herself ready . . . she should be arrayed in fine linen, clean and white."

The Ordinances of the Church

Despite the fact that some teach that there are seven ordinances, the Bible only teaches two ordinances of the church.
1 Baptism, Matthew 28:19,20; Mark 16:16; Acts 2:38-41; 8:36-40; 10:47,48.
2 The Lord's Supper, Acts 2:42-46; 20:7; 1 Corinthians 11:20-34.

VI The Purpose of the Church

1 To worship God and to glorify Him on the earth.
   Ephesians 1:4-6 ". . . to the praise of the glory of His grace, wherein He hath made us accepted in the Beloved."
2 To evangelize the world with the Gospel. Matthew 28:19,20 "Go ye therefore, and teach all nations." Mark 16:15. See also Ephesians 3:8.
3 To teach and instruct Christians. Ephesians 4:11-15 ". . . for the perfecting of the saints . . ." 1 Thessalonians 5:11; 1 Corinthians 12:1-31.
4 To witness constantly. Acts 1:8 " . . . witnesses in Jerusalem . . . Judaea . . . Samaria . . ."

VII Unity in the Earthly Church
Taken from Jesus' High Priestly Prayer

1 Unity because we worship the same Father, John 17:1-5.
2 Unity because the saved all belong to the Son, John 17:6-10.
3 Unity because all indwelt by the same Spirit, John 17:11a; 16:7; Romans 8:16.
4 Unity because the Father and Son are united and we ought to be, too, John 17:11b.
5 Unity because we live by the same Word, John 17:14-17.
6 Unity because it will cause unbelievers to believe, John 17:21,23.
7 Unity because we shall live together in heaven, John 17:24.

Conclusion

Why are there so many denominations? Each is probably like a variety of fruit and it takes many varieties to make an orchard. (Many spokes to make a wheel). Christ's desire is that the Church on earth should be clean, glorious and holy, Ephesians 5:27 "That He might present it (the Church) to Himself a glorious Church, not having spot, or wrinkle, or any such thing; but that it (you and I) should be holy and without blemish."

Review Questions

1 Which Church is the one true Church?
2 On the basis of Acts 15:14, what is the Church?
3 Distinguish between the Church and the kingdom; between the visible and invisible Church.
4 When and on what was the Church founded?
5 List five conditions of membership in the Church.
6 Explain briefly the three biblical symbols of the Church.
7 Name the Church ordinances.
8 Enumerate four purposes of the Church.
9 On the basis of John 17:1-26, give seven reasons for unity in the earthly Church.
10 Is it right or wrong to have so many denominations? Why?

67

Despising the Church

Introduction

Notes from *Some Vital Questions*, G. W. Truett.

1 Corinthians 11:22 "Or despise ye the Church of God?"

This thought or question is drawn from the Communion chapter where their bad behavior was a shame to the Church at Corinth.

In this lesson we will consider other ways that we sometimes despise the Church without intending to do it — not realizing the implications of our thoughtless actions.

In the Old Testament God dealt with a nation. In the New Testament He deals with a Church.

After Pentecost when the Spirit descended they were all baptized into His body.

The Church is more than an earthly organization. It is Christ's Body.

At conversion each one of us is baptized into this Body.

Some have prominent positions, eyes, tongue, hands, etc., but most Christians occupy a minor, insignificant, hidden place inside the body, probably a minute cell.

But if that hidden cell is damaged the whole body suffers.

The Church is the invisible body of believers. The visible Church is an earthly organization that includes good and bad, wheat and tares, saved and hypocrites.

The earthly Church is unfortunately divided into sects, denominations and isolated ones. Jesus' present occupation is building the Church, Matthew 16:18 ". . . upon this rock I will build My Church . . ." This is not an edifice of stone but a living Body. Do we despise this Church? To despise means to treat with contempt, to loathe, abhor.

I How may the Church be Despised?

1 The unbeliever or atheist ridicules the Church as a despicable, useless organization.

2 **The Christian, of course, would not despise the Church in this manner.**

Unfortunately the Christian adopts more subtle means. We despise the church by:

a Forsaking church attendance. Hebrews 10:25 "Not forsaking the assembling of ourselves together, as the manner of some is."

When we do not attend church it is a way of saying to the community, "Church attendance is not important. It is good to go to church if you feel good, the weather is good, you have no other engagement and you have plenty of time."

This is despising the Church for you are treating it lightly in that you recognize other things as having greater importance and prominence in your life.

Of course we recognize that those who are really ill cannot come to church, but we are speaking of those who get a headache at church time but it fades away in time to go out to dinner at noon.

b We despise the Church by accepting its benefits without accepting responsibilities:

1) We take our children there to be dedicated but never take them to Sunday School,

2) We take our young people there to get married but never erect a family altar at home,

3) We have our names on the Church roll but live like heathen or unbelievers,

4) We go to Communion once a year or once a month but never seek to win the lost,

5) We enjoy the Christmas and Easter programs but never learn the other truths of the Word,

6) We take our dead there to be buried but continue to live wickedly without preparing for death ourselves,

7) We despise the Church by reducing it to a social club for business, entertainment or matrimonial purposes.

c By failing to make preparation for the service.

We expect the preacher to study, pray and prepare well. Each member should also prepare. It is good and proper to come to Church dressed clean and neat, but the most important preparation is to come spiritually prepared by prayer and Bible study.

Come in the spirit of expectancy, expecting God to feed your

hungry soul. Bring your Bible, a pencil and notepaper to mark
or record your blessings.

d By failing to listen or being irreverent during the service.
God dislikes irreverence. Remember that you are in God's house
to worship Him.

It is not only what we hear but also how we hear.

e We despise the Church by lax religious beliefs, views and convictions regarding doctrine. There is no excuse for religious
uncertainty in the pulpit or pew.

We learn how to market, sew, cook, do business — everything
for the daily life — but can we prove the deity of Jesus Christ?

If we cannot prove the doctrine from Scripture then it is a shame
on us and the Church.

f By wrong and inconsistent lives. If I see a church member who
is a flagrant sinner, I say, "Shame on that church that cannot
make a better Christian than that."

As a member of this congregation you bear a heavy responsibility before this community.

To live wrongly after professing salvation is despising His
Church.

g By unworthy giving to the church. To a small child you give
₱2.00 for coke but only ₱1.00 to the Church. Is this showing
respect or disrespect?

If I recognize that giving to the Church is giving to the Lord, then
my gift reflects the extent of my love to Him, my Creator and
my Savior.

Under law we would expect to pay a tithe (one tenth). Under
grace we ought to give the tithe plus a love offering.

h By using our talents poorly. I sing for entertainment of
others but refuse to sing in the choir.

I speak at parties and entertain and exhort but never use this
talent for the Lord.

I have a splendid personality for my friends and business associates, but never use this talent for the Lord for soul-winning.

Consciously or unconsciously we are saying, "My talent is too
good to be wasted on that small church." Caution: False
humility is a form of pride.

I believe that this is despicable in the sight of the Lord.
Remember the Church is His body, not just a weak earthly
organization.

God and the Church ought to have the first claim on my life.

i By being a Christian detached from the Church. This is extreme separation. "The Church is not holy enough for me, too many hypocrites in it."

I sit at home and listen to Dr. Billy Graham on the radio instead of attending church. This is despising His Church, His Body.

Even if we cannot agree 100%, we can still have fellowship, one with another.

j By refusing to join the Church. That is saying, "I am too good for that church."

II Results of Despising the Church of God

1 The Lord Jesus must feel terribly hurt; we are sinning against Him.
2 The earthly organization is weakened. The Church needs you and you need the Church.
3 The sinner is stumbled and turned away from the Savior. A clean strong Church attracts sinners to Christ.
4 As a result the Christians who do attend are weakened and overburdened. The tasks are too great for so few people.
5 Basically the non-attender is the loser:
  a Spiritually, for your spiritual life is stymied.
  b Economically, God gives to those who give to Him.
  c Morally, You need the moral teaching and strengthening of the Church.
  d Physically, God requires that you leave work and worship Him one day in seven.

III Remedy for Despising the Church of God

1 Recognize your sin. You have despised the precious body of the Lord Jesus.
2 Confess the sin to the Lord Jesus, 1 John 1:9, and He will cleanse and forgive it.
3 Promise God that never again will you be careless in this important matter.
4 Pray and ask God to teach you how to honor and respect the Church, the invisible Body of Christ.
5 Tell your pastor that you have erred but that he can count on you to be a much better member in the future, beginning today.

Conclusion

It is a dangerous thing to despise the Church that Jesus Christ is busy building.

Review Questions

1 Define the word "despise" as used in 1 Corinthians 11:22.
2 What was the special object of God's care in the Old Testament? In the New Testament?
3 How do unbelievers despise the Church?
4 List ten ways that a believer may despise the Church of God.
5 What are we saying (consciously or unconsciously) when we do not attend Church?
6 Mention seven benefits that the Church offers to a community.
7 Of the ten points mentioned in question 4, which do you consider the worst? Why?
8 Give four results of despising the Church..
9 In what four ways is the non-attender the loser by not attending Church?
10 What is the remedy for despising the Church?

68

Church Discipline

Introduction

Church discipline is like the weather. We talk a great deal about it but seldom do anything about it. Paul expected Christians to use church courts, not government courts.

1 Corinthians 6:1-3 "Dare any of you, having a matter against another, go to law before the unjust, and not before the saints? Do ye not know that the saints shall judge the world? and if the world shall be judged by you, are ye unworthy to judge the smallest matters? Know ye not that we shall judge angels? How much more things that pertain to this life?" See also verse 12.

Discipline means taking corrective measures as punishment in order to maintain the good conduct of church members.

This is a practice seldom made effective in our churches today. Why?

Is it because we have grown weak and cold, and fear to act on our principles?

Is it because we have all attained a state of perfection and no longer require it?

Is it because our churches are afraid of losing church members?

Are we afraid that the church income will be reduced if we punish sin?

Do we love popularity, money, large churches, easy times, more than holiness?

Are we afraid of calling "sin" *sin*, thus condoning evil in the lives of fellow believers?

The Apostolic Church was strong because it was pure. Our modern church is weak because we have compromised our position and condoned sin in the members.

I When to Teach Discipline

I believe that it ought to be taught after conversion but before baptism. In baptism courses we set before the candidates our

Christian standards.

Alongside these we ought to teach the punishment for disobedience. We say to our children, "Clean up the mess or I will put you to bed hungry." The child then weighs the facts and acts accordingly.

Before entering the Church and its responsibilities the candidate ought to be informed on this important point. This ought to be comparatively easy in a Roman Catholic country where the people are accustomed to church authority, penance and excommunication.

II What to Teach regarding Discipline

1 **Basis of our authority to administer discipline** Matthew 18:15-17 "Moreover if thy brother shall trespass against thee, go and tell him his fault between thee and him alone: if he shall hear thee, thou hast gained thy brother. But if he will not hear thee, then take with thee one or two more, that in the mouth of two or three witnesses every word may be established. And if he shall neglect to hear them, tell it unto the church: but if he neglect to hear the church, let him be unto thee as an heathen man and a publican."

a   Go to the erring one alone to exhort him to repent.

b   If he resists, take with you two or three others as witnesses.

c   If he continues to harden his heart, inform the church.

d   If he insists on resisting consider him as a sinning heathen man.

2 **Occasions for discipline**

a   False doctrine. Titus 1:13 "This witness is true. Wherefore rebuke them sharply, that they may be sound in the faith."

Has your church ever taken this strong a stand against corrupt doctrine?

Our educational system needs a housecleaning of false teachers.

b   Open sin. 1 Timothy 5:20 "Them that sin rebuke before all, that others also may fear."

Has your church ever taken disciplinary action against flagrant sin?

Habakkuk 1:13 "Thou (God) art of purer eyes than to behold evil."

Romans 7:13 ". . . that sin by the commandment might become exceeding sinful."

Let us pray and ask God to make sin so terrible that we will strive to punish it or exclude it from our midst.

    c Immorality, 1 Corinthians 5:1-5. This man was excommunicated for he had committed fornication with his own mother or step-mother.

3 **Extent of discipline** Deliver the individual to Satan for the destruction of the body. 1 Corinthians 5:5 "To deliver such an one unto Satan for the destruction of the flesh, that the spirit may be saved in the day of the Lord Jesus."

1 Corinthians 5:13 "Therefore put away from among yourselves that wicked person."

1 Timothy 1:20 "Of whom is Hymenaeus and Alexander; whom I have delivered unto Satan, that they may learn not to blaspheme."

What does one do when the crime or sin does not merit excommunication?

If the guilty one shows genuine repentance, keep the guilty one from the Communion table or any public office for a set period of time (three months, six months, one year, in accordance with the crime committed).

This judgment would be handed down by the presiding church council.

III How to Teach Discipline

Firstly, the church and particularly the church council must live clean, disciplined lives themselves, above reproach in word and deed. What a responsibility!

1 **In humility** 1 Corinthians 10:12 "Wherefore let him that thinketh he standeth take heed lest he fall." Do not lord it over the fallen one.

If the temptations and circumstances were similar perhaps we would have committed an even greater sin.

Also our "besetting sin" may be much different from his. The point on which I would succumb to sin might be a strong point to this erring one.

This is no place for superior "holier than thou" feelings.

2 **In sincerity** Remove the beam from your own eye before you mention the mote in your brother's eye. Matthew 7:3-5 "And why do you look at the speck in your brother's eye, but do not consider the plank in your own eye? Or how can you say to your brother, 'Let me remove the speck out of your eye,' and look, a

plank is on your own eye?

Hypocrite! First remove the plank from your own eye, and then you will see clearly to remove the speck out of your brother's eye."

Some may take the attitude that "I am not perfect, therefore I will not discipline my brother."

This is wrong. If God gives me responsibility I am expected to exercise it.

3 **In love** 1 Corinthians 13:4 "Love suffereth long and is kind."

We certainly must deal in love. Love is our strongest lever against the one whom we are trying to bring back to the strict paths of righteousness.

He may respond to our love when he may resist our words and arguments.

"Suffer long." Be sure to exercise plenty of patience — "till seventy times seven" if there are signs of genuine repentance.

4 **By Scripture** Be sure that you can prove that that which he has done is sin from Scripture and not just transgressing "Western Culture."

The church is founded on Scripture and its actions must be the outworkings of the doctrines and principles laid down in the Word of God.

5 **By testimony** Be willing to share personal experiences on the subject. This will assist in establishing a friendly, brotherly confidence — a mutual trust.

This will help us to deal with him as a brother and not a dog beneath our feet.

6 **By experience** In Panhsiem, S.W. China, I recall three cases of church discipline.

a A man excommunicated for marrying the second wife (bigamy).

b A woman was kept from the Communion table of three months for dealing in opium, which was contrary to the laws of the land.

c A widow was disciplined for flirting with a young man - behavior unbecoming to a sober, mature church member.

Conclusion

May God give us the courage of our convictions to exercise discipline.

Acts 20:28 "Take heed therefore unto yourselves, and to all the flock, over the which the Holy Ghost hath made you overseers."

Review Questions

1 Is a Church Court Scriptural? Give proof.
2 What is the ultimate object of Church discipline?
3 Why is Church discipline seldom practiced today?
4 Outline the four steps in discipline mentioned in Matthew 18:15-17.
5 List three occasions for Church discipline.
6 Name various punishments that a Church Board may give.
7 How should discipline be taught?
8 What is required of the Church Board before dealing with the erring member?
9 When was the last time the Church Council in your Church administered discipline?
10 Should one postpone judgment on the basis of Matthew 18:22 (just forgive him 490 times)?

69

The Pastor

Introduction

The introduction is taken from "Christian Guardian," reprinted in Gospel Herald.

"The perfect preacher is never too long either in his prayers or sermons. He never forgets anything that he ought to remember and he never remembers anything that he ought to forget.

He knows just when to speak and when to keep silent.

His laughter is always well-timed and his tears are always shed at the precise moment of psychological correctness.

His sermons are always well-prepared, well-delivered and appropriate.

He is educated enough to be a college president and unassuming enough for a humble beginner.

He never has any financial embarrassments as he always manages to live comfortably on the smallest salary.

He never quarrels and yet he is always outspoken and courageous.

He is at once an ideal visitor and an ideal student.

He is a real leader of Israel's hosts and yet his enemies speak well of him.

His wife is absolutely without fault and his children are all just like her.

His theology is old-fashioned enough to please the most conservative and new-fangled enough to satisfy the most radical.

There is never any difficulty in stationing him, as any appointment is glad to get him and he is always willing to sacrifice himself for the good of all."

Perhaps that man is not born yet, nevertheless the standards set by congregations are very high and it behooves the prospective pastor to aim high. To be a pastor of a congregation is a high calling from God.

I Personal Life

The personal life of the pastor is of prime importance for people listen to his sermons on Sundays and watch to see how they are fulfilled through the week.

The pastor must be a man of piety — a pious, holy man who radiates the Lord Jesus Christ.

The unbeliever expects near perfection of a minister at all times.

The pastor must be a man of prayer. The Church expects him to spend considerable time in prayer daily — even hours.

The pastor needs this for his own personal attainment of holiness — remaining long in the presence of God until all the dross is revealed and removed.

1 Samuel 12:23 "God forbid that I should sin against the Lord in ceasing to pray for you: but I will teach you the good and the right way."

Samuel had a burden to pray for the flock. Each pastor ought to pray for the flock by name, person by person, if at all possible.

Colossians 1:9 "For this cause we also, since the day we heard it, do not cease to pray for you." This was the prayer life of the Apostle Paul.

Isaiah 52:11 ". . . be ye clean, that bear the vessels of the Lord."

The pastor must be a man with a passion for the lost and dying.

Acts 20:31 "Therefore watch, and remember, that by the space of three years I ceased not to warn every one night and day with tears."

Matthew 9:36 "But when He (Jesus) saw the multitudes, He was moved with compassion."

II Private Ministry

The pastor must be able to talk to people individually about salvation, personal problems, or to point out discrepancies in their testimony, Matthew 18:15-17.

The pastor ought to learn to comfort the bereaved and all who sorrow.

He ought to be able to enter into their personal lives and become a part of the family.

Romans 12:15 "Rejoice with them that do rejoice, and weep with them that weep."

The pastor must remember that he is, in a very special way, the under-shepherd, representing the Lord Jesus here on earth at all times.

III Public Ministry

As a pastor, his greatest ministry is to stand and preach the Gospel. This will involve education, experience and will require the blessing of God to be effective to the conversion of sinners and strengthening of believers.

He must remember to give the whole counsel of God, which will include evangelism, Bible doctrine, teaching, reproofs, exhortations and warnings.

Acts 20;27 "For I have not shunned to declare unto you all the counsel of God."

He must also learn to pray publicly, which can only be learned by much private prayer in the secret place. In the pastoral prayer he lifts a congregation into the presence of God in an atmosphere of sublime worship.

He must also learn to read the Scriptures clearly, reverently and distinctly, so that all can understand.

Nehemiah 8:8 "So they read in the book in the law of God distinctly, and gave the sense, and caused them to understand the reading."

He is commanded to "feed the Church of God," Acts 20:28, by preaching sermons and Bible lessons that are applicable to their individual needs.

It is also his responsibility to prepare candidates for baptism.

He is responsible for the sacraments of Baptism and holy Communion.

At the conclusion of the service he has the responsibility to bless the people from God. Numbers 6:23-26; Revelation 1:4,5; Luke 1;21 (the people waited for Zacharias to come out and bless them).

He is to protect the flock from false teachings and false teachers, Acts 20:29,30.

He has a special responsibility to care for the poor of his flock, Acts 11:29,30.

He has the privilege of teaching his members the need of reaching out into the unreached areas. He can best do this by example — taking them with him on trips.

In all things, he is an example of the Lord and godliness to the people.

IV Motives

The preacher must work with a correct motive — to glorify the Name of the Lord.

Paul's motive was not money or fame, but men — their salvation and grounding.

1 Corinthians 1:15-18, the urgency and passion was on Paul and he was forced to press on.

Let the pastor be prayerful, sincere, diligent and faithful at all times.

The wonderful message, the shortness of time, the nearness of death, the coming of Christ undergird his motive to do all to His glory, Colossians 3:17; 1 Corinthians 10:31.

V Adaptability

1 Corinthians 9:4, Paul was willing to forego eating and drinking if men would only believe.

Paul even refused a salary at Corinth to avoid suspicion and win more souls.

Paul was willing to change eating habits, to sacrifice liberty to win souls.

Paul adapted himself to various classes of men: To the Jew he was a Jew; to those under law as one under law; to those without law as one without law; to the weak he became weak, 1 Corinthians 9:19-23.

Paul was willing to forbear marriage, home and children if more people would be saved.

Paul was willing to regulate his social life and customs (but not his Christian principles) to gain men and avoid unnecessary offense.

VI Responsibility

He is responsible to God for the souls of his flock, Hebrews 13:17, "... for they watch for your souls, as they that must give account, that they may do it with joy, and not with grief."

The successful pastor must be temperate and constantly Spirit-controlled.

The pastor that begins well but turns aside, the Lord threatens with being a castaway, 1 Corinthians 9:27. Even the great Apostle Paul seemed to fear this.

Conclusion

2 Corinthians 2:16 "Who is sufficient for these things?"

2 Corinthians 3:5 "Our sufficiency is of God."

Luke 9:62 "No man, having put his hand to the plow, and looking back, is fit for the kingdom of God."

Review Questions

1   List ten standards set by the congregation for their pastor.
2   Tell five things about the pastor's personal life.

3 In your opinion which part of the pastor's work is most important? Why? Preaching? Private Counseling? Visiting? Public relations?

4 Mention four aspects of the pastor's private ministry.

5 List five things involved in preparation for the ministry.

6 Give six different things that a pastor should remember to cover in his preaching at least once a quarter (every three months).

7 Describe the scope of a pastor's responsibility.

8 Give one true and two false motives for preaching.

9 Should a pastor be adaptable? Explain.

10 To whom does the pastor owe the first responsibility? To the congregation? To the Church Elders or official Board?

70

Duties of Elders and Deacons

Introduction

God has declared that the Church should be governed by pastors, elders and deacons.

1 Thessalonians 5:12,13 "And we beseech you, brethren, to know them which labour among you, and are over you in the Lord, and admonish you; and to esteem them very highly in love for their work's sake."

We are exhorted to get to know them that labor among us. There are many advantages of knowing them intimately and personally.

They are godly individuals who can help you with your spiritual problems.

They labor (not play or idle away their time) among you, not for money but for the spiritual strengthening of the Church and its propagation.

God has placed them over us in the Lord. They are not cruel, harsh taskmasters, but kind, considerate leaders seeking to guide and help you.

They are to admonish us. Accept their rebuke as from the Lord.

Expect them to correct you. Say "thank you" with sincere appreciation.

In many churches the deacons look after the business and financial matters of the congregation while the elders look after the spiritual affairs.

I Deacons

1 What is a Deacon?

The first Board of Deacons consisted of seven men in Acts 6:1-6.

The Apostolic Church had all their goods in common. Some began to complain that they did not get a fair share of the food.

The apostles felt that their ministry was preaching and teaching, and that others should be appointed to look after this mundane but necessary task.

The apostles called the multitude together and chose seven men to do this work.

2 What are a Deacon's qualifications?

a Men of honest report, good reputation both inside and out of the Church. Acts 6:3 "Look ye out among you seven men of honest report."

b Men full of the Holy Ghost. Acts 6:3 "... full of the Holy Ghost..." Ephesians 5:18 "And be not drunk with wine, wherein is excess; but be filled with the Spirit." A drunkard or one not filled with the Spirit is automatically disqualified.

c Men full of wisdom, Acts 6:3, "... and wisdom, whom we may appoint . . . :"

We certainly need heavenly wisdom for this difficult task. If a capable man lacks wisdom it is his fault for James 1:5 offers wisdom to a Christian.

d Grave. 1 Timothy 3:8 "Likewise must the deacons be grave." That is serious, mature. Someone who is light, giddy, immature, flippant, is not qualified.

e Not doubletongued, 1 Timothy 3:8, "... not doubletongued..." That is, not say saying one thing to one person and something different to another one.

They must be qualified to speak with authority and command respect. Matthew 7:29.

f Not given to much wine, 1 Timothy 3:8. That is, not a drunkard and a waster.

g Not greedy of filthy lucre, 1 Timothy 3:8.Thus as they collected alms they would not be tempted to keep some of it for themselves, lest they become a Judas, John 12:6.

h Holding the mystery of faith in pure conscience, 1 Timothy 3:9. That is, true in doctrine.

i Husband of one wife, 1 Timothy 3:12. That is, only married once (does not mean bigamy).

j Ruling their children and houses (servants) well, 1 Timothy 3:12. If they do not control these well, how can they manage the Church of God?

3 What are the Deacons' duties?

a In Acts 6:1-6, to serve tables and minister food to the poor.

b Today they look after the business and financial needs of the church.

c Collecting church funds, banking or keeping the money, paying the pastor, janitor, electric and water bills. Repairing the church building.

d Taking care of the poor people. Assisting them whenever and wherever possible.

e They should be able to teach a Sunday School class.

f Examples in church attendance to the entire congregation.

g These are the men that someday will be promoted to become elders.

4 Deaconesses

Romans 16:1 "I commend unto you Phebe our sister, which is a servant (deaconess RV).

Romans 16:3, Priscilla probably was a deaconess, too. She is mentioned in Acts 18, too,

a Qualifications

1 Grave. 1 Timothy 3:11 — sober, mature, not young, immature and silly.

2 Not a slanderer. 1 Timothy 3:11 — not busybodies or gossips.

3 Sober. 1 Timothy 3:11 — mature, capable of sound judgment and good advice.

4 Faithful in all things. 1 Timothy 3:11 — Faithful in doctrine, faith, works and love.

b Duties

1 To assist at baptisms of lady candidates, as well as teaching the candidates.

2 To visit the sick, to give sound advice to the women and girls of the church.

3 To teach Sunday School, to teach children the truths of the Scriptures.

II Elders

1 What is an Elder?

He is one of the spiritual leaders of the Church of Jesus Christ.

In rank he is above a deacon but below a pastor or minister of the church.

He is generally ordained to this ministry by the laying on of hands.

Acts 14:23 "And when they had ordained them elders in every church, and had prayed with fasting, they commended them to the Lord, on whom they believed."

Titus 1:5 ". . . that thou shouldest . . . ordain elders in every city."

In some churches it is a life appointment. In other churches for a limited term.

2 What are the Qualifications of an Elder?

a Blameless, Titus 1:6 — a man of honest reputation, good character and standing.

b The husband of one wife, Titus 1:6 — having only been married once.

c Faithful children, obedient and under control, Titus 1:6. This is the test. If one rules one's household well, then he can govern a church.

d Not self-willed, Titus 1:7 — of a meek and quiet spirit; he is not a dictator.

e Not soon angry, Titus 1:7 — patient. There will be much that is trying, but anger and temper have no place here.

f Not given to wine, Titus 1:7. He must not be a drunkard nor a waster of money.

g No striker, Titus 1:7, satisfied, not murmuring and complaining.

h Not given to filthy lucre, Titus 1:7, lest church funds become a snare to him.

i A lover of hospitality, Titus 1:8, manifesting love to fellow-believers and strangers.

j Lover of good men, Titus 1:8, lover of all that is good, clean, wholesome and upright.

3 What are the Duties of an Elder?

a He is charged with the spiritual activities of the church.

b To attend church regularly and take an interest in all departments.

c To select a suitable pastor for the congregation.

d To supply the pulpit if the pastor is absent. Gain experience in house meetings.

e To arrange for special events like evangelistic campaigns, DVBS, etc.

f To assist the pastor in dispensing Communion.

g To visit the sick and pray for them according to James 5:14.

h Capable of leading in public prayer, including the pastoral prayer.

i To engage actively in church discipline (Lesson 68) — to sit on church council.

j To assist in examining candidates for baptism.

Conclusion

Let the elders have double honor, 1 Timothy 4:17. Obey them that
have the rule over you according to Hebrews 13:17. Pray for your
church leaders, 1 Timothy 2:1,2. Love them as God's servants,
1 Thessalonians 5:13.

Review Questions

1   What four things do we learn about Church officials from
1 Thessalonians 5:12,13?
2   What is a deacon?
3   List ten qualifications of a deacon.
4   Give six duties of a deacon.
5   What are the qualifications of a deaconess?
6   List some duties of a deaconess.
7   What is an Elder?
8   List ten qualifications of an Elder.
9   Mention ten duties of an Elder.
10   According to 1 Timothy 5:7; Hebrews 13:17; 1 Timothy 2:1,2; and
1 Thessalonians 5:13, what four things are we to give Church
officials?

71

The Layman's Place in the Church

Introduction

One reason for the failure of modern churches is that they become a one-man affair.

The pew-sitter leaves the work of evangelism, preaching, teaching, visiting, to the preacher. This has never been God's order. God's order has always been that every Christian should be a witness. Acts 1:8 "And ye shall be witnesses unto Me both in Jerusalem, and in all Judaea, and in Samaria, and unto the uttermost part of the earth."

John Wesley: "We are all at it (Evangelism) and at it always." This was the secret of the Moravian and Wesleyan revivals.

A layman is a person not of the clergy, one of the laity — an ordinary member of the church. The word does not appear in the Scriptures. It is a term that has arisen with the elevation of the clergy.

The answer to the problem of getting the ordinary church member to do personal evangelism is revival. The reason that we find personal evangelism so hard is that we are spiritually cold.

At Pentecost there were 120 praying but only a few of these were members of the clergy (the eleven disciples). There were women present also.

At Pentecost they preached in over 20 languages, so more than the disciples preached.

Acts 8:4 "Therefore they that were scattered abroad went everywhere preaching the Word."

It seems that the clergy stayed in Jerusalem and the laity were the ones out preaching.

Therefore it is fitting and necessary that each church member, each Christian, should be active for Christ.

I How Laymen can Prepare themselves to be Effective Witnesses

1 **By doing what you can** This is the story of Mary of Bethany in Mark 14:3-9.

The Lord asks you to use the talents that He has given you. Matthew 25:15 "And unto one He gave five talents, to another two, and to another one; to every man (me too) according to his several ability; and straightway took his journey."

The Lord does not ask anyone to be another Billy Graham. *I* must be *Alban Douglas*.

As we use our talents they and others will develop. The man with five talents gained five more.

2 **By prayer** Story of quiet praying of the two retired spinters aged 82 and 84 who faithfully prayed and received the revival in the Hebrides in October, 1951.

3 **By Bible study** Perhaps the opportunity will come to answer a perplexing question authoritatively from the Bible. You need not be a lawyer — just a witness.

4 **By seeking the guidance of the Holy Spirit** He knows the hearts of others, their needs and problems and can arrange "accidental" meetings for us.

5 **By a quiet, consistent Christian testimony** Eventually our unsaved friends will come to us in time of need. Perhaps to visit a dying person at midnight, Luke 11:5.

6 **By living out the preacher's sermon** Sinners listen to the preacher and then look to you, an ordinary layman, for the practical outworking in the daily life.

7 **By watching "senior" Christians** One day you will inherit their responsibilities. What a tremendous responsibility rests on us as "senior" Christians.

8 **By attempting small tasks first** Later as you become proficient (or semi-proficient) in these, you can expand your activities (testimony, YP message, preaching, campaigns).

9 **By reading biographies and autobiographies** Goforth of China was spurred on by reading the revival stories of Finney; and many others have been inspired by the story of Hudson Taylor books.

10 **By practice** You will never learn by only listening to lectures or only reading books.

II Effective ways for Laymen to Spread the Gospel

1 By bringing people to church by car, paying jeep fares and accompanying them to church, or by being willing to walk with a classmate.
Andrew brought his brother Peter to Jesus, John 1:40-42.
Andrew brought the boy with the five loaves and two fishes to Jesus, John 6:8,9.
Andrew brought certain Greeks to Jesus, John 12:20-22.

2 By joining the Bible Society and helping them in their great work.

3 By joining the Gideons to distribute Bibles in hotels and schools.

4 By joining a Christian Businessmen's organization, your church's Missionary Society, or other Christian organization to assist the cause of Missions or Christian work. (If you are a professional, discover if there is a Christian Association for members of your profession. Many such groups undertake community projects as part of their witness.)

5 By giving your money for missions at home and abroad. Story of R. G. Le-Tourneau.

6 By encouraging your pastor. Help him to keep actively fighting the battle. He, too, may become discouraged. Encourage him occasionally with a compliment, smile, handshake.

7 By organizing a Sunday School or Bible class in your home for the children on your street. Perhaps a local Christian organization can help by supplying more teachers.

8 If time and talents permit, teach a Sunday School class. Tell your Sunday School Superintendent that you are available as a substitute teacher at first, perhaps.

9 In Christian campaigns and rallies be a good "inviter" of others. Don't be discouraged if they say, "yes, yes," but don't come. Be cheerful and keep inviting them again and again.

10 By organizing and leading a prayer meeting in your home, pray for revival, etc.

11 By quietly inviting the person next to you in a campaign to receive Christ. The evangelist gives the invitation publicly. You give it personally. This is the secret of the personal touch which is quite irresistible.

12 By being willing to walk up the aisles with the penitents and stand with them at the front.

13 By being a counselor or helper. Be willing to share your testimony
    and point the sinner to Jesus Christ. Do not be afraid. You will
    learn by watching and doing.
14 By the use of good tracts. They are cheap but attractive and very
    effective, and readily accepted in the Philippines.
15 By talking about the Bible, turning a conversation in the beauty
    parlor or barber shop to the things of the Lord and the Truth
    as found in the Bible. Evan Roberts was a coal miner but an
    ardent student of the Scriptures and led Wales in the 1905
    revival.
16 By sharing your testimony. Tell about answers to prayer that you
    have just received. Psalm 50:15 "And call upon Me in the day
    of trouble: I will deliver thee, and thou shalt glorify Me." We
    can best glorify Him by quietly telling the story.
17 By a comforting ministry to the bereaved. This can be very
    effective if tact is used. Choose appropriate tracts, flowers,
    Christian literature, run errands for the sick.
18 By giving food to the hungry, water to the thirsty, clothes to the
    naked, visiting jails. Matthew 25:34-36 "Then shall the King say
    unto them on His right hand, Come, ye blessed of My Father,
    inherit the kingdom prepared for you from the foundation of
    the world: For I was an hungered, and ye gave Me meat: I was
    thirsty, and ye gave Me drink; I was a stranger, and ye took Me
    in: naked, and ye clothed Me: I was sick, and ye visited me: I
    was in prison, and ye came unto Me."
19 By caring for the fatherless (orphans) and widows. James 1:27
    "Pure religion and undefiled before God and the Father is this,
    To visit the fatherless and widows in their affliction, and to
    keep himself unspotted from the world."
20 By radiating happiness. Story of shoemaker measuring a lady's
    foot. He was very happy. She was a rich society woman, a
    friend of royalty, but very sad. "Why are you so happy?" "Jesus
    has forgiven all my sins and put song in my heart." The woman
    was convicted and later converted, and witnessed to many of
    noble birth including the Emperor of Russia.
21 By preaching when the pastor is sick or on leave. John Wesley
    listened four nights to a carpenter in Herrnhut in Germany
    during the Moravian revival.
22 By singing. Mr. Sankey controlled and quieted crowds that the
    great D. L. Moody could not handle. Sing in the choir, or sing

solos if God has given you that talent.

23 By painting a picture. The story of Stensburg's painting that led to Zinzendorf's consecration and the Moravian revival in 1727.

24 By doing what we can, as best as we can, all the time.

Conclusion

Then some day we will hear the words of Matthew 25:21,23 "His Lord said unto him, 'Well done, good and faithful servant; thou hast been faithful over a few things, I will make thee ruler over many things. Enter thou into the joy of thy Lord.' "

In verse 21 it was said to the man that was faithful with five talents.

In verse 23 it was said to the man that was faithful with two talents.

1 Corinthians 4:2 "Moreover it is required in stewards, that a man be found faithful."

Review Questions

1 Show from Scripture the division between clergy and laity.
2 How can we prevent a Church from becoming a "one man affair"?
3 What lesson for a layman can be learned from Mark 14:3-9?
4 List ten ways laymen can prepare themselves for Christian service.
5 Of the ten ways mentioned in question 4, which do you consider to be the most important? Why?
6 Mention a dozen things that an ordinary Christian can do to help spread the Gospel.
7 List three different ones that Andrew brought to Jesus.
8 Of the twenty-four things mentioned in point II of the lesson, how many have you personally tried?
9 Tell a personal experience of witnessing with a story of answered prayer. Psalm 50:15.
10 Will Matthew 25:21,23 be spoken to clergy or laity? Explain.

Revival

Introduction

A great deal of preaching is on this subject today. This is a very good sign.

The only way to avoid spiritual decay is by progress. (Evangelize or fossilize.)

From Psalm 24:3,4 we learn that a revival affects three things;

1 Hands. These must be clean. They represent our actions.
2 Heart. It must be pure. The heart represents our feelings.
3 Tongue. It must not be deceitful. It must be honest. It represents speech.

These three things, actions, feelings, and speech, represent our true character.

I What is Revival?

Revival means to come back to life, to return to consciousness, to return to vigor from a state of langour or neglect.

There is a difference between evangelism and revival. A sinner needs evangelism to bring him to the Lord. You cannot revive a dead person. He needs new birth.

But the twice-born Christian that backslides or sins needs to be revived.

A revival is the return of the Christian from backsliding.

It invariably includes a deep conviction of sin.

Revival is a new beginning of obedience to Almighty God.

It produces a great effect on all that the revived one meets.

It brings a deep sense of the presence, glory and wonder of God.

II When is a Revival Needed?

You will not purchase a hat unless you need it. You will not be revived unless you feel or desire a need for it.

When you hunger and thirst for revival, God will give it.

The river of God is flowing but you will not drink of it until you are thirsty.

Revival is needed when there is a want of brotherly love. Dissensions, jealousies, evil speaking, etc., are sure signs that a revival is needed.

Is my heart filled with bitterness or hatred? If so, then I need to be revived.

Worldliness is a sure sign. Do I love the comics more than my Bible? Would I rather go to a show than to Sunday School? Am I more interested in being popular than in humbly serving the Lord Jesus Christ?

Gross sin is an open sign that revival is needed. Stealing, lying, disobedience.

Revived Christians are concerned for the lost. Backslidden, cold Christians don't care if sinners go to hell or not.

III How to Get Revival

2 Chronicles 7:14 lays down four simple concise steps to revival: "If My people, which are called by My Name, shall humble themselves, and pray, and seek My face, and turn from their wicked ways; then will I hear from heaven, and will forgive their sin, and will heal their land."

The text first defines who may be revived: "My people . . . called by My Name," Christians are called after Christ: *Christ*ians or Christ-ones.

Only God's true children can be revived. Sinners need to be converted.

1 Humble themselves. This is not me humbling you, but you yourself voluntarily bowing in contrite submission. Humble is the opposite of proud. Away with pride.

2 Pray. God is waiting for you to open you mouth and start confessing. Lay aside the memorized prayer and just confess your individual sins.

3 Seek My face. To seek is to search diligently. Why search for His face? Because when we sinned He turned away from us. Confession restores contact.

4 Turn from wicked ways. This is true repentance. Ask God to give you a bitter hatred for sin. Sin crucified my Savior. It was my sin. I hate it.

The results of meeting these four conditions or requirements:
1 God will hear your prayers — hear in the sense of receiving graciously and answering.
2 God will forgive your sin. This is the most glorious thing in this world.
3 God will heal and strengthen your lives. The Spirit and the Son will direct you.

IV Why do we need Revival?

1 Peter 4:17 "For the time is come that judgment must begin at the house of God: and if it first begin at us, what shall the end be of them that obey not the Gospel of God? And if the righteous scarcely be saved, where shall the ungodly and the sinner appear?"

We need to be revived because of sin. Coldness and backsliding are results of sin.

"Scarcely be saved," the battle is terrific. Many fall by the wayside.

We need to love God more than parents or anything else. Only the revived man can love God with all the heart, soul, strength, and mind. Luke 10:27.

We need to love and read God's Word every day. The cold heart reads in a cold mechanical way but the revived one rejoices in the message.

We need to pray. Backsliders' prayers are cold, long, uninteresting, formal and dead. But the prayer of the revived Christian stirs others as it touches the Throne.

We need to walk circumspectly — being discreet, cautious, watchful and guarded.

The cold Christian is half asleep spiritually and an easy target for the devil.

We need to be disciplined. This is emphasized in Luke 14:25-33:
1 "Cannot be My disciple," if I love father, mother, wife, children, brethren, and my own life more than I love the Lord Jesus.
2 "Cannot be My disciple," if I refuse to bear the cross.
3 "Cannot be My disciple," if I refuse to forsake all luxuries, comforts, anything to save a soul for the Lord Jesus.

We need to be delivered from sin: big sins, little sins, open sins, secret sins, anger, wrath, filthy communication, lies, impatience, temper, dishonesty, coldness of heart, emptiness, dryness, hardness, fear, worry, liquor, gambling, pride, self-righteousness, unbelief, hate, self-pity, criticism, unkind thoughts, sharp words, jealousy, cheating, hypocrisy, strife, lust of the eye, evil or impure thoughts, selfishness, covetousness, gossip, worldliness, stealing, adultery, murder, Sabbath-breaking, disobedience to parents, fighting, cursing, revenge, testimony failure, failure to set a good example, neglect of the Bible, neglect of prayer, grieving or quenching the Spirit, etc., etc.

V. Results of a Revival

The Hebrides revival: People lost in the glory and wonder of God, a deep sense of the presence of God, men moving about with bowed heads, subdued in His presence, a deep sense of sin, conversion of sinners, preaching dealt on the severity of God, family worship to the fore, social evils swept away in a night as by a flood, very few backsliders from campaign.

The revival in Wales: Vested interests aroused to opposition, groups of revived ones went preaching everywhere, debts were paid, confessions were made, theater going dropped, interest in sports dropped, dance halls were deserted, open air Gospel services were held everywhere, miners treated their horses much better, and were filled with hymns and not with cursing, there was a great emphasis on singing.

The revival in East Central Africa: Great emphasis on the daily walk, brokenness of spirit, a new recognition of the terribleness of sin, moment by moment communion with the Spirit, instant confession, much emphasis on the Blood, a constant growth, spread and deepening of the revival.

The revival in China: Confessions, revivals, conversions, demons cast out, divisions in churches healed, cooperation among Mission Societies and churches.

The Moravian revival: A prayer meeting that lasted 100 years (1727 to 1827), in thirty years they took the Gospel to every country in Europe, pagan races in North and South America and Africa, then Greenland, founders of modern missions.

Conclusion

Do you hunger and thirst for revival? We may have it if we pay the price. Each one of us has an influence. The backslider for evil and the revived Christian both have the potential of great blessing to humanity.

Review Questions

1   What three parts of a Christian are affected by a revival? Psalm 24:3,4

2   Show the difference between revival and evangelism.

3   Define revival.

4   When does an individual (or Church) need revival?

5   List the four basic requirements for revival as set forth in 2 Chronicles 7:14?

6   Give results of meeting the four conditions of 2 Chronicles 7:14.

7   Does 1 Peter 4:17, include revival? Explain.

8   What is the relationship between discipline and revival?

9   List ten sins of which the average Christian is often guilty. Are you presently guilty?

10   List ten results of revival.

73

Love

Introduction

Notes from "Paul's Hymn of Love," D. M. Panton on 1 Corinthians 13.

We are acquainted with human love. We revel in the human love of parents. We delight in the love of classmates, friends and relatives. But their love is fickle and falls far short of the standards of love as set forth in 1 Corinthians 13, the love chapter of the Bible. 1 Corinthians 13:1-13 is an exposition defining the love of Christ.

The richest, highest possible attainments in a church are useless without true Christian love.

Verse 1, The oratory of men is useless in a church or life without true love.

Story of two preachers in Wiseton, Canada. One preacher was an orator, beautiful language, exquisite illustrations, but was cold, without love. The other man was a poor speaker but abounded in love. The people chose the second man as their pastor.

Therefore love is desirable both in:

1 Me — as the one giving this message.
2 You — as the one that will go out and live the Christ constrained love life.

I Love is Essential 1 Corinthians 13:2

1 **Love is more important than prophecy.** The Bible is full of prophecies but combined they are not as great as love.

Prophecy covers the whole range of eternity from creation to the end of Revelation. Prophecy is excellent, but it is useless without love.

2 **Love is more important than mysteries.** This includes the whole range of the unknown: Trinity, Incarnation, Election, etc.

A knowledge so great that could understand all these is useless without love.

3 **Love is more important than knowledge.** This includes the whole

range of possible learning: schools, universities and college degrees.

These are all wonderful *if* they are accompanied by love, the dynamic of life.

4 **Love is more important than faith** — the whole range of the inward devotional life of a man.

Faith as a grain of mustard seed would be wonderful, but useless without love.

Without love, man is nothing. He is a nonentity, a nobody.

Story: A missionary in North West China never learned to speak Chinese very well, but was deeply appreciated because he loved the people. The people knew it and said he smiled and spoke the language of love. And they loved him, too.

II Love is Generous 1 Corinthians 13:3

Giving without love is useless. To give with a harsh spirit is useless.

God manifested His love by giving. The gift of Christ to man was bathed in love.

Christmas gifts may be without love — just as a matter of courtesy.

1 Utmost possible sacrifices of property are useless if the action is not governed and immersed in love.

2 Utmost possible sacrifices of one's person (martyrdom) is useless without being impregnated with His love, divine love, the love of God.

III Love is Able to Suffer 1 Corinthians 13:4a

This I believe is the most outstanding quality of love.

Lovelorn columns in the daily papers are full of stories of offended lovers. Feelings are hurt and they think that they are no longer in love.

True love says, I love you and will go through fire, sorrow and trouble for you. True love is able to endure suffering and yet remain sweet and kind.

The Christian pathway is one of suffering, yet the Christian learns to love. Through suffering his Christian character matures and deepens.

Love that turns to hate overnight was mere human love or perhaps only infatuation. This is well illustrated in the story in 2 Samuel 13:15.

True love involved a Calvary. God loved us so much that His great love could find expression in nothing less than the suffering of Calvary.

IV Love is not 1 Corinthians 13:4b-6a

1 **Envious** "love envieth not" True love does not envy success, gifts, talents and possessions of others.
2 **Boastful** "vaunteth not itself." It does not show off. It maintains humility.
3 **Conceited** "is not puffed up." True love always prefers the other one to self.
4 **Rude:** "doth not behave itself unseemly." It is never coarse or offensive. True love is courteous at *all* times. (Lovers, remember this at all times.)
5 **Selfish** "seeketh not her own." Love sacrifices and gives generously.
6 **Irritable** "is not easily provoked." True love is not touchy. It absorbs much.
7 **Censorious** "thinketh no evil." It is not critical, reproving, carping, nagging, suspicious or blaming.
8 **Sin loving** "rejoiceth not in iniquity." True love hates and abominates sin.

V Love is 1 Corinthians 13:6b-8a

1 **Truthful** "rejoiceth in the truth." Love delights to tell the truth. Lovers are not afraid to confide their weaknesses to their partners for mutual benefit.
2 **Sustaining** "beareth all things." True love does not collapse under strain, emotional, mental or physical.
3 **Trusting** "believeth all things." True love thinks good motives (not suspicious).
4 **Hopeful** "hopeth all things." True love always expects the best.
5 **Enduring** "endureth all things." It endures through time, deception and even death.
6 **Successful** "Love never faileth." This is true because Romans 8:28 is true.

VI **Love is Eternal** 1 Corinthians 13:8b-12

1 Love will outlive prophecy. Prophecies will fail.
2 Love will outlive tongues. Tongues too will cease one day.
3 Love will outlive knowledge. Knowledge will vanish away.

God is *Love*. 1 John 4:16. Love is an attribute of the Almighty.

Heaven and earth may pass away but love will abide. Love is eternal.

When manhood comes, verses 9-12, we put away childish things for
   the adult things.

We put away the fleeting things of youth for the mature knowledge
   of adulthood.

VII **Love is Supreme** 1 Corinthians 13:13

1 Love is greater than faith. Salvation is wrapped up in faith, yet love
     is far superior. Love was the motive and power undergirding
     salvation.
2 Love is greater than hope. Romans 8:24 "For we are saved by
     hope." Heaven is so different from earth for it is controlled by
     love.

Christ, the One who indwells us desires that daily we should manifest
   this love.

The world is dying for a little bit of love. Let us share His love with
   others.

Conclusion

A story illustrating 1 Corinthians 13:13.

A mother loved her wayward son who was charged with a horrible
   murder.

1 Her faith was shaken when he frankly confessed the gruesome
     details.
2 Hope remained to the last for a pardon for her son.
3 After the execution her faith and hope were gone, but love
     remained.

   He was still her boy and she loved him just the same. This is the love
   of Christ that constrains us to serve Him day by day.

Review Questions

1 What is the main difference between human and divine love?
2 Of all the gifts or talents that one could choose, which is the

highest? Why?

3 List four things less important than love.

4 What is the greatest demonstration of love that the world has ever known?

5 What in your opinion is the most outstanding characteristic of love? Explain.

6 What characteristic distinguishes true and false love?

7 From 1 Corinthians 13:4-6, list the seven negative aspects of love.

8 From 1 Corinthians 13:6-8, list the six positive aspects of love.

9 When a man is converted, what two wonderful things does he then possess?

10 Illustrate how love can be greater than faith or hope.

74

Praise

Introduction

Notes from Mr. Earl Bittenbender and the *New Topical Text Book*, R. A. Torrey.

What is the most important thing in life? To earn a living? To get saved and go to heaven? To serve God? I believe the answer is to praise God.

The shorter catechism's first question "What is the chief end of man?" has this answer: "Man's chief end is to glorify God and to enjoy Him forever."

Isaiah 43:7 "Even every one that is called by My name: for I have created him for My glory." Created to praise and glorify the Lord day by day.

Our life should be a song of praise to the glory of God. 1 Corinthians 10:31 "Whether therefore ye eat, or drink, or whatsoever ye do, do all to the glory of God."

Is praising God a selfish desire on God's part? Certainly not. Praise was the purpose for which He created us. We ought to voluntarily give praise daily.

I The Meaning of Praise

Dictionary: To bestow approval upon; to honor; to worship; to glorify; commendation.

The Hebrew word *yadah* means, "To stretch out the hand," and is translated "praise." That is, to hold out the hands in reverence, to open the hands and let go of everything, just stand and praise God open-handedly

Our problem is to let go of things, to let go of our problems and service and give ourselves to praising the Lord.

We only praise something that we honor and prize highly. If we hold the Lord in the highest state of respect and admiration it will be easy to praise Him.

II Praise is Obligatory

1 *From angels.* Psalm 103:20 "Bless the Lord, ye His angels." See also Psalm 148:2.
2 *From saints.* Psalm 30:4 "Sing unto the Lord, O ye saints of His, and give thanks at the remembrance of His holiness." Psalm 149:5 "Let the saints be joyful in glory: let them sing aloud upon their beds."
3 *From nations.* Psalm 117:1 "O praise the Lord, all ye nations: praise Him, all ye people."
4 *From children.* Matthew 21:16 ". . . out of the mouth of babes and sucklings Thou hast perfected praise." See also Psalm 8:2.
5 *From high and low.* Psalm 148:11 "Kings of the earth, and all people; princes, and all judges of the earth."
6 *From young and old.* Psalm 148:12 "Both young men and maidens; old men, and children."
7 *From all creation.* Psalm 150:6 "Let everything that hath breath praise the Lord." Psalm 148:1-10, God gets praise from: the heavens, the heights, angels, hosts, sun, moon, stars, the earth, dragons, deeps, fire, hail, snow, vapors, stormy winds, hills, mountains, fruit trees, cedar trees, beasts, cattle, creeping things and birds.

III The Reasons Why we Praise the Lord

1 *Because of God's majesty.* Isaiah 24:14 "They shall lift up their voice, they shall sing for the majesty of the Lord."
2 *Because of God's glory.* Psalm 138:5 "Yea, they shall sing in the ways of the lord: for great is the glory of the Lord."
3 *Because of God's excellency.* Psalm 148:13 "Let them praise the Name of the Lord: for His Name alone is excellent."
4 *Because of God's greatness.* Psalm 145:3 "Great is the Lord, and greatly to be praised; and His greatness is unsearchable."
5 *Because of the Lord's holiness.* Exodus 15:11 "Who is like unto Thee, O Lord . . . who is like Thee, glorious in holiness, fearful in praise, doing wonders?"
6 *Because of God's wisdom.* Daniel 2:20 'Blessed be the name of God for ever and ever: for wisdom and might are his."
7 *Because of God's power.* Psalm 21:13 "Be Thou exalted, Lord, in Thine own strength: so will we sing and praise Thy power."
8 *Because of God's goodness.* Psalm 107:8, 15, 21, 31 "Oh that men

would praise the Lord for His goodness." This is important for it is repeated four times.

9 *Because of God's mercy.* 2 Chronicles 20:21 "Praise the Lord; for His mercy endureth forever." We are saved through His mercy.

10 *Because of God's loving-kindness and truth.* Psalm 138:2 ". . . and praise Thy Name for Thy lovingkindness and for Thy truth."

11 *Because of God's faithfulness and truth.* Isaiah 25:1 "O Lord, Thou art my God; I will exalt Thee, I will praise Thy Name; for Thou hast done wonderful things; Thy counsels of old are faithfulness and truth."

12 *Because He has provided salvation.* Luke 1:68,69 "Blessed be the Lord God of Israel; for He hath visited and redeemed His people, and hath raised up an horn of salvation."

13 *Because of God's wonderful works.* Psalm 150:2 "Praise Him for His mighty acts." See also Psalm 107:8,15,21,31. These works include creation, redemption, consolation, just judgment, true counsel, keeping His promises, pardon of sin, spiritual health, constant preservation, protection, answered prayer, the hope of glory, all physical, material and spiritual blessings.

IV How to Praise the Lord

1 With the understanding. Psalm 47:7 "Sing ye praises with understanding." 1 Corinthians 14:15.

2 With the soul. Psalm 103:1 "Bless the Lord, O my soul: and all that is within me."

3 With the whole heart. Psalm 9:1 "I will praise Thee, O Lord, with my whole heart."

4 With the lips. Psalm 63:3 "My lips shall praise Thee." Psalm 119:171.

5 With the mouth. Psalm 51:15 "My mouth shall shew forth Thy praise."

6 With joy. Psalm 63:5 "My mouth shall praise Thee with joyful lips."

7 With gladness. 2 Chronicles 29:30 "And they sang praises with gladness, and they bowed their heads and worshipped." Not mere mechanical praise, but joyful, heartfelt praise.

8 With thankfulness. Psalm 147:7 "Sing unto the Lord with thanksgiving."

9 Continually. Psalm 71:6 "My praise shall be continually of Thee."

10 To the end of life. Psalm 104:33 "I will sing unto the Lord as long as I live."
11 More and more. Psalm 71:14 "But I will hope continually and will yet praise Thee more and more." The longer we live, more and more praiseworthy things come to us.
12 Day by day. 1 Chronicles 30:21 "... and the Levites and the priests praised the Lord day by day, singing with loud instruments unto the Lord."

V Some Things for Which to Praise the Lord

We should praise the Lord in sickness, in adversity and in health and prosperity.

We should praise the Lord for anything and everything, Philippians 4:6.

The true Christian is one who can trust and praise the Lord even through blinding tears. It is enough to know that God plans and does all things well. Romans 8:28.

Conclusion

Perhaps we realize that we have not praised enough. Pray that God will teach us to praise Him much more in the future, beginning today. Psalm 51:15 "O Lord, open Thou my lips." Cause me to praise Thee more and more.

Praise is the precious privilege of every born again believer in Jesus Christ.

Sing a great deal. This is one good way to praise the Lord.

If people praise us for our accomplishments, let us be sure to pass the praise to *Him*.

It is easy to praise one who is truly worthy of praise, and Jesus is worthy, Revelation 5:9.

It is easier for God to get money or service than praise from His children.

Praise is an attitude of the heart. 1 Corinthians 10:31, Whatsoever we do — do for His glory.

Review Questions

1 What is the chief end of man?
2 What is the basic meaning of the Hebrew word, *yadah*?
3 List seven classes of people upon whom praise is obligatory.

4   To what extent is praise optional?

5   Mention ten things about God that we should praise.

6   What are the two basic works of God for which we should praise Him?

7   Name five parts of the body that should be utilized in praising God.

8   List two handmaidens of praise.

9   Is it true that praise reaches a crescendo at conversion and then tapers off? Explain.

10   Is this statement good or bad, "My child is sick — praise the Lord?" Explain.

75

The Grace of Giving

Introduction

2 Corinthians 8:7 "Therefore, as ye abound in every thing, in faith, and utterance, and knowledge, and in all diligence, and in your love to us, see that ye abound in this grace also."

The context shows that he is speaking of giving.

It is Christmastime which brings its joys and problems of Christmas cards and gifts.

Christmas is rightly a time of giving. Commercialization has almost ruined Christmas with stores advertising gifts, etc.

For many children the spirit of Christmas is lost: the attitude today is to *receive* gifts instead of giving and honoring the Savior on His birthday. The first Christmas was marked by *giving*. God the Father gave the Gift of His only begotten Son to this world.

In celebration and commemoration of this it is good for us to give, but we ought to remember that "it is more blessed to give than to receive," Acts 20:35.

In the Christmas story we have the wise men giving expensive gifts to Jesus.

I What the Wise Men Gave Matthew 2:1

In the story of the wise men we find a beautiful progression of faith:
1 Seeking. They saw the star in the sky and departed following it.
2 Finding. They went to Jerusalem enquiring of Herod where the Baby was.
3 Worshipping. They fall on their knees before the Savior in worship.
4 Giving. After worship, or as a part of their worship, they gave their gifts.

The gifts that the wise men gave are very interesting:
1 Gold. A fitting gift and tribute to a King. Jesus was King of kings.
2 Frankincense. A yellow substance used in incense. This would have been given as an acknowledgment of His divinity.

3. Myrrh. Used in perfuming ointments from a bitter herb. This was given as a tribute to the suffering Savior. See Mark 15:23, myrrh mixed with wine.

We may not be able to give gold, frankincense and myrrh, but what can we give?

II What we Ought to Give

1 Our bodies. Romans 12:1 "I beseech you therefore, brethren, by the mercies of God, that ye present your bodies a living sacrifice. . ." The Macedonians gave themselves to God, 2 Corinthians 8:5 "They . . . first gave their own selves to the Lord."

2 Ourselves wholly to the things of God. 1 Timothy 4:15 "Meditate upon these things; give thyself wholly (completely) to them."

3 Attendance to the reading of the Word. 1 Timothy 4:13 "Till I come, give attendance to reading, to exhortation, to doctrine."

4 Earnest heed to what we have heard. Hebrews 2:1 "Therefore we ought to give the more earnest heed to the things which we have heard."

5 Ourselves continually to prayer. Acts 6:4 "But we will give ourselves continually to prayer, and to the ministry of the Word."

6 Thanks for everything. 1 Thessalonians 5:18 "In every thing give thanks: for this is the will of God in Christ Jesus concerning you."

7 Money to the Lord. 2 Corinthians 8:2-4. The Macedonians out of their deep poverty gave liberally to the Lord, and Paul accepted the gifts as an act of fellowship.

III How are We to Give to the Lord?

1 **Systematically** 1 Corinthians 16:2 "Upon the first day of the week let every one of you lay by him in store, as God hath prospered him."

Not only giving at Christmas time but every week of the year.

Be businesslike in your giving and God will reward your honesty and scrupulousness.

2 **Individually** 1 Corinthians 16:2 "Let every one of you lay by him in store . . ."

Not only the head of the home, but mother and the children, too.

Giving is not only for the rich. It is for the poor, too.

The only difference will be in the size and quality of the gift.

Mrs. Hsi in China, a very poor peasant, ate less in order to save a bit of food in order to give to the Lord and the Lord abundantly blessed her spiritually.

3 Proportionately 1 Corinthians 16:2 ". . . as God hath prospered"

In the Old Testament, under the law, they gave a tithe — one-tenth of their income.

The tithe, Leviticus 27:30, was holy unto the Lord, and did not belong to the person.

We are not under law today. We are not forced to give a tithe of all that we receive. But we are under grace which is a covenant of love.

Which is stronger, the power of law or the power of love? It seems to me that love is greater, and that we ought to give the tithes plus offerings.

Personally we give our testimony that since 1940 we have faithfully tithed and God has blessed us spiritually and economically.

R. G. Letourneau gave 10%; then as God prospered him he increased the gift to 20%, and later even much higher.

God gives abundantly to those who give to Him. Prove God daily in this matter.

4 Cheerfully 2 Corinthians 9:7 ". . . for God loveth a cheerful giver."

"There's that collection plate again! Do I have to give something again?"

This is the wrong attitude. We ought to count it a great privilege and joy to be able to give something back to Him who gave so much for us.

God loves the one that gives willingly and cheerfully. We like to receive gifts that have been cheerfully given to us — not grudgingly.

5 Give as Christ gave He gave everything that he had, even life itself.

Let us abound in the splendid grace of giving.

6 Sacrificially. 2 Corinthians 8:2, they gave out of their deep poverty.

The widow gave two mites which was all her living.

God measures gifts by how much is left, not by how much we give.

God sees the heart of the giver rather than the size of the gift. Let us with gladsome hearts of love give to the Savior.

IV The Rewards of Giving

Philippians 4:18 ". . . the things which were sent from you, an odour of a sweet smell, a sacrifice acceptable, well pleasing to God."

Our gifts, though small, surely delight the heart of the Father in heaven.

Blessings follow generous giving to the Lord. The Father gives to us in return.

The blessing is not necessarily material abundance, though it very often is.

Acts 20:35 "It is more blessed to give than to receive."

Matthew 6:20 "But lay up for yourselves treasures in heaven." This is a command.

Malachi 3:10 "Bring ye all the tithes into the storehouse, that there may be meat in Mine house, and prove Me now herewith, saith the Lord of hosts, if I will not open you the windows of heaven, and pour you out a blessing, that there shall not be room enough to receive it." This is God's solemn promise.

We have faithfully tithed and when we have been in need the Lord has abundantly given to us.

V To Whom Should We Give?

Give to the poor and needy, to the orphans and widows, James 1:27; Matthew 5:42.

Give for the needs of the church and worship.

Give for the furtherance of the Gospel.

Conclusion

Inadequate giving is evidence of inadequate teaching or of inadequate spiritual life.

Review Questions

1   Give the fourfold progression of faith in the story of the wise men.

2   What three gifts did the wise men give Jesus?

3   What should we give the Lord before giving our money? Two Scriptures.

4   True or false: "The Lord expects the rich to give their money and the poor to give themselves." Explain the reason for your answer.

5   List five ways that we are to give.

6   If it is true that we are not under law, then isn't it advisable to give as the needs are presented? Explain.

7   Some Christians seem to be more generous than others. Does this mean that they have the gift of giving? Explain.
8   List three rewards of giving mentioned in Philippians 4:18.
9   Prove that giving is not optional.
10 What is the New Testament storehouse? (Malachi 3:10)

76

Divine Healing

Introduction

Notes from: *Miraculous Healing*, H. W. Frost; T. T. Shields' sermons; *Heresies Ancient and Modern*, O. J. Sanders; *Asking and Receiving*, John R. Rice; *J. F. B. Commentary*; and writings of Morris Cerullo.

Let us consider the passage 2 Corinthians 12:7-10. Here we have Paul the faith healer, praying three times for deliverance from sickness and it was denied him.

In Acts 28, Paul performs two miracles. In verses 3-6, the miracle of no harm from the viper bites and in verses 7,8, Paul healed Publius' father of a fever.

1 Purpose of the sickness, 2 Corinthians 12:7 — to keep Paul humble. Self-exaltation is indeed a very dangerous thing.

2 Source of the thorn or sickness — it was the messenger of Satan, but allowed by God.

Some sickness comes from the devil and some comes from the Lord.

3 What was the sickness? — a thorn in the flesh, verse 7. It was a bodily affliction that caused acute pain.

It is thought that it was a chronic ophthalmia — an eye disease inducing weakness and a repulsive appearance. Galatians 4:15, ". . . ye would have plucked out your own eyes, and have given them to me. Galatians 6:11 "Ye see how large a letter I have written unto you with mine own hand." That is, large writing due to failing eyesight.

4 Paul's prayer, 2 Corinthians 12:8, was for its departure and his own healing. He was so desirous of it that he prayed for it three times.

5 God's answer to Paul's prayer: "My grace is sufficient for thee." The Lord leaves the thorn but adds grace — the tender grace of the Lord.

6 Paul's reaction to this answer, verse 9, ". . . will I rather glory in my infirmities," and verse 10, "I take pleasure in infirmities."

7 The cause of Paul's rejoicing, verse 10, "For when I am weak, then am I strong."

In sickness we rely on God and are stronger than at any other time.

I Is God Capable of Healing Miracles?

The Bible is a supernatural book — a miracle book, and it tells the true stories of many miracles.

The lepers were cleansed; the eyes of the blind were opened; the deaf could hear; the lame could walk; the demon possessed were delivered; the dead were raised.

The greatest miracle is the resurrection of our Savior. All other miracles are inferior.

Our God is a miracle working God. *Jehovah Rophi* (Exodus 15:26) is one of His names.

Exodus 15:26 "I am the Lord that healeth thee." See Psalm 103:3.

Our God is the God of the impossible. Matthew 19:26 ". . . with men this is impossible; but with God all things are possible." Luke 18:27 "The things which are impossible with men are possible with God."

Could God have healed Paul? Yes, certainly. God could have healed him instantaneously.

Why didn't God heal Paul? It was not the Lord's will.

This is the important crucial question in a given case. Is it the will of the Lord?

II Does God Heal Miraculously Today?

Yes, He certainly does, if and when it is His will to do so.

My wife, Mrs. Douglas, was healed of eclampsia in West China in February, 1951.

Dr. H. W. Frost, in his book, *Miraculous Healing,* tells in detail of ten cases of sickness. Of the ten, five were miraculously healed. One was healed of strep throat; another of seasickness and complications; heart attack; insanity; nervous prostration.

It is usually God's will to heal. In a lifetime we are healed of many diseases. We only die of one sickness — the last one.

Healing is normal and generally to be expected.

Does God always heal? No. Paul was not healed.

If we were always healed, then we would never die.

III Is Healing in the Atonement?

The faith healers say that it is, and base their claims on Matthew 8:7, and Isaiah 53:5.

We understand this to mean soul sickness for bodily sickness is not mentioned by Peter referring to this passage in 1 Peter 2:24. "Who His own Self bare our sins in His own body on the tree, that we . . ." He didn't mention physical healing, but soul healing from the ravages of sin.

If healing is in the atonement, then all sickness is of the devil.

The sickness would be a sign of backsliding. But this is not true in the case of Job.

This teaching would take all comfort away from the sick-bed.

Then medicines and doctors would be wrong. But God told Hezekiah to use figs as medicine, and Paul told Timothy to use wine as medicine for his stomach.

If healing is in the atonement, both salvation and healing would be eternal. But history proves that even the very best of saints have to die.

The faith healer cannot answer this question: If healing is in the atonement, why do Christians die?

IV What are the Teachings of Faith Healers?

This is a summary of the teachings of Dr. A. J. Gordon and Dr. A. B. Simpson, faith healers.

1 All sickness is a direct consequence of sin and Christ came to save men from sin and all of its consequences.

2 Christ in heaven today delivers us from sin, bodily weakness and sickness.

3 The Christian has no need of doctors of medicine, for healing is in the atonement.

4 The healing ministry was intended for the entire church age.

5 It is the duty of the sick to call for the elders and be anointed with oil.

Observations: Both men experienced miraculous healing, personally and for others.

Both were overcome by sickness and died in spite of many contrary prayers.

Both fell under a spiritual cloud in sickness, concluding personal sin.

How much better to be resigned to the will of God and relax happily in the will of God.

V What is Taught in James 5:14-20?

James wrote as a Christian Jew to Christian Jews.

The sick were to call for the elders, a set, elected board, consisting of men only.

The elders are to pray over the sick and anoint him with oil.

The elders are to pray the prayer of faith, like Elijah's prayers that opened the heavens.

It is the faith of the elders, not necessarily of the sick one, that heals. See Mark 2:5 "When Jesus saw their faith, He said unto the sick of the palsy. . ."

James speaks of confessing faults one to another. ". . . *If* he have committed sins." It is possible to be sick without having committed sin. These sins will be forgiven.

VI What are the Objections to Public Healing Campaigns?

There is no record of such a thing in the New Testament.

Long thirty-minute appeals for money that rob the churches of tithes and offerings.

Fake healings bring much shame on the Lord's Name.

Many of the healings are mental, for the people were not physically sick at all.

Seventy-five percent of the sicknesses are recoverable without a doctor or medicine.

To throw away medical advice after following it for years can be suicide.

Some in the excitement think they are healed, but later realize the truth. This leads to disappointment, disillusionment and sometimes to despondency and hardness.

Sometimes people demand that God perform a miracle against His will because of Luke 11:10.

The wrong attitude to sickness is given. One ought not to struggle against Him, but yield to him.

VII What are the Blessings from Sickness?

Job learned to know God better than ever before.

The blind man had the miracle performed (John 9:1-38) showing forth the works of God.

Lazarus was allowed to die but was resurrected for the glory of the Lord, John 11:4.

Sickness kept Paul from self-exaltation, 2 Corinthians 12:7.

Sickness can be invaluable chastening which we all need, Hebrews 12:11.

A deathbed scene with the saint relaxed and happy in the will of God is the great capstone of the race. Jesus promises, "My grace is sufficient." — even in sickness.

Review Questions

1   From 2 Corinthians 12:7, answer the following: a) purpose of the sickness b) type of sickness and c) God's answer.
2   Mention five miracles recorded in the Bible.
3   What is the meaning of *Jehovah Rophi*?
4   Are there any genuine miraculous healings today?
5   Why is God not obligated to heal us every time that we get sick?
6   Is healing in the atonement? Explain.
7   Give five teachings of faith healers regarding sickness.
8   What is taught in James 5:14-20, regarding healing?
9   List seven objections to a public healing campaign.
10 Name five blessings from sickness.

77

The Lord's Day

Introduction

In America, Sunday has become a "fun-day"; a "holi-day" instead of a holy day.

Our experience is that those who honor the Lord's day are honored by God.

In West China we found that the church that kept Sunday with closed stores prospered spiritually.

The student who honors God with no secular study on Sunday will be God-blessed.

But the problem that faces us today is, Can we force Christians to keep the Lord's day the way the Sabbath used to be kept by law enforcement?

The Republic of the Philippines has laws that demand that certain types of business must close on Sunday, but unfortunately keeps the public markets, cockpits and entertainment houses open.

I The Origin of the Lord's Day

The Lord's Day (Sunday) is a new Testament fact, but it has its roots in the Sabbath of the Old Testament.

In Genesis 2:2,3 "And on the seventh day God ended His work which He had made; and He rested on the seventh day ... and God blessed the seventh day, and sanctified it; because that in it he had rested from all His work."

But the Sabbath was not given to man till 2500 years later in Exodus 20:8-10.

However, from Exodus 16:23, it would seem that some form of Sabbath was kept then.

At the giving of the law in Exodus 20, Sabbath keeping became part of the Decalogue.

The Old Testament Sabbath was a day of rest, not of sacrifice or worship. It was a day when beats of burden, slaves and humans all rested. It was not associated with temple attendance or any religious observance.

The Sabbath was given to Israel as a sign of the covenant. Exodus 31:13 "Speak thou also unto the children of Israel, saying, Verily My sabbaths ye shall keep: for it is a sign between Me and you throughout your generations."

Exodus 31:17 "It (the Sabbath) is a sign between Me (the Lord God) and the children of Israel for ever."

The Pharisees kept a perverted Sabbath in Jesus' day, for they had turned the Sabbath into a stern, hard, ritualistic day, hedged with strict limitations.

In the book of Acts we find the church keeping the first day of the week instead of the seventh day as a day of worship and good deeds.

II The Observance of the Sabbath under Law

1 Even the servants and cattle were forced to rest, Exodus 20:10.
2 No manner of work was to be done on the Sabbath Day, Exodus 20:10. Food was cooked on Friday.
3 No purchase was to be made on the Sabbath Day, Nehemiah 10:31; 13:15-17.
4 No burdens were to be carried on the Sabbath Day, Nehemiah 13:19; Jeremiah 17:21.
5 No harvesting was to be done on the Sabbath Day, Exodus 34:21.
6 Death was the punishment appointed by God for those who broke the Sabbath.

The man in Numbers 15:32-36 who was found gathering sticks to build a fire was commanded to be stoned to death.

III Christ's Attitude to the Sabbath Day

The Savior did many miracles of healing on the Sabbath day which angered the Jews and made them call Jesus a "Sabbath breaker."

1 Jesus taught that He was Lord of the Sabbath. Matthew 12:8 "For the Son of man is Lord even of the Sabbath day."

As Lord of the Sabbath day he was at liberty to set aside the seventh day and institute the first day of the week.

2 Jesus taught that the Sabbath was made for man. Mark 2:27 "And He said unto them, The Sabbath was made for man, and not man for the Sabbath."

3 Jesus taught that it was right to do good on the Sabbath day,

Matthew 12:11. The sheep that fell into a pit on the Sabbath day should be removed.

Matthew 12:12 "Wherefore it is lawful to do well on the Sabbath days." And Jesus went on and healed the man with the withered hand in verse 13.

IV The True Way to Keep the Sabbath Day
Isaiah 58:13, 14

1 To delight in the Lord. Make it a special day of worship, prayer, and praise.
2 To cease from your own pleasure. It is not a day for pleasure, sport, education, but a day to do *His* pleasure. visit the sick for *Him*.
3 To make it a day that honors the Lord. Six days we work and earn our living, but one-seventh of our time belongs to the Lord to be used for *Himself* alone.

V The Apostolic Church Kept the First Day of the Week

Acts 20:7 "And upon the first day of the week, when the disciples came together to break bread, Paul preached unto them." (Regular church services)

1 Corinthians 16:2 "Upon the first day of the week let every one of you lay by him in store, as God hath prospered him." (Sunday church collections)

Revelation 1:10 "I was in the Spirit on the Lord's day." That is, Sunday, the first day of the week. Sunday, the first day of the week, was chosen because Jesus rose from the dead on the first Easter Sunday morning.

Matthew 28:1 "In the end of the Sabbath, as it began to dawn toward the first day of the week . . ." they went to the tomb and found that Jesus had risen.

Jesus remained in the grave long enough to fulfill the Jewish Sabbath.

VI How Jesus Kept the First Christian Lord's Day

1 Jesus comforted weeping Mary, John 20:13.
2 Jesus walked seven miles with two disciples, Luke 24:13.
3 Jesus gave a Bible reading to these two disciples, Luke 24:24-31.

4 Jesus sent messages to the other disciples, Matthew 28:10.
5 Jesus had a private interview with Peter, Luke 24:34.
6 Jesus met with the ten disciples and ate with them, Luke 24:36-45.
These are excellent examples for believers to follow. Do not these six
   things not fulfill Isaiah 58:13,14 most beautifully?
1 Peter 2:21, Jesus left us an example that we should follow in His
   footsteps.

VII Contrast between the Sabbath and the Lord's Day

1 The Sabbath is the seventh day and the Lord's Day is the first day
   of the week.
2 The Sabbath commemorates God's creation rest while the Lord's
   day commemorates the resurrection.
3 On the seventh day God rested. On the first day Jesus was very
   busy.
4 The Sabbath commemorates a finished creation. The Lord's day
   commemorates a finished redemption.
5 The Sabbath was a day of legal obligation. The Lord's day is for
   voluntary worship.
6 The Sabbath was for the Jews and the Lord's day is for the Church
   of Jesus Christ.

Conclusion

Is the Christian obligated to keep either or both of these special days?
The Sabbath is part of the Decalogue and is obligatory to those under
   the Law.
But the Christian is no longer under the Law.
   Romans 6:15 "What then? Shall we sin, because we are not under
   the law, but under grace? God forbid."
However, though we are not under law, the principle of keeping one
   day in seven holy unto the Lord has not changed.
In giving we are no longer forced by law to give the tithe, but under
   grace we do more. We give the tithe and love offerings. The
   principle is the same here.
The fact that we are not forced to keep the day holy ought to rejoice
   our hearts to live this day and extra hours beside for the worship
   and work of God.

Hebrews 4:1-11 speaks of the blessedness of rest. Our bodies need a day of rest.

Review Questions

1 Who was the first to keep the Sabbath Day?
2 What is the basic requirement of the Sabbath Day?
3 What was the punishment for breaking the Sabbath?
4 What was Jesus' threefold attitude toward the Sabbath Day?
5 According to Isaiah 58:13,14, how should we keep the Sabbath Day?
6 What proof do we have that the early Church kept Sunday instead of Saturday?
7 List six things that Jesus did on the first Lord's Day.
8 List six contrasts between the Sabbath and the Lord's Day.
9 What do we learn from the Sabbath from Romans 6:15?
10 List five kinds of rest referred to in Hebrews 4:1-11.

78

Christian Marriage

Introduction

Notes from *The Home*, John R. Rice, and *A Guide for the Course in Marriage and Family Relationships*, Maria Fe G. Atienza.

Marriage was meant to be happy as it is the residue of sinless Eden, Genesis 1:28.

Proverbs 18:22 "Whoso findeth a wife findeth a good thing, and obtaineth favor of the Lord."

Marriage has been ordained of the Lord for the procreation of the race and the establishment of homes for children where happiness and joy can reign.

Marriage is the oldest human institution. It is older than the church or human government.

We live in a day of low moral standards, when marriage vows are easily broken and divorce is considered common. God's laws and standards do not change.

I Reasons for Marriage

1 To obey the command of God. Genesis 1:28 "Be fruitful, and multiply, and replenish the earth."

2 For fellowship. Genesis 3:18 "And the Lord God said, It is not good that the man should be alone." The exception seems to be the pioneer missionary like the Apostle Paul in which 1 Corinthians 7:32 is true.

3 For partnership. Ecclesiastes 4:9-11. Two are better than one, for if they fall, one will lift up the other. It takes the two to make "one flesh," Genesis 2:24.

4 To satisfy biological desires. Man is born with certain desires that are good, holy and legitimate but can only be satisfied in marriage.

5 For the propagation of the human race, Genesis 1:28, Genesis 9:1.

II Whom to Marry

Christians may only marry Christians.

2 Corinthians 6:14-17 "Be ye not unequally yoked together with unbelievers."

In God's sight it is a travesty for a godly person and an ungodly one to be united in holy matrimony to be one flesh. How can they be *one* when one serves God, holiness and righteousness, while the other serves sin and Satan?

How can these who are so different form a true partnership and have fellowship?

Christian ministers of the Gospel ought not to perform mixed marriages.

Generally a boy should choose a girl of mature Christian character with similar background, tastes, education, religion and interests, a little younger than himself.

The girl accepts the proposal from a man who is of the same religion, background, education, likes and dislikes, who is a gentleman at all times.

III When to Marry

1 When God guides you into marriage after much prayer and seeking His will.

2 When you know the other person sufficiently well to know his or her likes and dislikes, good points and bad points. Hasty marriages are dangerous.

3 Wait for love. Infatuation is not sufficient. Marriage is for life, and it will take godly love (1 Corinthians 13) to make a happy home.

4 Wait until you are old enough to marry. Marriage is for adults, not for children, for it carries heavy responsibilities requiring maturity and experience.

5 Wait until moral problems are settled. Never marry a man to reform him. It is better to never marry a man whose habits can only mean bitterness and a ruined marriage and an unhappy home.

6 Wait for health. Marriage requires strong bodies. If after marriage sickness comes to you, your marriage vows require constant and loving care of the stricter member.

7 Wait for the approval of your parents. This is very important.

8 Wait for a measure of financial stability, not wealth, but some security.

9 Let both wholeheartedly agree to keep the marriage vows at any cost. If one partner is reluctant, then delay marriage, waiting for maturity and assurance.

IV Principles of a Happy Marriage

1 A successful marriage is based on genuine heart agreement of the couple.
2 They must be willing to establish a Christian home, with the husband as head of the home, the wife a pleasant helpmeet, and with the family altar.
3 It must be based on a lifetime anticipation, "till death do us part." Marriage is not an experiment for a short time. It is permanent.
4 The successful marriage should have the blessing of children. Psalm 127:3-5 "Lo, children are an heritage of the Lord . . . happy is the man that hath his quiver full of them."
5 Genuine love is an essential to a happy marriage. Ephesians 5:25 "Husbands, love your wives." Titus 2:4, wives "to love their husbands."
6 An honorable engagement tends to promote a happy, successful marriage. Young ladies, beware of the man who wants a secret engagement!
7 Insist on a public Christian wedding. Never for a moment consider elopement or a secret marriage. Marriage is far too sacred for this.
8 Let both learn to pray together over every problem and misunderstanding.
9 Let each continually express his or her love for his or her partner, both by act and word.

V Engagement and Courtship

An engagement is the honorable announcement to the community that the couple plans to marry soon — likely within a year.

To the couple, it is a time of getting better acquainted and ascertaining whether or not they are prepared for marriage and are really meant for one another.

It is natural that engaged couples will be together, talk together, and will exchange views on marriage, children, birth control, likes, ambitions, etc.

But they must not take liberties one with another, for they are not married.

Marriage privileges *must* be reserved until after marriage, lest love turn to hate and mutual respect be lost completely, 2 Samuel 13:15.

Avoid petting and caressing lest passion override reason and will, and ruin it all.

Let the couple be honest and sincere with one another.

Do nothing that will hinder your private prayer life or Christian testimony.

It is very important for future happiness that both be virgins at marriage.

VI Adultery

Exodus 20:14 "Thou shalt not commit adultery." See also Exodus 20:17.

Only by seeing how God hates adultery can we see the sanctity of marriage.

Marriage is properly called "holy matrimony" for it is indeed a holy union.

God commanded the death penalty for adultery (death for both) Leviticus 20:10.

Adultery, the scarlet sin, is the only Scriptural ground for divorce, Matthew 19:9.

Venereal disease is the physical plague that God uses to punish guilty ones.

Adultery and fornication lead to hell, Proverbs 7:27; 9:13-17; 1 Corinthians 6:9,10.

VII Divorce

Divorce was not in the original plan of God for mankind, Matthew 19:8.

Marriage is a lifetime contract. Matthew 19:6 "What therefore God hath joined together, let not man put asunder."

For one who receives a divorce for any other reason than adultery and marries another commits adultery, Matthew 19:9.

The wife that is put away, may remarry, Deuteronomy 24:2.

Six reasons from 2 Corinthians 6:14-17, why a believer should not marry an unbeliever:

1 God's command, Do not be yoked together with unbelievers.

2 Righteousness has no fellowship with unrighteousness.

3 Light has no communion with darkness.

4 Christ has no concord with Belial.
5 Believers have no part with infidels.
6 God's temple has no agreement with idols.

Conclusion

Make Christ the Head of the home — both Lord and Savior of the home.
Let the husband maintain a tender love for his wife and children.
Let the wife develop the unselfish love of a wife and mother.
Let engaged couples and young people be much in prayer about this important subject.

Review Questions

1 What is the oldest human institution?
2 Give two reasons for seeking a wife on the basis of Proverbs 18:22.
3 List five reasons for marriage.
4 List six reasons from 2 Corinthians 6:14-17, why a believer should not marry an unbeliever.
5 What six things should a man consider in choosing a wife?
6 Mention nine things to consider in the timing of marriage.
7 Give nine principles of a happy marriage.
8 What great lesson can we learn from 2 Samuel 13:15?
9 What penalty does God impose on adultery?
10 What do we learn about marriage from Matthew 19:6,8?

The Christian Home

Introduction

The Christian Church cannot flourish without the Christian home.

The Christian home is the backbone of the nation, the salt of civilization.

A Christian home is an institution where parents are bound together by Christian love; where children are welcome and Scripturally instructed, and the Lord Jesus is not only the supposed Head of the home, but the actual Head; where parents and children gather daily for family worship.

A Christian home is a place where members of the family enjoy rest, privacy, a sense of security; and learn to work, play, pray, and plan together.

A Christian home is one in which the members learn to regard one another as having equal rights; where loyalty, honesty and cooperation are practiced and learned by each member of the family team.

A Christian home is one that radiates Christ; welcomes strangers; and dispenses hospitality without measure.

A Christian home consists of God-fearing father, God-fearing mother, and God-fearing children.

Genesis 18:19 is one of the best pictures in the Bible of a Christian home.

God first recognized Abraham's success in the home, and then granted him greater responsibilities.

I God-fearing Fathers

God has placed the husband as head of the home, Genesis 18:19. Abraham commanded his household faithfully. The household includes the wife, children and servants.

Ephesians 5:23 "For the husband is the head of the wife, even as Christ is the Head of the church."

This is God's order, and the home that reverses it breaks God's plan and destroys the peace of that home.

This does not mean that the wife is a slave beneath the husband's feet. She is his helpmeet taken from his side, to remain at his side, an equal partner.

It is the husband's duty to love his wife, Ephesians 5:25 "Husbands, love your wives, even as Christ also loved the church, and gave Himself for it."

This isn't mere respect. This is the tremendous love of 1 Corinthians 13, loving in health, in sickness, in poverty and in prosperity.

The husband is required to be faithful to his wife. We live in an age of lax moral standards and easy divorce and infidelity.

The standards of God have not changed. God still demands honesty, frankness and faithfulness between the partners contracting marriage.

It is the husband's duty to comfort his wife in times of sorrow, 1 Samuel 1:8.

He ought to consult with his wife on business matters, for they are a team.

By virtue of marriage, they two have become one — a single unit — Genesis 31:4-7.

Jacob's wives rightly reply in verse 16, "Whatsoever God hath said unto thee, do." That is, we are yours, we belong to you, we obey you now.

The Christian husband will always put Christ first in his life, Luke 14:26.

He must love his wife, but he must love Christ more.

The husband is priest of the family and is responsible to establish a family altar for daily family worship. He is responsible for grace at meals.

Job offered sacrifices for the whole family, Job 1:5.

II God-fearing Mothers

Almost all great men have been made great by one or two loving women — a godly mother or a devoted wife. They are tremendous assets.

The wife's first duty is to love and serve Jesus Christ, Luke 14:26.

The wife's second duty is to obey her husband, Ephesians 5:22 "Wives, submit yourselves unto your won husbands, as unto the Lord."

Sarah was exemplary, 1 Peter 3:6 "Even as Sarah obeyed Abraham, calling him lord . . ." This is a hard lesson for the modern wife, but she can never be a happy, God-pleasing woman, until she submits to the plan of God.

The reason for this is given in 1 Timothy 2:11-15, that Eve was first in the transgression in the Garden of Eden. See also Genesis 3:16.

If the husband is unsaved she will have to become the spiritual head of the home, yet in subject to her husband. God will give wisdom and grace.

God's ideal Christian home is where both parents love Jesus.

Wives are not only to respect and obey their husbands, but they are to love them, too: Titus 2:4 Husbands need a great deal of affection, too.

The woman is not to be adorned with ornaments, 1 Timothy 2:9,10 — that is, *outward* adornments, but she ought to be adorned with good works, including:

1 Modesty and sobriety, 1 Timothy 2:9, so sadly lacking in this day and age.

2 A meek and quiet spirit, 1 Peter 3:4,5.

Good wives and good mothers are wonderful gifts from the Lord. They become a tremendous blessing to their husbands and families, Proverbs 31:10 "Who can find a virtuous woman? for her price is far above rubies."

Proverbs 31:12 "She will do him good and not evil all the days of her life."

Wives need appreciation and praise occasionally, Proverbs 31:28 "Her children arise up, and call her blessed; her husband also, and he praiseth her."

III God-Fearing Parents

A home cannot be happy without children. The parents who deliberately hinder the birth of a family are disobeying God and waiting for judgment.

God's order, "Be fruitful, and multiply, and replenish the earth," Genesis 1:28.

In some cases God closes the womb and even though parents pray for children their prayers are denied, temporarily or permanently (Hannah).

Parents are to realize that their children are a precious heritage from the Lord.

Parents are to love their children, Titus 2:4.

Parents are to bring their children to the Lord at an early age, Matthew 19:13,14.

Parents are to train and discipline their children for the Lord, Proverbs 22:6 "Train up a child in the way that he should go; and when he is old, he will not depart from it."

Parents, be sure that you bring your children to Sunday School and church.

Teach the children Bible stories at home and give them a part in family prayers.

Teach the children to obey God and the laws of the country, Deuteronomy 32:46.

Eli was punished because he couldn't control his wicked sons.

Parents are to provide for their children — food, clothing and opportunities for an education and means to choose their own life vocation under God, 1 Timothy 5:8.

Parents are not to provoke their children to wrath, Ephesians 6:4. sometimes when the parents quarrel, the frustrated one releases pent-up feelings by whipping the children. This is very wrong.

Above all, let godly parents pray for their children. Pray that they will be saved.

Pray that they will overcome sin, etc.

IV God-fearing Children

Exodus 20:12 "Honor thy father and thy mother: that thy days may be long upon the land."

Isaac was exemplary in Genesis 22 in carrying the wood without murmuring.

Samuel was most exemplary with instant obedience even in the middle of the night.

Jesus as a child was obedient to his parents, Luke 2:51.

V God-fearing Servants

Titus 2:9,10 "Exhort servants to be obedient unto their own masters, and to please them well in all things; not answering again; not purloining, but shewing all good fidelity; that they may adorn the doctrine of God our Savior in all things."

Conclusion

The secret of a successful Christian home is in the family altar where Christ is crowned as Head of the home. Love is the second secret.

Review Questions

1 Do you think it is possible to build a successful Church with only students?

2 If Christ is the Unseen Head of the family, what is the visible symbol of unity in the family?

3 Name the four individuals that comprise a happy Oriental home.

4 What member of the family is responsible for the family altar and table grace?

5 Describe the happy relationship between husband and wife. (Five things)

6 Is a wife's first duty to her husband or to the Lord? Why?

7 On the basis of 1 Timothy 2:9 and 1 Peter:4, 5, what things should adorn a woman?

8 In this age of population explosion does Genesis 1:28 still apply?

9 Which one of the ten commandments has a promise attached to it?

10 On the basis of Titus 2:9,10, is it wrong to have household servants? How should they act?

Law and Grace

Introduction

There are many Christians who are saved by grace but try to *keep* saved by obeying the law or keeping the commandments.

This was the error of the Galatian church which Paul seeks to correct in his Epistle to the Galatians.

Galatians 3:3 "Are you foolish? having begun in the Spirit (saved by grace), are ye now made perfect by the flesh (keeping of the law)?"

Paul answers this provocative question in Galatians 3:11 "The just shall live by faith": We are saved by faith; we live by faith.

But does this allow us to become a law unto ourselves and brake the law of God and sin wilfully? Paul answers this question in Romans 6:1,2 "God forbid..."

It is sometimes hard to keep a balance between the teaching of Paul and of James. James says in James 2:14, "What doth it profit, my brethren, though a man may say he hath faith, and have not works? can faith save him?"

James 2:20 "But wilt thou know, O vain man, that faith without works is dead?"

Paul answers this is Philippians 2:12,13 "Work out your own salvation with fear and trembling. For it is God which worketh in you both to will and to do of His good pleasure." By faith we yield to the indwelling Christ and He uses out bodies to do good works. The Savior works through us.

Our work is to yield. He is the one who performs the works of righteousness.

After conversion we do good works because we are saved already, not in order to be saved. A dog barks because he *is* a dog, not in order *to become* a dog.

I What is the Law?

1 The law includes the ten commandments of Exodus 20:1-17, and all other commands.

Romans 7:16 "Wherefore the law is *holy*, and the commandment holy, and just and good."

Psalm 19:7, 8 "The law of the Lord is perfect, converting the soul . . . the statutes of the Lord are *right* . . . the commandment of the Lord is pure . . ."

Thus we see that the law is holy, just, good, perfect, pure and right.

2 Grace is unmerited favor, the kindness and love of God our Savior toward us.

Under law God demands righteousness. Under grace God gives righteousness.

Ephesians 2:8, 9 "For by grace are ye saved through faith; and that not of yourselves: it is the gift of God: not of works, lest any man should boast."

II What Does it Say?

1 The Law says, Obey me and live. Leviticus 18:5 "Ye shall therefore keep My statutes, and My judgments: which if a man do, he shall live in them."

Romans 10:5 ". . . That the man which doeth those things (law) shall live by them."

The problem is this: Who can keep the law perfectly? The answer is clear from Romans 3:9-23, that only Christ could fulfill every jot and tittle of the Law.

2 Grace says that whosoever hears and believes on Jesus Christ has passed from death unto life, John 5:24 — a miracle that the Law could not perform.

Grace offers pardon and peace to sinners through the death of another — the Savior.

Grace says that those who receive eternal life will never perish, John 10:28.

III What does it do?

1 Law condemns every individual ever born into this world for all have broken at least one commandment on one occasion. James 2:10 "For whosoever shall keep the whole law, and yet offend in one

point, he is guilty of all."

Romans 3:19 makes the whole world guilty before God, "... that every mouth may be stopped, and all the world may become guilty before God."

The Law sets up a standard, but people are helpless before it.

Galatians 3:10 "Cursed is every one that continueth not in all things which are written in the book of the law to do them."

2   Grace is willing and ready to save the lost, the guilty, the law-breaker.

Grace brings salvation. Titus 2:11 "For the grace of God that bringeth salvation hath appeared to all men."

Grace restores righteousness that law took from us through the gift of God.

Grace is God's riches at Christ's expense in favor of the guilty sinner.

Grace not only saves the sinner, but more grace is added daily to sustain him.

IV What it Cannot Do

1   The law could never justify a guilty sinner. Acts 13:39 "And by Him all that believe are justified from all things, from which ye could not be justified by the law of Moses."

The law could not make anything perfect. Hebrews 7:19 "For the law made nothing perfect."

To get to heaven the sinner needs to be both justified and made perfect through the blood of Christ and the atoning work of the cross.

2   But grace through faith can bring justification to the sinner. Romans 3:24 "Being justified freely by His grace through the redemption that is in Christ Jesus."

Grace can teach us to deny ungodliness and worldly lusts and to live soberly, righteously and godly in this present world, Titus 2:11,12.

V Why Was it Given?

1   The law was given to show us our transgressions.

Galatians 3:19 "Wherefore then serveth the law? It was added because of transgressions."

Without law man would have no knowledge of sin. Romans 3:20 "... for by the law is the knowledge of sin."

The law was a schoolmaster to bring us to Christ. Galatians 3:24 "Wherefore the law was our schoolmaster to bring us unto Christ, that we might be justified by faith." Justified by faith, for we cannot be saved by works or law.

2 Grace was given to man not because man merited it, but because God loved the world of sinners. John 3:16 "For God so loved the world, that He gave . . ."

Grace is given to us for we are too weak in ourselves to keep saved, to keep the law or to do good works. 2 Corinthians 12:9 "And He (Jesus) said unto me, My grace is sufficient for thee: for My strength is made perfect in weakness."

VI By Whom was the Law Given?

1 The law was given by Moses, John 1:17; Exodus 20:19; Hebrews 12:18-21.

2 Grace came from Jesus Christ. John 1:17 "For the law was given by Moses, but grace and truth came by Jesus Christ."

Conclusion

Is Christianity a mixed system of law and grace? No, it must be all of faith.

Romans 4:4,5 "Now to him that worketh is the reward not reckoned of grace, but of debt. But to him that worketh not, but believeth on Him that justifieth the ungodly, his faith is counted for righteousness."

Is the believer under law after conversion? *No.* Romans 6:14 "For ye are not under the law, but under grace." Scripture could not be plainer.

How ought a true believer to walk before his fellowmen? As Jesus walked. 1 John 2:6 "He that saith he abideth in Him ought himself also so to walk, even as He walked."

1 Peter 2:21, following in His steps.

Those who are in Christ while not saved or kept by the law, nevertheless love the will of God and do from the heart those things which please him, not for salvation nor by constraint, but for love's sake, as they walk in the Spirit. (Goodman)

Galatians 5:18 "But if ye be led of the Spirit, ye are not under the law," Romans 8:4, 5.

To be saved by faith and then to return to works is to fall from grace, Galatians 5:4.

Review Questions

1 What was the error of the Church at Galatia? (3:3)
2 Does following grace allow us to sin more in order to enjoy more grace? Explain.
3 What is the great consoling truth of Philippians 2:12,13?
4 What is law? What is grace?
5 What is the message of the law? Of grace?
6 What does the law actually do? What does grace do? One Scripture for each.
7 If the law cannot save, why did God give it?
8 How can a person merit grace?
9 True or false? "Salvation is by grace but is continued by works." Explain.
10 A New Testament believer under grace may ignore the law. True or false? Explain.

Life

Introduction

In John 11:25 and 14:6, Jesus says that He possesses life and that He is life.

John 11:25 "Jesus said unto her, I am the resurrection, and the life."

John 14:6 "Jesus saith unto him, I am the way, the truth and the life."

Story: Some years ago Nehru of India was visiting United States and requested the pleasure of visiting Einstein who was probably the greatest brain that ever lived. Request granted. They talked of politics, travel, etc., and then Nehru said, "Mr. Einstein, the question that I came to ask is this, Have you found the meaning of life?" Einstein bowed his head and replied, "No, I have not found the meaning of life."

Does the Bible give us the answer to this question? Men and women are asking, "Why was I born? Why did God make me? Why am I here? What is the purpose of life?"

I Definition of Life

Dictionary: "It is the union of soul and body." This is true of humans, but not of plants.

"The state of being alive." This is true, but very ambiguous.

"The period between birth and death." This is not true for life exists before birth.

"Life is the property of a plant or animal that involves growth, nutrition, respiration and reproduction."

The truth is that life is very difficult to define.

Life is a trust, a loan from God for a short period of time. Job 1:21 "The Lord gave and the Lord hath taken away; blessed be the Name of the Lord."

Life is an intangible gift from God. We can neither see it, feel it, or bargain with it.

Life is an unsubstantial flimsy thing. It is here today and gone tomorrow.

II The Origin of Life

Where did you get life from? From your parents. And where did they get it from? Inevitably one goes back to Eden and the creation of man.

Genesis 2:7 "And the Lord God formed man of the dust of the ground, and breathed into his nostrils the breath of life; and man became a living soul."

All life comes from God. 1 John 5:20 "This is the true God, and eternal life."

Life is a characteristic, an attribute, the very nature of the Almighty God.

III Kinds of Life

The Bible speaks of three kinds of life:
1 Physical life which was given to man at the time of creation.
2 Spiritual life. This is the new life that God gives to the believer in Jesus Christ.

Ephesians 2:1 "And you hath He quickened, who were dead in trespasses and sins."

This new life is a gift from God to the repentant sinner.
3 Eternal life. This is the nature and characteristic of the Lord God.

IV Length of Life

In Genesis 5, before the flood, the life span was an average of 846 years.

In Genesis 11, after the flood, the life span was reduced to 393 years.

In Moses' time, Psalm 90:10 "The days of our years are threescore years and ten (70); and if by reason of strength they be fourscore years, yet is their strength labor and sorrow."

Psalm 89:47 "Remember how short my time is."

Job 14:1 "Man that is born of a woman is of few days."

James 4:13-15, Life is like a vapor that quickly vanishes away.

Life is limited to a set time. Job 7:1 "Is thee not an appointed time to man upon earth?"

God in His sovereign will has set the span (length) of our lives.

A wise man told his disciples to prepare for death the day before they died. "But," they objected, "we may die tomorrow." "True," he replied, "then prepare today."

V Comparisons

1 **Life is like a journey** Genesis 47:9, Jacob talking to King Pharaoh, "The days of the years of my pilgrimage are an hundred and thirty years: few and evil have the days of my life been." Life is a journey from earth to eternity; from the cradle to the beyond.

We are travelling on this journey whether we like it or not. Birth is an automatic start. To some it is a long, long journey. To others it is a very short one.

2 **Life is like a dream** Psalm 73:20 "As a dream when one awaketh." How long is a dream? Only a few seconds. Can you recall a dream? No. Life is short, fleeting and transient.

3 **Life is like a shadow** Ecclesiastes 6:12 "For who knoweth what is good for man in this life, all the days of his vain life which he spendeth as a shadow?"

A shadow is such a poor imitation of the real thing. Can you recognize a person by his shadow? Shadows can be so deceiving, so long, so short. Life is like that.

4 **Life is like vapor** James 4:14 "What is your life? It is even a vapor, that appeareth for a little time, and then vanisheth away."

If all that we knew about water was what we saw in steam, how limited our knowledge of water would be. You cannot drink steam. Water and ice are other forms.

Life on earth is like a bud that will open and develop in eternity. Life is too short.

5 **Life is like a tale** Psalm 90:9 "For all our days are passed away in Thy wrath: we spend our years as a tale that is told."

Life is like an interesting story that is soon told and the people look for another form of entertainment. This was Shakespeare's observation, too:

> "Out, out, brief candle, life's but a walking shadow,
> A poor player that struts and frets his hour
> Upon the stage and then is heard no more.
> It is a tale told by an idiot, full of sound
> And fury, signifying nothing."

6 **Life is like water spilt on the ground** 2 Samuel 14:14 "For we must needs die, and are as water spilt on the ground, which cannot be

gathered up again."

In a moment the earth absorbs the moisture and it disappears.

7 **Life is like a flower.** Job 14:1,2 "Man that is born of a woman is of
few days, and full of trouble. He cometh forth like a flower, and is
cut down: he fleeth also as a shadow, and continueth not."

First we see the blade, then leaves, and afterwards the beautiful bud.
Slowly it opens and we gasp at its beauty. Then it withers and is
gone — gone so soon, so quickly.

Some flowers never bloom. They are cut down in their prime.

VI The Purpose of Life

Life is a moment of time in which to prepare for the long, long,
eternity.

In this brief, fleeting, second of time we are asked to answer one
question.

The question: "Where do you wish to spend eternity?"

There are two great eternities. We must choose one or the other. No
neutral ground.

1 The blessed privilege of living forever with the Lord Jesus in
heaven.

2 The terrible anguish of living forever with Satan in a burning hell.

The purpose of life is to let you personally choose the abiding place
of your soul.

Conclusion

Paul said in Philippians 1:21, "For to me to live is *Christ*." Christ is life.

Jesus said to Martha, "I am . . . the life . . ." Jesus is God and possesses
eternal life.

Today make the right decision to be with Christ forever in heaven.

When I invite Jesus to come into my heart, then He comes in and
I am indwelt by God's life, eternal life.

When Jesus comes into the life He takes away the sin and cleanses the
heart.

With Christ within I am indwelt by eternal life and can never perish.

Decide today to invite Jesus into your heart and life, Revelation 3:20.

The mystery of life is solved in the revelation of Jesus Christ to man.

Review Questions

1 What kind of life does Jesus refer to in John 11:25, and 14:6?
2 Define life.
3 Where did life come from?
4 List three kinds of life.
5 What was man's average life span: before the flood; immediately after the flood (Genesis 11); in Moses' time?
6 What verse teaches that God sets the length of life of a human being?
7 List seven comparisons or pictures that the Bible gives regarding life.
8 In what two ways is life like a dream?
9 What are the three dimensions of life and water?
10 What is the purpose of life?

82

Death

Introduction

In Lesson 81 we considered "Life." We tried to define it and understand it.

We decided that life was a moment of time to prepare for eternity.

Life is saddened by the fact that it must end sooner or later in death unless Jesus returns to rapture the Church.

We found it difficult to define life. Can we define death?

Death is the departure of life — the cessation of life.

Death is the change from the animate to the inanimate.

Death is when the heart stops, when the breath ceases, when the body is a stiff corpse.

Can you be assured of long life?

Story: Boy asked mother, "At what age do people die?" She told him to go to the cemetery and examine the graves. His conclusion, "They die at all ages."

To humans, death is the separation of body, soul and spirit:

1 The body goes to the grave and disintegrates.

2 The spirit goes back to God. Ecclesiastes 12:7 "Then shall the dust return to the earth as it was: and the spirit shall return unto God who gave it."

3 The soul in Luke 16:19-31, goes to one of two places:

   a The soul of the wicked to hell, Luke 16:23.

   b The soul of the righteous to paradise, Luke 16:22 (Abraham's bosom), Luke 23:43. The thief was with Christ in paradise.

I The Origin of Death

There are two kinds of death and both of them come from the Garden of Eden.

1 **Spiritual death.** Genesis 2:17 ". . . for in the day that thou eatest thereof thou shalt surely die."

In Eden, Adam and Eve did not die physically when they ate the forbidden fruit.

They died spiritually. Ephesians 2:1 ". . . quickened, who were dead in trespasses and sins."

2 **Physical death.** Genesis 3:21, God killed animals to get skins to cover Adam and Eve.

The first human to die was Abel the son of Adam, murdered by his brother Cain.

Genesis 4:8 "Cain rose up against Abel his brother, and slew him."

II The Cause of Death

Spiritual death was caused by disobedience to God. James 1:15 "When lust hath conceived, it bringeth forth sin: and sin, when it is finished, bringeth forth death."

Death is the direct result of sin.

In the case of physical death the doctor may write any one of many things on the death certificate, but the real answer is *sin*.

Sin is the basic cause and the disease the immediate agency that God used to execute the sentence that was pronounced on mankind in the Garden of Eden.

Ezekiel 18:20 "The soul that sinneth, it shall die."

Romans 6:23 "For the wages of sin is death."

Hebrews 9:27 "And as it is appointed unto men once to die, but after this the judgment."

III A Description of Death

Physical death is described as:

1 Sleep. John 11:11 "Our friend Lazarus sleepeth." 1 Thessalonians 4:14.

2 As requiring the soul. Luke 12:20 "Thou fool, this night thy soul shall be required of thee."

3 As putting off this earthly house. 2 Corinthians 5:1 "For we know that if our earthly house of this tabernacle were dissolved. . ."
2 Peter 1:14 "I must put off this my tabernacle."

4 As going to a place of no return. Job 16:22 "When a few years are come, then I shall go the way whence I shall not return." See also Luke 16:31.

5 As going down into silence. Psalm 115:17 "The dead praise not the Lord, neither any that go down into silence."

6 As yielding up the ghost. Acts 5:10 "Sapphira", and in Luke 23:46, of the Savior.

Eternal death is known as banishment from God. 2 Thessalonians 1:9 "Who shall be punished with everlasting destruction from the presence of the Lord." That is, eternal death.

Eternal death is also called alienation from God. Ephesians 4:18 "Having the understanding darkened, being alienated from the life of God . . ."

IV The Remedy

Modern science and doctors can do a great deal to prolong life. The life span is lengthening, but that is merely postponing the day of death.

We are "appointed to die," Hebrews 9:27. We are born with an appointment to meet death. We must keep that appointment.

The one true remedy is found in the Lord Jesus Christ.

Spiritual death is cured by believing on the Lord Jesus Christ.

John 5:24 "Verily, verily, I say unto you, He that heareth My Word, and believeth on Him that sent Me, hath everlasting life, and shall not come into condemnation; but is passed from death unto life."

When we believe on Christ, the Holy Spirit works the miracle of regeneration in our lives, transforming us into children of God, John 1:12.

Physical death can be avoided by the rapture of the Church.

But Christ has promised to walk with us (Christians) through the experience of death.

Psalm 23:4 "Yea, though I walk through the valley of the shadow of death, I will fear no evil: for Thou art with me."

(Those that can truthfully say, "The Lord is *My* Shepherd," can also claim this promise.)

V The Death of Christ

Why did Jesus die on the cross? Was it an accident? Certainly not.

God's Word said that someone must die for sin. Jesus volunteered to be the One to die. He died the death that *You* and *I* ought to have died.

Hebrews 2:9 ". . . that He by the grace of God should taste death for every man."

Jesus tasted the bitter dregs of death for you. Oh, reject Him no longer.

Jesus died on the cross as a sacrifice for you and me. Ephesians 5:2 ". . . and hath given Himself for us an offering and a sacrifice to God."

The death of the Savior was necessary for the redemption of mankind. Luke 24:46 ". . . Thus it is written, and thus it behooved Christ to suffer, and to rise from the dead the third day."

What is the Gospel? 1 Corinthians 15:1-4 defines it as that Christ suffered for our sins according to the Scriptures, that He was buried and that He rose the third day. That is, the Gospel includes death, the death of the Savior for sin.

Conclusion

The death of the righteous is precious to the Father. Psalm 116:15 "Precious in the sight of the Lord is the death of His saints."

The death of the wicked is unpleasant to God. Ezekiel 33:11 "I have no pleasure in the death of the wicked . . . that the wicked turn from his way and live: turn ye, turn ye from your evil ways."

I implore you today to turn from your sins, to repent and turn to the Lord.

Revelation 3:20, Jesus is knocking at the door of your heart seeking entrance. *Open Now!*

Story (*Born Crucified*, page 15) of George Wyatt, married man with six children, was drafted. Richard Pratt, a bachelor, volunteered to take his place. He was accepted, went to war, and was killed. Wyatt said, "He died for me."

Jesus died for you on the cross. Receive Him as your Savior *today*.

Review Questions

1 Define death.
2 What happens to tripartite man at death?
3 What are the two kinds of death and where did they originate?
4 What is the basic cause of death?
5 List six Scriptural descriptions of death.
6 What is the cure for spiritual death?
7 Why is Psalm 23:4, so precious to the seriously sick?
8 Do you think that Jesus died as a martyr? Why?
9 What is the Gospel?
10 What is the contrast between Psalm 116:15, and Ezekiel 33:11?

83

Resurrection

Introduction

Notes from *Handfuls on Purpose; The Christian After Death*, R. E. Hough; and *The Resurrection of the Human Body*, N. H. Camp.

At the parting with a loved one several questions come to our mind that demand answers: Job 14:14 "If a man die, shall he live again?"

Job answers his own question in Job 19:26 "And though after my skin worms destroy this body, yet in my flesh shall I see God."

What becomes of the body at death? Will a lame, ugly man of 80 look that way in the resurrection? Will the body burned in an accident be like that forever?

Do both the believers and the unbelievers get new bodies?

Will we recognize one another in heaven? Yes, because:

1 We will be known there as we were known on earth. 1 Corinthians 13:12 "For now we see through a glass, darkly; but then face to face: now I know in part; but then shall I know even as also I am known."

2 Our names are recorded in heaven and we will be known by these names. For example, Moses and Elijah in Matthew 17 were known by their earthly names.

3 The rich man recognized Lazarus in Luke 16:23.

4 The disciples recognized Jesus after His resurrection.

5 On earth we recognize people with our imperfect faculties. There our faculties will be perfect. Peter, James and John recognized Moses and Elijah in Matthew 17:4, though they had never met before.

I The Resurrection of Christ

There were some in Corinth who taught that Jesus did not rise from the dead, 1 Corinthians 15.

Paul gives a definite answer in 1 Corinthians 15:20, "But now is Christ risen from the dead."

There were many who witnessed Jesus' bodily resurrection:

1 Jesus first appeared to Mary Magdalene, John 20:17.
2 Jesus appeared to the women, Mark 16:1-3.
3 Jesus appeared to Peter, Mark 16:7; see also Luke 24:34.
4 The disciples on the Emmaus Road, Luke 24:16.
5 The eleven disciples, Luke 24:33; see also Acts 1:23-26.
6 The disciples including Thomas in the upper room, John 20:25-28.
7 The disciples at the sea of Tiberias, John 21:1.
8 To the eleven disciples on the mountain, Matthew 28:16.
9 To five hundred brethren, 1 Corinthians 15:6.
10 To the eleven at Bethany where He ascended, Luke 24:36-51.

II The Resurrection Hope
1 Corinthians 15:17, 18

Our entire faith rests or falls with the resurrection. If Christ did not die and was not raised from the dead, then:

1 Your faith is vain.
2 You are still in your sins.
3 All who have died have perished.
4 Then there will be no future reunions with loved ones, *but Christ did rise from the dead!*

Because Jesus rose we have a positive hope of reunion.
Because Jesus rose from the dead, every man, woman, and child shall rise from the dead.

III The Resurrection of the Dead

The resurrection seems to be in stages:

1 Christ, the first fruits, was the first to rise, 1 Corinthians 15:20.
2 Matthew 27:52,53 "And the graves were opened; and many bodies of the saints which slept arose, and came out of the graves after His resurrection and went into the holy city, and appeared unto many "
3 The resurrection of life. John 5:28,29 "Marvel not at this: for the hour is coming, in the which all that are in the graves shall hear His voice, and shall come forth; they that have done good, unto the resurrection of life; and they that have done evil, unto the resurrection of damnation."
   Revelation 20:5 "But the rest of the dead lived not again until the thousand years were finished. This is the first resurrection."

This coincides with the rapture.

4 The resurrection of damnation. John 5:29, quoted above.

Revelation 20:13 "And the sea gave up the dead which were in it; and death and hell delivered up the dead which were in them. . ."

Therefore all *must* and *shall* rise from the dead. Some will rise to eternal blessing, while others will rise and be cast into hell forever.

IV The Resurrection Body
1 Corinthians 15:35-49

There are some who deny the resurrection of the body, saying that the post-resurrection product will be a spirit only.

1 Corinthians 15;44 says it is raised a spiritual body, not a spirit without a body.

1 Corinthians 15:35 asks two questions: "How are the dead raised up?" By God's power.

"And with what body do they come?" Paul proceeds to answer the second question:

1 It is not the same body, verse 37. The dead body is like a seed planted in the ground and the plant is different from the seed that was planted.

The crippled or burned body at death will not be like that in the resurrection. It will germinate and mature as the other bodies.

There will be no aged, deformed, crippled or ugly bodies in heaven.

2 It is a God-given body, verse 38. It is according to the sovereign will of God.

John 3:2, "When He shall appear, we shall be like Him." (that is, perfect.)

3 It will be a body suited in every way to the individual spirit, verse 38, ". . . to every seed his own body." Verses 41,42, the stars differ, and so will our bodies.

4 It will be an incorruptible body, verse 42. This body will be incapable of death or decay. Those condemned in hell will need this kind of body to endure forever and forever in hell. This human body would disintegrate there.

5 It will be a glorious body, verse 43. Probably like the glorious bodies in Matthew 17 at the Transfiguration — radiant in white glory.

6 It will be a body of power, verse 43. It will not be subject to the laws of 'earth.

Jesus' body passed through locked doors and solid walls. Jesus ascended easily.

7 It will be a spiritual body, verse 44. Jesus' earthly body was one of flesh, blood and bones. Jesus' resurrection body had flesh and bones but it did not have blood. The blood was poured out on the cross. Luke 24:39 "Behold My hands and My feet, that it is I Myself: handle Me, and see; for a spirit hath not flesh and bones, as ye see me have."

After this Jesus ate fish and an honeycomb, Luke 24:42,43.

V The Resurrection Mystery
1 Corinthians 15:51-54

The mystery: It is not necessary for all of us to die. Some will be alive when Jesus returns and will be raptured.

The living shall be changed, verse 52, "And we shall be changed," proving that the resurrection body is different, yet likely similar to our present bodies.

The living body must put on incorruption, 1 Corinthians 15:52, and immortality, 1 Corinthians 15:53.

VI The Resurrection Song
1 Corinthians 15:54-57

Verse 54 — death is swallowed up in victory.
Verse 55 — the sting of death is gone.
Verse 55 — the grave has lost its victory.
Verse 57 — victory is ours through Christ.

Conclusion

The wicked dead will rise with eternal, incorruptible bodies, but likely minus the glorious aspect of the bodies of the saints.

Norman H. Camp describes the bodies of the resurrection damned as "bodies of abhorrence" Isaiah 66:23,24.

Review Questions

1 What is the relationship between Job 14:14 and Job 19:26?
2 Give five reasons why we believe that we will recognize one

another in heaven.

3   How do we know that Christ rose from the dead?

4   What would be the four tragedies if Jesus had not risen from the dead?

5   List the four stages of resurrection.

6   Tell seven things about the resurrection body from 1 Corinthians 15:35-49.

7   What is the mystery of 1 Corinthians 15:51-54?

8   Name the four facts of the resurrection song.

9   Describe the resurrection bodies of the unsaved.

10   Give one valid reason why a person would reject a glorified body and choose a "body of abhorrence."

84

The Bema

Introduction

Hebrews 9:27 "And as it is appointed unto men once to die, but after this the judgment."

2 Corinthians 5:10 "For we must all appear before the judgment seat of Christ."

As there is more than one resurrection, there is more than one judgment.

Because Adam sinned, all die. Because Christ rose, all must rise to be judged.

God has appointed His Son Jesus Christ to be the Judge of all the earth.

The Bible speaks of at least seven different judgments:

1 The Savior on the cross being judged for our sins.
2 The believers' self-judgment. 1 Corinthians 11:31 "For if we would judge ourselves, we should not be judged." At Communion and daily the saint judges himself.
3 The judgment of the believers at the *Bema* — the subject of this lesson.
4 The judgment of the nations, Matthew 25:32, division of the sheep and the goats.
5 The judgment of Israel, Ezekiel 20:30-44, post-tribulation.
6 The judgment of angels, Jude 6. They are reserved in darkness, waiting.
7 The judgment of the wicked dead, Revelation 20:12 — the great White Throne Judgment.

I Description of the *Bema*

In 2 Corinthians 5:10 it is called the "judgment seat of Christ."

It is generally conceded that this judgment will take place in the air. This fact is probably drawn from 1 Thessalonians 4:13-17, which speaks of the Second Coming, the first resurrection and then says,

". . . to meet the Lord in the air: and so shall we ever be with the Lord."

II Time of the *Bema* - the Judgment Seat

1 At the first resurrection. Luke 14:14 ". . . for thou shalt be recompensed at the resurrection of the just."
2 At the Second Coming of Christ. Matthew 16:27, "For the Son of man shall come in the glory of His Father with His angels; and then He shall reward every man according to his works."

III Who will be Judged at the *Bema* ?

Only believers will be judged. In 2 Corinthians 5, the pronoun "we" is used 26 times and in each instance it refers only to believers.

IV What is Being Judged at the *Bema* ?

The judgment is not a trial to decide the fate either of the saved or unsaved.

The Bible is very plain, John 3:16-18, that salvation is not the issue here. That issue is settled in life.

The believer is being judged for his works. The returning Lord examines the servants in the use of the one, two or five talents that He has entrusted to them.

Sins committed before conversion will not be judged. Hebrews 10:17 "And their sins and iniquities will I remember no more." To judge them, God would need to remember them, to dig them up from the lowest sea, etc.

The next chapter (Hebrews 11) sees the saints as perfect, for all their sins and imperfections were hidden beneath the blood of Christ.

The believer's sins committed and confessed after conversion will not be judged at the *Bema*. 1 John 1:9, confessed sin is forgiven and cleansed forever.

1 Our works will be judged. 1 Corinthians 3:13 "Every man's work shall be made manifest . . . and the fire shall try every man's work of what sort it is."

Ecclesiastes 12;14 "For God shall bring every work into judgment."

2 Our words. Matthew 12:36,37 "That every idle word that men speak, they shall give account thereof in the day of judgment."

3 Our thoughts. Matthew 15:19,20 "For out of the heart proceed evil

thoughts. . . these are the things which defile a man. . ." See Matthew 5:28 ". . . looketh . . . lust. . ."

4 Our secrets. Romans 2:16 "In the day when God shall judge the secrets of men by Jesus Christ according to my Gospel."

5 Our motives:

    Correct — Constrained by His love, 1 Corinthians 5:14.

    Wrong — Self glory, 1 Corinthians 3:21 "Therefore let no man glory in men."

V How will God Judge at the *Bema* ?

The test will be by fire. 1 Corinthians 3:13 "For the day shall declare it, because it shall be revealed by fire; and the fire shall try every man's work of what sort it is."

This will be a fair impartial public display of justice. No one will be able to say that God showed favoritism.

Galatians 6:7,8 "Be not deceived; God is not mocked: for whatsoever a man soweth, that shall he also reap."

VI What are the Results of the *Bema* ?

For the works that remain, there will be rewards. For that which is burned, the individual will suffer loss. 1 Corinthians 3:15 "If any man's work shall be burned, he shall suffer loss: but he himself shall be saved; yet so as by fire."

The Bible does not tell what that loss will be.

    If the reward is a crown, the loss of a reward or loss of a crown will bring shame, for we will not have a crown to lay at the feet of Jesus Christ.

Building materials are of two classes:

1 Fireproof — gold, silver and precious stones

2 Combustible — wood, hay and stubble

What works are represented by fireproof materials?

1 Righteousness, a clean pure life in the sight of the Lord

2 Honesty, not only before men but before God

3 A life of faith, faith in God, Christ, the Bible, etc.

4 Love, true love, "1-Corinthians-13" love. Love to God and love to man

5 Patience. 2 Peter 1:6 a highly desirable and praiseworthy virtue

6 Meekness and humility, Matthew 11:28,29, being molded and fashioned like our Savior

7 Peaceful, Matthew 5:9; 2 Timothy 2:22 ". . . follow. . . peace. . ."

What works are represented by combustible material?

1 All forms of sin and wickedness
2 Cheating, graft and bribery so common on earth, so hateful to the Lord
3 All forms of dishonesty will be quickly burned
4 Influence benefits will crumble in the flames
5 Yielding to youthful lusts, 1 Timothy 6:9-11; 2 Timothy 2:22; Joseph in Genesis 39:12
6 Good things done with wrong motives
7 Pride is perhaps the most reprehensible sin in the sight of the Lord

VII How can I be prepared to Meet the *Bema* ?

By constant communion with my Savior Jesus Christ. By much self-examination.

By constant confession of my sins (Don't confess the same sin twice. God forgives after the first honest confession.)

By much prayer and meditation on the Word of God. By constant attention to the will of the Holy Spirit.

By having a conscience void of offence before God and men, Acts 24;16.

Conclusion

To the Christian the *Bema* should hold no terrors, it ought to be the best day he has ever had. It will be his crowning day.

1 Corinthians 4:5 "And then shall every man have praise of God." Much of our works may be burned, but God will find at least one thing to praise.

Review Questions

1 List the seven different judgments mentioned in the Scriptures.
2 What is the *Bema*?
3 When will the *Bema* take place?
4 Who will be judged at the *Bema*?
5 What five things will be judged at the *Bema*?
6 How will God judge at the *Bema*?
7 What is the relationship between Luke 12:47 and 1 Corinthians 3:15?
8 What seven works are represented by the fireproof materials?

9   What seven works are represented by the combustible materials?

10 How can we be prepared to meet the *Bema*?

85

The Judgments

Introduction

In our last lesson we spoke about the certainty of judgment and listed seven different judgments in the introduction.

In this lesson we propose to outline briefly some broad details of these seven events, as they have transpired or will transpire in the world. We will study these under five basic points for each judgment: subject; time; place; basis; and results.

These are not the only judgments; there was the judgment by flood in the days of Noah and the judgment of confusion of languages at the Tower of Babel. There have been lesser judgments that have fallen upon individuals, nations or even groups of nations at various times.

Perhaps the first major judgment was the catastrophe that fell on the pre-Adamite race between the first two verses of chapter one of Genesis.

I The Judgment that Fell at Calvary

1 **Subject** Christ bearing our sin, John 1:29 "Behold the Lamb of God, which taketh away the sin of the world." Also Hebrews 2:9; 1 John 2:2.

2 **Time** About A.D. 30, when Christ was on the cross.

3 **Place** Calvary, John 19:17,18, the actual crucifixion; Romans 1:18, "For the wrath of God is revealed from heaven against all ungodliness and unrighteousness of men."

   This wrath was revealed at Calvary; God pulled down the curtain of darkness, Matthew 27:45.

4 **Basis** The law, Romans 6:23 "For the wages of sin is death." Also 18:4, "The soul that sinneth, it shall die." Sin was judged by the perfect law, James 1:25.

5 **Results** Physical death for Christ; justification for believers

— 1 Timothy 4:10 ". . . who is the Savior of all men, specially of those that believe."

II Daily Self Judgment

1 **Subjects** The saints judge themselves, 1 Corinthians 11:28 ". . . but let a man examine himself, and so let him eat of that bread . . ."; Psalm 26:1,2 "Judge me, O Lord. . . examine me, O Lord, and prove me; try my reins and my heart."

2 **Time** Anytime, not only Communion but daily, particularly in our morning Quiet Time.

3 **Place** Any place; let us be constantly in communion with the Lord and ready to heed the rebuke or pleading of the Holy Spirit.

4 **Basis** Sonship, Hebrews 12:6,7 "For whom the Lord loveth He chasteneth, and scourgeth every son whom He receiveth. If ye endure chastening, God dealeth with you as with sons."

5 **Results** Purging, delivered from weakness, sickness and death — 1 Corinthians 11:30.

Forgiveness to the believer with joy and peace, John 1:9 "If we confess our sins, He is faithful and just to forgive us our sins, and to cleanse us from all unrighteousness."

III The *Bema*, The Judgment Seat of Christ
(See Lesson 84)

1 **Subject** The saints are being judged for their works.

2 **Time** At the Second Coming of Christ, Luke 14:14, and after the first resurrection, Matthew 16:27.

3 **Place** In the air, 1 Thessalonians 4:16,17.

4 **Basis** The believer's works, 1 Corinthians 3:13.

5 **Results** Rewards and crowns for the faithful, 1 Corinthians 3:14. Loss to those who produce hay, wood, and stubble, 1 Corinthians 3:15.

IV The Judgment of the Jews

1 **Subjects** The Jewish nation or people, Exekiel 20:34-38

2 **Time** During the Great Tribulation.

3 **Place** Jerusalem and vicinity.

4 **Basis** Rejection of the God-head, 1 Samuel 8:7; Luke 23:18; Acts 7:51.

5 **Results** The conversion of the Jews and their acceptance of Christ as Messiah.

V The Judgment of the Nations

1 **Subjects** The Gentile nations, Matthew 25:32 "And before him shall be gathered all nations: and He shall separate them one from another, as a shepherd."
2 **Time** At the second coming of Christ, Matthew 25:31 "When the Son of man shall come in His glory, and all the holy angels with Him, then shall He sit upon the throne of His glory."
3 **Place** The Valley of Jehoshaphat, Joel 3:2 "I will gather all nations, and will bring them down into the Valley of Jehoshaphat."
4 **Basis** Treatment of the Jews, Matthew 25:40 "Inasmuch as ye have done it unto one of the least of these My brethren, ye have done it unto Me."

Christ's brethren were the Jews.
5 **Results** Punishment for the goat nations, Matthew 25:41 "Depart from Me, ye cursed, into everlasting fire, prepared for the devil and his angels."

Blessing for the sheep nations, Matthew 25:34 "Come, ye blessed of My Father, inherit the kingdom prepared for you from the foundation of the world."

VI The Judgment of the Fallen Angels

1 **Subjects** The fallen angels.
2 **Time** Unknown (probably at the time of the Great White Throne Judgment).
3 **Place** Unknown.
4 **Basis** Probably the rebellion led by Lucifer, Ezekiel 28:12-19; Isaiah 14:12-17; Revelation 12:4. 1 Corinthians 6:3 "Know ye not that we shall judge angels?"

Jude 6 "And the angels which kept not their first estate, but left their own habitation, He hath reserved in everlasting chains under darkness unto the judgment of the great day."

2 Peter 2:4 "For if God spared not the angels that sinned, but cast them down to hell, and delivered them into chains of darkness, to be reserved unto judgment."

VI The Judgment of the Wicked Dead

1 **Subjects** The wicked dead, Revelation 20:12; those who have never been born again; those who do not rise at the first resurrection or have not been raptured.

2 **Time** After the thousand year millennial period, Revelation 20:5 "But the rest of the dead lived not again until the thousand years were finished."

3 **Place** At the Great White Throne, Revelation 20:11 "And I saw a great white throne, and Him that sat on it."

4 **Basis** Whether or not the names were recorded in the book of life and the works of these individuals.

Revelation 20:12 "And the books were opened: and another book was opened, which is the book of life: and the dead were judged out of those things which were written in the books, according to their works."

5 **Results** Revelation 20:15, the ungodly are to be cast into the lake of fire.

"And whosoever was not found written in the book of life was cast into the lake of fire."

Conclusion

The Great White Throne judgment is personal and final; it is not a trial to discover whether the person is guilty or not; it is a pronouncement of judgment by the Lord God Almighty on the ungodly and doomed.

Differences between the Great White Throne judgment and an earthly court case.

1 One of the living; the other of the resurrected dead.

2 One with witnesses; the other has no witnesses, lawyers, juries.

3 One with questions; the other, no questions to answer (information recorded).

4 One with rebuttal; the other with no speeches, law books, cross-examination.

5 One with human law; the other with Divine law.

6 One with physical death; the other with eternal death.

7 One with bribery; the other with absolute justice, honesty and full measure.

8 One presents evidence; the other produces evidence filed and recorded years, before while the person was living; probably

with films, tape recorders and machines that visualize the thought life of the prisoner.

Review Questions

1   List three major judgments that fell in the book of Genesis.
2   Was Jesus judged for the billions of human beings or just for those who would be saved? (1 Timothy 4:10)
3   Is self-judgment of believers compulsory? Explain.
4   What is the relationship between John 15:2, and Hebrews 12:6?
5   Is Ezekiel 20:34-38, history or prophecy? Explain.
6   Does Zechariah 12:10-13:1 explain Isaiah 66:8? How?
7   What part does the Church have in Matthew 25:31-46?
8   When will the Great White Throne Judgment take place?
9   Will some be judged righteous at the Great White Throne judgment and go to heaven?
10   List seven differences between the Great White Throne judgment and an earthly court case.

86

Future Glory and Rewards

Introduction

2 Corinthians 4:17 "For our light affliction, which is but for a moment, worketh for us a far more exceeding and eternal weight of glory."

I believe that the rewards to be given at the *Bema* will consist of crowns and other glorious things.

2 Corinthians 4:17 speaks of the momentary light affliction which is a very descriptive picture of this world of sorrow, pain, tears, problems, etc.

The moment that we cross to the other side this moment of affliction will be exchanged for an "exceeding and eternal weight of glory."

What does this strange phrase mean? Can you *weigh* glory on scales? Perhaps it is a figure of speech comparing the two opposite words, "light" and "weight."

If the reverse were true then we as believers would be most miserable, 1 Corinthians 15:19.

One of the first blessings is the believer's death — a death from which the sting has already been removed, John 8:51, 1 Corinthians 15:55.

Death to the believer is just falling asleep in Jesus Christ, John 11:11; 1 Thessalonians 4:14.

Then the person suddenly awakes in the Lord's presence. Philippians 1:23.

I The Future Glory of Believers

1 To be with Christ: John 14:3 "And if I go and prepare a place for you, I will come again, and receive you unto Myself; that where I am, there ye may be also."

We are all happy to be in the presence of a great person.

2 To behold His face: Psalm 17:15 "As for me, I will behold Thy face in righteousness. I shall be satisfied, when I awake, with Thy likeness."

2 Corinthians 4:6 ". . . the glory of God in the face of Jesus Christ." We'll behold it!

What glory it will be just to be able to gaze on that wonderful face. Revelation 22:4 "And they shall see His face."

3 To behold the glory of Christ: John 17:24 "Father, I will that they also, whom Thou hast given Me, be with Me where I am; that they may behold My glory which Thou hast given me."

Everyone loves to view a beautiful bride! What a far more wonderful sight is this!

This would be a pre-incarnation, Matthew 17:2, transfiguration scene. Wonderful!

4 To be glorified with Christ! Romans 8:17,18 "And if children, then heirs; heirs of God, and joint-heirs with Christ; if so be that we suffer with Him that we may be also glorified together. For I reckon that the sufferings of this present time are not worthy to be compared with the glory which shall be revealed in us."

We don't know what this means but it surely is going to be marvelously wonderful!

5 To reign with Christ. 2 Timothy 2:12 "If we suffer, we shall also reign with Him."

In the Matthew 25:20-23 parable of the talents, the faithful ones were made rulers over many things.

In Luke 19:12-19, the parable of the nobleman and pounds, the man with one pound gained ten more and was given to rule over ten cities.

Another man with one pound gained five more and was granted to rule over five cities.

6 To inherit all things. Revelation 21:7 "He that overcometh shall inherit all things; and I will be his God, and he shall be My son."

Acts 26:18, the Christian is one with an inheritance up there in the glory land.

7 To shine as the stars. Daniel 12:3 "And they that be wise shall shine as the brightness of the firmament; and they that turn many to righteousness as the stars for ever and ever."

II Crowns that Believers may win

I once visited the Tower of London to see the Crown Jewels.

The Queen's Imperial State crown contains 3,000 diamonds and 300 other jewels.

The Imperial State crown contains 6,000 diamonds and other stones.

Revelation 19:12 "On His head were many crowns." (The head of the Savior, Jesus Christ.)

How many crowns do you expect to win? It is possible for believers to win several.

1 **Crowns for runners** 1 Corinthians 9:24,25 — an Incorruptible Crown. "Know ye not that they which run in a race run all, but one receiveth the prize? So run, that ye may obtain. And every man that striveth for the mastery is temperate in all things. Now they do it to obtain a corruptible crown; but we an incorruptible."

Hebrews 12:1 "Let us run with patience the race that is set before us."

An incorruptible crown, not one made of cheap material like the barrio fiesta queen's, but an eternal one.

2 **Crowns for soul winners** 1 Thessalonians 2:19 — the Crown of Rejoicing, "For what is our hope, or joy, or crown of rejoicing? Are not even ye in the presence of the Lord Jesus Christ at His coming?"

Perhaps each convert will be a jewel in that crown. How many jewels will you have in your crown? You ought to have one for each year of your Christian life.

3 **Crowns for anticipators, Crowns of Righteousness** 2 Timothy 4:8 "Henceforth there is laid up for me a crown of righteousness, which the Lord, the righteous Judge, shall give me at that day: and not to me only, but unto all them that love His appearing."

Everyone ought to win this crown. Each one of us ought to be watching and waiting for the coming of our Lord Jesus Christ.

4 **Crowns for faithful ones** Crowns of Life: James 1:12 "Blessed is the man that endureth temptation: for when he is tried, he shall receive the crown of life, which the Lord hath promised to them that love Him."

There seem to be three conditions to winning this crown:

a Enduring temptation, overcoming evil.

b Loving Him. This ought to be easy, to love Jesus.

Revelation 2:10 "Be thou faithful unto death, and I will give thee a crown of life."

c Being faithful unto death, enduring to the end. Not only being faithful to death, the end of life, but "unto death" even to martyrdom.

5 **Crowns for true pastors, Crowns of Glory** 1 Peter 5:4 "And when the chief Shepherd shall appear, ye shall receive a crown of glory that fadeth not away."

This is the crown for the elders, the under shepherds, the pastors, missionaries, teachers.

To be faithful over the Lord's heritage and to hear His "well done" and receive this crown, too.

6 **Crowns for all of the redeemed, Crowns of Gold** Revelation 4:4 "I saw four and twenty elders sitting, clothed in white raiment; and they had on their heads crowns of gold."

Not only earthly kings and queens have crowns. Redeemed men have theirs too.

Conclusion

The challenge is to faithfulness. Revelation 3:11 "Behold, I come quickly: hold that fast which thou hast, that no man take thy crown."

It is possible to earn a crown and then to lose it again. Wouldn't that be a terrible tragedy? My God grant that it will not happen to us.

John 19:5, a mock coronation when they crowned the Lord Jesus with a cruel crown of thorns. What a demonstration of the depravity of fallen man.

In Revelation 4:10-11 the elders take their crowns and give them to Jesus saying "Thou art worthy, O Lord, to receive glory and honour and power . . ."

I want to have crowns to lay at His feet at that time. O the utter shame of a Christian who does not have at least one crown to lay at His feet.

He wins the crown for us as we yield to Him. The crown is rightly His, for He has won. I desire to be able to lay many crowns at His blessed feet.

Review Questions

1 Explain the contrast in 2 Corinthians 4:17.
2 What is the blessing in 1 Corinthians 15:55, to which the Christian can look forward?
3 List seven things that could be included in the future glory of believers.
4 Which one of the seven things in question 3 do you consider to be the greatest? Why?

5   Name five different crowns that a believer may wear.
6   Linking James 1:12 and Revelation 2:10, what are the three conditions for winning the crown of life?
7   What are the conditions for winning the incorruptible crown?
8   Which one of the crowns do you think will be the easiest to win?
9   Is it possible to win a crown and then to lose it later? Explain.
10   What do you expect to do when Revelation 4:10,11 becomes a reality?

Heaven

Introduction

Notes taken from D. L. Moody and others.

Carpenter Kao Panhsien, West China, "The Buddhists talk a lot about hell because they are going there; we talk a lot about heaven because we are going there."

D. L. Moody's favorite sermon subject was "Heaven."

"We are nearer heaven tonight than we have ever been before in our lives."

Story: A man kept shouting "Amen" during the sermon. A visiting preacher was coming and someone offered him a pair of boots if he would keep quiet during the sermon. He accepted the proposal. The preacher spoke on heaven and all its wonders and finally the man, unable to contain himself any longer cried, "Boots or no boots, I must shout, Amen, Hallelujah."

I The Origin of Heaven

It was created by God in the beginning. Genesis 1:1 "In the beginning God created the heaven and the earth." When or how long ago is a mystery hidden from man.

Heaven will abide forever. 2 Corinthians 5:11 ". . . an house not made with hands, eternal in the heavens."

Heaven is a prepared place (John 14:2) for a prepared people.

II What is Heaven?

Heaven is the home of the Lord God. Matthew 6:9 "Our Father which art in heaven . . .

2 Corinthians 12:2 speaks of a man caught up to the third heaven. The first heaven is the area where birds fly. The second heaven is where spacecraft go. The third heaven is the home or throne of the Lord God.

Heaven is a building. 2 Corinthians 5:1 "For we know that if our earthly house of this tabernacle were dissolved, we have building of God, an house not made with hands, eternal in the heavens."

Heaven is a building of God. It is not man-made, 2 Corinthians 5:1.

Heaven is called a garner. Matthew 3:12 ". . . gather His wheat into the garner." This occurs at the division of the wheat (good going to heaven and the chaff being burned).

Heaven is called the kingdom of God and of Christ. Ephesians 5:5 ". . . hath any inheritance in the kingdom of Christ and of God."

Heaven is called the Father's House. John 14:2 "In My Father's house . . ."

Heaven is called a place of rest. Hebrews 4:9 "There remaineth therefore a rest to the people of God."

Heaven is called paradise. 2 Corinthians 12:4 "And I knew such a man . . . caught up into paradise."

III The Size of Heaven

It is immeasurable. Jeremiah 31:37 "Thus saith the Lord; If heaven above can be measured. . ."

Revelation 21:1 "And I saw a new heaven and a new earth: for the first heaven and the first earth were passed away; and there was no more sea."

Some have erroneously considered the New Jerusalem of this chapter as heaven.

The New Jerusalem is of equal length, width and height. That is, 12,000 furlongs.

Someone (possibly Bob Ripley) figured the cubical contents at being capable of holding 49,679,308,800,000,000,000 (49.5 pentillion) people.

But that does not allow space for trees and the river of life.

From creation to 1928, 302 hexillion people born. (302,231,454,903,657,293,676,543)

From creation to the present about 78 generation of people have lived (42 before Christ and 36 after).

If these were all alive they would cover the earth to a depth of 113,326 miles.

There were enough people born between Christ and Columbus to fill the New Jerusalem.

Mr. Ripley says that if the New Jerusalem *is* heaven, you had better get your reservation in early!

However, I'm sure that this is not heaven, for the New Jerusalem comes out "from" heaven, but is not heaven itself, Revelation 21:2,10.

But heaven is for the limited few who are holy and pure, and the mansions are definitely limited so it is very wise to book a mansion this very day.

IV Characteristics of Heaven

Heaven is a high place. Isaiah 57:15 "I dwell in the high and holy place."

Heaven is a holy place. Psalm 20:6 "He will hear him from His holy heaven."

Heaven is a happy place. Revelation 7:17 "God shall wipe away all tears."

Heaven is a place without death, tears, sorrow, crying or pain. Revelation 21:4 ". . . and there shall be no more death, neither sorrow, nor crying, neither shall there be any more pain: for the former th things are passed away."

Heaven is a place without night or darkness. Revelation 22:3-5 ". . . and there shall be no night there . . . neither light of the sun: for the Lord God giveth them light. . ."

Heaven is a place without hunger, thirst, excessive heat. Revelation 7:16 "They shall hunger no more, neither thirst any more, neither shall the sun light on them, nor any heat."

Neither will it be too cold like North China or Canada.

V Inhabitants of heaven

1 Negative
   a The devil will never enter there, Revelation 20:10.
   b Thieves will never enter there, Luke 12:33.
   c Revelation 21:8 "But the fearful, and unbelieving, and the abominable, and murderers, and whoremongers, and sorcerers, and idolaters, and all liars. . ."
   d Galatians 5:19-21, the seventeen fruits of the flesh will never enter heaven's perfection.
2 Positive
   a God the Father lives there, Matthew 6:9.
   b Jesus went there after His ascension, Acts 3:21.

c Angels, myriads of these created beings are there, Matthew 18:10; 26:53.

d Enoch and Elijah, who were translated, are there, Genesis 5:24; Matthew 17:3; 2 Kings 2:11.

e All those who have died trusting in Jesus will be there. 1 Thessalonians 4:14 ". . . even so them also which sleep in Jesus will God bring with Him."

f Moses who was buried by God, is there, Matthew 17:3.

VI Heaven is a Perfect Place Revelation 22; 1-5

Notes taken from H. W. Peeler, Millar Memorial Bible Institute.

1 A place of perfect satisfaction, Revelation 22:1,2, a pure river of water of life, a tree with twelve kinds of fruit. A picture of perfect leisurely comfort.

2 A place of perfect provision, Revelation 22:2, the leaves of the trees for the healing of the nations. Everything good, gloriously provided.

3 A place of perfect sinlessness, Revelation 22:3, no more curse. The curse of Eden removed forever from man. Can you imagine such sheer joy?

4 A place of perfect government, Revelation 22:3, ruled by God, the just One, and the Lamb.

5 A place of perfect service, Revelation 22:3 ". . . and His servants shall serve Him." Does this thought spoil the picture of heaven? Certainly not. We serve with joy.

6 A place of perfect communion, Revelation 22:4 "And they shall see His face." Wonderful!

7 A place of perfect possession. We will belong to Him alone. Revelation 22:4 ". . . and His Name shall be in their foreheads." No divided loyalty. His, all *His*.

8 A place of perfect glory, Revelation 22:5. No artificial light there. Together they shall reign forever and ever.

Conclusion

Do you want to go to heaven? Are you prepared? Heaven is for prepared people.

An unbeliever would find it very uncomfortable in heaven because of its holiness.

Story: A king gave to his clown a walking stick in honour of his being the best clown, the biggest fool. It was only to be given to one who was a greater fool. One day the king was dying and the clown came to visit him. The clown asked him what preparations he had made for going to heaven. "None." Then solemnly the clown gave the king and walking stick remarking, "You are the greatest fool."

Review Questions

1   Distinguish the three heavens.
2   Which heaven is referred to in Genesis 1:1?
3   Is heaven a state or place? Explain.
4   How big is heaven?
5   Is the New Jerusalem of Revelation 21:16,17, heaven? Why?
6   List seven characteristics of heaven.
7   Name eight classes of people who will not be in heaven according to Revelation 21:8.
8   List seventeen fruits of the flesh that will never enter heaven.
9   Who is living in heaven today?
10   Describe heaven from Revelation 22:1-5.

Hell

Introduction

In Lesson 40 we were studying about Satan and found that hell or the lake of fire was his final destiny.

It seems that even the angels that sinned with Satan are now in hell waiting for judgment. 2 Peter 2:4 "For if God spared not the angels that sinned, but cast them down to hell, and delivered them into chains of darkness, to be reserved unto judgment. . ."

The Bible teaches that the wicked who finally reject Christ will be turned into hell.

Psalm 9:17 "The wicked shall be turned into hell, and all the nations that forget God."

Is there an everlasting hell? The Bible declares that there is, in very dogmatic language. Hell is a reality, an awful fact to be realized.

There are 162 texts in the New Testament alone which speak of the doom that awaits the unrepentant, and over 70 of these were uttered by the Lord Himself.

I Definition

What is Hell? Hell is banishment from the presence of God. 2 Thessalonians 1:9 "Who shall be punished with everlasting destruction from the presence of the Lord, and from the glory of His power."

Hell is a place of torment and punishment. Luke 16:23 "And in hell he lift up his eyes, being in torments."

Some scoff and say, "Where is hell?" The Bible says it is "down," Isaiah 14:9.

Ezekiel 32:27 ". . . which are gone down to hell . . . "

Numbers 16:30-33, the earth opened and they went down alive into the pit (Sheol).

One of the problems in the study of hell is the various terms that are used.

In the original language three terms are used:
   1) Sheol 2) Hades 3) Gehenna.
Unfortunately in English these have been translated: hell, pit, grave.
These translation lose something of the force of the original, and
give Jehovah's Witnesses and others a loophole to say that hell is
only the grave.

II The Origin of Hell

Hell was originally prepared for the devil and his wicked angels.
Matthew 25:41 "Depart from me, ye cursed, into everlasting fire,
prepared for the devil and his angels."
Hell was never intended for man but if men insist on rejecting heaven
through the Savior, Jesus Christ, then they must accompany Satan
forever.

III Dimensions of Hell

Because of man's insistence on going there, God has had to enlarge
hell.
Isaiah 5:14 "Therefore hell hath enlarged herself, and opened her
mouth without measure."
Proverbs 27:20 "Hell and destruction are never full."

IV Descriptions of Hell

1 It is a place of punishment. Matthew 25:46 "And these shall go
away into everlasting punishment: but the righteous into life
eternal."
2 It is a place of torment. Luke 16:23 "And in hell he lift up his eyes,
and being in torments. . ."
3 It is a place of fire, Matthew 13:42,50; Revelation 20:15; 14:10;
Matthew 3:12; Isaiah 33:14.
4 It is a place of worms. Mark 9:44,46,48 "Where their worm dieth
not, and the fire is not quenched."
5 In Luke 16:23, the man had the ability to recognize others.
6 In Luke 16:27, the man had the ability to pray, though the prayer
was denied.
7 In Luke 16:24-27, the man still had desire. He desired water to drink
and a missionary to go and preach to his brethren, warning them
not to come.

V Duration of Hell

The Bible repeatedly says that both heaven and hell are eternal, everlasting.

Matthew 25:46 "And these shall go away into everlasting punishment: but the righteous into life eternal."

We may not be able to understand it, but we accept it as true, for God says so.

This doctrine is in harmony with the deeply rooted inborn conviction of men. Few object to the fact that heaven is eternal, why object to eternal punishment? If one ceases so much the other.

VI Objections to this Doctrine

1 This doctrine is "inconsistent with the love of God."
    Answer: The same Bible that speaks of the love of God also speaks of the justice and holiness of God. God is balanced, both loving and just.

2 Is there any need of eternal punishment? Won't all sin be paid for eventually?
    Answer: The punishment for each sin is death. Romans 6:23 "For the wages of sin is death. . ."

3 Is it not unjust to sentence men to eternal punishment for one sin?
    Answer: Everlasting punishment does not mean equal punishment. The time may be the same, but the degrees of punishment will vary.

4 Won't the doomed repent and seek the Lord and be forgiven in hell?
    Answer: Salvation is limited to this life. All prayers of the doomed are denied, Luke 16:24-27. prayers for deliverance and salvation will be denied forever.

5 Is it not cruel to think of the doomed being driven into perdition?
    Answer: The ungodly are relieved to get away from the holy presence of a righteous God.

6 The word "eternal" does not always mean forever and ever.
    It is the same word use in relation to God, Romans 16:26 "The everlasting God," to life, John 3:16 "everlasting life," of rewards, Hebrews 9:15 "eternal inheritance."

7 Surely you do not believe in a literal lake of fire?
    Whether it is literal or symbolical the point is that it is a place of punishment for the bodies and souls of men, angels and devils

that reject him.

8 Surely you don't teach that God tortures the lost!

Conscience and memory will torture one in hell.

9 Don't you think hell is a state and not a place?

Perhaps hell is both a state and a definite place.

10 Doesn't "hell" mean the 'grave' where both the good and the bad must go?

In Luke 16, both men died and both men went to the grave, for both were buried, but the abodes of the souls of the two men were different. One was in a place where he was comforted, the other in a place of torment, and the two were separated by a great gulf to prevent travel back and forth.

11 Does "hell" or "hades" or "Gehenna" or "Sheol" mean annihilation only?

The annihilationist says that in 2 Thessalonians 1:9, "Who shall be punished with everlasting destruction from the presence of the Lord . . ." refers to "the results or consequences" of the punishment.

We sincerely believe that it is the punishment that is eternal and the subject must be conscious to be punished. you cannot punish a stone (Evans).

12 Will there not be a probationary period after death?

Certainly not. Consider Hebrews 9:27; Mark 9:42-50; Matthew 18:8,9,25-46.

VII Degrees of Punishment in Hell

Deuteronomy 32:22 "For a fire is kindled in Mine anger, and shall burn unto the lowest hell, and shall consume the earth with her increase . . .'

Matthew 10:15; Mark 6:11; Luke 10:12 "More tolerable for Sodom and Gomorrha than for . . ."

The justice of God demands degrees of punishment. Perhaps those who will suffer the hottest flames of hell are those who reject Him the most times.

Conclusion

How does one get to hell? by neglect. Hebrews 2:3 "How shall we escape, if we neglect. . ."

How does one avoid hell? By receiving Jesus as His personal Savior, Proverbs 15:24.

Review Questions

1 Who will be in hell according to Psalm 9:17?
2 What is hell according to 2 Thessalonians 1:9, and Luke 16:23?
3 If hell is "down" to the Chinese, American and African, where *is* hell? (Isaiah 14:9)
4 What is the origin of hell?
5 What does Isaiah 5:14, teach about hell?
6 Give a sevenfold description of hell.
7 How do we know that both heaven and hell are eternal?
8 True or false: "Hell is inconsistent with the love of God." Explain.
9 Would it be possible for a doomed soul in hell to repent, and seek the Lord and forgiveness? Why?
10 What can we learn about hell from Deuteronomy 32:22, and Matthew 10:15?

Missionary Motives

Introduction

2 Corinthians 5:14 "For the love of Christ constraineth us. . ."

All believers are, or ought to be, constrained by the love of Jesus Christ to serve Him from conversion to death or the rapture. Unfortunately, many Christians have vague ideas as to why they should serve Christ, but no definite, concrete thinking on this very important matter.

Meaning of "constrained": It means compelled, impelled, driven forward.

In the Old Testament men were compelled by law and in the New Testament we are compelled by love. Which is the greater power? I believe Love is.

Many believers would be willing to serve Jesus if He called them to Bible School and full time service, but while waiting for this special call they do not feel any particular need or urge to serve the Master, Jesus Christ the Savior!

To understand a text one must study the context. The context of 2 Corinthians 5:14 gives us several incentives for service:

I The Empty Mansions in Heaven
2 Corinthians 5:1-4

Death is an unpopular topic, yet one that we must constantly face.

In verse 1 Paul speaks about the building of God in heaven. See also John 14:2 "In My Father's house are many mansions."

Luke 14:23 "Go out into the highways and hedges, and compel them to come in that My house may be filled."

I believe that the second coming of Christ is delayed, waiting for the mansions to be filled — for souls to be saved and the heavenly inheritance claimed.

I believe that God gave me a title deed to my mansion at my

conversion in 1936.

How many of your friends, loved ones, acquaintances do not have the title deed?

As a Christian I am constrained to persuade men to be definite about the possession of that home NOW.

Can I be selfish and keep this without sharing it? No. I must tell others.

II The Simplicity of Faith
2 Corinthians 5:7

Verse 7 "For we walk by faith. . ." The way and plan of salvation is so simple.

Everyone of my friends, the aged, the young, the illiterate, the simple-minded, everyone can meet this simple condition of salvation by faith in Jesus Christ

Every Christmas, the poor in Metro Manila (indigents) get their share of gifts from the government and civic-oriented groups. The simple requirement is poverty, and many apply and receive the food and clothes.

If God required that each pay one hundred pesos for salvation, then many would be excluded. But God only requires faith which everyone possesses.

All can meet this requirement — all can believe. But someone must tell them the wonderful story of Jesus and the cross before they can believe it.

III The Desire to Please the Savior
2 Corinthians 5:9

Verse 9 "Wherefore we labour, that, whether present or absent, we may be accepted of Him."

The heartfelt cry of every believer is to please His Master Jesus Christ.

We no longer live to please ourselves. We long to please our new Master.

Story: A violin player was applauded, but showed no sign of response. His eyes were glued on a spot in the balcony. He was watching his teacher sitting there. Finally, after the third encore, the *teacher* applauded and the violinist smiled and responded. you and I are waiting for *His* smile of approval.

Let us do our best to serve Him faithfully, not mere men pleasers but working with an eye single to His honor and glory.

IV Coming Judgment
2 Corinthians 5:10,11

This is the judgment of you and me, the believers, at the *Bema*. See Lesson 84.

We will not be judged on our acceptance of Christ. We will be judged on the superstructure that we build on the foundation (Christ) 1 Corinthians 3:11.

All of our works will be tested by fire. If we have served Him faithfully He will reward us. Some will win many crowns and stars.

The unfaithful will not only lose rewards, but they will suffer loss and the "terror of the Lord" may abide on them, 2 Corinthians 5:11.

The fact that someday I will be judged makes me walk circumspectly and serve diligently. It is not only negative, that I am afraid of punishment. It is positive, for I want rewards and crowns to lay at the feet of the Savior, Revelation 4:10,11.

V Christ Died for All
2 Corinthians 5:14b

"Christ died for all." This is the blessed Gospel story.

This is the reason why I left the comforts of life in Canada to go to China. I knew that Jesus loved all the Chinese and that He died for each one.

This is the reason why I came to the Philippines. I am not afraid to preach to anyone, wondering if he or she was included at Calvary.

Furthermore, if Jesus died for all, then each has a right to know about it.

We serve Jesus by informing them of this great fact. To us it is a well known fact, but many have not heard or realized it as yet.

All need a Savior. Jesus died for *all*. Then let us tell everyone.

VI The Moral Obligation to Live for Others
2 Corinthians 5:15

The life of service is an unselfish life, not serving self but serving others.

I left farming, for it seemed to be such a selfish way of life. Working hours, days, weeks, and never helping anyone but yourself.

Verse 15 ". . . should not henceforth live unto themselves. . ."

Today I give my life to Jesus Christ to serve Him. He has saved me.

He has purchased me. he has redeemed me. I belong to Him. He must have all I possess.

If salvation were the object of life, then we could be translated at conversion straight to heaven. If that had happened who would have brought us the Gospel?

We are saved to serve — to serve not ourselves but *Him* and our neighbours.

He is the potter — I am the clay. He is the Master — I am the servant. He is the Lord, and I must obey orders.

I believe that the happiest life is an unselfish life. The selfish individual is a miserable creature, always jealous lest others get more gifts or praise. The one serving others rejoices in all the successes and pleasures that come to the lives of others.

VII We are Ambassadors with the Word of Reconciliation 2 Corinthians 5:18-21

Verse 19 ". . . and hath committed unto us the word of reconciliation."

Reconciliation infers that two people were enemies. This is very true. The two parties were God and the sinner.

To us as believers has been given the task of bringing the news of the reconciliation won on Calvary to the sinner hiding from God.

Verse 20 calls us ambassadors. We are the official representatives of the government of heaven to the sinner whose back is turned against God.

Wouldn't you like to be a Filipino ambassador? But to be *an ambassador of the court of heaven* is a far greater honour and responsibility.

We are not to be retired ambassadors, but ambassadors on active duty.

Conclusion

Because of these seven reasons I am constrained to serve the Lord Jesus Christ today.

The sphere of service or type of service is not important at this moment. The important thing is, "Am I faithfully serving Him where He wants me to be?"

Review Questions

1   Define "constrained" as it is used in 2 Corinthians 5:14.
2   List seven reasons why we should serve Jesus Christ.

3   What is the connection between Luke 14:23 and John 14:2?
4   In what way is 2 Corinthians 5:7 an inducement to serve the Lord Jesus?
5   Why didn't the violin player respond when the audience applauded?
6   Explain the expression, "the terror of the Lord," in 2 Corinthians 5:11.
7   List those excluded from 2 Corinthians 5:14b.
8   Is farming necessarily a selfish way of life? Explain.
9   What high position is automatically given to each believer?
10 Which one of the reasons given in question 2 do you consider to be the greatest? Why?

90

Missionary Challenge

Introduction

Refer also to *Operation World*, P.J. Johnstone, 1986 edition, and *Ten Sending Churches*, MARC Europe.

There are more people alive today than the total number of people who have ever lived on planet earth.

There are 5 billion people in the world today. At least one half of these have never once heard the Gospel. It is estimated that 80,000 unsaved people die every day, approximately 55 people every single minute.

More than one third of the world's population is communistic (1,558,430,000).

Moslems are advancing rapidly, with the new confidence that oil wealth has given Muslim nations.

There are only 85,000 active Protestant missionaries in the world today.

The Philippines is a great mission field, with unreached islands, barrios and tribes.

Of the 50 million people in the Philippines, probably 36 million are Roman Catholic; 4.2 million Aglipayan, 4 million Muslims, 1 million pagans, with only 6 million Protestants - and many of these only nominal professing believers.

Surely this presents a tremendous challenge to spread the pure Gospel.

There are at least 87 languages spoken in the Philippines, so it is impossible to reach everyone by radio or foreign missionaries.

Foreign missionaries are hindered by the heat of the tropics, and language barriers.

Filipinos are born linguists and find it comparatively easy to live on the meager diet of rice, fish, and bananas of the remote islands and forests.

Filipinos have precious souls and need salvation through the Lord Jesus Christ.

It behooves the true Filipino to arise and give the Gospel to every island and tribe scattered on the 700 inhabited islands (out of 7,000).

I Missionary Objectives

Notes from *Ambassadors for Christ*, Misses French and Cable.

1 The wrong objectives

a To teach the true brotherhood of man. This is wrong for it overlooks the vital sin question.

b To reconcile the Filipino to God. Jesus has already accomplished this on Calvary.

c To seek the uplift of the pagan people by civilization. Education and civilization cannot save one soul from an eternal hell.

d Pleasure, adventure, escape from boredom, an easy task, are false and unsteady motives that will quickly wear off in a few months of arduous service.

2 The right objectives

a Obedience to the command of Christ. Matthew 28:19 "Go ye therefore, and teach all nations." Mark 16:15 "Go ye into all the world, and preach the Gospel to every creature."

b Acceptance of the will of God for our lives. Ephesians 2:10, God has ordained that we believers ought to walk in certain "good works." Romans 12:1,2.

c A passion for the souls of men. Psalm 126:6 "He that goeth forth and weepeth, bearing precious seed. . ." Matthew 9:36.

d A desire to preach the Gospel, to beseech men to turn from sin to God, Acts 3:26. Ezekiel 33:11 "Turn ye, turn ye from your evil ways."

e To teach the whole counsel of God, to establish Christians in the truth, Hebrews 5:12.

f To establish indigenous churches that will become self-propagating, Titus 1:5.

II Missionary Motives

Notes from *Progress of Worldwide Missions*, Glover and Kane.

1 External motives

a The spiritual condition of the lost — bound by a false religion, spiritually lost for they are wicked sinners in the sight of a holy

God, Ephesians 2:12.

b **Their moral condition** — filthy and degrading habits, abominable practices, unmentionable cruelties, moral corruption, slavery, withchcraft, immorality, polygamy, etc.

c **Their temporal condition** — dire poverty, poor homes, long toil, intellectual ignorance, unrelieved sufferings.

2 Internal motives

a **Loyalty to the Master we serve.** He longs for these lost sheep, John 10:16. Let us go and rescue them for him, even as the men got the water from the well of Bethlehem for David, 2 Samuel 23:15,16.

b **Gratitude to the Savior who has redeemed us.**

c **Love.** Constrained by His love to serve *Him.* Jesus said to Peter, If ye *Love* Me feed My lambs and sheep, John 21:15-17.

III Missionary Principles

"Progress of Worldwide Missions"

1 The aim of missions is to make Christ known to all men as the Savior from sin.

a It is a distinctive aim, a spiritual aim. Our work is not commercial, political, philanthropic. Let us hold steady to our original course.

b It is a unique aim. It claims that all men irrespective of class, race or color are lost and need to be saved in exactly the same way, by having their sins cleansed in the Blood of Jesus Christ.

c It is a determining aim. It ought to rule our spirits and control our methods. All our energies are to be bent in this one direction.

2 The policy of missions is to widest diffusion.

The Lord Jesus taught that the field is the world. Our commission is to the world, Mark 16:15, to all nations, Matthew 28:19, to every creature, Mark 16:15.

In the Book of Acts God used persecution to scatter the Christians and reach greater areas with the blessed Gospel.

3 The responsibility of missions rests upon every member of the body of Christ.

The Savior's command was individual and personal, "Go ye."

When God calls one to service He calls by name, Genesis 22:1; John 21:15.

God has called you and me by name into this glorious soul-saving task of reaching Filipinos for Christ.

Romans 11:29 "For the gifts and calling of God are without repentance."

God doesn't change His mind on such important subjects.

God may change your field but not your occupation. He may change the visa but not the passport.

Paul was a Jew, loved the Jews, was called to Jewish work (Acts 9:15c), fitted for it, prepared to live and die for it, but God sent him far away to the Gentiles when the Jews rejected the message, Acts 22:21.

The Overseas Missionary Fellowship was called to China. We loved the Chinese, and were called to Chinese work, prepared to live and die in China. But after 85 years God said "I will send you out of China to the peoples of Southeast Asia."

IV Requirements of a Missionary Candidate

1 He must be born again. This is the first and greatest requirement.
2 He must be willing to bear the cross. Missionary work is not easy, Luke 9:23.
3 Youth is highly desirable that he better adapt to the new surroundings.
4 Boldness is necessary to preach the Gospel in the open air or everywhere.
5 Health is of prime importance for living conditions are poor and disease rampant.
6 He must be zealous for His Master, always putting the Lord first in everything.
7 He must be humble, teachable, willing to learn daily from the Master how to act.
8 He must be sincere for others will soon see through a mock hypocrisy.
9 Straightforwardness and honesty before God and man is desirable, Acts 24:16.
10 Education is important to prove his perseverance and the enlarging of his mental faculties.
11 Experience is highly desirable, for missionary work abounds with problems.

Conclusion

The challenge is to wait upon the Lord for the revelation of His will for your life and then obey it regardless of the price, Luke 9:62.

Review Questions

1   What is the present world population? (in round figures)
2   Would you consider the Philippines a Mission field? Why?
3   List four wrong missionary objectives.
4   Mention six correct missionary objectives.
5   Name three external missionary motives.
6   What are the three highest missionary motives?
7   Describe the aim of Missions.
8   What is the scope of Missions?
9   Upon whom does the missionary responsibility rest?
10   List seven requirements of missionary candidates.

91

Conscience

Introduction

Notes from *Conscience*, Dr. Hallesby; *Systematic Theology*, Chafer; and the *Homiletic Thesaurus*, Vol. 3.

What is conscience? A little girl replied, "It is grandmother!!!"

"Conscience is a thinking man's filter" — Readers' Digest.

The *Oxford Dictionary* says, "It is an inward knowledge or consciousness; the faculty that passes judgment on the moral quality of actions or of individuals."

The *Winston Dictionary* says, "The moral sense or consciousness within oneself that determines whether an action is right or wrong, good or bad."

Hallesby says, "One can have peace with God without a good conscience but this experience would not be a happy one"; I trust this is not our story.

Is conscience the voice of God created within man? No, definitely not. Conscience is something inborn and universal rather than an acquired faculty.

Who has a conscience? Educated and civilized people only? No, all have consciences.

2 Corinthians 4:2 ". . . commending ourselves to every man's conscience. . ."

Conscience cannot be the voice of God, for sometimes it leads people to do things contrary to the will of God as revealed in the Holy Scriptures. Conscience will direct a heathen man to bow down to idols of wood and stone. Conscience approves of acts of sexual license in the temple in honor of the gods.

Sometimes conscience insists that a man must murder the one who killed his father. Sometimes it causes him to forsake the sick, believing them to be cursed by deity and therefore to be left alone. Conscience instructs heathen to throw away twin babies and do many frightful things.

The word "conscience" does not appear in the Old Testament; in the Old Testament the word "heart" is substituted — 1 Samuel 24:5 "David's heart (conscience) smote him."

Conscience is an internal judge examining all that I do and say.

Conscience expresses itself before, during and after the act.

Some feel that conscience will be the main tormentor in hell ("Son, remember..." — Luke 16:25).

I An Evil Conscience

Not all consciences are good — in fact, since the fall, they are depraved.

The conscience of man suffered terribly in the Fall in the Garden of Eden. Ephesians 4:18 describes the unconverted man as "having the understanding darkened because of the blindness of their heart (conscience)."

Romans 1:18-32 is a sad commentary of what happened when, "their foolish heart was darkened," verse 21; sin had clouded the pure Adamic conscience of mankind.

1 Timothy 4:2 warns of the last days when men have "their conscience seared with a hot iron"; They are almost without a conscience, seared and warped.

Titus 1:15 ". . . but even their mind and conscience is defiled."

Let us pray the prayer of Hebrews 10:22, "Let us draw near with a true heart in full assurance of faith, having our hearts sprinkled from an evil conscience."

Let us recognize the past and pray for continual deliverance from an evil conscience.

II A Convicted Conscience

Romans 2:15 "Which show the work of the law written in their hearts, their conscience also bearing witness, and their thoughts the mean while accusing or else excusing one another." This is the work of the conscience of man.

The judgment of conscience is categorical, without giving reasons; it is absolute for it neither bargains nor compromises, and it is definitely individualistic.

John 8:1-11 is a picture of the conscience in action; each man left with the stab pricks from its mighty prongs, bringing confusion of face and shame.

III A Purged (Cleansed) Conscience

Hebrews 9:14 "Purge your conscience from dead works to serve the
   living God."

First realize the evil of a depraved conscience; let conviction lead to
   a conversion of the standards of conscience.

No longer silence your conscience but pray for its enlightenment by
   the Word of God.

Let conscience maintain a high standard of righteousness and then
   stick to it.

Some have suffered torture, loss of property, reputation and even
   martyrdom rather than offend conscience.

A good conscience gives meaning to life, richness, fulness, purpose
   and pleasure.

Spiritual awakening is the awakening of the conscience of man
   Godward.

Let the Word of God daily instruct the conscience about the will and
   plan of God. The awakened conscience brings pressure on the
   personal life to conform to the knowledge of sin and righteousness
   derived from the study of God's Word.

IV A Pure Conscience

1 Timothy 3:9 "Holding the mystery of the faith in a pure conscience . . ."

2 Timothy 1:3 "I thank God, whom I serve from my forefathers with
   pure conscience."

At conversion not only the soul is saved but the conscience is
   converted, too. This change of conscience is often a gradual process
   as the individual is instructed more perfectly in the will of God.

The conscience is cleansed by the Blood of Christ; this is taught in
   Hebrews 10:2-10, where the blood of animal sacrifices was a type
   of Calvary's Blood.

The new birth does not oppose conscience but rather re-establishes
   normal order.

The unconverted consider conscience is a burden but to the saved
   conscience is a help.

To the saved the conscience is a friend to know and love; a messenger
   from God.

The standard of the conscience is perfection, Matthew 5:48, which is
   God's standard.

V A Weak Conscience

The young convert may find that his conscience is too weak to rely upon. 1 Corinthians 8:7 "And their conscience being weak is defiled." Also 1 Corinthians 8:10.

Conversion is the re-creation of conscience which has been long silenced.

This weakness can be overcome by prayer, Bible study and constant obedience.

The problem is to recognize it, for the solution is very plain and simple.

Often converts blame other things: environment, education, friends, etc.

The Lord desires to strengthen and build up the weak conscience.

VI A Good Conscience

This is the desire of God for every Christian.

Do not be at war with your conscience but be at peace; agree with the enlightened conscience and obey it implicitly.

1 Timothy 1:5 ". . . charity out of a pure heart, and of a good conscience. . ."

1 Timothy 1:19, Paul charged Timothy to hold faith and have a "good conscience."

1 Peter 3:16 "Having a good conscience"; live to rebuke those who abuse you.

The message of conscience is directed to the will; if the will obeys, the conscience will grow and develop. If the will resists, the conscience will be weakened; and more easily silenced.

Pray that the Lord will give you a good conscience; a tender conscience.

Beware of the attitude of the scribes who had a tender conscience in small matters but overlooked the weightier matters of the law, Matthew 23:23.

Conscience is a living thing, subject to growth and development.

VII A Conscience void of Offence

Acts 24:16 "And herein do I exercise myself, to have always a conscience void of offence toward God and toward men."

I believe that this is one of the highest goals in a Christian life.

Beware of a pathologically *over*sensitive conscience that keeps the individual in continuous conflict. The result of justification is peace, not conflict.

Pray much for a conscience that listens to the will of God as revealed in Scripture.

In prayer and during the Quiet Time stop to listen to conscience speaking.

The believer is indwelt by the Holy Spirit and the Spirit works through conscience.

A sensitive conscience produces Christians who are conscientious, dependable and usable in the kingdom of God.

An insensitive conscience produces careless saints, the weakening influence in the Church today.

Conclusion

What is our reaction to this study on conscience? Have we learned anything?

Have we ever analyzed our own conscience?

Is my conscience evil? convicted? purged? pure? weak? good? void of blame?

No medical doctor can find the organ called conscience but we know we have it.

Do we spend time trying to silence or kill conscience with plausible reasonings?

Let us determine now to let God examine and control our conscience.

One student wrote in an examination, "Beware of conscience — it will come again!!!"

Do we want peace? Let conscience be obeyed and we will have heart *peace.*

Review Questions

1   What is conscience?
2   Is conscience the voice of God? Why?
3   List seven kinds of consciences listed in the Holy Scriptures.
4   What type of conscience will men have in the latter days?
5   What two things does the conscience do according to Romans 2:15?
6   How can a conscience be purged (cleansed)?
7   Is the "pure conscience" of 2 Timothy 1:3, and 1 Timothy 3:9, the same? Why?

8 Should a convert or young Christian always trust his conscience? Why?
9 Is there a distinction between the "pure heart" and "good conscience" of 1 Timothy 1:5?
10 What are the vertical and horizontal areas in which conscience works?

Divorce

Introduction

Notes chiefly from *The Home, Courtship and Marriage* Dr. John Rice; *What The Bible Says About Divorce*, William W. Orr; *Question Box*, Dr. C.I. Scofield.

Today in the United States, one marriage in two ends in the divorce court.

Divorce represents one of the major problems facing homes today.

Most of these divorces could have been prevented if sane counsel regarding marriage had been sought before marriage.

Today divorce is granted for many reasons including adultery, cruelty, desertion, drunkenness, neglect to provide, vagrancy, conviction of crime, separation, bigamy, incompatibility, fraudulent representation, misconduct, etc. (Orr).

Let us approach this subject by attempting to answer a number of questions:

I How long is a Marriage Contract?

"Till death breaks it." Matthew 19:6 "Wherefore they are no more twain, but one flesh. What therefore God hath joined together, let not man put asunder."

In marriage God performs a miracle when two individuals become one person.

Only God is permitted to break that union by taking one of the partners in death.

II What Constitutes a Marriage?

If a couple in a state of intoxication or infatuation have a civil ceremony are they legally married? Is such a marriage null and void?

1 The marriage is legal because the law says that marriage duly performed is a legal ceremony. If the proper documents are signed, they are officially man and wife, an inseparable unit.

2 According to 1 Corinthians 6:16, sexual union constitutes marriage. "What? know ye not that he which is joined to an harlot is one body? for two, saith He, shall be one flesh."

Marriage is twofold: It is both legal and spiritual; sealed by God Himself.

III Is there any Scriptural Ground for Divorce?

Yes. There is one and only one legal reason and that is fornication.

Matthew 19:9 "And I say unto you, Whosoever shall put away his wife, except it be for fornication, and shall marry another, committeth adultery."

What does the word, "fornication" mean in this passage? Some newer translations translate it "unfaithfulness." The basic meaning is illicit sexual relations with a third party before marriage according to Deuteronomy 24:1-4.

Dr. Rice and Dr. Orr suggest that it means only if the other person has become a habitual fornicator; ordinarily the innocent party would forgive the guilty party upon confession and the couple would be reunited.

However, for chronic cases the Lord permitted a writing of divorcement.

IV Should the Innocent Party Demand a Divorce if Matthew 19:9 Becomes True?

No. Divorce is never *commanded*; it is *permitted* in unusual and extreme cases.

Divorce was not in the original plan of God — Matthew 19:4,5.

Why then are there divorces? Jesus explained it this way in Matthew 19:8, "Moses, because of the hardness of your hearts, suffered (permitted by a special dispensation of grace) you to put away your wives: but from the beginning it was not so."

V If a Divorcee marries again, and then Becomes a Christian, should he or she Return to the Original Marriage Partner?

Definitely not. The second marriage is legal and to try to dissolve it would create many other complex problems.

The Scripture says, "Let every man abide in the same calling wherein he was called," 1 Corinthians 7:20. This is the principle followed by missionaries; life begins at conversion.

VI If a Wife is Divorced and Marries someone else who later Dies, may she Return to her First Husband?

Definitely not; this is an abomination in the sight of the Lord. Deuteronomy 24:1-4, would clearly forbid any such action.

VII Should a Divorced Person Remarry?

If the persons were divorced on Scriptural grounds, they would be free to remarry.

Naturally, they would be much more cautious the next time. Deuteronomy 24:2.

If they were divorced on unscriptural grounds, then the second marriage would be "living in adultery."

VIII Why should People avoid Divorce?

1 Consider the welfare of the children who suffer the most.
2 Consider the shame connected with divorce and the scandal that it engenders.
3 Some churches deny church privileges to divorced people.
4 Many Christians look on divorce as sinful, regardless of the circumstances.
5 Economic disaster often follows divorce.
6 Divorce is a public admission of utter failure.
7 Divorce is the ruination of love and happiness in marriage.

IX May the Innocent Party in a Divorce Remarry?

It is doubtful if there is such a thing as an innocent party in the sight of God, for probably the "innocent" party failed in some way which caused the partner to go further allied for satisfaction.

Dr. Ironside says the innocent party would need to prove his or her innocence with two or three witnesses, 2 Corinthians 13:1.

Deuteronomy 24:2, permits the innocent party to remarry.

X Is it Permissible for a Divorced Person to Hold a Church Office?

If the person were innocent and the divorce granted on Scriptural grounds then the answer would be, yes.

If the person were partially guilty or received the divorce for other than Scriptural grounds, then the answer would be a strong, "No."

XI Why is there a Stigma against Divorce?

Because it represents a tragedy that has undermined the home, the basis of society.

Because of the misery that follows in its path: broken homes, bruised and broken hearts, bewildered homeless children, delinquent youth, mountains of loneliness, oceans of tears and even suicide and insanity.

XII What about Young People Anticipating Marriage but Afraid of Divorce?

Divorce should never be considered and will not be necessary if the marriage is made in heaven.

To prevent divorce, be sure that both parties are Christians, of the same religious faith, with mutual interests, and private guidance to enter into marriage.

Commit everything to the Lord and He will choose both well and satisfactorily, Psalm 37:4.

XIII What about Married people who are Contemplating Divorce?

Let both husband and wife solemnly renew their vow for "better or worse, till death do us part."

Let each get right with the Lord and then with one another; confession and repentance with mutual sharing will make any marriage a success.

Let them spend time in prayer individually and as a couple.

Little children are often the solution to marital problems; preventing children leads to childlessness, dissatisfaction, frustration and quarreling.

Let the husband be the actual head of the home (not merely a figurehead).

Let wives be subject to their own husbands.

Let husbands and wives continually woo each other; each needs a great deal of affection.

Continuously ask God for a holy love for each other.

XIV Can there be Love when there is no Respect?

Dr. Rice says "Yes," for God loves the unlovely sinner, whom He cannot respect.

Many a mother loves a drunken, murderous son.

The *Father* in Luke 15 still loved the prodigal.

Love that is unselfish and godly can be deep and powerful even with those whom we cannot respect.

Jesus even goes further when He says, Love your enemies" — Matthew 5:44.

Review Questions

1   How long is a marriage contract?
2   In what two ways may a marriage be contracted?
3   What is the Scriptural ground for divorce?
4   When was divorce first recognized?
5   Should a missionary force Christians to return to their original marriage partners? Why?
6   Is it possible for a divorcee to return to her husband:
   a) if neither have remarried?
   b) after a second marriage?

7   Why should people avoid divorce?
8   Should divorce be a major consideration in planning a marriage?
9   What advice can you give married people contemplating divorce?
10   Can there be love when there is no respect for the other party? Explain your answer.

Fasting

Introduction

Material drawn from *Studies in the Sermon on the Mount,* Dr. D. Martyn Lloyd Jones; *Dictionary of the Bible,* Dr. James Hastings; Tillotson and "Unger."

"Should we spend more time fasting?"; "Is fasting the forgotten grace in the New Testament Church?" "Do you fast? How often? Why?"

This lesson is an attempt to answer some of these basic questions.

Fasting is not found in the Pentateuch but often in the historical books.

Apparently the first recorded fast is in Judges 20:26, about 1400 B.C.

Because Roman Catholics and Mohammedans fast frequently, Protestants have gone to the opposite extreme and seldom or never fast.

In passages like Leviticus 16:29-31; 23:27-32, the Bible speaks of "afflicting the soul," and in the light of passages like Psalm 35:13, this is interpreted as fasting.

Psalm 35:13 "I humbled my soul with fasting."

The book of Nehemiah (7:73-9:38) records a general fast.

During the captivity Israel added four fasts in addition to the one for the Day of Atonement — Zechariah 7:3-5; 8:19.

1 A fast to commemorate the capture of Jerusalem
— the 17th day of the 4th month.

2 A fast to commemorate the burning of the Temple
— the 9th day of the 5th month.

3 A fast to commemorate the murder of Gedaliah
— the 10th day of the 7th month.

4 A fast to commemorate the siege of Jerusalem
— the 10th month.

In the New Testament the Pharisees kept two weekly fasts (Monday and Thursday).

The present Jewish calendar permits 22 fasts plus the Day of Atonement.

I The Old Testament Standard of Fasting

According to Tillotson, it included six things:
1 Strict abstinence from food (some say lentils could be eaten).
2 Humble confession of sins to God.
3 Earnest seeking of God's face — this often included sackcloth and
   ashes, Daniel 9:3.
4 True intercession for themselves and others.
5 Giving alms to the poor.
6 Living as one prayed and vowed.

II Old Testament Reasons for Fasting

To express deep mourning 1 Samuel 31:13, fasting seven days for
Saul.

To avert Divine wrath 2 Samuel 12:16-17, fasting to keep the baby
alive.

To express repentance and sorrow for sin Jonah 3:7, the city of
Nineveh.

III The Wrong Kind of Fasting

It is possible to take a perfectly good thing and abuse it; to cause it to
   degenerate to a mere external form without sincere heart meaning.
In Isaiah 58:3-5; God reveals the sin of the mere form of outward
   fasting:
1 As a display for God to see, verse 3.
2 Merely afflicting their souls, verse 3, abstaining from food.
3 For personal pleasure, verse 3, something to boast about, Luke
   18:12.
4 To exact full labor (oppress employees to get full daily output of
   goods verse 3
5 For strife or debate, verse 4.
6 To smite with a wicked fist, verse 4.
7 To make God hear their voices, verse 4; to obligate God to hear their
   prayers.
8 To bow the head as a bulrush, verse 5.
9 To sit in sackcloth and ashes, verse 5: an outward show of fasting.

IV Right Fasting Isaiah 58:6-9

Correct fasting would demonstrate itself in a life of practical daily holiness.

1 To loose the bands of wickedness, verse 6.
2 To undo the heavy burdens, verse 6.
3 To let the oppressed go free, verse 6.
4 To break every yoke, verse 6.
5 To give bread to the hungry, verse 7.
6 To restore the poor from thy house, verse 7.
7 To clothe the naked, verse 7.
8 To reveal yourself to your relatives, verse 7.

These eight things could be summarized in the words of James 1:27.

V Jesus and Fasting

He was not legalistic in regard to fasts but probably kept the main Jewish fasts.

He fasted forty days and forty nights just prior to the great temptations, Matthew 4:2.

He warned against the abuse of fasting, Matthew 6:16.

He taught that His disciples would fast after His departure, Mark 2:20.

He gave some instructions regarding proper fasting, Matthew 6:17,18.

He associated prayer with fasting, Mark 9:29.

He said that certain demons could be cast out only by prayer and fasting, Matthew 17:21.

VI Fasting in the New Testament

The Apostle Paul fasted, 2 Corinthians 6:5; 2 Corinthians 11:27.

The Church fasted before prayer in Acts 13:3, before separating Paul and Barnabas for ministry as missionaries.

The Church fasted before appointing elders in Acts 14:23.

In Acts 10:30, Cornelius fasted for four days.

In 1 Corinthians 7:5, fasting seems to include not only abstinence from food but from legitimate, normal love relations between husbands and wives by mutual consent.

VII Value of Fasting Today

Speaking from the medical or physical point of view it is excellent for the body; most of us eat far too much and to rest the digestive system periodically is good.

People who are overweight or obese would be well advised to fast in order to reduce. One American doctor has written, "After you feast, you should fast."

Students who face strenuous examinations find it highly desirable to fast in order to increase the blood in the brain area; it gives more clarity of thought.

Some who fast for extended periods say that the first three or four days are the hardest but after that the mind becomes unusually clear.

Christians seeking the will of God could profitably spend time in prayer and fasting. With the mind clearer they would be able to think more logically and evaluate the various circumstances and interacting factors. Furthermore, fasting demonstrates to the Lord the depth of our sincerity; that we are willing to importunately (Luke 11:8) knock and keep on knocking till light comes.

"Praying Hyde" of India gives a classic example of prayer and fasting; he would leave his bed unslept in and the food untouched simply because he was so engrossed in intercession that he forgot to eat and sleep.

Matthew 6:17,18 (the Sermon on the Mount by the Lord Jesus Himself) infers that we are to fast secretly, surreptitiously, without any telltale signs.

The basic meaning of fasting is abstinence from food for spiritual purposes.

Dr. Jones pointed out the clear distinction between fasting and discipline; discipline is something that we do every day, all day long, while fasting is something quite special for unusual circumstances.

Fasting is something that we do in order to reach a higher spiritual realm in prayer, meditation or finding the will of God.

Conclusion

Never fast with the thought of obligating God, saying to yourself: "Because I fast the Lord is forced to bless me or make me a great blessing."

Our fasting, praying or tithe does not obligate God and make Him our servant.

We should never engage in fasting as a means of obtaining blessing; the value of fasting is indirect and not direct.

Why, then, should a Christian fast? Because he feels impelled to do so for some spiritual reason or reasons.

Fasting should never be routine or mechanical; it should be prompted by the Holy Spirit and engaged in at His command for the duration that He dictates.

Review Questions

1 What was the original Old Testament fast?
2 Did Israel do right or wrong in adding four fasts?
3 What was the Old Testament standard of fasting?
4 List three main reasons for fasting in the Old Testament.
5 Describe the degeneracy of fasting in Isaiah 58:3-5.
6 What eight things would result from true fasting according to Isaiah 58:6-9?
7 What was Jesus' teaching and attitude toward fasting?
8 Did the New Testament Church practice fasting?
9 What is the value of fasting today?
10 Will fasting obligate God to bless me? Explain.

Capital Punishment

Introduction

Material taken from various sources including articles by Jacob J. Vellenga, John H. Yoder; C. S. Milligan; G. H. Clark, writing in "Christianity Today."

Many States now have abolished the death penalty and others never demand it though it is still on the statute books.

The question of the abolition of capital punishment has been before the Canadian parliament for several years.

Worldwide protests flowed in when Caryl Chessman died in the gas chamber on May 2, 1960, after fighting the death penalty for twelve years.

Open forums in newspapers both secular and religious have debated this controversial issue for some time.

One Canadian columnist says, "Not one authenticated case is known of a person being deterred from murder from fear of the consequences."

A man confessed to me, "I'd kill that man (and humanly speaking he had good reasons to do so) but the authorities would just take my life," and that murder was never perpetrated.

I Arguments of those Favoring Abolition of the Death Penalty

Capital punishment is immoral; it is repulsive to modern concepts of society.

Some progressive nations limit the death penalty to heinous crimes and offenses like treason.

The death penalty is expensive for it involves endless appeals, hoping to find technicalities in the law to delay the execution or obtain a new trial, even when the individual is undeniably guilty.

Actually records show that only 2% of convicted cases are actually executed; many with money or friends escape the death penalty via "insanity" or similar excuse.

The 2% who die are the poor and friendless and not necessarily the most vile or wanton.

Up to 5% of those convicted are actually innocent; they have been convicted on mistaken identity, circumstantial evidence, prejudiced juries or over-powerful appeals by lawyers.

Capital punishment brutalizes society by cheapening life. It is morally indefensible; it is not a deterrent to murder.

Capital punishment makes it impossible to rehabilitate criminals.

Those favoring capital punishment are stigmatized as heartless, vengeful and lacking in mercy.

II Arguments Upholding Capital punishment

Capital punishment is based on Scripture and must be upheld. Genesis 9:6; Romans 13:4.

Civil governments are instituted by God and are duty bound to execute murderers.

The government must consider the protection of society, not only the welfare of the criminal.

Justice must be maintained and this will instill standards of right and wrong among the people.

Governments based on the Bible are to maintain high moral and ethical standards.

The opposition is based on modern philosophical systems; sociological studies.

Capital punishment is not a social evil like segregation, racketeering, the liquor traffic or gambling.

Capital punishment is a matter of jurisprudence established for the common good and benefit of society.

III Old Testament Teachings on Capital punishment

Genesis 9:4-6 "Whoso sheddeth man's blood, by man shall his blood be shed."

Exodus 20:13, God's law, "Thou shalt not kill."

The warden who performs the execution does not commit murder in the taking of a life according to Numbers 35:27, for he is the Lord's appointed "revenger of blood."

Numbers 35:27 "And the revenger of blood kill the slayer; he shall not be guilty of blood."

Numbers 35:31 "Moreover ye shall take no satisfaction for the life of a murderer, which is guilty of death: but he shall surely be put to death."

Death penalty only given after the evidence has been confirmed by more than one witness — Numbers 35:30 "Whoso killeth any person, the murderer shall be put to death by the mouth of witnesses: but one witness shall not testify against any person to cause him to die."

The Bible makes a distinction between premeditated murder and an accidental killing — Exodus 21:12-17; no death penalty for an accidental killing.

Leviticus 24:14-17 capital punishment for blasphemy, cursing and murder.

Numbers 35:15-34 cities of refuge for the murderers who committed murder accidentally.

Numbers 35:16,17,18,21,30,31 — the murderer to be killed.

Deuteronomy 17:6,7 testimony of two or more witnesses essential to give death penalty.

Deuteronomy 19:11-13 authority to take the individual guilty of first degree murder from the City of Refuge and slay him.

The Old Testament gave the death penalty for:

Outright, premeditated murder, Numbers 35:16.

Stealing and selling people, Exodus 21:16.

Cursing father or mother, Exodus 21:17.

Ox and owner to be killed if owner knew of the tendency of the animal to kill and didn't curb it, Exodus 21:29.

Witches, Exodus 22:18.

Those sacrificing to a false god, Exodus 22:20.

Adultery, Leviticus 20:10; Harlot and whoremonger both to die, Deuteronomy 22:24.

Blasphemy, Leviticus 24:10-14.

Breaking the Sabbath, Numbers 15:32.

IV New Testament Teachings on Capital Punishment

Jesus Christ came to fulfill the law, Matthew 5:17-20; He did not come to change or abrogate the law.

Matthew 5:21,22 men are liable "to the judgment" which would include capital punishment.

Some argue that the New Testament is based on love even to loving one's enemies, Matthew 5:44.

They say that we are to love our neighbors (even criminals) as ourselves, therefore, we ought not to execute them.

The opponents of capital punishment quote the story in John 8:1-11, where the woman was taken in adultery and brought to Jesus for passing of judgment. The law demanded the death penalty but Jesus forgave the woman. Why didn't Jesus demand justice? If the woman were actually taken in adultery then both she and the man should be stoned together. Jesus said that the one without sin was to cast the first stone: perhaps they were all guilty in this affair and the woman the least guilty.

Others quote the story of Paul requesting leniency for Onesimus the runaway slave, who deserved the death penalty according to Roman law. Paul pleads for leniency because of Onesimus' conversion.

Romans 13:1-4 establishes the right of governments to use the sword if necessary to revenge evil. The sword would certainly include the death penalty.

Romans 12:19-21 the grieved individuals were not to take revenge as they did in the Old Testament but allow the constituted authorities to execute proper judgment.

Romans 13:1 "Let every soul be subject unto the higher powers." We are to obey them.

Conclusion

Some feel that a definite conclusion is not possible but continue to wait for the mind of Christ to better understand the problem. Personally I feel that capital punishment is God's divine order for today; this principle antedates the giving of the law by 800 years (Usher).

The argument that capital punishment rules out the possibility of repentance for crime is ridiculous. If a man does not repent with a death sentence over his head I doubt if he ever will under a "life sentence."

Physical life is less important than eternal life; a man has to die sometime.

Hebrews 9:27 "It is appointed unto men (every man) once to die..."No one can deny that the execution of a murderer is a terrible spectacle

but we must not forget that murder is certainly far more horrible.
If one accepts the authority of the Scriptures, the issue is clear
— capital punishment is essential to a safe community.

Let us not be led astray by modern naturalistic ideas of sociology and
penology. Let us study the Bible and obey it completely, remembering that the God of the Old Testament is the same as the God of
the New Testament; the basic principles of God and His government will never change, Hebrews 13:8.

Review Questions

1   What do we mean by capital punishment?
2   What do you consider the most humane form of capital punish-
    ment?
3   List some arguments against the death penalty.
4   What is the main reason why Christians uphold the death
    penalty?
5   What are the two sides to consider regarding a criminal's future?
6   What is the difference between first degree murder and man-
    slaughter?
7   List three Scriptures to uphold the death penalty.
8   Could a guilty murderer safely remain in the City of Refuge?
9   List eight things for which the Old Testament gave the death
    penalty.
10 Explain Romans 13:4, in relation to capital punishment.

Compromise

Introduction

Material drawn from an editorial in *Moody Monthly* by Dr. James M. Gray, and other sources.

The word "compromise" does not appear in the Holy Scriptures, though it is a common word in our evangelical vocabulary today.

Dr. C. I. Scofield outlines the section in Exodus 5:3; 7:16; 8:25-28; 10:11,24-27, as *"The four compromises offered by Pharaoh to Moses and Israel."*

Compromise is a common word in politics and in the settling of a labour dispute.

In a labour strike where the men want an increase in pay of one dollar per day and management offers only twenty cents, an arbitrator begins to bargain with both sides seeking a compromise at probably a sixty-cent raise.

Both sides compromise and it is considered "good business" to accept the result.

Neither side may be too happy, but they feel that it is the best that they can do under the circumstances and accept it as an honorable solution.

Can we use this principle in religion? In our relationships with God? the world? sin? etc.

Compromise according to the dictionary means, "A settlement of a dispute in which each concedes."

Compromise involves conceding, concessions, sacrifice of principles; as Christians may we do this? No, ten thousand times *No!*

Compromise involves the partial surrender of one's position in concession to another party, (in our case the enemy, Satan, and his cohorts).

Illustrations of compromise:

1 God told Joshua to destroy the inhabitants of Canan (Joshua 9:24), but the Gibeonites tricked Joshua and got a compromise —

they became his servants.

2 God told Saul to utterly destroy Amalek and all his possessions (1 Samuel 15:3) but Saul compromised and saved some to sacrifice (15:15). For this ungodly compromise he was severely reprimanded and the kingdom was taken from him.

There are many illustrations of compromise today:

1 Evangelicals compromising with modernists.
2 Christians compromising with sin.
3 The Church compromising with the world.

I First compromise offered by Pharaoh
Exodus 8:25 "Sacrifice in the land"

God's command was clear — Exodus 5:3 "Let us go, we pray thee, three days' journey into the desert, and sacrifice unto the Lord our God."

Exodus 7:16 "Let My people go, that they may serve Me in the wilderness."

God's commands are specific; God intended it to be obeyed to the full extent, in every detail.

Pharaoh's compromise was but a partial fulfillment of the will of the Lord God.

God's command specifically required that Israel be separated from Egypt by a three-day journey. Why three days? Likely it was to be a picture of living on resurrection ground, separated from death and the world by three days, as Christ was.

Today God is issuing the same order of separation; Luke 5:4 "Launch out into the deep." Go as far from the world and the place of sin as possible.

Have you heard the story of the boy who fell out of bed and explained it this way, "I stayed too near where I got in." Similarly, in the Kingdom, people stay too near where they enter, compromise, and lose out spiritually with the Lord.

Beware of compromise: Launch out into the deep of divine strength; the deep of God's infinite love; into the deep of His faithfulness.

For Israel to have sacrificed in Egypt would have been an abomination to the Egyptians and would have resulted in riots and stoning for Israel; to sacrifice sheep and goats before the Egyptians would have been anathema, for these were sacred animals to the Egyptians.

The story is told of a Roman ambassador who was torn to pieces for accidentally killing a sacred animal in Egypt.

Moses will accept no compromise; he demands 100% obedience; true worship requires separation; separation from that which is wicked, profane and ungodly.

Politically the Israelites were slaves in Egypt but in matters of religion they must be free; completely free.

If Israel had sacrificed in Egypt, men would say, "I see no difference between us; our religions are the same; our aims and objectives are identical."

The average man today feels that all religion is good as long as one is sincere; it is only by an uncompromising life that we can prove otherwise.

Men today prefer a compromise; a bit of religion, a little bit of the world and sin; the devil also wants a compromised, watered-down religion.

Launch out into the deep and away from a compromising, mediocre Christianity.

II Second Compromise offered by Pharaoh
Exodus 8:28 "Go not very far"

Instead of three days into the wilderness, go just over the border; just a mile or so outside of Egypt.

It sounds good! Separated, no more Egyptians. Did Moses accept it? Certainly not!

Pharaoh was afraid that once outside the land they might try to escape to Canaan. He wanted to keep an eye on them and bring them back if necessary.

Moses rejected it for the line of separation was too close; too limited; too near Egypt and the world.

After conversion launch right out; don't compromise; be baptized and maintain a bold testimony; burn all the bridges behind you so that you can't return to the world.

When you get converted burn the cigarettes, smash the liquor bottles, destroy gambling paraphernalia; make a loud profession for Christ and stand by it.

Make the division between you and the former life as great as possible.

Don't be like the boy who took a bathing suit in case he was tempted to go swimming in forbidden waters.

Romans 13:14 "Make not provision for the flesh."

To follow Christ and then return to the world is a terrible thing; Satan is well pleased with "borderline Christians."

What is God's reaction to these borderline individuals? He says they are neither cold nor hot (Revelation 3:15,16) and He will spew them out of His mouth. If you are a "borderline Christian," quickly rebuke Satan, quit compromising and launch way out into the deep.

III Third Compromise offered by Pharaoh
Exodus 10:8-11 "Let only the men go"

Pharaoh and Satan knew that if the men went the full three days into the wilderness to sacrifice that they would soon return to their wives and families and slavery.

The devil will let you go to Church if you go back home and serve him in the same manner afterwards — i.e. giving God *one* hour a week and self and 167 hours to Satan.

This is a subtle compromise; parents serving the Lord but not including their children; they are our precious gift to give back to the Creator.

Men in the wilderness and children in Egypt — What an anomaly! Can one serve both? No.

A friend of mine in Swift Current, Canada, has claimed the promise of Acts 16:31, "and thy house," for all his children and grandchildren, and God has faithfully, abundantly caused them all to serve God as one happy united family.

O parents, let's not just get the children saved; let's get them out of Egypt — away from the borderline; out beyond the camp with the Lord Jesus Himself.

Beware of the compromise of sending a delegate to Church or prayer meeting; take the whole family; Moses said everyone must go, male, female, old and young.

IV Fourth Compromise offered by Pharaoh
Exodus 10:24-27 "Let the people go
but not the cattle"

Would Moses accept this wonderful offer? Everybody could go, even to make the three-day journey to the very spot where God wanted them to go and worship ... No. Moses rejected it for it represented incomplete obedience; incomplete obedience means compromise. How could they sacrifice without animals? Impossible!

How can we worship without presenting our possessions to give Him as He requires?

A man being baptized discovered that he had left his wallet in his trousers, took it out and gave it to a friend saying, "Please hold this — it has nothing to do with the baptism." The minister rightly replied, "I either baptize you with the wallet or not at all."

Here is one point where we cannot permit compromise; God told them to go and worship with sacrifices but didn't specify which animals or how many.

God demands us unconditionally — all that we have; our wives, children and possessions.

There can be no compromise; we cannot bargain with God: He is Lord of *all* or not Lord at all.

Jesus is worthy of all — let not one hoof remain behind; everything to Him we give.

Gladly my all to Him I give — my mind, strength, heart, soul, body, and possessions.

Conclusion

Note the subtleness of Satan's compromises:

a) Sought to keep Israel in the land; b) Sought to keep Israel near the land; c) Sought to divide Israel and d) Sought to send them forth empty-handed without the ability to serve the Lord.

Moses refused to accept the four compromises and held out for 100% obedience which was finally granted after the death of the firstborn on that first Passover night.

When Paul was converted he made a clean break with his past life.

James 1:27 speaks of "Pure religion and undefiled," pure, not mixed, not watered down, no compromise.

Separation from the world is an indispensable quality in true service for Christ.

A salvation that left Israel in Egypt would have been a failure.

May a Christian compromise? No. Why? Because compromising is sacrificing principles.

Review Questions

1   Define the word "compromise."
2   Illustrate compromise from the business world.

3 Is it permissible in Christianity to have a dialogue with the enemy for the purpose of coming to an amiable solution? Why?
4 Did God accept Saul's fine compromise in 1 Samuel 15?
5 List three modern illustrations of compromise.
6 What were the four compromises offered by Pharaoh to Moses?
7 Why a separation of three days' journey into the wilderness?
8 Why was it impractical for Israel to worship in Egypt?
9 What is the connection between Exodus 10:11 and Acts 16:31?
10 List three ways that evangelical Christians often compromise today.

Abstinence, Not Temperance

Introduction

Many Christians believe in temperance, being moderate in the consumption of alcoholic beverages, but are strongly opposed to excessive drinking.

What is the Christian's position? The safest, most Scriptural answer is complete abstinence, for temperance may get broader than one can control.

Some say that since Jesus changed the water into wine in John 2:1-11; that the Savior gave permission for wine at a wedding.

What kind of wine did Jesus create in John 2? The Greek word is "*oinos*" meaning grape juice, while the word for intoxicating liquor is "*shekar*." Both of these words are used in Luke 1:15, "For he (John the Baptist) shall be great in the sight of the Lord, and shall drink neither wine (oinos) nor strong drink (shekar)."

In 1 Timothy 5:23, Paul exhorts Timothy to use wine as a medicine, "Drink no longer water, but use a little wine for thy stomach's sake and thine often infirmities." The word used here is "*oinos*" (grape juice).

The USA now has more than five million alcoholics, and three million pre-alcoholics, tottering on the brink of social helplessness. The financial loss to the nation exceeds 700 million dollars annually.

Dr. Andrew Ivy of the University of Illinois says, "Alcoholism is now the nation's number three health problem from the viewpoint of lives lost and people disabled.

I Why do People Consume Alcoholic Beverages?

If liquor clouds the brain and makes a fool out of a person why does he drink? If alcohol makes the driver reckless and a potential killer why does he drink?

The Manila Times (Philippines), listed 13 answers given by drinkers.
1 Popularity; if you don't drink you are unpopular and ostracized from society.
2 Conformity to the crowd; everybody drinks, why shouldn't I?
3 The thought of power; it gives you nerve and courage to do what you ought to do.
4 As a gesture of friendship; it is considered anti-social and impolite not to drink.
5 As a show of manliness; this is particularly true of the teen-ager trying to attain.
6 As an escape from problems; in actuality liquor merely doubles the problems.
7 To overcome shyness; it is better to be shy and sober than drunk and talkative.
8 As public relations; it is essential to go to night clubs to close a "big deal."
9 Because they are disgusted with their ordinary, mediocre life; for a few hours they want to live in the world of imagination, excitement and action.
10 Loneliness; strangers and students in a far-away city drink for entertainment.
11 To get confidence; some men drink before asking the boss for a raise in pay.
12 "Because it's my business to live as I please and I can drink if I want to"; this may be true, but remember Romans 14:7; our lives do affect others.
13 Social occasions like toasting a dignitary demand it; this is not true, for they can be toasted with water as easily as with liquor.

II What Great Men Have Said about Alcohol

Shakespeare "Alcohol is a poison men take into the mouth to steal away the brain."

British statesman and Prime Minister, Gladstone "Strong drink is more destructive than war, pestilence and famine."

Sir Wilfred Lawson "The devil in solution."

Abraham Lincoln "A cancer in human society, eating out its vitals and threatening its destruction."

Robert Hall "Distilled damnation."

The English statesman Lord Chesterfield "An artist in human slaughter."

The British critic John Ruskin "The most criminal and artistic method of assassination ever invented by the bravos of any age or nation."

The American WWI General, Pershing "Drunkenness has killed more men than all of history's wars."

General Robert E. Lee commander of confederate forces in American Civil War "My experience through life has convinced me that abstinence from spirituous liquors is the best safeguard to morals and health."

President Taft "He who drinks is deliberately disqualifying himself for administration."

III What God has to Say about Liquor Indulgence

Proverbs 20:1 "Wine is a mocker, strong drink is raging: and whosoever is deceived thereby is not wise." In God's estimation only fools consume liquor.

Proverbs 23:29-35 is wise Solomon's earnest exhortation to his sons not to consume liquor. He says, "Look not thou upon the wine when it is red ... at the last it biteth like a serpent, and stingeth like an adder." Beware, BEWARE!

Genesis 9:21 is the first mention of wine in the Bible and tells of Noah being drunk — and the calamity that fell on his son Ham and his descendents (the black race).

Isaiah 28:7 condemns wine as sidetracking the priests, and causing them to err in judgment due to a marred vision.

Hosea 4:11 "Whoredom and wine and new wine take away the heart"; wine and immorality nearly always go together.

1 Corinthians 6:10 lists those who will not enter the kingdom of God and mentions thieves, covetous, drunkards, revilers and extortioners.

Galatians 5:21 also lists certain things that will not inherit the kingdom of God and mentions envyings, murders drunkenness, revellings and such like (liquor leads to all these related sins and evils and is a damnable curse in our land).

IV Reasons why I Believe in Abstinence rather than Temperance

1 My body is the Temple of the Holy Ghost and not to be defiled with poison or anything that would defile it in any way. 1 Corinthians 6:19

2 I am a witness for Christ and if I should take one tiny sip my weaker brother might be tempted thereby to take a larger portion.

3 I am my brother's keeper — Genesis 4:9; I have a responsibility to help my brother (friend, neighbor or acquaintance) to live a noble, upright, righteous life.

4 I am a steward of my money and I have absolutely no right whatsoever to squander it for that which is not bread or profitable for me. Isaiah 55:2

5 My Bible reveals the effects of liquor, therefore, as a Christian I heed its advice and refuse to allow one drop of the filthy stuff to contaminate me.

6 I need not yield to the temptation to drink either socially or moderately; with every temptation God guarantees a way of escape, 1 Corinthians 10:13

7 I have been redeemed from sin, therefore, I refuse to return to its slavery; in Christ I am master over evil. Romans 6:14

8 As a Christian my life is to be a living witness of the power of God; if I live an intoxicated life I'm an insult to the grace and goodness of God.

9 I want the world to be better because I have lived; if I'm living on the straight and narrow way, Matthew 7:14, then I'll lift others to higher standards.

10 If I have to drink to be popular then I'm living with the wrong crowd; liquor is absolutely unnecessary in clean Christian circles.

11 For the sake of my loving wife, devoted children and the community that I live in, I refuse to touch one drop of liquor.

12 For the safety of others on the highway I refuse to imbibe, lest I become a menace and thoughtlessly bring tragedy into the lives of other people.

V A Noble Example to Follow

Daniel in Daniel 1:8-20, purposed in his heart that he would not defile himself with the portion of the king's meat, nor with the wine which he drank.

God honored Daniel tremendously and advanced him to high positions because he was a complete abstainer; God honors those who obey Him implicitly.

Daniel was strong physically, morally and spiritually. How did Daniel attain this unusual strength?

1 By purpose (determination) Daniel 1:8; Daniel purposed in his heart to abstain.

2 By prayer Daniel 6:10; pray diligently for victory over this social menace.

3 By self-denial He could have lived like a king on royal dainties which would have led to fatness, laziness and a dull mind.

4 By devotion He kept close to God by constant meditation and obedience.

Conclusion

Because one taste leads to another, one glass to another, the only safe, Scriptural conclusion is complete abstinence always under *all* circumstances. A taste for liquor is easily developed but breaking of this vicious habit is a task superior to most men and only successful by the power and goodness of God.

Rev. William McCarrell outlines his lesson on liquor this way: Liquor indulgence is wrong because it:

1 Leads to other sins, Deuteronomy 21:18,20 (disobedience, disrespect, stubbornness).
2 Aids in breaking homes, Deuteronomy 21:18-21.
3 Leads from the seemingly harmless to chronic drunkards, Deuteronomy 21:20.
4 Brings severe judgment, Deuteronomy 21:21.
5 Because it is costly, Deuteronomy 21:18-21.
6 Because it is linked with debauchery (sensual indulgence), — Proverbs 23:20 (drunkenness, riotous fleshliness).
7 Tends to poverty, Proverbs 23:21 (eventually, if not immediately).
8 Causes one to miss God's kingdom, 1 Corinthians 6:9,10.

Review Questions

1 What type of wine did Jesus make in John 2:9?
2 What type of wine was Timothy to use as a medicine in 1 Timothy 5:23?
3 Which one of the thirteen reasons why people consume

alcoholic beverages do you consider 1) the most logical; 2) the most illogical?

4   Of the ten sayings of the wise men about alcohol which do you consider 1) the best; 2) the weakest.

5   Why shouldn't one look on the wine when it is red? (two reasons)

6   What does God call wine in Proverbs 20:1? What does this mean?

7   Prove that drunkards will not go to heaven.

8   List ten reasons why one should practice abstinence.

9   What prophet was abundantly rewarded because he was an abstainer?

10   What do you learn about the results of liquor consumption from Deuteronomy 21:18-21?

Temptation

Introduction

Temptation is one of the most familiar experiences of the true child of God, but some seem to be tempted much more than others.

No one can escape from temptation; Adam, Lucifer and Christ were tempted.

The Lord taught us to include this petition in our daily prayer, "And lead us not into temptation, but deliver us from evil."

Some saints are greatly troubled when they are tempted for they think they must be so wicked; to be *tempted* is not sin; sin is *yielding to temptation*.

> "Yield not to temptation, for yielding is sin,
> Each victory will help you, some other to win."

We cannot stop birds from flying over our heads but we *can* stop them from nesting in our hair; we cannot stop evil thoughts from passing through our minds but we need not accept them nor dwell upon them.

Someone asked a little girl what she did when temptations come. She replied, "Temptations are like Satan knocking at my heart, and when I see him there I tell Jesus to answer the door!!"

Satan flees when the mighty conquering Jesus appears and speaks of Calvary.

James 1:12 "Blessed is the man that endureth temptation," i.e., resists it and becomes the victor through the Blood of the cross.

1 Corinthians 10:13 "There hath no temptation taken you but such as is common to man: but God is faithful who will not suffer you to be tempted above that ye are able; but will with the temptation also make a way to escape, that ye may be able to bear it."

I Source of Temptations

1 It is *not* in God — James 1:13 "Let no man say when he is tempted, I am tempted of God: for God cannot be tempted with evil,

neither tempteth He any man."

In the case of Job, God gave Satan permission to tempt Job within certain restricted boundaries, Job 1:12; 2:6.

2 Four sources of temptation:

a **Satan** — Matthew 4:1, Satan tempting the Lord Jesus.

b **The flesh** — James 1:14 "But every man is tempted, when he is drawn away of his own lust, and enticed."

This is manifested in three specific forms:

   i   The lust of the flesh — 1 John 2:16

   ii The lust of the eyes — 1 John 2:16

   iii The pride of life — 1 John 2:16

c **Evil associates** — Proverbs 1:10 "My son, if sinners entice thee, consent thou not."

d **Christian friends** — Matthew 16:22,23, Jesus rebuked Satan speaking through Peter, "He turned and said unto Peter, Get thee behind Me, Satan: thou art an offence unto Me."

II Reasons for Temptations

1 **As a test of our faith** James 1:2,3 "My brethren, count it all joy when ye fall into divers temptations; knowing this, that the trying of your faith worketh patience."

Dr. Haldeman's story of a railway company testing a new bridge in the mountains. Two locomotives arrived on the bridge at full speed, then pulled the brakes and left the engines running at full throttle for half a day to let the vibrations jar the bridge to its deepest foundation. The bridge stood firm and no one doubted the ability of that bridge to carry heavy loads.

Because Jesus was severely tempted here on earth, He can help us in time of need.

2 **As a test of obedience** Genesis 22:1 "And it came to pass after these things, that God did tempt (test) Abraham, and said unto him ... Take now thy son, thine only son Isaac ... and offer him ..."

God tests men to know the depth of their love and sincerity of their obedience.

Words are easy; we say we love God and that we would obey Him under all circumstances, but how can this be proven except by some form of testing?

III Load-limit of Temptations

1 Corinthians 10:13 "... not suffer you to be tempted above that ye are able ...." God knows our load limit; He knows how much we can take; how much pressure or strain we can withstand.

Sometimes we see a sign on a bridge, "Load limit, ten tons"; this means that heavier vehicles must detour to a stronger bridge or unload to specified weight.

God limits our temptations in several ways:

1 He sets the time limit of the temptation—He knows whether in one more hour we might have yielded to that insiduous attack.

2 He sets the timing of the temptation; He only allows it when we are mature enough to withstand that particular type of temptation.

3 He guides the stress or amount of pressure during the actual temptation.

The eyes and counsels of the Lord watch over us each moment.

Just when we think we will weaken and sin the Lord removes the pressure and makes a way to escape.

IV Methods of Temptations

1 **Through poverty**   Proverbs 30:9 "Lest I be poor, and steal, and take the Name of my God in vain. . ."

2 **Through prosperity**   Proverbs 30:9 "Lest I be full, and deny Thee, and say, Who is the Lord?"

3 **Through worldly glory**   Balaam in Numbers 22:17 "For I will promote thee unto very great honor. . ."

4 **Through discouragement**   Psalm 42:11 "Why art thou cast down, O my soul?"

Elijah desiring suicide under the Juniper tree — 1 Kings 19:4.

V Types of Temptations

1 **To unbelief**   Job 2:9 ". . . curse God, and die"; also the "If" in Matthew 4:3.

2 **To presumption**   Matthew 4:6; Jesus to cast Himself down from the temple and presumptuously expect the angels to protect Him (subtle temptation to suicide).

3 **To worship the god of this world**   Matthew 4:9, Satan to Christ, "Fall down and worship me."

4 To pride Nebuchadnezzar in Daniel 4:30 "Is not this great Babylon, that I have built. . ."

5 To pleasure Demas in 2 Timothy 4:10 "For Demas hath forsaken me, having loved this present evil world."

6 To power Simon Magus in Acts 8:19, money to get the power of the Holy Spirit to regain the community popularity and power that he once possessed.

7 To society Lot's wife in Genesis 19:1-6.

8 To possessions Achan in Joshua 7:1-24, earth, gold, silver and garments.

9 To sex Solomon in Nehemiah 13:26; and David in 2 Samuel 11:2-4.

10 To money Judas Iscariot in John 13:21-30.

11 To false humility "I'm no good, I can't do anything, I can't preach, sing, etc."

VI Results of Temptations

1 If yielded to, they become sin — 1 Timothy 6:9, and the saint is weakened in testimony.

2 If resisted, the Lord is glorified and the saint grows stronger to resist other temptations; the person grows in faith and maturity; obedience is confirmed.

VII How to get Victory over Temptations

1 By the faithfulness of God 1 Corinthians 10:13, Revelation 3:10 "I also will keep thee from the hour of temptation."
We can rely on the faithfulness of God, 1 Corinthians 1:9; He changes not.

2 By using the Word of God appropriately Jesus quoted Scripture three times in Matthew 4.

3 By the intercession of Christ Luke 22:31,32 "I have prayed for thee that thy faith fail not."

4 By personal prayer Matthew 26:41 "Watch and pray, that ye enter not into temptation."

5 By fleeing 2 Timothy 2:22 "Flee also youthful lusts," Proverbs 4:14,15 "Avoid it, pass not by it, turn from it, and pass away."

6 By resisting James 4:7 "Resist the devil, and he will flee from you."

7 By accepting the way of escape 1 Corinthians 10:13.

Conclusion

Temptations are common to all men; every Christian must expect to be tempted.

Praise the Lord for the possibility of victory and bringing glory to His Name.

Beware of yielding to sin; to fall is easy but scars often remain.

Be conscious of immediate restoration through confession, repentance and the Blood of Christ — 1 John 1;9.

Review Questions

1   What type of people are subject to temptations?
2   What do you consider the greatest verse in the Bible regarding temptation?
3   Explain the conflict between James 1:13 and Genesis 22:1.
4   List four possible sources of temptations.
5   Give two reasons for temptations.
6   Suggest three ways that God guarantees that we will not be tempted above that which we are able.
7   Mention four methods of temptations.
8   List ten types of temptations.
9   What are the positive and negative results of temptations?
10   How may one get victory over temptations?

Planned Parenthood

Introduction

Some may ask: Why discuss so delicate, intimate and personal a problem as this?

There are several answers to this question, and the most common one is the alarming population explosion in the world today.

It is a very popular subject in magazines both religious and secular and we ought to have some knowledge of Bible teaching on this particular subject.

It is difficult to discuss this in a mixed audience; we must learn to be frank but extremely cautious in our phrases and terms.

I The Meaning of Planned Parenthood

It means the voluntary limitation of possible offspring by the use of contraceptives, artificial means of various types including pills.

Parents must be impressed with the basic purpose of marriage — procreation and continuance of the human race: "Be fruitful and multiply and replenish the earth."

Some men consider woman simply as a "baby machine" without due consideration of her physical or mental health; Christian men are very considerate.

Planned parenthood is an intelligent approach to a major family problem today.

II Reasons in Favor of Planned Parenthood

1 To prevent unnecessary or premature deaths (deaths to mothers with serious ailments).
2 To give wives sufficient rest between pregnancies.
3 To prevent high death rate among babies (well spaced babies are stronger).
4 To prevent the transmission of communicable diseases from

parent to child.
5 To prevent the birth of children with inheritable diseases (feeble-minded, etc.).
6 Society may demand the curtailment of families if parents cannot feed, clothe and educate themselves and their children.
7 To curtail world population. (Previously population explosions were controlled by diseases, famines, plagues, war and pestilences.)
8 Planned parenthood is not a device to protect the immoral, or the social parasites or those too lazy or too selfish to raise a family.

III Methods of Planned Parenthood

Historical research says that birth control has been practiced more than 2,000 years.
1 Infanticide — the killing or abandoning of the newborn infant (outlawed today).
2 Sterilization — a process (generally through surgery) to render a person unproductive.
3 Coitus interruptus — Genesis 38:9; this practice is abnormal and leads to frustration.
4 Abstinence — the voluntary or partial abstaining from all sexual intercourse for a time.
5 Abortion — the termination (generally medically or surgically) of a pregnancy, generally before the expiration of the seventh month.
6 Rhythm method — having intercourse during the sterile time in a woman's menstrual cycle.
7 Contraceptives or artificial means such as pills, douche or IUD (Intrauterine contraceptive device).

IV The Catholic Position on Planned Parenthood

1 The sexual function has only one purpose — the propagation of the human race.
2 Birth control by artificial means is directly opposed to the laws of nature.
3 Birth control exerts an evil influence on morality and religion.
4 Pope Pius XI called birth control a horrible crime and vicious.
5 Birth control destroys the difference between prostitutes and respectable women.

6 Birth control leads to infidelity by destroying self-restraint and self-discipline.
7 Birth control is a refusal to co-operate with God in His production plans.
8 Birth control leads to selfishness by substituting personal pleasure for God's will.
9 Birth control is a crime and no excuse is acceptable; it is intrinsically evil.

V The Bible Teaching on Birth Control

A true Christian yields all (including sex) to the Lord, seeking His will alone.

Theologians have argued the question for generations and have differed widely.

The answer may vary from person to person or situation to circumstance.

The Bible is surprisingly silent on this major problem; God is both the author and preserver of life; if He gives life, He can easily care for it.

Life and human personalities are exceedingly precious to the Lord.

The Bible does not command marriage for all, or set the number of children per family.

1 Genesis 38:9,10 is a condemnation of the *refusal to raise children for a brother* rather than a condemnation of a form of birth control.
2 Genesis 1:28 doesn't apply now for the world is well populated.
3 Romans 1:24-28 is dealing with homosexuality and not with birth control.
4 Psalm 128:3 and Psalm 127:3-5 would certainly encourage large families.

VI Marriage and its Purpose

Marriage is honorable (Hebrews 13:4) and all transgressions are violations of God's laws.

Man was created in the image of God to operate not by instinct but by intelligence, emotion and will Deuteronomy 6:6,7; Ephesians 6:4; Genesis 1:27.

God is the author of marriage for both companionship and procreation.

VII Basic Questions on Planned Parenthood

1 Can planned parenthood ever be considered right and permissible for Christians, or is it basically wrong and immoral? Birth control is not a violation of God's creation order; nowhere in the Bible is birth control forbidden. Sexual intercourse is not limited to procreation; 1 Corinthians 7:3-5,9 permits coitus as the highest possible expression of physical love.

2 May Christians voluntarily limit the number of children? The Bible does not hint as to the desirable number of children per family; however, parents must never use their liberty for selfish purposes or as irresponsible license.

3 When and under what circumstances are parents free to use contraceptives? Circumstances and conditions may vary from case to case; parents may need to consult the family physician, pastor, psychologist or psychiatrist to get the best possible answer.

4 Do the principles applicable to the use of contraceptives also apply to abortion? An emphatic *No*, for abortion is a form of murder, the termination of a life.

5 Catholic theologians and some Protestants recommend either abstinence or the rhythm method. Are these sufficient? Abstinence is either partial or complete cessation from sexual intercourse. Paul, in 1 Corinthians 7:7-9, recognizes this as difficult and only to be temporary.
The rhythm method is far from foolproof for the mathematics are difficult to determine, and some women actually never have a period that is absolutely sterile or safe.

6 May parents before marriage determine the number of children — say 2 or 4?
No, for this would presumptuously seize the prerogatives of the Lord Himself. God could punish such a couple with childlessness or by taking some of the children early in life; no couple have sufficient knowledge to make this decision which is sealed in the sovereignty of Almighty God.

7 If birth control becomes acceptable will not the evil and unmarried take advantage of it to satisfy their own lusts and passion? There are always people who will turn liberty into license; the abuse of a good thing does not vitiate its proper use.

8 Will an acceptance of contraceptives not give an acceptance to immorality, too? No, for Christians are guided by the principles of

Scripture and not by fear or changing social codes of behavior; we act on the basis of God's Word.

9 Would birth control lead to race suicide and economic disaster? Yes, if carried to ridiculous extremes, but certainly not if followed in moderation.

10 What advice do you have for Christian couples who feel that it is *not* morally right to practice birth control? By all means avoid it; do not act contrary to your conscience — Romans 14:23.

Conclusion

Marriage is a divine ordinance, a precious gift to mankind from the Creator.

The precious gifts of marriage, sex and children belong to the home.

Home is a relationship where parents are respected and honored and children are wanted and loved; a Christian home is one permeated with Divine love.

This kind of home does not grow by itself. It requires effort and co-operation between husband, mother and each child.

Happy is the home where no contraceptives are used, but if they must be used for medical reasons let it be with extreme care and moderation.

(Much of this material is outlined from *Birth Control*, A. M. Relwin.)

Review Questions

1 Give the meaning of planned parenthood.
2 List seven reasons in favor of planned parenthood.
3 Name seven methods of planned parenthood.
4 What is the Catholic position on birth control?
5 Does Genesis 38:9,10 teach that birth control is wrong? Explain.
6 Do you feel that Genesis 1:28 is applicable today? Why?
7 Is birth control a violation of Scripture? Proof?
8 Is birth control justifiable on economic grounds? Why?
9 Why is it wrong for parents to predetermine the number of children that they will have?
10 If my conscience says not to use contraceptives and my doctor says to use them what shall I do?

99

The Offence of the Cross

Introduction

Notes taken from a sermon preached by Rev. Leo Calica, in Manila; a message preached by Bishop Marcus Loane in Baguio; and other sources.

Galatians 5:11 "And I, brethren, if I still preach circumcision, why do I still suffer persecution? Then the offence of the cross has ceased."

In Christian circles we often speak about "the offence of the cross" but do we know what we mean? Has it become a trite saying without significance?

The cross has always been a stumbling block to the Jews (1 Corinthians 1:22-24), and foolishness to the Greeks but to the child of God it is both the power of God and wisdom of God.

I What is the Offence of the Cross?

It is the shame and scorn that is heaped on the head of the evangelical who still believes in salvation through the precious Blood of Christ.

The "modern" Christian today calls this "an old-fashioned, slaughterhouse religion," and disdains the ignoramus living in "ancient history."

This individual, depending on good works, philosophy, religiosity and formalism to save him, feels so much more enlightened than us "back-numbers."

II Where is the Offence of the Cross?

It is the doctrine of the atonement; it hurts man's pride to be told that he is a sinner utterly helpless to save himself; natural man wrongly imagines that he is "basically pretty good" with but a few minor "weaknesses" that can easily be offset by meritorious deeds of charity, benevolence and almsgiving.

It attacks the pride of man; it takes considerable humility to confess that "all our righteousnesses are as filthy rags" Isaiah 64:6; and that "the whole head is sick, and the whole heart faint. From the sole of the foot even unto the head there is no soundness in it; but wounds . . . bruises . . . purifying sores . . ."

It goes against the wisdom of man; man's wisdom says that everything and everyone has a price and that somehow man ought to be able to reimburse God for the debt of sin and be reckoned righteous on the basis of a suitable purchase price.

The Cross was the death blow to human pride and worldy honor. To be identified with a so-called "criminal" brings shame and ignominy.

III The Manifestations of this Offence

Because the crucifixion was surrounded by scandal, men have tried to erase this "offence" by music, poetry and art.

Men attempt to beautify that which was once an ugly instrument of death.

People like hymns with a sentimental appeal, "On a hill far away, stood an old rugged cross". . . a cross glittering with gold edges and garlanded with flowers.

Centuries of tradition have attempted to remove the offensive odor from the cross.

The cross that Paul glorified in (Galatians 6:14) was far different; he preached a salvation by the ignominious cross of shame, sorrow, anguish and pain.

Peter in Acts 5:30, says, "The God of our fathers raised up Jesus, whom ye slew and hanged on a tree." Impolite language? offensive? This is the true cross!

The writer of the book of Hebrews (13:13) catches this thought of shame when he says, "Let us go forth therefore to *Him* outside the camp, bearing (sharing) His reproach." This is a gentle invitation to every child of God.

This was the place of the outcast, the criminal and leper; in their filth, disease, and misery they called out, "Unclean, unclean."

This doctrine is not merely a New Testament revelation, for Hebrews 11:26 tells us that Moses chose "the reproach of Christ" rather than the riches of Egypt.

IV Blessedness of the One not Offended in Christ

Matthew 11:6 "And blessed is he, whosoever shall not be offended in Me."

Does our faith rise to the crescendo of Peter in Matthew 26:33? "Though all men shall be offended because of Thee, yet will I never be offended."

Why were the disciples (including Peter) later offended, departing from Him? Because of His association with a terrible cross and the awful glory sight.

No Jew could think of crucifixion apart from shame, for God had said, "Cursed is every one that hangeth on a tree" Deuteronomy 21:22,23; Galatians 3:13.

He who was held accursed for me, rose from the grave; now shall I be offended in Him? Will I be willing to absorb the scandal, shame and offence of the cross?

Dare I do less? If I fail to daily accept this offence I am unworthy to be a disciple.

V Meaning of the Cross to a Believer Today

The cross stains the pride of human glory; to the Gentile the cross was a mental affront for it offended his intellect.

The Greeks didn't think of the curse of the cross but only of its shame; the law of Caesar reserved it only for the worst of criminals.

Think of the disgrace and shame of hanging naked; Hebrews 12:2 "Jesus. . . endured the cross, despising the shame"; counting this cost not too great to redeem us. Natural man cries out, "How could one who died in shame on a Roman gallows be the Son of God? be the Messiah and Redeemer of mankind?" The expression, "The blood of the cross" is considered cruel, repulsive to polite society today; they consider it a hangover of ancient religion.

Saul of Tarsus rebelled against the cross and looked on the crucified Nazarene as a blasphemer and consequently set out to persecute and imprison the Christians.

The Apostle Paul acknowledged his error and learned to glory in the cross.

VI What the Cross Really Is

1 It is the power of God unto salvation to all who will believe
    — 1 Corinthians 1:23,24.
2 It is the exceeding greatness of His power to us-ward who believe
    — Ephesians 1:19.
3 It is the wisdom of God — 1 Corinthians 1:23,24.

VII Bearing the Offence Today

This represents the inner conflict between the self-life and the new
    nature — 2 Peter 1:4.

Victory comes when we are willing to crucify self, accept the cross and
    bear the shame.

It is a daily (moment-by-moment, experience-by-experience) accept-
    ing the stigma of being different joyfully, for the glory of our
    matchless Redeemer, Luke 9:23.

Perhaps we are walking along the street and the Holy Spirit tells us
    to join a group of Christians having an open-air meeting. But our
    inner respectable self says that would be too undignified; your
    neighbors would be horrified; you have to protect your noble name
    in this community!! But we need to resist this temptation and in the
    Name of Christ identify ourselves and give our testimony.

Every occasion that tests our self-surrender and exposes our old
    nature to further shame and death may be considered as accepting
    the offence of the cross.

Providential circumstances (sent by the Savior's hand) bring us up
    against choices which will antagonize the old nature; daily we will
    be given opportunity to die.

Some of these things may be ordinary routine matters like juggling of
    the daily schedule; extra accumulation of duties; unexpected
    interruptions when we are facing immediate deadlines; unwel-
    come distractions, though beneficial and pleasant at other times.

Is there any particular area in your life where you have secretly said
    to God, "Anything, Lord, anything, but not that"? For you, that may
    represent the offence of the cross in its deepest meaning. Why the
    hesitation? Are you afraid of the shame and ridicule that it might
    bring you? Put self on the altar and Christ on the throne of your
    life; accept the "cross" gladly and dying to self, magnify Christ.

To some it might be immersion after years of being satisfied with
    baptism by sprinkling; to many this represents a humiliation

beneath their dignity.

Rev. L. E. Maxwell says, "Our cross is the voluntary embracing of a path which exposes self to fresh denial, disgrace and death and which may actually cost us our life."* Blessed death if Christ can be seen in the resurrection.

For some it may be speaking out boldly against sin; the flesh would say, "Keep quiet, it really isn't your business," but the Holy Spirit must be obeyed.

*Born Crucified, p. 144

Conclusion

It is folly to attempt to avoid the offence; His grace is sufficient to endure the shame, 2 Corinthians 12:9; Embrace it gladly and serve Him acceptably.

Bearing the offence is part of the price of discipleship — Luke 14:27.

In Matthew 27:32, Simon (an African from present-day Libya) was forced to carry the cross after Jesus. He was a stranger and would not understand the spiritual significance of the event. But with us it is so different; we are not *compelled* to bear the cross but we daily accept it prayerfully as we acknowledge our identification with the Savior.

Review Questions

1   Is the expression "The Offence of the Cross" Scriptural? Proof?
2   What is the offence of the cross?
3   Where is the offence of the cross? Explain.
4   Name three ways that men have tried to erase this offence.
5   What is the reproach of Hebrews 13:13?
6   What does Matthew 11:6, offer to the true followers of Christ?
7   What is the meaning of the cross to believers today?
8   Illustrate the possibility of bearing the offence of the cross today.
9   Is self on the throne or on the cross in your self?
10 Do you envy or pity Simon in Matthew 27:32? Why?

100

The New Morality, Immorality and Morality

Introduction

We are living in the last days; times when men are trying to change the standards and moral codes that have been set down centuries ago by God.

God is holy and just and changes not; neither will His standards adapt to meet the imaginary "progressiveness" of the twentieth century.

The so-called "new morality" professes to restate codes of conduct in the light of modern knowledge and science, when in actuality it returns to the morality of Romans 1:18,24,28. Instead of progress, it is retrogression.

I The New Morality

Proponents of the new morality suggest two "alternative lifestyles."

1 For unmarried people to live together as husband and wife on a "trial marriage" basis to test their ability to live happily together.

2 For married people to go outside the marriage bond and enjoy extramarital relationships to satisfy their unfulfilled lust.

This teaching says that if one indulges in these sexual experiences (in or out of marriage) that it will give you the ability to feel at one with the universe and with God! What utter and reprehensible nonsense.

They say that right and wrong are relative terms, with the standard being the *desires* (needs) *of man* rather than the strict codes of *the law*.

They say that sex is an expression of love and should not be prohibited or curtailed.

Homosexuality (or lesbianism) is merely an expression of love between members of the same sex, and therefore should be legalized in order to let people express themselves to one another in a way that seems the most natural.

In the name of compassion the new morality condones adultery, fornication, etc.

However, the Scripture says, "Whatsoever a man soweth, that shall he also reap"; Galatians 6:7.

Promiscuity leads to venereal disease and other problems.

The commands of the Lord still stand — Exodus 20:14 "Thou shalt not commit adultery," and Mark 10:19 "Thou knowest the commandments, Do not commit adultery."

II Immorality

Sometimes we are asked: How can immorality destroy a nation? The answer is because immorality is sin, a transgression of the laws of God Almighty.

Proverbs 14:34 "Righteousness exalteth a nation: but sin is a reproach to any people."

The word "immorality" does not appear in the Scriptures but it has two basic meanings in modern usage: 1) Sexual impurity and 2) Deceit and falsehood.

1 Sexual impurity

a Adultery — Forbidden in Exodus 20:14; sexual union when at least one partner is married.

b Fornication — Forbidden in Acts 15:20; sexual union of unmarried people.

c Effeminacy — Forbidden in 1 Corinthians 6:9; for a male to become like a woman, soft, delicate.

d Masturbation — Forbidden in 1 Corinthians 6:9; ". .. abusers of themselves with mankind."

e Whoremongering — Forbidden in Ephesians 5:5; a man who practices fornication.

f Inordinate affection — Forbidden in Colossians 3:5; doting love that is immoderate, excessive, intemperate and disordered.

g Homosexual sin — Romans 1:27; the sin of sodomy, Genesis 19:5; men sexually involved with men.

h Lesbianism — Romans 1:27; women sexually involved with other women.

i Lewdness — Condemned in Judges 20:6; wicked thoughts and devices; licentiousness.

j Nakedness — Exodus 32:25; the state of undress follows

immorality and idolatry; caution against short skirts, low neck-lines and immodest bathing suits.

k Divorce — The woman in John 4:17, 18, was living in adultery for she had had five husbands and her present man was not her husband.

l Evil sensual appetite —Condemned in Colossians 3:5; 1 Thessalonians 4:5; lustful, sensual desires.

2 Deceit and falsehood

a Cheating — Condemned in Amos 8:5; giving short change and poor measure.

b Dishonesty — Renounced in 2 Corinthians 4:2; shame, deceit, unfairness, unchaste.

c Bribery — Fire to destroy bribery, Job 15:34; Amos 5:12; refuse bribes, Isaiah 33:15.

d Gambling — The prodigal wasted his substance with riotous living, Luke 15:13.

e Corruption — 2 Peter 2:19, false teachers promise liberty but being servants of corruption they are unable to produce it. The child of God is to be delivered from the bondage of corruption, Romans 8:21.

f Extortion — 1 Corinthians 6:10, says that extortioners shall not inherit the kingdom of God. The Scribes and Pharisees were condemned for being full of extortion by our Lord in Matthew 23:25 (extortion means to exact unlawfully).

g Fraud — Condemned in James 5:4; Psalm 10:7; keeping back wages by trickery.

h Slothfulness —Condemned in Proverbs 15:19; 19:24; 21:25; 22:13; 24:30; 26:13-15. Romans 12:11 "Be not slothful (lazy, indolent) in business." wasting the master's time, property and business.

3 Distinction between morality and immorality

Sometimes this is hard to decipher but God uses His plumbline in Amos 7:7,8; and He, judging the heart, is able to discern between black and white, good and evil, dark and light grey. Learn to respect God's plumbline!

4. How immorality destroys a nation

a. Only righteousness can exalt a nation, Proverbs 14:34. God honors those who honor Him with clean, pure, upright lives.

b Sin is a reproach to any people, Proverbs 14:34, "Righteousness exalteth a nation: but sin is a reproach to any people."

c Immorality eats away the heart of the nation:

Daniel 5:30, 31, immoral Belshazzar gives way to Darius; Babylon to Media-Persia. The great Roman Empire disintegrated through internal moral corruption.

d God cannot tolerate immorality — Habakkuk 1:13 "Thou art of purer eyes than to behold evil, and canst not look on iniquity."

e God blesses morality (Deuteronomy 28:1-14) and punishes immorality (Deuteronomy 28:15-68).

f Immorality cannot be hidden from God — Numbers 32:23 "Be sure your sin will find you out."

g A possible result of the new morality would be a plague of venereal disease.

h Morality leads to heaven — Luke 10:27,28 "This do, and thou shalt live."

Immorality leads to damnation — Revelation 21:8.

III God's Standard of Morality

The Apostle Paul rebuked the Church at Corinth because of immorality, 1 Corinthians 5:1, for a member had his stepmother as his wife.

We have been called to glorify God in our bodies (1 Corinthians 6:20), and this can only be done as we maintain the standards of holiness and righteousness set forth in the Holy Bible, particularly in the Ten Commandments.

Romans 1:18 condemns the new morality and all immorality with these words, "For the wrath of God is revealed from heaven against all ungodliness and unrighteousness of men."

God's standard of morality is set forth in 1 Peter 1:15,16 "But as He which hath called you is holy, so be ye holy in all manner of conversation; because it is written, Be ye holy; for I (the Lord God) am holy," Leviticus 11:44; 19:2; 20:7. This standard is also set forth in the Sermon on the Mount in Matthew 5:48, "Be ye therefore perfect, even as your Father which is in heaven is perfect."

As Christians we have been called on to renounce the 17 works of the flesh enumerated in Galatians 5:19-21; and to bear the ninefold fruit of Galatians 5:22,23.

1 John 2:17 teaches that the lusts of the flesh will pass away but he that does the will of God shall abide forever.

1 Timothy 5:22 "... neither be partaker of other men's sins: *Keep thyself pure.*"

This would include both external purity (committing acts of immorality) but also internal purity in the realm of the mind, Matthew 5:28. This is why the Apostle Paul says in 1 Corinthians 7:1, "It is good for a man not to touch a woman." Girls: Don't let a fellow touch you until you are married.

Conclusion

The so-called new morality is putting women back hundreds of years by giving a free rein to the lusts of evil men.

The late Dr. J. D. Unwin in *Sex and Culture*, confirmed scientifically the historic fact that productive social energy is proportionate to the sexual discipline by the two previous generations. His investigations covered the customs of 80 primitive peoples and 16 civilizations over a period of 40 centuries. There were no exceptions.

Rev. Harold J. Ockenga in the Sunday School Times says, "The answer to the New Morality is not only theological but personal. It lies in a clean heart, made so by the cleansing blood of Christ, 1 John 1:7,9; in a commitment to the will of God, to abstain from fornication (immorality), 1 Thessalonians 4:3"

Let us accept our liberty in Christ as liberty to resist all immorality and never as license to cater to the lusts and whims of the flesh.

Review Questions

1   What two things are included in the new morality?
2   What is the imagined goal of the new morality?
3   Will God re-interpret Exodus 20:14, and Mark 10:19 for modern youth? Why?
4   What, basically, is immorality?
5   Give the two modern meanings of immorality.
6   List and define briefly ten manifestations of sexual impurity.
7   List and define briefly seven forms of deceit and falsehood.
8   How should one distinguish between morality and immorality in difficult cases?
9   How can immorality destroy a nation?
10 What is God's standard of morality?

Selective Bibliography and Recommended Reading

Certain of the references mentioned in earlier editions of *One Hundred Bible Lessons* are no longer easy to obtain, but in some cases other books provide the same information. This present list includes several books from the original selection, while adding new titles more widely available today.

The Adversary. Bubeck M I
Backsliding. MacDonald W
Between Christ and Satan. Koch K
Biblical Demonology. Unger M F
Born for Battle. Matthews R A
Certainties of Christ's Second Coming. Sanders J O
Counterfeit? Platt D
Creative Bible Teaching. Richards L O
Decision Making and the Will of God. Friesen G
The Divine Art of Soul Winning. Sanders J O
Dr Dobson Answers Your Questions. Dobson J
The Fight. White J
Filipino Spirit World. Henry R
Get Your Church Involved in Missions. Griffiths M
God's Powerful Weapon. Lane D
The Gospel in Filipino Context. Maggay M
Great Doctrines of the Bible. Evans W
Guidebook to Discipleship. Hartman D et al
Heaven. Moody D L
The Holy Spirit. Torrey R A
How We Got Our Bible. Earle R
Issues Facing Christians Today. Stott J R
Keep in Step with the Spirit. Packer J
Know the Truth. Milne B
Know What You Believe. Little P
Know Why You Believe. Little P
The Legacy of Jesus. MacArthur J
Life and Love. Narramore C
Local Church and Missions. Williams T
Love and Courtship. Miranda-Feliciano E
Major Bible Themes. Chafer L S et al
Meet Yourself in the Parables. Wiersbe W
The Master Plan of Evangelism. Coleman R

The Ministry of the Spirit. Gordon S D
Miraculous Healing. Frost T H
Missionary Call. Sanders J O
On Being a Real Christian. Weiss G
The Perfect Will of God. Weiss G
Pictorial Introduction to the Bible. Deal W
The Prayer of Faith. Fraser J
Prayer Power Unlimited. Sanders J O
The Second Coming of Christ. Larkin C
The Seduction of Christianity. Hunt D et al
Studies in the Sermon on the Mount. Lloyd-Jones M
Tell the Truth. Metzger W
Train Up a Child. Sala H
Trinity - Take a Second Look. Espinosa N
A True View of You. Baldwin S
Twelve Dynamics of Bible Study. Warren R
What Can Christian Women Do? Javalera E
What Every Christian Should Know. Eims L
Why Do Christians Suffer? Epp T
Worship. Gibbs A P

Systematic Theology - various titles available

Index